MANY HEADS
AND MANY HANDS

James Madison's

Search for a More Perfect Union

By Mau VanDuren

For Joan Long

Comrade in arms!

Mau VanDuren

Northampton House Press

To Jackie and Maggie,
who have complicated my life
into a permanent state of bliss.

MANY HEADS
AND MANY HANDS

James Madison at the time of his presidency

Contents

The past is just as difficult to predict
as is the future

*Learned Institutions ought to be favorite objects with every free people.
They throw that light over the public mind which is the best security against
crafty & dangerous encroachments on the public liberty.*

James Madison to W.T. Barry, August 4, 1822.

Prologue

One September night in 1982 I was the front seat passenger in a big, old and rusty Detroit Dinosaur on its way to Princeton, New Jersey. The car was a Rent-a-Wreck special at ten dollars a day. The five-foot-nothing driver was my Peace Corps sweetheart. It was my first time in the United States. Looking back after thirty years, that first day is a blurry mix of elation and anxiety — elation to be reunited with the woman I had met in Botswana, Africa, and whom I loved beyond description; anxiety because of the difficulties I had had as an unemployed Dutchman to get into her country. And there were the typical uncertainties of a future in a strange place. After leaving JFK International Airport in New York, we made a wrong turn and got lost. The tree-less, concrete neighborhoods, where old cars lined dilapidated streets, reminded me of the depressing scenes of the 1970s TV crime series *Kojak*. Once back on the right road, the broken concrete strip of US Route 1 led us through the rust belt and smoke stacks of northern New Jersey. And then it got dark.

The student house where we stayed the first few weeks was close to the University and the center of town, so while Jackie was in class I could explore my new surroundings and become less of a stranger. To my surprise the place was more familiar than I had expected.

The oldest building at Princeton University, New Jersey, carries the name Nassau Hall. The name came as a pleasant surprise. Nassau in Germany is the ancestral home of the Orange-Nassau royal house of my native Netherlands. The largest stone building in the colonies at the time, it was built in 1756 for the College of New Jersey and was named after "the Glorious King William the Third who was of the Illustrious House of Nassau.[1]" This was the William of "William and Mary," who was responsible for the Glorious Revolution in England in 1688 that had brought, among other innovations, the Bill of Rights, the Tolerance Act regarding religious belief, and the permanent parliament. In the following weeks I learned that Nassau Hall had served as the Capitol of the United States from June to November 1783. It is where the Continental Congress received official word of the signing of the Treaty of Paris that formally ended the Revolution and affirmed, internationally, the independent status of the United States

Nassau Hall, Princeton University (Photo Smallbones)

of America. And it is where Congress received the first foreign minister, as ambassadors were then called, accredited to these United States, Pieter Johan van Berckel[2] from the Netherlands.

I almost felt at home already. But it also made me curious. What was the nature of this apparent close connection, in 1783, between the 200 year old Dutch Republic and this brand new North American republic? Was it because the Dutch had an axe to grind with the English? Not really. Relations were not bad at that time. Or was it cultural? As far as I could tell, the cultures of the Netherlands, England, and the United States seemed rather similar. Although I got engaged in trying to make a living and a future in this country, the questions kept coming back when I encountered other reminders of a possible close link between my adopted country and the country of my birth. The term Roman-Dutch law popped up in New York -- not that I understood what it meant at that time, so we will get back to that later. My wife's grandmother had a Dutch maiden name. Many waters or towns in the area had the Dutch word "kill[3]" in their names. Santa Claus was so similar to Sinterklaas, the Dutch colloquial for Saint Nicolas, the patron saint of "more causes than any other saint[4]."

It wasn't until 2008 that I decided to do some serious research and find out where all the familiar American customs, notions, inventions, laws, and aspects of governance came from. Did Americans invent them out of nothing as many Americans apparently think their Founding Fathers did? Did the British come up with them first as so many wanted me to believe? Did the Dutch bring them to these shores? If so, did they invent these concepts? Or was it not that simple? Was it an amalgamation of many customs and ideas that each had developed in different places and had been built upon in other places before some of them landed on the shores of America? Although we read about revolutions in our history books, there is no such thing as a revolution of ideas. Concepts develop slowly and only when people implement them to replace older systems can they lead to revolutions.

The first concept that caught my attention was that of a slogan that became a battle cry of the American Revolution: "No taxation without representation." In this country it is hailed as perhaps the defining ingredient of American Exceptionalism. But was it? After a bit of searching, I found a reference in Watertown, Massachusetts, in 1708. An earlier reference was in 1669 in Hempstead, Long Island, New York[5]. The actual phrase was not coined but the sentiment was clear. There was another reference in New Amsterdam, now New York, in 1639. Before that, in 1632, the issue came up in Massachusetts. These are references to events that all took place on the American continent and it is obvious that the sentiment was widespread here. This makes it very likely that the colonists were familiar with the concept and brought it with them from Europe. Digging further I eventually found a document in which the concept is spelled out as a right granted by a ruler to his subject provinces and cities, who, by the way, already had bestowed that right on their citizens. The document was known as the Great Privilege. It served as a functional constitution that defined the relationship and the rights of the provinces of the Netherlands with each other and with their head of state, the Duchess of Burgundy. The year was 1477.

Even then the concept was not new. There are earlier references in the city states of northern Italy, cities in Western Europe, and surely elsewhere, giving taxpaying merchants and tradesmen a voice in government. The phrase, "pay to play," comes to mind.

Next to the concept of representation stands that of tolerance of religious affiliation. Many wars were fought in the name of religion. Many violent conflicts still rage in its name. The United States justifiably prides itself on the fact that it is a multi-denominational country that is at peace with itself. There is no state sanctioned religion and the separation of church and state is well defined in the Constitution. Ours is one of the few such countries in the world. Believe it or not but the official religion in both England and the Netherlands is still a version of Protestantism. This is a leftover from the Reformation when both countries were at war with Catholic Spain and it now applies to their respective royal houses only. So, is the concept of religious toleration another unique aspect of Americana or did the idea originate elsewhere? Toleration of differing religious practice or belief was discussed in various parts of Europe after the onset of the Reformation in the 16th century. In the midst of the turmoil, some municipalities in Germany distributed existing, and formerly Roman churches, among the active religious denominations. If there were not enough church buildings, then the structures were shared. These were expedient solutions that did not lead to a blanket tolerance in the various German states. The Polish-Lithuanian Commonwealth enacted religious tolerance in the Warsaw Confederation of January, 1573, and was the first country in Europe to do so. The Dutch Republic enacted religious tolerance six years later in the Union of Utrecht. There were some similar attempts in England but the bloody fight between Catholics and Protestants lasted a while longer and caused such distrust that religious tolerance was not established until 1689 under King William the Third, the same after whom Nassau Hall in Princeton was named. And even then it extended to Protestant denominations only and not Roman Catholics. The colonies on the eastern shore of North America pretty much followed the policies of the home country although some did better than others. Massachusetts sanctioned vicious persecutions, particularly against Quakers. With some ups and downs, Maryland, founded as a Catholic colony, set a better example. However, the first explicit appeal for tolerance in the American colonies came on Long Island in 1657 in a document called the "Flushing Remonstrance." It is interesting to note that:

The petitioners were all English

They asked for an exemption to the ban on Quaker worship

None of the signers were Quakers themselves

The ban existed in the Dutch colony where Dutch law, including freedom of religion, was supposed to be officially in place.

We will revisit this remarkable event in more detail later on.

The Founders of this nation took it one step further and prescribed Freedom of Religion in their Constitution. Considering the turmoil that religious competition had caused until then you may wonder if they really had not meant to call it Freedom from Religion. The United States had no state sanctioned religion and the separation between state and church was enacted in the Constitution.

Had I known, back in 1982, that the primary author of our Constitution, James Madison, had attended the College of New Jersey, now Princeton University, I might have landed on these concepts and their origins a bit earlier. But the limited knowledge might also have been confining. What I did learn however was that the participatory nature of American politics, much more so than in Europe, was characteristic right from the start. Listening to NPR[6] and watching the McNeal Lehrer News Hour[7] on PBS[8], I learned about town hall meetings large and small, conventions, elections, campaigns, and an active civic engagement. On the University grounds I attended a speech by Alexander Haig, recently Secretary of State. The critical questions from students during the Q & A session, and the way that Haig answered them, were wonderful examples of political engagement. It all was so exciting.

In 1986 my wife's cousin decided to run for circuit court judge in northern Michigan. He needed campaign workers. Could we help? Campaigns were a lot simpler in those days and were often family affairs. We did not have lists of voters to work with. I went out with little more than a map of the county, a few yard signs, and the message that he was a good guy. There was no party affiliation, although he had represented the district in the State House as a Republican. The month went by quickly with countless doors knocked, many signs placed, and lovely engagements with voters, many of whom wondered, "Who is this guy with a Dutch accent we have never seen before?" Often people invited me into their homes. Some offered coffee and conversation about issues of concern to them. I learned and I was hooked.

Back in 2008, when curiosity led me to the research for this book, I was blissfully unaware of some facts. I say blissfully because this ignorance sent me on a journey into semi-charted and uncharted waters that led to discoveries that otherwise I would not have made. These events reached ever farther back in time from the North Atlantic colonies back across the ocean to England and Holland, from there south into medieval Burgundy and the dark-age land of the Franks, occasionally touching on the influences of the Renaissance, and eventually exploring the beginnings of the rule of law and governance in one small outpost of the flourishing Roman Empire.

All the while, there were people engaged in the practices of governing, who identified flaws, and who attempted to improve their lot and that of their fellow men and women by urging and implementing small and large changes. By extension we will explore the human condition in the absence of governance and law and see how human desires for structure and equity led to the creation of some of these institutions. In the pages that follow, I will present the events in the order in which they occurred rather than the order in which I found them. This narrative will take a look into the so-called "Dark Ages" of Europe, long after the Roman Republic and Ancient Greek City States. It will not spend time on the well-known stories of the Italian Renaissance, Magna Carta, or of philosophers such as Hobbes, Locke or Rousseau. Also, this narrative will stop when the hammer falls at the opening of the Constitutional Convention in 1787. Plenty has been written about all that and subsequent events in American history that I do not dare touch. And then, hopefully, when that hammer, in the steady hands of General George Washington, comes down at the end of this book, we should have a better understanding, and appreciation, of how we came to our current system of government. Because, for one to understand the present, one has to know its history.

That last phrase might as well have been coined by James Madison, that Princeton student of whom I once was unaware. Even in the far away Netherlands he was mentioned in high school history classes as one of the Founding Fathers of that intriguing country called the United States of America. But our knowledge of its history was overshadowed by news stories of race discrimination and what we now call hate crimes, the murders of a sitting president[9], his brother[10], and a black Baptist minister and civil rights leader[11]. America's conduct in Vietnam and the protests at home were daily fodder and there was the horrifying news of the killings of students at a college in Ohio[12]. And then there were shows like *Bonanza*, *Gun Smoke*, the earlier mentioned *Kojak*, and a slew of others that added up to a violent and negative picture. I had a lot to overcome that first year in Princeton. Objectivity is hard to achieve when you have been on a diet of shallow newscasts.

After my campaign experience in Michigan we went overseas for work. Reengagement with American politics had to wait. But then our daughter was born and I learned quickly that raising a child did not leave time for much else. In 2004 a local issue drew me back into activism. The previous experience in Michigan had been about no more than a cousin who was "a nice-guy-running-for-office." Having a tangible issue was new for me. There were some people in our extended neighborhood who wanted to form a municipality. The reason they gave for this was that trash collection, fall leaf cleanup, and winter snow plowing would be more efficient and that we could do it cheaper than the County. And, they pointed out, we had only to look at nearby municipalities to see how wonderful it all was. I was adamantly against. Imagine amateur government, neighborhood fights, stinking trash trucks rumbling through your streets twice a week instead of once, favoritism, and petty ordinances. If you take a little time you can likely think of a few more reasons to abhor the prospect. In addition the tax structure in Maryland is such that a large amount of revenue would be diverted from the county to the relatively wealthy new municipality. This makes for bad public policy. We formed a group, knocked on doors, did research, analyzed data, wrote a lengthy report, lobbied the county council, and eventually defeated the proposal with a nine to nothing vote in the council. An activist was born.

I became curious. If a few devoted people with a reasonable cause can have so much influence in the larger system of governance, then surely this has been done before. Of course I had read about popular movements and their various levels of success. But until now that had all been abstract to me. This was real. By living the action the historic ones came to life as well. A whole new world of historic realities opened up.

And what were the men who created the United States before they were statesmen? Activists. Their activism was directed against the government of Great Britain and their grievance was, in a nutshell, the unequal status they were held to as British subjects. First they protested, then they revolted, and next they were saddled with the task of forging a nation out of a collection of differing colonies.

How effective were they? The founders lived over two hundred years ago. In 1776, people did not know what we know now. There were only two nation republics back then, Switzerland and the Netherlands (there were more city republics). Most countries were ruled by potentates. Even the Dutch Republic was increasingly controlled by one family, the House of Orange-Nassau, and began to look more and more like a monarchy. With the benefit of some hindsight we can say that the founders left some things rather ambiguous (i.e. human rights, states' rights, gun rights, free speech). If this means that the founders did not deal with these issues then you could say that they did poorly. However, they did address them but they could not muster the votes to pass precisely defined rules. The people were just not ready for such progressive issues. Therefore, they left some texts ambiguous, expecting that future generations would be forced to address the issues and bring clarity and resolution[13]. By doing so they effectively counted on future activism. With some reluctance you could say that they were right with regard to slavery and civil rights, even though it took a civil war to move the matter along. The Commerce Clause was eventually used to regulate the power of the States. Many other issues are continuously being discussed. Political activism has been a part of the fabric of this nation since its inception and you could say that our system of government requires it. We as a people struggle to introduce what we consider improvements to an incomplete means of governance. This is the natural process. Political scientists and public finance economists would say it is an inherently unstable process giving rise to new combinations of factions forever and ever. The advantage of a democratic republic is the ability to allow for those changes to take place peacefully and with a sense of legitimacy based on the active participation of "We the People."

Many people have engaged in it before us and many will engage in it after we are history. Our student James Madison, as was his friend Thomas Jefferson, was one of those thinkers and doers of his time. As a well-read student of history he had the benefit of hindsight, too. As it is in every age, knowledge was limited to what was available then. Fortunately Jefferson's and Madison's libraries were not limited to texts in English. Madison knew Latin, French, and Italian and read books in those languages. He learned some Hebrew. He was particularly interested in the subjects of human nature, law, and governance. Many of those works had been published in the old city of Leyden in the Netherlands. His generation of intellectuals was dominated by keen students of human nature who applied a good measure of common sense. This is evident from the rich texts they wrote. Madison wrote that people were "much more disposed to vex and oppress each other than to cooperate for their common good."[14] Alexander Hamilton, who founded the publication *The Federalist*, said, "Take mankind in general, they are vicious. Take mankind as they are, and what are they governed by? Their passions. There may be in every government a few choice spirits, who may act from more worthy motives. One great error is that we suppose mankind more honest than they are. Our prevailing passions are ambition and interest; it will ever be the duty of wise government to avail itself of these passions, in order to make them subservient to the public good."[15] Under the pseudonym Publius, the Federalists wrote that just like men, it "is too true, however disgraceful it may be to human nature, that nations in general will make war whenever they have a prospect of getting anything by it." Under the pseudonym The Maryland Farmer, the Anti-Federalists wrote, "Our people are capable of being made any thing, that human nature was capable of, if only we have a little patience and give them good and wholesome institutions."[16] A large part of the discussions among the founders rested on their view of human nature[17]. Those wanting a strong union were generally more pessimistic about their fellow humans than those who favored a looser union.

Back in January of 1783, Madison, Thomas Mifflin, and Hugh Williamson had drawn up a list of books for his proposed Library of Congress[18]. A fellow delegate, Williamson was well-read and had completed the study of medicine in Utrecht, the Netherlands, where he had been exposed to the governance of that republic and the province and city of Utrecht. There were 309 titles divided over thirteen subject areas. Loren Smith suggests that they proposed a "statesman's library" with an overwhelming proportion of works on history, politics, political theory, and an extensive list of "Americana" that amounted to a rudimentary national archive. In subsequent years, Jefferson, who was ambassador to France, purchased a great number of books for Madison and had them shipped in crates to his friend. Jefferson also provided about two thirds of the suggested titles from his own catalogue. The list of 1783 was partially a wish list. But by 1786, the acquisition of the list must have been near completion.

This was the year when Madison locked himself up for two months at his home near Orange, Virginia[19]. His personal library at Montpelier was richly stocked with authors and philosophers such as Descartes, Locke, Grotius, and Hobbes. There were many books on governance that spanned from the ancient Greeks to the then modern Netherlands, Germany, England, and Scotland. The private library included a great many books on the subject of human nature. It was a popular subject in this time of enlightenment. As his notes show, Madison supported his case for a change in the way the American Confederation functioned, with a thorough analysis of the republics of antiquity as well as the contemporary republics. Although an empire and not a republic, the German Union did not escape his scrutiny[20]. The notes point out the various systems of government and their strengths and weaknesses.

He and his friend Jefferson were perhaps the most well-read men on the continent. It is small wonder that the personal library at Madison's home at Montpelier was a cramped affair with clusters of books spread over the entire house. Mary Cutts, a niece, wrote of the various library spaces[21]. "Enter the library," and there are, "plain cases, not only round the room, but in the middle with just sufficient room to pass between, these cases were filled with books, pamphlets, papers, all, every thing of interest to our country before and since the Revolution."

Since Madison's days many more studies have been carried out. With the benefit of hindsight we can attempt to accompany Madison on his journey through time. So, let us go back to a period when human nature was less constrained by rules and laws and examine how we as a species came to apply increasing doses of common sense that would benefit increasing proportions of humanity. Let us stand with James Madison as he reaches up into his bookcase to retrieve and consult one of the over four thousand volumes, open it to expose its ornate print, rich prose, and promising bouquet.

Knowledge will forever govern ignorance.
James Madison to W.T. Barry, August 4, 1822.

Timeline

Year	Event(s)
163,000 BCE	Blombos People, South Africa
ca. 500 BCE	Democracy in Greece
ca. 450 BCE	Democracy in Rome
ca. 60 CE	Roman armies occupy territory as far north as the mouth of the Rhine
104	Romans grant market rights to Noviomagus on the Rhine
122	Romans grant market rights to Forum Hadriani on the Rhine
ca. 400	Romans retreat
ca. 470	Franks occupy Paris area
496	Frankish King Clovis converts to Christianity
511	Lex Salica (law of the Sea Franks) written up in Latin
615	Edict of Paris spelling out rights of nobles and clergy
648	Clovis II and Balthild married
650	Landri Bishop of Paris
667	Marculf dies after completing his Formularae
ca. 800	Netherlands part of Charlemagne's empire
ca. 850	Leyden first mentioned (as Leithon)
11 th c.	Formation of Waterschappen, or water boards, in Holland
ca. 1200	Leyden a city. Institutes civic government
1215	King John signs Magna Carta
13 th c.	Holland most densely populated area in Europe
1355	The "De cura reipublicae et sorte principantis" implemented in Holland
1384	Burgundian expansion into Netherlands
1425	First assembly of Estates of Brabant, Holland, and Zeeland

1433	Single currency in Burgundian Netherlands
1477	Great Privilege of the Burgundian Netherlands
1517	Martin Luther publishes his Theses
1533	William of Nassau born
1536	Anabaptists settle in England
1547	John of Barneveld born
1555	Netherlands under Spanish rule
1561	Edwin Sandys born
1566	Iconoclasms in the Netherlands
1568	Dutch Revolt against Spain and start of 80 Year War
1584	William of Orange-Nassau assassinated
1607	Jamestown founded. Pilgrims settle in Holland
1609	Twelve Year Truce between Spain and the Netherlands begins
1618	Adriaen van der Donck born
1619	Barneveld executed, Virginia Articles of Government passed
1620	Mayflower Compact, Plimoth Plantation founded
1621	80 Year War between Spain and the Netherlands resumes
1624	New Netherlands founded Virginia a Royal colony
1629	New Hampshire and Maine founded
1630	Massachusetts founded
1633	First school in America opened in New Amsterdam
1634	Maryland founded
1635	Connecticut founded
1636	Rhode Island founded
1638	Delaware founded
1643	United Colonies of New England
1647	Rhode Island constitution allows separation of Church and State
1648	80 and 30 Year Wars end

1649	King Charles I executed in England Petition of the Commonality of New Netherlands; Remonstrance of New Netherlands
1649	Toleration Act in Maryland
1653	Cromwell becomes Lord Protector of England Municipal Charter for New Netherlands North Carolina founded
1657	Flushing Remonstrance
1660	English monarchy reinstated, Charles II King
1663	South Carolina founded
1664	British take New Netherlands, New York Founded New Jersey founded
1676	Bacon's rebellion in Virginia
1682	Pennsylvania founded
1732	Georgia founded and birth of George Washington
1750	English Parliament passed the Iron Act limiting American production
1751	English Parliament passed the Currency Act banning New England's paper money
1754	French and Indian War erupted
1759	British control all of Canada
1764	English Parliament passed the Sugar Act increasing tax burden on America. It also passed the Currency Act banning the issuing of paper money in America
1765	English Parliament passed the Stamp Act taxing all printed materials. Quartering Act forced colonists to house British troops. Patrick Henry presented seven resolutions Sons of Liberty forced all stamp agents to resign Stamp Act, Congress asserted that only colonial legislatures can tax colonists
1766	New York refused to comply with some stipulations of the Quartering Act. King George repealed the Stamp Act Parliament passed the Declaration Act asserting total control over the colonies

	Violence broke out between colonists and British soldiers
1767	English Parliament passed the Townshend Revenue Acts imposing new taxes on the colonists
1768	Massachusetts protest Boston and New York boycott English goods Boston residents urged to arm themselves British infantry set up permanent residence in Boston
1769	Boycott of British goods spread to New Jersey, Rhode Island, and North Carolina
1770	Violence between colonists and soldiers in New York Boston Massacre Townshend Acts repealed Quartering Act not renewed
1772	British customs schooner burned
1773	Virginia initiated joined exploration of complaints against the British New Hampshire, Rhode Island, Connecticut, and South Carolina followed Boston Tea Party
1774	English Parliament passed the Coercive Acts (called the Intolerable Acts in America) Also passed another Quartering Act First Continental Congress met in Philadelphia Export ban to Britain
1775	Hostilities broke out in Massachusetts. The Revolutionary War started
1782	The United States of America were officially recognized by the Dutch Republic
1783	The Treaty of Paris confirming British acceptance of American independence
1786	Annapolis Convention
1787	Constitutional Convention in Philadelphia
1790	Rhode Island last state to ratify the Constitution

If men were angels, no government would be necessary.
James Madison in The Federalist No. 51

Chapter 1: Rules, Trust, and Laws

In the timeline of human history, democracy as we know it is a recent invention. For modern humans that timeline started around 165,000 years ago. Recent excavations in a cave near Blombos, South Africa[22], revealed that its occupants exploited seashells, used ocher (perhaps for adornment), and made very small, sharp stone blades by a method of careful heating and chipping. One stone, from a later date layer, showed geometric lines that were very regularly spaced. The communities survived long-term adverse climatic conditions during which many species went extinct. They were pretty clever folks, these ancients, which is good for us, because they were our ancestors. The skills needed to make the blades point to a level of specialization through diversification. In other words, each member of the community contributed to the whole by doing some tasks while relying on others to carry out theirs. To make that work they had to have rules and to make them stick they had to have an enforcement mechanism.

Until very recently the San people of Southern Africa had a lifestyle that resembled that of the Blombos people. They scavenged and hunted and they had a division of labor[23]. They usually worked in groups and they shared the proceeds with the whole community. In fact, to this day the sharing of resources reassures membership. However, sharing does not always happen and the fear that you might receive nothing is strong. The rules are simple and mostly enforce themselves. But what could the primitive communities do about a thief, murderer, or a mentally ill person? There the rules were simple, too. Since there was no prison or hospital, such a person would be banned or, if he returned, killed. It was the only remaining option.

These rules did not just appear out of nowhere. Necessity was the mother of invention. A community, or someone in it, must have found it necessary to introduce or impose a rule. This system evidently served our ancestors well. Otherwise evolution would have left the systems, and our ancestors who relied on them, in the dust of history.

It became a bit more complicated when people transitioned from hunting-gathering communities to agricultural settlements. Stationary communities did not just scavenge the land. Clearing land, plowing, sowing, weeding, and harvesting were long-term investments that required protections. Rules regarding rights or ownership needed to be enforceable and that in turn required an entity strong enough to evict usurpers or punish perpetrators. By the time the Roman historian Cornelius Tacitus studied the Germanic people and wrote about them in 60 CE[24], agricultural societies in northern Europe had developed intricate systems of law and governance.

The feudal system of government did not have a large bureaucracy. Administration was in the hands of a few, presumably distrustful, individuals. The single biggest line item in the budget (if they bothered to maintain one) was the army. The overlord promised to protect his subjects from other warlords. He often employed a certain level of terror and collected his taxes by (threat of) force. It was akin to the modern-day protection racket. Like the inner city gangsters of our age, the overlord would harm those who refused to pay. If you paid the overlord then he would protect you from himself. On the whole the system provided a measure of security from outside raiders since a destroyed farm wouldn't yield the overlord anything. But, protection against external threats was not guaranteed. Another uncertainty was the fair imposition of justice. Laws were mostly unwritten and, in any case, ultimately enforced exclusively by the whim of the overlord.

German tribal warrior

In such an environment trust may seem outright foolish. Voluntary transactions will mostly be limited to those between close relatives. Business will not flourish. The condition may rise to the level of culture and can endure for generations. In his book *Making Democracy Work: Civic Traditions in Modern Italy*[25], Robert Putnam examines the functioning of civic institutions and compares governmental functioning in north and south Italy some ten years after the introduction of a new "county" or "province" layer of government. In a nutshell, he finds the following: In the north people are generally content with the responsiveness of government. People vote, parliamentary discussions are lively and constructive, and representatives have a sense of doing something useful. In the south it is practically the opposite. In addition, the north is wealthy, the south is poor.

Why is that? To find an answer, Putnam goes back hundreds of years and observes that there was a fundamental difference in the way these two areas developed. Communities such as farms and towns in the north instituted a common defense against invaders and bandits. The successful interaction and interdependence also stimulated government by committee and a certain level of participatory rule. People created civic institutions and expected that they serve them.

The south didn't see this development. There, government was in the hands of feudal lords who tolerated no civil input and who were often at war with each other. As a consequence, no flourishing merchant class developed and what wealth there was accumulated in the hands of a few. It is no accident that the Renaissance started in the north and spread to places that were receptive through familiarity – Germanic Europe, such as parts of France, Germany, the Netherlands, and, later, England. In short, we see that strong civic institutions are a prerequisite for the development of commerce and cities. They gained wealth through activities that required cooperation and trust: manufacturing and trade.

Roman soldier

Why were some parts of Europe more receptive? Upon their arrival in Western Europe, the Romans introduced a level of civic organization that had not previously been present. Taxation wasn't based on robbery and protection wasn't based on extortion. In fact most taxes were collected on roads and rivers in the form of tolls. The Romans also introduced a more reliable form of justice since it relied on written, and thus verifiable, laws. They codified and applied their laws to all levels of society.

As a result, two important things happened around the Roman settlements: the relative safety of their forts attracted goods, and as a result, they attracted people. The forts were in need of labor for tasks that the occupants preferred not to do themselves. This may have included laundry service, cooking, cleaning, and, no doubt, prostitution. The forts also provided a measure of protection that made living in their proximity desirable. The forts and settlements needed supplies of food and other goods and attracted local farmers and traders.

One example of how this developed is the granting of a special privilege by Emperor Trajanus in the year 104 to establish a market in a new town near the fort *Noviomagus*. Now called Nijmegen and located in the Netherlands, this town was a replacement for the nearby capital of the *Batavieren* (Batavians) after the Romans put down their revolt in 70 CE. Similar privileges were extended to many towns in the Roman Empire, including in France and Britain.

However, the Romans did not arrive in a barren land populated by primitive people. The historian Tacitus described how Germanic fighting men elected their leaders and how local councils settled disputes and decided on matters concerning the tribe, town, or village. The Germanic peoples already had strong democratic customs.

Trade is a tricky business. If there is an immediate exchange of goods then the safety of the location and the road home are important. If the exchange cannot be immediate and a promise is involved, then it is safer to trade with relatives or people of the clan or village rather than strangers from elsewhere. With the former there is enforcement through social control and the imposition of repercussions by elders or leaders. Strangers may never be seen again. But, as business opportunities increased, so did transactions between people who were not family. The increase in risk must have been worth it. In his book *The Company of Strangers* Paul Seabright[26] examines this dynamic and observes that we can trust because we have created the necessary social and legal structures. The foundations of these structures are quite logical and allow for a rational cost-benefit analysis. Reciprocity makes sure that kindness is repaid with kindness and betrayal with revenge. Under such a system we can treat strangers as honorary relatives or friends. Rules are enforced by proscribed incentives, learned through practice and education, which make opportunistic behavior less comfortable.

The process that led to this kind of trust must have been a slow one. We pretty much have the same brains as did our ancestors of tens of thousands of years ago. They lived in a very dangerous environment where animals and competing bands of people posed a threat. The trusting of strangers probably grew in fits and starts. There had to be a benefit, otherwise the trait would not have survived human evolution.

Trust originated in the family group. This is no coincidence. Families share genes that they protect and carry forward. Because of the differing role in procreation, the strategies of men and women differ. The number of pregnancies she can bring to completion limits the offspring of women. They will look for a good provider and protector and may, on occasion, stray to share offspring with a healthy, good-looking man. Men, on the other hand, can have offspring with as many women they can mate with, and, in the absence of social or other constraints, they will (i.e. military during war, male staff in prisons for women, abuse of drunken young women in college). This behavior of the sexes may be confirmed in our time where men in prestigious positions appear to have better access to more women than ordinary men.

In his book *King of the Mountain* Arnold Ludwig[27] ponders on page one why people would want to rule others. He dismisses the obvious reasons such as power, privilege, and perks or the high minded motives of patriotism, duty, and service. Instead he goes on to show that the aforementioned reasons are mere rationalizations by aspiring rulers for seeking high office and that the real reasons are socially and biologically driven. He writes, "Just as the orgasmic pleasures associated with sex ensure procreation and contribute to the preservation of the species – regardless of the reasons people give for copulating, such as doing it for love, intimacy, or fun – the rewards that come with the ultimate power likewise serve as powerful motivators for would-be rulers to do Nature's bidding."

Ludwig looked at 1941 rulers of 199 countries in the 20th century and made his case in abundance. He also found that the urge to procreate was so strong that (aspiring) rulers took enormous personal risk to get to, and stay at, the top. Their life expectancies were seriously shortened as a result. But their surviving genes, in the form of plentiful offspring, were their reward.

How do men gain access to women? In peaceful, ordered societies rape is not a good option. Men have to make themselves attractive to them. The best way to accomplish that is by rising to the top of some heap. In primitive societies there is usually one small heap for a chief to sit on. But, it is his heap alone. As long as he (for it was almost always a male) could fulfill his desires by command, his heap would continue to be monopolistic. He might have been able to conquer territories from other small rulers and so enlarge his heap and broaden his access to women. Eventually he would come upon objects that he could not obtain by command or conquest. He would have to purchase them by exchange of goods or moneys. Matt Ridley, in his book *The Rational Optimist*, writes, "At some point, after millions of years of indulging in reciprocal back-scratching of gradually increasing intensity, one species, and one alone, stumbled upon an entirely different trick. Adam gave Oz an object in exchange for a different object."[28]

Trade was born.

For trade to continue it has to benefit all parties involved. Otherwise it will just dry up. A successful trade between individuals inserts the expectation that future trades could be beneficial as well. Successive successful trades firm up that expectation. Repeated trades establish a method by which the exchange takes place. Eventually the method formalizes, and expectation has risen to the level of trust.

If institutions were an essential requirement for the development and maintenance of trust between strangers, then it follows that the benefit (or profit) motive must have induced humans to create these institutions.

At some point in our evolution we must have realized that some people were better at certain tasks and that by having them perform the task we would benefit. Reciprocity helped continue such an arrangement and a system of diversification of skills ensued, creating a specialization and division of labor. But such a system could only be maintained if there was a way to enforce reciprocity. Altruism does not guarantee it and, in any case, would be quite destructive to the altruist if there were no rewards. It makes sense therefore that a set of rules developed that were enforced by a powerful entity such as a leader or a collective council. A justice system of sorts codified violations and repercussions to be imposed on a transgressor of the rules.

In short, the desire for goods encouraged trade. Trade necessitated enforceable rules, which led to institutions, and institutions empowered ordinary people. To extrapolate from Ludwig's metaphor, "Mountains" flattened while many small heaps dotted its slopes and surrounding plains. Each had someone at its top who ruled and defended his or her domain (professions or crafts such as blacksmithing, masonry, tailoring, farming, etc.).

Caninefaten

... there may be occasions on which the evil may spring from the
[Government]
James Madison to Thomas Jefferson, 17 Oct., 1788.

Chapter 2: A Saxon in Paris

Timeline

Year	Event
451	Attila the Hun invades Gaul (France)
464	Childeric the Frank conquers Paris
481	Clovis I succeeds his father
486	Clovis I defeats the last Romans in Francia
496	Clovis I converts to Christianity
508	Clovis I makes Paris his capital
655	Clovis II King of Neustria and Burgundy

Both Madison and Jefferson were familiar with the *Encyclopedie ou Dictionaire Raisonne* ... etc. that John Adams owned[29]. The successor volumes, to be published from 1782 onward, featured as number one on the library list. The issue featured three interesting Frankish characters who were responsible for a significant change in both the treatment of slaves and the ownership of real estate. As a slave owner and an owner of real property James Madison must have found the revolutionary accomplishments of these Franks compelling. The English philosopher, David Hume, in his Political Essays of 1764 observed, "... the Gauls had no fixed property in land; but that the chieftains, when any death happened in the family, made a new division of all the lands among the several members of the family." Imagine the upheaval among the peasantry who were totally dependent on the whims of the ruling families.

Roman rule did not last in Western Europe. Germanic tribes overran both England and the Netherlands from the east[30]. The Saxons settled in the Netherlands north of the Rhine River and the Franks to the south. However, some Saxons were later squeezed out by the Frisians to the north and moved across the Channel and North Sea to England. The three Germanic tribes enjoyed a remarkable level of civic organization and were more democratic than later feudal times would suggest. Tacitus[31] wrote that the election (!) of a king took place at a gathering of all the shield and spear bearing men of the tribe. The king, as leader in case of warfare, was elected by the (literal) stakeholders. Smaller councils dealt with local matters Headmen proposed policies that were approved by a clashing of arms or rejected by a murmur of disapproval. Councils heard accusations and prosecuted crimes. Such councils also elected the "hundred" chiefs[32] who functioned as the administrative heads (*gouwvorsten*) of a canton (*gau*). The Germanic peoples recognized three classes: nobles, freemen, and slaves. Later they added a fourth class: half-free, which is somewhat comparable to the indentured servants of later times. There were pagan priests but, since not much has been written about them, their influence was presumably small. Marriage was monogamous and followed strict rules. The wife received a dowry from her husband and the marriage promise was of great importance.

The legends of King Arthur and their various modern day permutations notwithstanding, the Romans left very little of their governmental institutions behind. Gaul was overrun by the Franks while Albion was invaded by the Saxons and the Angles. All three were Germanic people and they brought with them their customs and institutions. When, in the Fifth century, King Clovis the First led the Franks to conquer land as far south as the Loire River in France, he found it inhabited by a hodgepodge of peoples. In little more than a century after the Romans officially left, invaders had caused much destruction.

However, the wagon train of the Romans had brought a passenger who proved more enduring, and who did not leave with the legions. It was the Church of Rome and it had survived in pockets with monasteries and churches. Its priests and monks were versed in Latin and their libraries were filled with writings in that language. There were bibles, of course, but there were also books about the laws of the church, Canon Law. Others described the laws of society, Roman law.

After Clovis converted to Christianity in 496 CE, the country reintroduced Roman customs and law, of which the church had become the heir. The inclusion of bishops in the council of advisors to the King encouraged the Romanization of the kingdom. The Franks produced two bodies of law known as the *Lex Salica* (Law of the Sea Franks) and the *Lex Ripuaria* (Law of the River Franks). The first was drawn up before 511 CE and was written in Latin, showing the hand of ecclesiastics. Although much of it was based on old Frankish law, the writers used old Roman law to give interpretation and/or clarification. The work is informative of Frankish organization and mostly deals with the administration of justice. The Laws of the River Franks were probably compiled in the late sixth century and are very similar to that of the Sea Franks.

South Saxon, spring of 643

England was nothing like today[33]. Thick forests covered its gentle hills, valleys, and much of its plains. Its human inhabitants had developed the scarce open terrain into small fields where oxen-powered wood ploughs stirred the topsoil. Wheat, barley and rye grew unevenly in the shallow furrows. Young boys and girls herded cattle, pigs, goats, and sheep along the edges of the forest and in fields that lay fallow for a year. In the evening they returned to safe enclosures for the night. The people lived in small hams[34] of perhaps a hundred souls or less who formed a large extended family with strong ties. The community provided protection from wild animals such as wolves and bears that prowled the forest by day and the fields by night, and their numbers helped discourage outsiders from stealing, robbing, kidnapping, or murdering. Their homes were made of wood, wattle, and mud. Thatched roofs of grasses or reeds kept them dry from the wet elements.

Compared to today, the climate was cold in the 7th century, and winters were anything but pleasant in these primitive living conditions.

Saxons

For warmth, families usually shared the one room dwelling with their farm animals. Clothing was made from wool and linen. The men wore short or long pants and shirts. Leather straps kept leggings in place. Against cold or rain they wore cloaks. The women were dressed in long garments covered with long tunics and mantles for warmth.

The majority of Saxons were churls[35], who were freemen. The wealthier lived in huts with multiple rooms and slept on beds made of wood and straw while the poor had to make do on the ground. Much of their wellbeing depended on the whims of the ruling class. Only the thanes[36] had the right to hunt, and they controlled most cultivated land. Some churls owned their own land, but most paid a rent for the privilege of using a thane's fields. Either the payment was a portion of the harvest or it could be in the form of labor. And there were slaves. Some had sold themselves to repay debts or to survive a famine. Destitute parents sold their children as a way of improving the prospects of survival for all family members, including the enslaved ones. The frequent famines were so bad that parents would abandon children in the woods or along roads. Others trekked to the coast to sell their children and stray ones they picked up along the way. Traders would transport them as far as North Africa. Others would steal children from more fortunate families and sell them. The Church increased its purchase of these children for the benefit of their salvation. Some churches put the slaves on their balance books and became active participants in the trade[37].

The larger villages enjoyed a diversification of skills. They might have a blacksmith who made tools and weapons for local use. Or the goods could be traded against those from other villages. Some people specialized in making pottery used for food storage, containers for water, pots for cooking, or beakers for drinking.

The old Roman roads had fallen into disrepair and were overgrown. Travel and trade were limited to coastal areas and rivers large enough to support a boat. Villages were relatively isolated so that most farming was for subsistence. The population was very dependent on the good fortunes of the weather and harvests varied greatly from year to year. Famines and disease were common, life was harsh, and life expectancy short. Let us picture a Saxon village.

⊕ It is spring. The sun is out and brightens the young green shoots of grain in the fields. A gentle wind pushes occasional wafts of warm air from the fields and cold wafts from the nearby forest. The air is filled with the smells of mold from the thatched roofs, smoke from fires in open stone-ringed hearths, manure, and rancid odors from unwashed bodies and rotting meat. You would not particularly notice them though. You are used to them. But there are also sweet hints of the growing season. The scent of flowers fills your senses with the promise of a new growing season, fresh food and honey. Apple trees and some berry bushes are in full bloom. The hives are swarming with worker bees that seem to get in each other's way as they fly in with nectar and out with fresh information about the best sources. Men go out to the forest and return with materials to repair their huts. Women work in small fields to plant carrots, cabbages, and other vegetables. Mothers nurse babies and toddlers[38]. Young children play between the huts, poking sticks in abundant mud puddles, chasing after insects, discovering what is edible or not, or playing house. Older children help their parents with the daily chores, assist in the forest and the fields, herd the

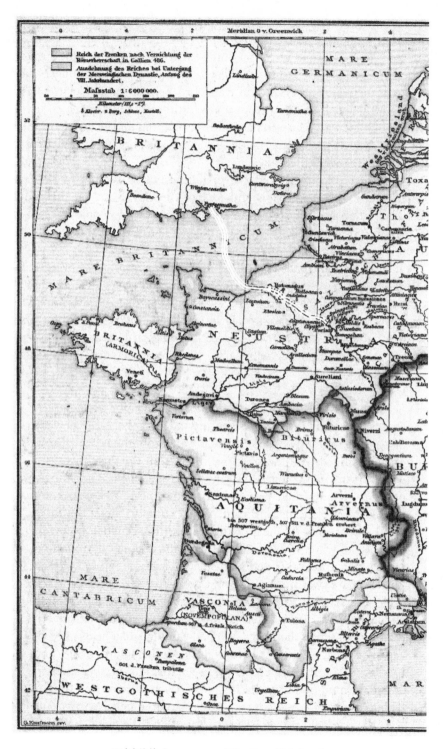

Balthild's journey and the Frankish lands

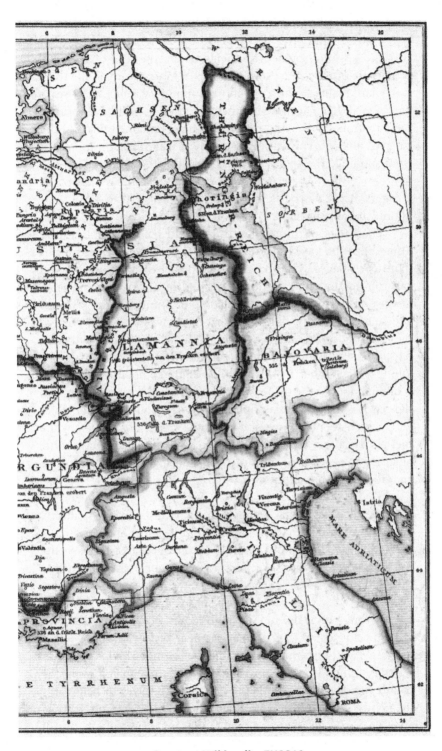

Courtesy Wikipedia, ZH2010

animals, and in between do what kids do best: chase each other, do mock sword fights with sticks, get into real fights, break a pot or two, and get into trouble with their elders. And in all this hopeful activity that carries the promise of a continuing lease on life there is the hard reality of shortage. If the community is lucky, last year's harvest will have been abundant. Stored grain will have escaped the attention of mice and rats; it will have remained dry and not suffered any rot. The salting of the meat was sufficient to keep it from spoiling. The apples are not infested with worms or covered in mold. In short, there are a many conditions to the welfare of the villagers. Any failure in just one of them will lead to a full-scale famine. It happens often.

When there are too many mouths to feed, the options are limited[39]. If you have tradable items, and there is a harvest surplus in nearby villages, you can purchase food. If you are powerful, you can rob nearby villages and estates and let them starve instead. Disease and epidemic can reduce your numbers. You can sell yourself into slavery, but that offers no guarantee. Slaves were at the very bottom of Saxon society. They had no rights and were not protected from willful bodily harm. There was no penalty for killing a slave other than to provide some compensation for the economic loss to the owner. So, you could sell your children into slavery. It is the unpleasant option of choice. You receive tangibles with which to purchase food for your remaining family while there is a chance that the traded child will survive and have some offspring to perpetuate your line. Considering the alternatives it is an understandable solution.

One such family has a daughter of about nine years, Balthild. She is a precocious child and fairly good-looking. She is a middle child for which the family has little need. An older sister plays the role of mother and housekeeper and her younger siblings include at least one boy, who is destined to take over the farm and care for his parents when they get old. If she has younger sisters, then they are too young to be useful. But Balthild has all the skills necessary to run a household. If the village is near or on navigable water, her father will know of some traders who might be interested in purchasing her. It is also possible that traders regularly roam the country in search of commerce and acquire slaves to help carry the goods. Once in the ports, they can easily be sold off. And so a young Saxon girl begins a frightening journey in the hands of strange men. Taken away from her family, her neighbors, her friends and the familiar sights, sounds and smells of her village, she is among other children, girls mostly, and enters a world harsher even than the one in which she grew up. However, the traders recognize her value as she cares for the other six children in their possession, all between the ages of five and nine. She proves to have plenty of spunk and energy and she appears intelligent. Her village priest had taught her the virtues of Christ and how to be a worthy follower by caring for children, the poor and the elderly. Her father's involvement in the village council had taught her to be thoughtful and respectful and to obey her elders. Her mother had showed her how to cook, mend and make clothes, avoid and heal illness, and how to tend to wounds. Her adventure could have unfolded thus.

Finally the forest opens as they get to a wide river. She is awe-struck. Never before has she seen a large body of water. She notices a number of people near the water. As they get closer to the shore, she sees a large boat below at the bank. She has heard of them, but the sight of the sleek, eighty feet long wooden boat frightens and excites her at the same time. The bow and stern are pointed and a beam sticks up from each. There are long oars on the far side and a longer one near the stern. One score men are loading crates, baskets, clay vessels, goats, and bundles of cloth. Others mill around the grassy shore. Her group passes two men who are loading an ox cart. A half dozen women stand around some baskets and crates near the cart and one woman on the bank is in loud negotiation with a man on the boat, possibly the captain. A few horses rest under a large tree. The leader of her group orders the children to sit on the bank near the stern and instructs Balthild to look after them. He walks to the boat and starts a conversation with the captain. Balthild is very tired. So are the other children. Their bare feet are unaccustomed to such long journeys and received scrapes and bruises from fallen branches and rocks that were hidden under last fall's leaves. The walk from her village to the river had taken most of yesterday and all of this morning. They had spent the night in the forest. The children had all huddled together seeking each other's warmth and comfort. Some sobbed, some cried, others were quiet, their glassy eyes staring into the depths of fear and sorrow. Balthild had brought them food and drink. She had wiped their dirty, tear-streaked faces, escorted them among the trees for their bodily functions, and cuddled the youngest ones and rocked them to sleep. This morning they had awakened to a light drizzle.

Their wool and linen clothes are damp. Two lightly dressed girls are shivering and again Balthild takes charge and finds some morsels and water to share with the children and again she huddles them together under a worn tarp. When the men have finished their loading, they order her to bring the children on board. Not knowing or caring who the tarp belongs to she tucks it under her arm. Nobody protests. They walk down to the water's edge and up the roughly hewn gangplank. The captain directs them to the bow where they find a small place free of cargo. She settles the children on and between the boat's ribs and beam and covers them with the old tarp. The bottom of the boat gently moves them up and down and back and forth. She hears a few more yells and drifts off into a comatose sleep.

She wakes up. A regular banging against the boards follows the movement of her world. It is dark. To the right of the bow a large, full moon sits above the water and spreads its silvery glitter over the waves toward her. A sour smell spreads under the tarp. A few children are throwing up clear liquid from their empty stomachs. Balthild feels nauseated, too, but takes a few deep breaths of the fresh air above the tarp. She watches the two rows of men pulling large oars in unison. Cargo is lined up on the center beam between the men who sing softly in the rhythm of the oars. One man stands in the stern. He is holding a large oar that he keeps steady in the water behind him. A few more men appear to be sleeping near the standing man. The sounds of breaking waves and rushing water come from below her and she sinks back into sleep, heart aching from the loss of her familiar life. ⊖

Paris, winter of 642/3

A citizen of Paris today would be a complete stranger to the Frankish city. Perhaps from the air he would recognize the flow of the river Seine that, coming from the east, curves first to the north, then to the west before dipping a little south and then west again. Near the top of this bow he would perhaps identify a small group of islands, the largest of which has a great wall around its perimeter. Two small islets at either end are overgrown with bushes and ringed with reeds. Together those three islands would later form the *Île de la Cité* in the center of the 21st century metropolis. Let us descend to the ground and approach the small city from the south[40].

⊕ The old Roman road from Genabum[41] shows the signs of age and poor maintenance during the past 250 years. Cart wheels have left deep ruts in the pavement stones. In many places, two-tracks veer off where travelers have preferred the rough banks to the deep mud holes caused by blocked drainage and a softened road base. Where the plateau narrows between the Brièvre river valley

Medieval Paris

to the east and the plain of the Seine valley to the west, the road descends almost unnoticeably on a long ridge that runs north to where it almost meets the Seine itself. Continuing north, the leafless trees of the forest are replaced by wintry fields and a small village. In the distance the white and grey stones of Roman ruins contrast with a patch of light blue sky on the northern horizon. As the land opens up we see more ruins. Of most only the giant stones of their foundations remain. In others you can recognize the original shape, and a number of pillars still stand. There are no houses and no people. It is a desolate necropolis.

As we keep walking, a large walled-in compound appears to our right. This is the *Palais des Thermes,* where Rome's emperors stayed as they visited or lived in the city. As the name implies, the vast complex was built around the hot springs that the Romans so much coveted. Many of the buildings are still intact but much of the walls have been removed. As we pass the structures, we see the mixed colors of the large wall of an island in the Seine. Large towers interrupt its regular flow. Above the wall we make out a few church towers; most of them in the center and east of the island. On the west side are the four white towers of the palace, two of which are set in the city wall. A smoky haze hangs in the still winter air above the island.

As we approach the end of the ridge, the ruins make way for a small suburb. Some houses are built with the stones from the Roman buildings behind us, but most are of wood. Nearly all have thatched roofs where thin lines of smoke rise from their chimneys. Two small churches stand to our right, the largest of which is made with stone from the same Roman sources. The ridge continues for a short distance to end at a bluff not far from the river. The road descends and meets with the road that connects Paris with Rouen. The joined roads level with a wooden bridge that crosses the narrow arm of the Seine to a large gate between two towers in the city wall. This is the Petit-Pont[42].

We have an unobstructed view of the great wall. It is about 100 feet tall above the river and separated from it by a deep, gently sloping bank on which grow bushes and a few gnarled trees, damaged by the frequent harvesting of their branches. The old stones are gray and recent repair work shows in patches of white or gray stone or fired red brick. Except for some missing stones, the top of the wall is completely level. The large round towers are in the same condition and are only slightly taller. Large numbers of crows fly above the city; their caws echo across the water.

We mix with the ox carts and foot traffic and cross the bridge. A few mail-clad soldiers linger at the gate by a small fire. Under round iron helmets they wear wool hoods. Their long hair pours over their shoulders. As they warm their hands, spears rest against their arms or against the wall, while their swords hang in leather straps from their waist belts. They ignore us when we enter the darkness of the gate. Young men and boys, presumably pickpockets, hang out in the gloom.

With our hands on our wallets, we pass through the thirty-foot tunnel and enter the Rue Savaterie. Smells of smoke and human waste immediately halt our breath. But there is no escaping it so we move on. This road, which is the original Roman main road through the island to the Grand-Pont[43], and the north beyond, is the only paved public surface in the city. Tall, wooden houses crowd against its entire length. Their protruding second and third stories limit the light that reaches down.

Few buildings are older than 70 years. The invasion of Attila's Huns and the Frankish conquest left much of Paris outside of the small island a dead zone. Then it suffered a series of misfortunes, such as civil wars, a major flood in 583, and a fire in 586 that destroyed almost all private structures on the island. The Franks did engage in large building projects but their architects lacked the sophistication of the Romans and the resulting structures are crude in comparison. Using the remains of the old city for materials, they engaged in extensive repairs and the construction of churches and monasteries. And they made rough repairs to the 4th century Roman perimeter wall around the old island.

At the first opportunity we turn right. The street is muddy and the smell of urine and feces is strong. Regular houses line the left side of the street while the ones on the right are built against the city wall and have their thatched roofs summit against it. Windows that have shutters have them shut; ones without show drawn drapes.

A door opens. A woman comes out, walks three paces, and, as if she did not notice us, empties a wooden cask in the center of the street right in front of us. We step around the steaming human waste and continue to the church of St. Etienne[44]. It is the oldest church in Paris and was once its basilica. Built on the site of a Roman temple, it has many of the latter's stones in its walls. Right behind the church the city wall curves to the north before turning west. We follow the streets beside it and walk via the Rue Chanoinesses to the Rue Marineusets. Here the street separates from the wall, which can now only be seen at the end of little side streets. One such is the Rue Gastines where the bishop has his oratory and where he prefers to live.

Everywhere the houses are densely packed, making the streets dim. Half frozen mud and waste is scattered all around and sometimes piled up at street corners. The smells meet us in strong wafts. From behind a house we hear the sounds of pigs being fed. After two more short blocks we return to the Rue Savaterie and cross into the Rue Draperie. We pass the church of St. Croix on our right. We're startled by the clatter of hooves behind us and manage to duck into a narrow alleyway just in time. Frankish soldiers race by, galloping their oversized horses through the narrow street. The mail-clad ruffians have little regard for the common man, woman, or child, let alone dogs, hogs, goats or any other creature that lives in the dark, stinking streets. It was more than mud that the large hoofs sent flying. But, we escaped the worst of it and continue our foray in the Neustrian[45] capital.

A tiny square with a lone, bare tree shows us the church of St. Pierre des Assis before we reach the Cours du Palais, the large square in front of the Royal Palace. The open area allows for some ventilation, and the rancid smells fade somewhat. The façade of the old Roman palace is white, with darker streaks of fire and battle. Here it stretches the entire width of the walled-in city while the remaining three palace walls are incorporated into the city wall as it curves around from west to east. The windows are tall and topped with arches. Behind them, closed, thick, faded curtains are all that stand between the residents and the cold outside. The large double doors to the palace's internal courtyard are closed, but a small man-door in one of them is open. Soldiers linger inside. Smoke rises from the many chimneys. There is no roof structure other than the flat stone top. This is where the young king Clovis II was born and where he lives with his mother, the dowager Queen Nanthild. The boy's father, King Dagobert I, died several years ago. Clovis is now eight years old; his mother is in her early thirties and still an attractive woman. Others who live here are Erchinoald, the powerful mayor of the palace, and his wife. There are various underlings, advisors, officers and soldiers, and staff. ⊖

The third and last wife of the Frankish king Dagobert, Nanthild had been a Saxon slave at his court in Burgundy. Presumably the promiscuous king liked the young and pretty woman well enough to make her his wife and queen. Fate, or design, had it that all but one of the sons by his former wives had died, putting her first born, Clovis, in line for the succession. That succession was not guaranteed. Frankish politics were chaotic. Between the kings of other Frankish kingdoms, mayors of their various palaces, and the many nobles, their schemes, designs, and conspiracies often determined the outcome of untimely royal deaths, or even determined the deaths themselves. With the help of her palace mayor, Aeges, she had managed to hang on and protect her son. Upon Aeges's death, she had worried, but the new mayor, Erchinoald, proved an intelligent ally. He valued order and justice as much as she.

However, Nanthild had been taken ill.

As a matter of course the Frankish kingdoms went through much turmoil. Being Germanic peoples, the Franks adhered to a communal use of land. Personal ownership was unknown, although the nobles claimed land for their own use, built estates on them, farmed them using the labor of slaves and farmers in their sphere of influence, and decided which persons or families could use the land. The people who worked the land, and were dependent on the proceeds, were therefore uncertain of its continued use. The shifting of political alliances, pacts between nobility, even personal favors, could remove a farmer from the land and the fruits of his labor. This same instability was found up and down the entire social ladder.

But, with their arrival in Gaul, the Franks were exposed to one important institution that had survived the roughly one hundred years since the demise of the West-Roman Empire. It was the Christian Church. Once their powerful King Clovis I had converted, the Church came out of its obscurity and began to exert influence. As the adherent to Canon Law and the keeper of Roman texts, it encouraged the slow introduction of Roman law into Frankish society. Quite possibly the Church had managed to maintain Roman law in the provinces, but among the foreign overlords it was novel. The first clear sign of success was the writing of Frankish Salic law in the Latin language. This had happened around 130 years before the events that we visit here.

When Nanthild took on the regency of her son Clovis II it was not a certainty that she would get him on the throne of Neustria and Burgundy. Clovis's older half brother was king of the eastern kingdom of Austrasia. He could now be made king of Burgundy or even Neustria as well. However, the nobles of the latter two regions decided that their advantage lay with the dowager queen and they supported her son's ascension. The Neustrian mayor of the palace, Aeges, was a strong supporter and very powerful. That settled, it was important to keep the peace and hold on until Clovis came of age. Unfortunately, Aeges died that same year and the search was on for another supporting mayor. They settled on a relative, Erchinoald. He was possibly a maternal cousin of Nanthild's father-in-law, King Dagobert; this is not certain[46]. But he was powerful and skillful and some peace returned to the land. Particularly, Burgundy had seen much violence with a succession of murders of mayors and would-be mayors. Traditionally, the method of choice for bringing political change in the Frankish lands was murder.

As it was, Nanthild died just two years into her regency, leaving the ten-year-old Clovis under the influence of Erchinoald and his clan. Nothing is known about the boy's life at the palace. Later descriptions of his actions include the word "weak". It could indicate a gentle character or a scrawny physique. We can imagine his being taught the ways of his world by learned clergy - monks usually. Carefully selected clan members instructed him in the art of politics while Erchinoald's officers taught him military matters. He probably played with the children who lived at the palace, but did not venture into the city often for fear of kidnapping or murder. He may have traveled occasionally under the protection of a large entourage of soldiers.

Paris, late spring, or summer of 643.

There is no direct account of the events that follow. That a human transaction took place we are certain of. Let us explore a plausible scenario.

⊕ A ship under the power of many oarsmen moves up the Seine and passes under the Grand-Pont that connects the Île du Palais to the right shore before it moors on the north shore of the river at the Grève, the old port of the Nautae[47]. It is a merchant ship. The high bow and stern of the long boat identify it as Saxon. Between the two rows of oarsmen are crates, bags, and earthenware containers. A few more men stand near the stern while a group of children in the bow stare in astonishment at everything they see. They never saw

Saxon ship

a burgh before, let alone a city. A few days earlier, they had passed Rouen and had seen the close-spaced buildings as they glided by, but this, these great walls, the towers, and the bridges, was even more magnificent.

The captain climbs onto the wooden pier. He turns and conveys instructions to his deputy. It is late afternoon and too late to move the children. They are to be cleaned up and fed and they must have a good night's sleep so they'll be ready for market[48] in the morning.

Another man gets off the boat onto the dock. His dress is richer than the unadorned, bland garb of the others. A sword hangs from his hip. He wears a Saxon helmet of forged iron with a tall gilded point on top, short gilded ear protectors, and mail for the neck. The gold ornaments on his helmet show he is a soldier of considerable rank. He carries a small bundle wrapped in linen, held by a leather strap. The Saxon officer nods to the captain and exchanges a few words before walking off. He is keenly aware of the old relationship between the two and that his queen is Erchinoald's daughter[49]. He has carried their correspondence for years. He avoids people, animals, and merchandize as he walks the length of the dock and steps onto the quay. Before him the Place de la Grève stretches several hundred feet to the north. On the right are the offices of the Nautae, where the captain will pay his docking and trading dues tomorrow. The building of the city administration is next to it. He turns left and follows the riverbank to the bridge, and enters the city from the gate opposite the one our earlier travelers used, and enters the Rue Savaterie. From there he turns right into the Rue St. Croix, to the Neustrian palace.

The mayor, Erchinoald, receives the courier warmly. They embrace. The mayor takes the bundle, peels off its linen wrapping, and unties the ribbon, revealing letters from the Kentish king. The stack of parchment documents topples and the letters slide onto the heavy waxed oak table. He calls a servant to bring food and wine. There is a small celebration to be held and the courier must be hungry.

They sit on large wooden chairs with high backs and talk. The courier reports on the welfare of his royals, his country, and the political situation in Britain. The diverse tribes that had found their way to the islands live in conflict. You cannot even count on your own kinsmen. Angles, Saxons, Jutes, Frisians, and Danes all vie for territory. Frequent famines and outbreaks of disease plague the lands, too, and the past winter has been bad. Then the courier relates his journey from Kent to Paris and mentions the slave children. One young girl has caught his attention. Erchinoald jokes that he is not surprised, but the courier says, "Yes, she is pretty, but she is only about ten and quite smart." He reports that she might have saved a couple of the children's lives by looking after them during the boat journey. The mayor nods. He remembers his wife wants a girl for her quarters. So he instructs the soldier to ask the captain to bring the girl to the palace, so he can evaluate her. ⊖

And the rest, as they say, is history. Erchinoald did purchase the young slave, Balthild, and she did go to live at the palace in the employ of the mayor's wife. She developed a student/teacher relationship with a monk who served the palace. Since she shared the young king's home, it is certain that the young slave and the young man knew each other. A precocious girl would have explored her living environment and made sure that she would spot the boy-king somewhere. And, if she did not meet him deliberately, then conceivably the young man could have caught her spying.

Balthild's hagiographer[50] reports that Erchinoald's wife died a few years later and that the mayor wanted Balthild as a bed warmer. Since "the form of her body was pleasing, very slender, and beautiful to see," and, "her expression was cheerful and her gait dignified," the mayor was probably somewhat aroused in his deprived widower situation. But the story tells of how Balthild avoided this fate by hiding until he gave up and found another wife.

However, he had a better idea that would strengthen his relationship with the young king. He offered Balthild to Clovis for a wife. The adolescent was probably salivating at the prospect of bedding such a beauty. The two married in 648 when they were only 15 years old.

When Balthild became pregnant, she worried her child might not be a boy. After all, it was her duty to provide the royal house with an heir. Her ecclesiastic mentor assured her that she would bear a male, and she did. In fact, she had two more in quick succession.

The combination of beauty, dignity, intelligence, a serious devotion to her husband, a tolerance of his extramarital sexual pursuits, and the fact she had guaranteed him heirs would have raised her standing in the palace considerably. Her choices of action became defining. Her strong sense of justice drove her to get involved with affairs of the church. The teachings of Christ compelled the church to look after the wellbeing of the poor and that of the slaves. Having been first poor and then a slave herself, it was only natural that she became an important benefactor of others who shared the same plight. The death of the bishop of Paris provided her with an opportunity. She appointed a bishop who shared her concerns.

Balthild's ideas of governance may not have been very developed beyond the desire to do something about the endless squabbling and fighting that accompanied every succession, royal, noble, or commoner. Both the Saxons and the Franks were Germanic, and their customs were very similar. So were their laws with regard to property ownership and inheritance. Most real property was owned communally. Tribes, nobles, farmers, villagers, etcetera, had use-rights, rights that could shift with every political shift. The nobles divided their rights among all male heirs. When any of them thought the division unequal, they would fight. The same fate befell the Frankish kingdoms.

Balthild was determined not to have Neustria split into three small kingdoms with each of her three sons on respective thrones. To the contrary, she formed a plan that would unite all Frankish ruled territory under one king, preferably her oldest, Clotaire. For that she employed the legal skills of church scholars. Educated in the old monasteries, these scholars advocated Roman laws that had clear definitions of ownership and inheritance. Many of these laws had been in use by the commoners since their introduction by the Romans some seven centuries earlier, but they were still not accepted by the Frankish rulers. With the implementation of these laws in the Frankish system, some stability could be obtained, which would help the rulers as well as the ruled.

Paris, 650

With the Edict of Paris around 615, Clotaire II, the Merovingian king of the Franks, had codified the rights of the nobles and the clergy. After expelling the Jewish advisors from the Palace, the clergy were the only literate people left. Consequently, their influence increased vastly. These two facts compelled the Frankish nobles to position their sons in high church offices such as bishoprics. The most powerful was that of Paris, right at the king's palace.

Only a century earlier, high church office had been the domain of the Romans. Thomas Smith writes[51]:

In the first ages of the Frank conquest, the ministers of the Church were exclusively Roman. As the barbarians, glad to avail themselves of Roman cultivation in order to carry on the ordinary business of life, placed the Cadastre, the revenue, and every part of public employment which required intellectual refinement, in the hands of Roman clerks or laics, so Roman bishops appear prominent in state affairs, particularly in embassies and negociations. ...

If, however, the Romish clergy were, in the first century of Frank Herrschaft, without exception Roman, the monasteries were open to the illiterate Franks[52]. ... When once the current of barbarian zeal set in that direction, parents, in crowds, devoted their children to the service of the altar, with which was combined the blessing of instruction in the rudiments of letters. ..... Among those families were the houses of Burgundy and Hainault.

This course of events is no surprise if we consider the author Maria H. Lansdale's observation[53]:

The war band of Clovis numbered some 8,000 men, and the whole nation of the Burgundians but 40,000. These comparatively small forces came into a Gaul of millions upon millions[54]. They could not ... change its language, nor could they even greatly change its institutions.

No doubt Landri, the freshly appointed Archbishop of Paris, had been proud of his elevation to the priesthood and the years as a missionary priest in "Castellum Meltis" and Haumont[55]. Nine years he had spent there. His appointment to Paris in 650 had been a surprise. Landri's heritage is not known with certainty, but the fact he was recommended by an uncle[56] at the Court in Paris indicates he was a Frank of some standing. He was flattered and warmed by the idea that his uncle remembered him and proposed his appointment to Queen Balthild. It was she who was the main force behind the throne and it was she who maintained contacts with the church. She directed many of its affairs. She was a remarkable woman whom Landri respected and admired and with whom he would find a strong common cause: improving the lives of the commoners.

Icon of St. Balthild

Soon their convictions were put to the test. In 651, Paris experienced a severe famine. Balthild and Landri put their money where their mouths were. Without hesitation Landri sold most of his earthly wealth, robbed the monastery of St. Denis of many of its relics[57], and hired the Nautae to go in search of provisions and bring them back. The forays were successful and the citizens of Paris were saved from complete starvation.

Perhaps because of this event the duo realized that plugging holes or fighting fires was not a good way to deal with the plight of the poor. Something more permanent needed to be done. Some of the poverty was the direct result of political upheaval. The quickly shifting control of land caused many displacements of people that had found their livelihood there. Controlling the nobility was in any case in the interest of the palace. Upon the death of Clovis II, Balthild's stature did not weaken. On the contrary, she ruled with a stern, but just, hand and with Erchinoald's help, managed to keep the kingdom at peace with itself. Good diplomacy and the example she set in Neustria helped maintain good relations with the other Frankish kingdoms. But she needed more if she wanted to keep the peace and eventually see her son Clotaire on the throne. For that she had to stabilize the status quo and take away the main reason for upheaval: the uncertainty of land control.

She started with the church lands.

The church did not form a completely coherent organization. Different components had differing interests. The country churches were fairly independent because of their distance from the power centers of the bishops. The population was thinly distributed over vast tracts of land that consisted mainly of forest, putting many communities effectively out of reach of the top church hierarchy. The same was true for some of the monasteries and convents.

However, many of those were in, or close to, urban areas so the monks and nuns could do their work of salvation for the poor and destitute. The bishops were all of noble descent. They were used to being in control and many, if not all, treated their diocese as a fief. As we saw, the monastery of St. Denis paid the price for this reality by having many of its treasures removed by bishop Landri. Indeed, he had done that for a good cause, but they had rather made the decision themselves and not see so many relics disappear.

In 653, Balthild summoned the Neustrian bishops to Clichy, now a part of Paris. At that meeting they formulated the first worldly[58] delineation of powers within the church. The bishops disapproved of Landri's plunder of St. Denis, and with Bathild's backing decided that the Monastery of St. Denis should no longer be under his control. Sometime during or after the meeting he declared, "The request of the King is for us like a command which it is extremely difficult to resist." It proved a clever move. With this precedent set by the bishops themselves, Balthild acted quickly to separate all monasteries from their bishops. But what was Landri's role leading up to the synod, and how did they walk the bishops into this trap?

There are no surviving records of the meeting, but we have some insights concerning Landri's character. It is inconceivable that the order would have passed without Landri's consent. More likely, Balthild and Landri agreed that clearly defined ownership of land was the best defense against fiefdom and the willy-nilly behavior of its rulers that it invited. They must have decided to set a precedent by making St. Denis the owner of its properties, including the land. Landri put up a token public resistance and then proceeded to convince his colleagues that resistance was futile. Hence his eloquent phrase. And the bishops accepted it, probably because on the face of it, it affected only him. Little did they know that it was part of an elaborate plan to curb their own power.

Another way to help the poor was to provide direct services. Also here Queen and Bishop worked together. Landri founded a hospital on the south side of the Île du Palais. It was named Maison Dieu[59], House of God. It stood on the Rue St. Christophe next to the church of that name. The poor could receive free medical care and a place to rest while (if) they healed. Landri supposedly financed the entire operation, but it is likely that Balthild contributed considerable sums. It is even possible that the Nautae, too, donated, if only to keep in good standing with the Queen and the Bishop. In any case, the Queen's work was good for peace and peace was good for business.

At some point Balthild, Erchinoald and Landri must have decided that the best way to proceed was to establish rules that would support the concept of land ownership. The law of the Franks did not recognize this, so new laws needed to be devised. There are no documents that show how they planned to go about this, but it's clear they could not just create one new law that would affect everyone and expect it to find approval. It had to be done slowly and carefully. It had to be based on existing law, and it would be best if the whole concept was a small item in a long list of supporting case law. But, where to start?

Paris, 654[60]

Monasteries were the primary depositories of classical knowledge. Their libraries contained hand written[61] documents dating back centuries. The librarian monks prided themselves on the vast collections in their care. They were aided by scribes who diligently copied the texts onto new parchment either for their monastery's use or for others. Not all scribes were well schooled. Some documents were in old Greek, but most were in Latin, the language of the learned. When they did not understand the text and could find no one to help them, they had no choice but to give it their best guess. Their interpretations were often off the mark. Sometimes they took shortcuts and introduced their version of Latin, now known as Vulgar Latin. Many of the books dealt with law. As a result, some of the librarians, scribes, or other monks became experts in the jurisprudence of the old Romans. And often their knowledge caused them to be consulted. In the country, away from the Frankish overlords, their influence was greatest and the application of Roman law most widespread. Landri probably knew of this from his years as a priest in the relatively small towns of present-day Belgium. He searched his own diocese and found just the man he needed.

Marculf[62] was already quite old when his Bishop inquired about him. He was humble, self-effacing even, but considered an authority on Roman and German (Frankish) law. Also important, he was of simple origin and probably not a Frank but rather a Gaul[63]. Where Marculf came from is not entirely clear. Some originate him in Bourges, in central France; others think he came from Meaux, east of Paris. Smith explains:

In this manner, in the course of time, did such cultivation as the age supplied make its way among monks of barbarian race. Some became practitioners of medicine ; some proficients in the art of copying manuscripts ; some devoted their time to the composition of the annals of their monastery; some, like Marculfus, composed forms for facilitating the simple legal business of their neighbourhood, according to Roman or barbarian practice. Marculfus himself was a Frank, or some kindred race. These accomplished persons must have been brought up from early youth in their monasteries; but a ruder class found also admission within their walls.

Bishop Landri

At a minimum Marculf was a scribe but, having been entrusted with such an important project, this aging man was either the librarian of the monastery or, most likely, a recognized legal scholar and the prime legal advisor to the bishop. The two volumes he wrote became known as the *Formularæ Marculfi* and represented a marriage of Roman and Frankish law. The collection was revolutionary for the Franks in that it addressed property rights not only for church and nobility, but also for commoners. Although unknown in Germanic culture, the concept of property rights in other cultures is as old as written language. It can be found in Sumerian, Persian, and Greek texts. Aristotle gives a strong defense for individual property rights in his *Politics*:

….that which is common to the greatest number has the least care bestowed upon it. Every one thinks chiefly of his own, hardly at all of the common interest; and only when he is himself concerned as an individual. ….. If they do not share equally enjoyments and toils, those who labor much and get little will necessarily complain of those who labor little and receive or consume much. But indeed there is always a difficulty in men living together and having all human relations in common, but especially in their having common property.

However, J.W. Wessels[64] observes:

Originally the Germans did not recognize individual ownership of the soil. The land belonged to the tribe and was parceled out by lot from time to time to the various families. ...

The nobles in all probability did not take part in this division. At a very early period they seem to have had tracts of land allotted, on which they built their strongholds, with dwellings for their followers and slaves.

Early in their history, the Romans borrowed legal statutes from the Greeks, including those pertaining to private property. As the Frankish kingdoms increasingly came under the influence of the Church, so also concepts of Roman law found their way into Frankish society and into Marculf's *Formulae*. Henri F. Muller and Pauline Taylor in their "A Chrestomathy of Vulgar Latin", published in 1990, examine three cases. In the first the heirs of an estate ask a king's envoy to allow a division of property. In the second a woman gives a dowry to her future daughter-in-law and, in the third, a rich man exchanges real property with a church. Clearly, people owned land and the transactions show that it was valued.

Whether or not Landri ordered Marculf to include laws dealing with the commoners we do not know. It is almost certain that the bishop intended to establish a clear set of laws that would govern the nobles, and that he was more than willing to pay the price of losing fiscal power over monasteries in return. Ultimately, Marculf's work described a large swath of law in the Frankish lands. Smith's Essay states:

The Formulae consist of drafts or forms for every species of legal writing, whether they relate to the appointment of counts and bishops by the king, or to the most ordinary traffic between man and man.

The volumes were composed when Salic[65] Law (*Lex Salica*), written under Clovis I around 510, was already slowly fading. It is unclear when Landri instructed Marculf to begin his project.

Rather suddenly, the king was dead. It was a familiar situation; the crown prince was very young and the widowed queen was a former Saxon slave and very young. But, in contrast to Dagobert's death, Clovis II was just 23 when he died. The young Clovis was possibly insane and he may have been murdered[66]. We can only speculate, but it was not unusual to remove a person by means of poison (he would be 'taken ill') or arranged accident. However, in those days, a mere knife cut or even the common cold could kill, and there were more incurable diseases to worry about. As it was, the event did not appear to make much of a difference in the power of the palace. The assessments of Clovis being weak were probably quite accurate. Balthild took on the task of dowager queen as regent to her son Clotaire, who was then around seven years old. Her power increased and in her newfound freedom she involved herself in church-driven charity more than before. That freedom may have been somewhat limited, however. After all, there was the mayor of the palace, Erchinoald. But he seems to have indulged or even encouraged her. The Vita Domnae Balthildis[67] (VDB) states:

And the king, taking care of her faith and devotion, gave his faithful servant, Abbot Genesius, to her as support, and through his hands she served the priests and the poor, fed the hungry, found clothing for the naked, and conscientiously arranged the burial of the dead. Through him she sent the most generous alms of gold and silver to the monasteries of men and women.

This cooperation continued until her retirement. Shortly after Landri's death in 661, she founded the monastery of Kala[68] (Chelles) and bestowed it generously. It was quite customary that queens eventually retired to a monastery, voluntarily or forcibly, and that may have been her retirement plan.

The oldest of the three by far, Marculf continued to work on the law books. The project had taken on a life of its own and he felt dedicated to his former patron[69]. Balthild surely also had an interest in seeing it through, although by that time the most important work had already been done.

Eventually her former owner and protector, Erchinoald, died. The new mayor of the palace, Ebroin, was from a clan Erchinoald had opposed. Possibly Balthild encouraged his appointment to win over other clans. Ebroin was ambitious. He loved power for the sake of power. Some unrest reentered Frankish society, but Ebroin's designs eventually helped the Queen achieve her goals. She managed to unite the Frankish kingdoms[70] with her eldest son Clotaire on the throne. She codified the independence of the monasteries and their protection by the crown (as first done with St. Denis). She attempted to abolish slavery and, short of that, imposed rules that would improve the treatment of slaves. She continued to give away much of her wealth in support of monasteries and the poor. But when Clotaire came of age[71] in 664, Balthild retreated to her monastery of Kala, a move that

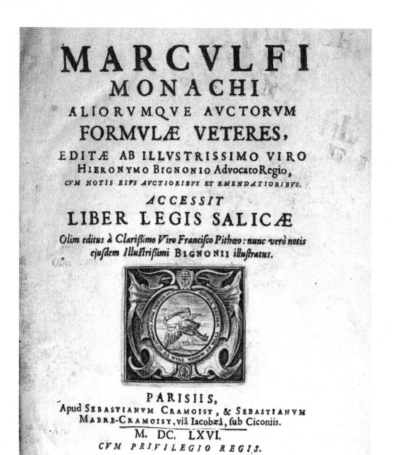

Printed copy of Marculf's Formulae, 1666

presumably had the strong encouragement of Ebroin, who must have found the young Clotaire more pliable than his mother. Considering her "take charge" personality it is almost certain that she kept abreast of state affairs and dispensed her advice, sought or not. She died at Kala in 680 and was canonized two centuries later.

Perhaps Balthild, Erchinoald, Landri and Marculf were visionaries, the first three for ordering the compilation of civil law and the fourth for doggedly, but competently, continuing the work after Landri's death. A very old man, he died in 667. After ten hard years of research and writing, he had exhausted his sources, and himself.

Different interests may have motivated each of the collaborators. As a senior church official, Landri had every reason to clarify the property rights of religious institutions and, being of their caste, marry them to the interests of the nobles. This action would benefit his ultimate goal of the protection and welfare of the commoners and the poor among them. Under Frankish law the king could allocate land, and anything on it, for use (as a fief), but he could not give it away as property. Usually the award went to a noble for the duration of a year.

The introduction of Roman law, and pressure from church and nobility, expanded the use rights to longer periods of as much as a lifetime, and eventually, in perpetuity, through hereditary rights. This established *de facto* ownership. Marculf, however, came from more humble beginnings. He understood that artisans, farmers, and traders had property interests, too. It may well be that he started with the compilation of cases pertaining to the higher strata of society — nobles and church — and introduced the common cases only after Landri's death. The important fact remains that Marculf did commit them to parchment and, by doing so, laid a solid foundation for later developments in civic society.

Both commerce and industry require real property as collateral against loans, and as a stable place to locate. They also require a clear legal system in whose protection to operate and grow. The Frankish kingdoms of the dark ages were the only societies in Western Europe where Roman law still breathed. As they grew, so did these concepts, which spread to take root, especially in those areas where commerce and industry could develop: the shores of the River Rhine and the maritime parts of the Netherlands.

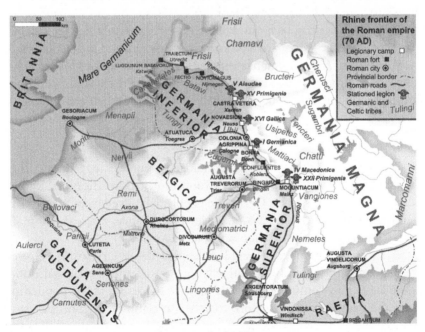

Courtesy Andrei Nacu

A watchful eye must be kept on ourselves lest, while we are building ideal monuments of renown and bliss here, we neglect to have our names enrolled in the Annals of Heaven.
James Madison to William Bradford, November 9, 1772.

Chapter 3: A Realist in the Wet Lands

Timeline

Year	Event
57 BCE	Romans arrive in Holland
860	First mention of Leyden (Leithon)
1047	Leyden sacked by Holy Roman Emperor Henry III
1266	Leyden receives city rights
1328-1350	Philip VI King of France
1328-1347	Louis IV Emperor of Holy Roman Empire

Thanks to the efforts of a former Saxon slave, a Frankish priest, and a Gaul monk, Roman law was firmly established in the Frankish lands. As the Neustrian Franks expanded their territories, so, too, did Roman law. By the time of Charlemagne, around 800 CE, the Frankish influence reached north into territories that are now known as Belgium and the Netherlands. Eventually, concepts of Roman law mixed with Saxon concepts to form what is known as Roman-Dutch law. To understand why these lands were such fertile ground for new thinking, we will have a look at their conditions.

Early Holland

Waterways swelled, withdrew, changed course, clogged up. They brought life and then, in one stormy swoop, took it away. The oldest known inhabitants were Frisians, a Germanic people, who lived from present day Denmark in the north to present day Northern France, where the Romans first encountered them two thousand years ago.

A surprising number of people occupied the watery world between the dry lands of Brabant and Utrecht to the east and the coastal dunes to the west. Tiny communities could survive there. But as the population grew, the people needed to work together to claim land from the water and to protect the gains from it. Farms and settlements occupied the sand walls that themselves were old riverbeds, and often lay alongside newly carved streams. People built small dams, dug trenches, and piled up dirt to form *terps*[72]. In times of flood, they retreated to the man-made high ground, bringing stock and possessions. In good times they enjoyed the fruits of their cooperation and in bad they found comfort in their common plight. The area was not only a boundary between land and water where both conditions ruled intermittently, it was also a border between various tribes, cultures, and overlords that penetrated, retreated, and mixed. The Frisians were pushed back from the south and east first by Roman allies[73], the Batavians, who came from Germany, and the Cananefaten, who were their vassals.

Model of a Roman fort. Photograph by Vincent van Zeijst

After a number of failed attempts to subjugate the Frisians, the Romans built a series of forts along the Rhine, and around 50 CE that river became the northern border of the Empire. Roman engineers connected the Rhine to the Maas with a canal, named the Fossa Corbulonis, and put the fort Matilo[74] where it entered the Rhine. These borderlands were already densely populated. Sources of subsistence were chiefly cattle and sheep but people also grew barley, rye, and beans.

The arrival of the legions had a major effect on the economy. Soldiers did not grow food and would have to buy it. Even if they had families, soldiers did not bring them. But they did want access to women. And so the local people moved up from subsistence to production farming. A service industry developed that included small manufacturing and prostitution. In return, they received goods, or coin with which to purchase goods. They valued the quality and novelty of the items these newcomers brought: fine garments, cloth, tools, pottery, bronze objects, and jewelry. Along with these goods, new ideas made their way north. Culture, religion and other values of these more sophisticated Romans spread and took hold.

This is perhaps most visually evident in the shape some terps took. Traditionally round, some were now square with steps on all sides. The only "city" in the area, Forum Hadriani, was built that way. It was the administrative center of the district of the Cananefaten and situated on the newly dug canal near a place called Leithon. In 122 CE it received market rights and around 150 CE city rights. These are proof of a rapidly evolving economy and of the significant fact that civil organizations, instituted by merchants and manufacturers, were recognized as governmental partners by the Romans. We do not know exactly how the civic government was organized at the time. It was probably a mixture of traditional Germanic communal rules and new Roman public and private law.

The political stability lasted only a few hundred years. The coastal area came under attack from Frankish and Saxon raiders. The first came down the Rhine from the east and the latter along the coast from the north. Around the year 400 all vestiges of the West Roman Empire disappeared. The area saw an almost total economic collapse and fell into obscurity. Did any of the imported culture and institutions survive here?

From archeological finds, historians conclude that the population of the old Frisian coast decreased very significantly. In addition to the removal of the Roman-induced social stability, large swaths of land were removed by the sea and by the actions of man himself. The relatively warm climate was also turning colder and stormy. However, evidence shows that the area in the vicinity of Leithon proved better for continued habitation than others. To the south, particularly the current province of Zeeland, the sea had removed most of the bog land and replaced it with sediments, only to attack it again in a series of huge storms. To the north, man exploited the peat bogs for fuel, which left large lakes. Although there is no direct evidence, Leithon still must have been inhabited. Forum Hadriani was reduced to a village and some forts became farmsteads. In other words, the remaining population resorted to the old tradition of living on terps. The absence of Roman institutions shows that the Church never took hold this far north. There had been no monasteries to preserve documents on law and governance. As opposed to Gaul, the locals were not exposed to these concepts. Apparently tribal conditions had returned and the Frisians[75] had been able to reassert their power. Sixteen generations without Rome-inspired institutions were too many. Their reintroduction had to wait until the 7th century when the Franks expanded their empire northward to include the whole of the Netherlands in the 8th.

Although little, if anything, of the Roman influence had taken root in these parts, this history shows that:

- Alien culture with its unique forms of governmental, religious, or mercantile organizations does not automatically transfer. We see that clearly in our own day, where after hundreds of years of colonial rule and fifty years of development aid, much of the developing world has only reluctantly adopted some of our institutions and has given them their own distinct flavors. Western institutions and culture grew in tandem and each may be unsuitable for others.
- The path of institutional development is a thin thread that can easily be broken. Roman law went underground in Western Europe and reemerged only because it hitched a ride with the fortunes of the Christian Church.
- The culture of cooperation, that had to exist for a population to be successful in a place as naturally hostile as the swamps of Holland, formed a fertile ground for civic institutions to sprout, develop, and thrive. We will witness this in the coming chapters.

The Frankish kingdoms first united into one nation that grew slowly. In the 8th century, Charles the Great (Charlemagne) expanded its territory into Italy, Iberia, Germany, and the Netherlands. And then, by uniting his State with the Church, Charlemagne completed the re-Romanization of this part of Europe. Because church officials had become the interpreters and makers of law, it was logical that they consulted canon law and the old Roman civil law and thus spread both. It should be mentioned, though, that Charlemagne allowed annexed territories to retain their own traditions, laws, and order so that, as a conqueror, he caused little immediate disturbance. The organization of his government[76] reflected that.

Case law shows that as early as the 7th century a mixture of Frankish and Roman law was used as precedents for judicial procedure[77] in Holland. It is almost certain that jurists at the time reached back to Roman law when Frankish law failed to adequately address the issues at hand. This increasingly provided the consistent application of the rule of law, which is essential for the development of trust between strangers[78]. The higher power that can be relied upon to administer stable rules over a large territory assures that anyone engaging in transactions with another person enjoys protections against dishonesty while also having a strong incentive to honor one's own promises. In such an environment, the stakes are allowed to grow so that an ever-increasing movement of goods and services can bring more wealth to more participants.

Leithon, the Netherlands, Middle Ages

A cluster of houses, a farmstead, was situated around a small, artificial hill at the confluence of two rivers, the Oude Rijn and the Nieuwe Rijn (Old Rhine and New Rhine). The hill was a leftover of a Roman fortification from the 4th century. The surrounding land was swampy and subject to flooding. Tall reeds, grasses, rushes, bushes, and trees lay in all directions. The primary mode of transportation was the boat, with sail, oars, or stake. This was the Rhine delta, where waterways swelled or withdrew, changed course or clogged up. People lived there for generations, bearing children, nurturing them, helping them to settle in places of their own and raise their own families. And so the settlement slowly grew while converting the wetlands to arable lands.

Leithon was first mentioned in documents of the 11th century as being a farmstead. Although the area was part of Frisia at the time of the Romans, we do not know from which tribes exactly the eventual inhabitants descended. Rhineland, as it is still known, was a border country between Frisians, Saxons, Franks, and Batavians (who might have been Frisians themselves). Many of the Frisian place names have survived. It is not clear whether this is because Frisians remained there or later arrivals kept the names. It's no surprise that in these remote and inaccessible swamps, the people were removed from central rule and very independent. Although Holland, as it became known, alternated its possession between the Franks, Germans, and Burgundians[79] it held on to a culture of tenacity, which proved important for its future.

The creation and maintenance of defenses against the water could not be accomplished by one family alone and required cooperation with neighbors. Without it the country would not exist. Because of the increasing scope of such works, the cooperation was increasingly between people who did not previously know each other. This could be accomplished only in an environment controlled by strong civic institutions. It is no surprise that the oldest of these were the *waterschappen* (water boards). These water management councils formed the first civic councils that were made up of stakeholders and they still exist today[80]. The stakeholders contributed labor and funds to build dikes, watering channels, and, eventually, water-pumping windmills. By necessity, cooperation became a hallmark of Dutch culture.

The farms of Leithon were situated at the confluence of two rivers and it became a trading center rather quickly. Just as quickly, the settlement's success attracted outside attention. By the year 1100, the count of Holland had installed an overlord (*burggraaf*[81]) by the name of Kuik who built a castle. The relationship between the Kuiks, the Count, and the inhabitants of Leyden, as it was then known, was good. The town acquired a charter early, giving it the right to organize civic government and be free from toll duties. In return, the city made a single payment to the Count. Leyden's oldest surviving charter dates from the 12th century and refers to an earlier grant. As with other towns in Holland, it was ruled by *schout en schepenen*, sheriff and aldermen, who were appointed by the count and who collected revenue and administered justice in his name. By the early 13th century, Leyden was the fourth largest city in Holland[82].

Settlements grow because they attract people who do not make their living in agriculture. In order to survive, the newcomers have to be able to sell skills that the other settlers have a demand for. On the farm, everyone is expected to apply similar skills. The farmer lived in a dwelling that was built by a farmer, most likely himself. Building materials were limited to wood and reeds and houses on the wet lands lasted not much longer than twenty years. The farmer wore clothes that his wife had made and shoes that he had made himself. Most of his implements may also have been homemade. The quality of all these commodities was limited since no person could possess good skills in so many different fields or possess the best tools. In a settlement, it was logical to get a plough from an experienced blacksmith, shoes from a skilled cobbler, clothes from a good tailor, and beer from the best brewer. There was a specialization of skills. Various trades developed. The quality of all manufactured goods went up and with it the welfare and quality of life.

As these settlements grew, they served an expanding hinterland. A farmer discovered that his neighbor's town-made implements lasted longer than his homemade ones. A fisherman would buy his nets from a manufacturer who could make them to consistent specifications[83] and quality. And, since the craftsmen were specialized, they were likely to produce these items at a lower cost. They bought larger quantities of raw materials, were better aware of the quality of those materials, were able to manufacture faster, and deliver a better product. The settlement grew into a town.

A community needed laws and leaders or institutions to enforce them. And a community needed an entity that could provide the kinds of services and infrastructure that benefited all, such as roads, walls for protection, navigable waterways, etc. Those kinds of public services required funding.

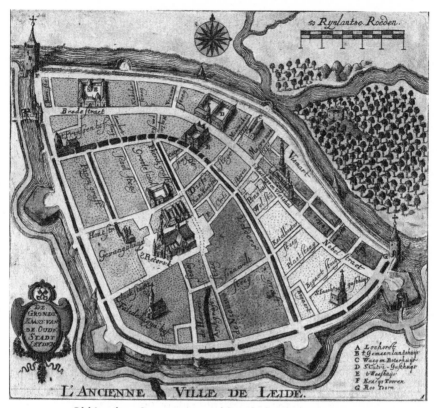

**Old Leyden. Courtesy www.historischeplattegrond.nl -
reproductions of historical maps**

The simplest way to collect funds was to charge tolls. Tolls could be levied on anyone passing a specific point, be it a bridge (both land and water traffic) or a gate. The latter could be a land or a water gate and it could be located in a city wall or some other strategic place. The town of Leyden requested, and received, from the Count, permission to form a local government. The organization and its rights were codified in the city's charter and mostly dealt with matters of justice. As was customary in those days, the city paid the Count for the charter when it was issued. With a change of ruler, the charter expired and had to be renewed and once again paid for. It was thus in the city's interest to support the Count and have him around for as long as possible. This arrangement tied the two firmly together. Renewal often included new and expanded rights, again, at a cost. In Leyden's charter the Count granted all *poorters*[84] free passage of all the Count's tolls in Holland. This provided the city's traders with an advantage and contributed to the city's rapid development and growth.

The Count was, however, not the only power the city had to contend with. There was also the *burggraaf* who represented the Count. This *burggraaf*, who lived in the castle on the old mound in Leyden, also had the privilege to bestow rights on the city in return for favors. The city regarded him as a parasite of little value to them. There were frequent conflicts, sometimes violent, between the city and the *burggraaf* and the Count often had to intervene. It is no surprise that the power of this *burggraaf* diminished over time while that of the city increased along with its wealth and size.

The growth of Leyden was not constant. The bogs of Holland were increasingly used for agriculture to supply the growing populations in the cities. The cultivation required better water management. The drier bogs began to sink and water management became more difficult. The growing of crops was replaced with cattle grazing on wetter lands until the need for fuel in the cities, combined with better water management methods, encouraged the exploitation of peat. Since the land was barely above high water to begin with, the removal of the thick top layer of peat created extensive lakes. This forced many farmers to migrate to the cities whose populations rose rapidly. By the 13th century, Holland was the most densely populated area in Europe.

While the town grew, the number of skilled artisans increased as well and a further diversification and specialization of skills ensued. To protect themselves from competition, the artisans organized, and set strict rules that governed the number of artisans allowed in one particular trade. Where the Nautae in Frankisch Paris had formed an early trading monopoly, the Guilds, as these organizations were called, formed an early manufacturing monopoly. They regulated who could be hired for training as assistants, where workshops could be located and, presumably, what prices should be asked for particular goods and services. In addition, they provided a safety net for old or sick members by giving aid in the form of money or labor, helping with succession of the business, and financially supporting retired tradesmen. To make interaction and cooperation easier, each trade had its own general neighborhood in the city. This imposed close social and commercial control. The Guilds were important civil organizations within the community. With their officials elected from among the members, they were among the first democratic institutions in Europe. Perhaps surprisingly, and in spite of their prominent position in the neighborhoods from which they sprouted, the Guilds did not rise to the level of city governance in Leyden as they did in some other cities. A wealthier group of people claimed that privilege, the merchants.

As we have seen, the Count appointed[85] a *schout* and eight *schepenen* (sheriff and aldermen). Together they formed the court of the town, but they were also responsible for civic administration and the collection of revenue on behalf of the count. It was in the interest of the town to have this court or council chosen from among its own so that they were familiar with the goings on and would advocate the interests of the city's patricians. Eventually the appointment of the *schepenen* was exclusively from a group of sixteen citizens who, once every year, chose eight for the job while the remaining eight were in reserve should a *schepen* fall ill, be removed, or die. These sixteen citizens were chosen once a year by the *vroedschap*[86] from among themselves. Of course these wise men also happened to be the wealthiest in the city.

In time, this group evolved into the so-called *veertigen*, or forties, which, as the name implies, was a group of forty outstanding men. This was really an oligarchy. The method for appointing a *schout* was not much better. In the 13th century the Count found it much easier to sell the position more or less by auction. The idea was that the *schout* would pay a hefty sum, which he then had to recoup from the proceeds of taxes, fines, etc. This became an expensive proposition for the city. Eventually it appealed to the Count to allow the city to purchase the position so it could make the appointment itself. The Count granted the privilege, but occasionally intervened with his own appointments. However, while the privilege was in effect, the city's position to govern itself was enhanced. From the Count's point of view this arrangement had the unintended effect of improving city government and city unity and, as a consequence, city power.

As the city grew and as its leaders took on more responsibility, it became necessary to diversify its administration. The first new positions were those of burgomasters who took the responsibility for public works and tax collection while the *schout* and *schepenen* remained responsible for law and order. All these positions had to be purchased and the office holder expected to recoup this expense by the powers of his office. Accounting records do not show how this was done. We have to assume that the officials engaged in the kind of rent-seeking that, in today's world, we refer to as corruption (Allegedly the public sector in many developing countries still operates this way[87]). When the appointment for these offices was the right of the Count or the *burggraaf*, the buyers paid them. After the city purchased the appointment rights from the Count the office buyers paid into the city coffers. However, the officeholders were personally responsible for any financial deficits that the city incurred. As a result, it became customary that new officeholders pay off the old by covering the debt.

It is no surprise that the city elders were looking for expanded sources of revenue. Most revenue came from taxes on alcohol and the importation of goods that were also locally produced (protectionism was well known and widely practiced). A new source of funds came from the sale of annuities[88], a financial instrument first created in ancient Rome[89]. In this case the city would receive a one-time sum of money from private individuals who would in return receive a percentage of that every year for the rest of their lives[90]. The risk was reflected in the percentage rate. These annuities could be bought for oneself, one's children, and even for three persons where the annuity had to be paid until the last one died. Rates varied from 2% to 15% per year. The concept must have been fairly new in Holland since there appeared to be no local takers. Annuities were sold to subjects of other nations, including the English.

Over time the complexity of the city's financial transactions became such that the burgomasters recruited the help of accounting clerks and auditors. Eventually these positions became permanent in a Clerk's Office. With the ever more complicated financial dealings and increased responsibilities of the city fathers, the complexity of law compelled them to hire legal advisors. Most often these jurists were church educated. Latin was the language of law and, as we have seen in previous chapters, articles of law were based on Roman traditions.

As the city's wealth increased, so did its power and it was the wealthy who controlled it. 15th century records[91] show that the various office positions were revolving between the same people and the same families. These families also delivered the clerks and jurists. Leyden had a plutocracy. The richest families in town were the merchants, followed by a few producers of textiles. By the 16th century these entrepreneurs had become the main powers in the city. In some ways it was a blessing that the group was small and that they often had to attract "new blood", which made the arrangement somewhat more democratic[92]. This kind of arrangement, where the commercial stakeholders are the ruling class, was in effect synonymous with corporate governance. Since there was little or no influence from titled nobility in the direct affairs of the city, this kind of government was patently republican. Both these characteristics of city government became synonymous with city life. The system by which stakeholders elected their leadership, decided issues by majority vote, and governed and taxed themselves could not be taken away without also ruining the city itself. When Count and City saw an opportune moment, they abolished the position of *burggraaf*.

And when cities could govern themselves in this way, why not provinces, or even countries?

Often referred to as the Calamitous Century, the 14th saw economic stagnation, famines, wars, and epidemics. A low-level civil war in Holland went on for 150 years. France and England started their 100-year war. In the periods of peace between battles, private armies roamed the French countryside in search of loot. The black plague and its subsequent shadow waves[93] reduced the population by half. In Holland, a combination of factors created political instability that in turn led to economic uncertainty. While commerce had increased the wealth of the cities, frequent warfare by the counts and their subsequent needs for financing had forced the counts to borrow money, sell rights to sources of income (tolls, mills, fisheries, etc), sell annuities, and sell lucrative government offices. The weakness of the counts became the strength of the cities, nobles and moneylenders (primarily Lombards from Italy where lending had started much earlier). The County saw a Balkanization as small powers made deals and agreements among some to the exclusion of others. In that same period a struggle for power among factions of the ruling family led to further concessions to respective allies.

Holland, 14th Century

One particularly determined young man grew up in the chaotic world of the 14th century. Philips van Leyden was advantaged. For generations his family had been part of the ruling merchant class in the city of Leyden. His father and many of his relatives had served the city government in various capacities. At a young age, Philips was familiar with the concepts of governance and its purpose. He learned how families vied for power in the city, how the city's interests were in conflict with those of nobles or other cities, and how the city negotiated the treacherous relationships with the larger powers such as the Count of Holland and even the King of England[94]. He must have had a strong preference for order. With the chaos around him his natural curiosity drove him to a search for proper organization – everything in its place. His studies suggest that he attended the Latin School of Leyden. There he would have been exposed to Latin texts. Latin was the language of learned discourse and most discourse concerned religion, church law (Canon), and Roman law. The logic and clarity of Canon and Roman law must have appealed to him. He went on to seminary and joined the large contingent of Dutch students at the University of Orléans in France. It was then the most prominent law school north of the Alps. The city was growing fast and had just completed an extension of its walls around the western suburb[95]. The bridge across the Loire surely impressed our young student as he crossed it from the north. Houses and shops were built on its sides and water mills under its twenty arches. Each end had a drawbridge. On a small island in the middle of

City of Orléans by Martin des Batailles, 1690

the bridge stood a new *bastille* (fortification). At the south end the large, recently strengthened, fortification of *Les Tourelles* protected the city from any army that had succeeded in crossing the bridge.

Philips had a big-picture view of the world and the cutting edge thinking in academia provided him with the tools he needed.

The university broke new ground when it advocated Roman law over Canon law. The first was the law of civil society and the latter that of the church. Whether the first serious foray into Roman law some seven hundred years earlier by Landri and Marculf was still of direct influence we cannot be sure. However, jurists referred to Marculf's writings and it is inconceivable that academics, who had laid the foundations for this new thinking one hundred or so years earlier, were unaware of them.

In Orléans the young Philips joined the French and Flemish student organization and not the Dutch one. He considered the first more serious and studious. A contributing factor was probably that critical thinking about law and its role in society had advanced more in France than in Holland. The application of Roman law was deeper in France while Holland still used Germanic common law where that was applicable. We have seen how, in the days of Queen Balthild, some of the Germanic concepts were not beneficial to commercial development and contributed to uncertainty and that Roman law found its way into the Frankish lands as a matter of improvement. The Roman concepts that Philips learned about were those referring to classes of property:

Private: house, farm, land
Common: air, flowing water, sea, beaches
Public: all navigable rivers, harbors

Corporate: theaters, racecourses

Nobody's: sacred and subject to divine right

In Philips's time there was no effective separation of the last four kinds of property. Cities, nobles, and even clergy controlled portions of some, or all, and were benefiting from the proceeds. Today we would call these arrangements corrupt. Philips thought so, too, and he borrowed and expanded on the Roman concept of the respublica[96] which he introduced in his *De Cura Reipublicae et Sorte Principantis*. This translates to "About the administration of the public interest and the role of the ruler." This is no small title. He had the audacity to suggest that the ruler had duties with regard to the public interest. However, as opposed to his academic contemporaries, Philips was no dreamer. He did not come up with revolutionary concepts, other than the few he needed to reconcile some seemingly contradictory opinions. He was a realist who wanted to create stability in his turbulent world. To accomplish this, he wanted order and a balance of power between the players. The closest to the concept of democracy that he was acquainted with was the corporate nature of the city governments with their mayors, aldermen, sheriffs, and judges, and their operations could be quite messy with their politics and intrigues. The councils of nobles and city representatives that the Count of Holland occasionally called were no better. So he looked back to Roman law and found comfort in the notion that the Emperor himself was bound to care for the public interest, and, crucially, that he could not alienate that which was considered public and common. The Emperor could not sell any of it; he could not give it away because he did not own it. He was only its keeper.

Of course there was no longer an emperor in Rome. But there were kings and counts. Where those rulers were the *de facto* highest powers they were functionally keepers and therefore all these laws applied to them. He wrote, "The Empire is torn up, therefore the lower lords have to perform [the emperor's] duties!" Philips developed these ideas in Orléans and worked on them after obtaining his degree in Canon law in 1349 and his return to Holland.

The journey home must have been dangerous. Northern France and Flanders were the scenes of fierce battles between French and English armies. The devastation, the displaced people, and the banditry that followed cannot but have affected him. He accepted the position of priest in Middelburg in Zeeland and quickly became involved in local affairs. Holland, of which Zeeland was then a part, became the scene of a power struggle between the young Count William V and his mother, Margareta, sister of the German emperor. Various battles were fought, but eventually

William won out in 1355. Curiously, Philips van Leyden entered in the Count's employment that same year. How could that have come about? Let us look at one plausible scenario.

'sGravenhage, the Netherlands, 1350s

Gerard Alewijnsz had served the Counts of Holland almost continuously since 1316[97] as land agent, accountant, and keeper of records in Zeeland and Holland. Alewijnsz had a difficult job with the family feud raging around him. William V had become Count in 1349. Presumably following the advice of Alewijnsz, William asserted control over his territories of Hainault, Zeeland, and Holland and introduced some reforms concerning nobility and cities. However, upon her arrival in Holland, his mother, Margareta, claimed control and undid much of William's progress. Alewijnsz was exasperated with the chaos. Already in his fifties, with the wisdom of a man who had seen it all, he grew impatient and searched for ways to serve his young master better. One day in 1351, Alewijnsz received a letter from a young clergyman in Middelburg addressed to Count William.

ϴ We imagine him putting the letter aside, figuring it could not be very important. About one week later, after he had taken care of the urgent business of the young Count, he sat in front of his large oak desk. It had three large drawers in the bottom adorned with ornamental knobs and large keyholes set in bone inlays. The top had a large door that covered the whole surface of the top. It, too, had a large inlaid keyhole. It folded on a horizontal hinge above the top drawer. Just between the hinges and the drawer at either end were two knobs. He pulled them out to reveal two foot-and-a-half long supports. He folded the door toward him to form a writing desk. Several rows of small drawers were facing him while in the space before them stood small stacks of correspondence and parchments containing records he was working on. He broke the seal on the letter from the young clergyman, unrolled the parchment, and started reading.

He had expected to find either a petition for funds or a complaint about Zeeland's and Middelburg's plight. It was neither. The text was in Latin and carefully written. It was easy to read. After the short introduction the writer went straight into what ailed governance. And then he went on to tell the reader about how to fix it. He spoke of divine rights and duties. He wrote about the public good and the Count's duty to protect it. He pointed out what the Count needed to do to restore order to the County. He went on how it would benefit the Count and then explained why the Count had every right, and even a duty, to assert his authority.

Alewijnsz went over the lines again. It was a most unusual letter. His eyes went to the name of the author. It was signed by one Philips van Leyden, clergyman in Middelburg, Zeeland. Who was this man who had the audacity to tell his ruler what to do? The suggestions were entirely unapologetic. The old man raised his eyebrows and shrugged. It came from a youthful, innocent, and overenthusiastic soul. He rolled it back up and put it away.

In the months that followed Alewijnsz was repeatedly reminded of the various points made in the letter and how they touched on the issues he and his master struggled with. Was there merit after all in the somewhat utopian but logically presented solutions? He decided to read the letter again. The opening argument considered the concept that the ruler was the guardian of God's garden[98] on earth. The public was a part of that garden. In order to be an effective guardian, he had to be able to exert absolute control over the parts that made up the garden and that was possible only if he were powerful[99]. It explained that this garden represented the Public Good. It was no one person's property. It served all and it belonged to all. Therefore the ruler could not sell it. He could not even exchange privileges on that Good in return for benefits for himself since that also constituted a sale. The letter pointed out that so much of the current turmoil in the County was caused by the proliferation of privileges and alienated (sold) rights. It urged that the Count take control and rescind all such privileges.

The old man decided to write back. He would challenge his uninvited advisor with a number of counter points based on his long experience and current troubles. If the response was as thoughtful and clearly stated as the first letter, then, perhaps and despite his long years, he could learn something from a younger mind? He was careful to present everything hypothetically. After all, he did not know this clergyman and could not trust him with real affairs of state. His letter was answered quickly with interesting arguments about what constituted the Public Good. A lively correspondence developed that was interrupted only when Alewijnsz was too occupied with the consequences of the fight between his master and his master's mother. But he did find the time to mention the concepts and arguments to Count William.

The Count, too, thought them interesting and worth exploring. Eventually the old advisor invited the creative young man to 'sGravenhage (the Hague).

Middelburg, the Netherlands, 1355

We can imagine Philips witnessing the whole unsavory power struggle from his domicile in Zeeland. To his delight, an exchange of ideas had started. Alewijnsz was well known for his able administration and positive energy. Being invited by this great man to come to the Count's seat of government was an honor. He packed two bags and decided to walk the short distance from the rectory to the harbor. At first light he stepped out of his house opposite the small church of St. Peter where he preached. It was a crisp fall day. The sun colored the eastern sky orange. There were few clouds. He headed south and on his left passed the long dead-end street leading to the Plague House. Only a few years earlier he'd spent much time there giving last rites to the dying. More uplifting were the small houses and chapel of the Beguines. Most of the elderly women were widows who were maintained by the church and had committed their lives to the service of others. Next he passed the gate to the city militia. It was a large, walled in space where the soldiers had pitched their tents around a rectangular pond. With most members on active duty on the walls or in the country, it was very quiet there. On the right the street opened up into a small square from where he could see the impressive structure of West Munster Cathedral towering over the two or three story houses.

He turned left and followed the curved street that led to the harbor where he would try to find a ship that could take him north. Half a dozen cogs[100] of various sizes were being loaded or unloaded. Groups of men were milling near the two hand-powered cranes. Philips walked into the office of the harbormaster where all merchants had to report their origins and destinations and what they were carrying. It was still quite dark inside but the men crowding around the clerk's desk wanted to set sail while the tide was still high. At low tide the harbor was often dry. Philips raised his voice, "Who is going to 'sGravenhage?"

A few heads turned but no one responded. "Who is going to Rotterdam or Delft?"

"Who wants to know?" a tanned, blond man asked as he turned away from the desk. In his hand he held a few sheets of parchment.

"A priest," Philips said. The blond man looked the clergyman up and down and spotted the bags. He smiled. "I am going to Rotterdam," he said, "and you travel for free." Without waiting for a reply or permission he grabbed one of Philips's bags and headed for the door. The young priest scurried after him.

Outside Philips caught up with the man, who turned to him. "My name is Klaas[101]," he offered, "and we're sailing right away."

Cog ship. Courtesy Heinz-Josef Lücking

"Philips van Leyden."

Klaas was about thirty, well built, but short. They rounded the Dam at the head of the harbor and turned toward the far end near the South Gate where a loaded cog was waiting. The one man on board had already rigged the trysail[102]. Philips could not but notice how much this man resembled Klaas. Seeing his glance, Klaas explained, "My brother Jan[103]. Jan, this is Father Philips." He threw the bag on board and jumped after it. Then he took Philips's bag and helped the young priest step off the quay. Before Philips could find a place to sit, Klaas had cast off. Each grabbing an oar, the brothers rowed through the opened bridge and the harbor gate until they were out in the channel that led to open water. They stowed the oars and Jan let out the sail. A light breeze caught the canvass. With seventy miles to go, they were under way. Depending on the weather, the trip could be completed in two days or as much as a week, and maybe longer.

As the treeless shore slowly drifted by, Philips settled comfortably on a soft bail placed against the low wall of the raised stern. Klaas was at the rudder while Jan trimmed the sail. The cog was perhaps forty feet long and fifteen feet wide at the beam. The deck was loaded mainly with gunnysacks. Philips had no idea what was in them and did not ask. His mind wandered off to the purpose of his trip. How would he convince the Count to give up worldly power? The concept that Philips tried to sell applied to Roman emperors, not relatively lowly counts. Indeed, Holland was part of the Holy Roman Empire, but the Emperor was far away and had little influence in the bog lands of the western Netherlands – less so now that the Count's mother, and the Emperor's sister, was facing defeat. Could he make the case that it was therefore the Count who acted as emperor; that he had the rights and duties of an emperor? It made sense, but would Alewijnsz buy it? Would Count William adopt it?

The sun was up over the bow and lent its warm glow to the three men on board the cog. Jan got up and handed the sheet[104] to Philips. The priest took it gingerly. "Just hold it firm," Jan instructed and stepped through a small opening into the small space under the poop deck, if the tiny area could be called that. Soon smoke appeared from the opening. Jan came back out and sat down facing the fire he'd lit inside. Philips leaned over. The fire was contained by four large bricks. Presumably there were bricks under the fire too. An iron pot sat on a few iron bars that ran across the bricks. "Soup," Jan said. Philips nodded. These pots were never cleaned. If the contents ran low, one just added more water and whatever vegetables, grits, or turnips were available. On good days you might even find a couple of bones or pieces of meat. With the pot doing duty twice a day there was no time for the food to spoil.

The cog had reached open water. Jan took the sheet from Philips and Klaas turned the bow to the north-east. As the wind moved from lee board to starboard the sail traveled across the deck to the left. Philips ducked to let it pass. It had gotten choppier and the wind had picked up. Jan gave the sheet back to Philips. "Hold firmly!" he advised.

'sGravenhage, the Netherlands, 1355

Surely Alewijnsz was eager for the young man to arrive. Intuitively, he knew that van Leyden was right in his thinking, but the old man had not been able to explain it very well to Count William. Before having his master make up his mind against the proposals, Alewijnsz needed van Leyden to explain them himself. In his correspondence the young man had been to the point, firm, and convincing. The timing would be good. William had just sent notice of his impending return from the military campaign in the north.

On the waters of Zeeland, 1355

By mid day the small ship had reached the deep waters of the Zuydt Vliet just south of Noord Bevelandt. Although the wind was strong the going was slow. They had been traveling against the outgoing tide and were pointing into the wind. The ship had to tack a lot as they passed the small island of Wolfersdyck. But the pace picked up considerably when they entered the Noort Oort and Cats Rac and turned north. In the distance behind him, Philips made out the church towers of Goes and beyond the bow he spotted the towers of Zierikzee. Klaas and Jan initially had planned to overnight in the bustling little city. But, with the favorable weather and the progress they'd made, they decided to press on into 't Slaeck and the Volckerack. The incoming tide would help carry them east so that they could reach the tiny harbor of Ooltgensplaet van Vloyhil[105] at the eastern tip of Overflackee before nightfall.

Philips was enjoying the voyage even though the spray from the breaking waves on the bow regularly rained down on him. The open water of the Volckerack was much rougher than that of the more protected 't Slaeck. Again sailing mostly in an easterly direction, Klaas had to tack often. Jan entrusted the young priest with the sail and told him, "If you ever decide to leave the priesthood, Father, you got a job waiting for you!" The sailor stayed close enough to intervene should it become necessary. But, Philips felt good. Some of the anxiety he harbored about his visit to 'sGravenhage ebbed away. The tranquility of his watery surroundings let him float his thoughts freely. The approach he would use and the arguments with which to convince the Count settled more firmly into his mind. His confidence increased. There was, after all, no alternative if the County was to thrive, or even survive.

With the sun resting on the western horizon, the cog turned west and entered the narrow channel of Ooltgensplaet, where the wind pushed them to the small village ahead. Its position was quite precarious in the unprotected flats. A few small fishing boats were moored at the small man-made rise in the land. The place was only recently settled and the tiny wattle and mud houses were fairly new. That is how it was in the water lands. One storm could wash boats, animals, houses, and people away. Then, after a number of years of favorable weather and currents, the land would slowly build up again. Grasses would grow, birds would nest and bring seeds, and shrubs appeared whose roots would strengthen the soil. Next, a few hardy souls found the courage, or desperation, to graze livestock and, eventually, settle.

On the embankment a small man and a large woman, arms folded, stood watching as the cog moored off. They had already recognized the ship when it sailed up the channel. During earlier visits, Klaas and Jan had established a good relationship with the villagers and the couple greeted them warmly. Once on shore they looked Philips up and down. "Who are you bringing?" the man asked. He was very short and skinny. His dark wool clothes showed their age. The knees of his pants were patched and his vest was too large. On his head he wore a long wool cap with its tail hanging down to his shoulder. "A priest on a mission, Danker," Klaas offered.

Soon the three travelers found themselves inside one of the tiny houses where a fire burned in a small brick stove. A pot much like the one on board ship spread a smell of fish, cabbage, and onions. They had all exchanged names. Maatje[106] occasionally stirred the brew. Her robe reached from the straps at her neck down to her ankles. It had lost much of its blue dye and was torn around the bottom edge. What was not covered by her wool vest showed many patches of darker material. Just like Danker's[107] vest, it had no buttons. Wool straps kept the sides together over her sizable bosom. She was much larger than he. "Pray tell, Father, what your errand is?" she asked. Philips hesitated. But, since he had already told the brothers, he decided to tell them.

"Count William's counsel, Alewijnsz, invited me," he said. She nodded and glanced at the little man. A person that high up had never been discussed in her home. Much less had she ever had a visitor like this and she was not sure if it was a good thing. After all, the village was clandestine. They had not asked for permission to settle here. As far as they were concerned, the flats were no-man's land. But they also knew that in time the lords of Overflackee would claim the new land. "Hmm" she said, "the war?" She hoped to divert the attention away from the village.

Philip van Leyden's journey. Map by Kaerius, 1617

"Well," Philips replied, "in a way, yes, I think so." Sensing that his audience was waiting for a clarification of his ambiguous answer, he continued, "It is a matter of law that could end the quarrels between our lords and I think I have a solution."

"Never not!" Maatje said firmly. "Those folks will never give up their greed." She stirred the pot more vigorously. Danker had not said a word. Philips had decided she was the boss and that the little man was perhaps dim-witted. But then Danker opened his mouth.

"Well wife," he addressed Maatje, "the good Father here must think there is a way?" He turned to Philips. "Is there, Father?"

Philips nodded and decided to keep the explanation simple. He raised his arm and let his hand indicate the water of the Volckerack behind them. "Who owns that water?"

His four companions looked puzzled. Were they supposed to say that the Count owned it?

Maatje spoke first. "Count William controls it."

Philips nodded. "He does control it," he confirmed and looked around at the faces in the small circle. "But does he own it?" he challenged them. They looked from one to the other hoping for a clue. If the Count controlled it, did he then not own it?

After some silent moments Jan spoke up. "Father, who do you think owns it?" he asked.

Philips raised shoulders and eyebrows. "That is indeed the question," he said.

Jan continued, "All right. My brother and I sail up and down these waters and you could say that we own them. We live on them and depend on them."

"But so do other sailors," Klaas protested.

"And fishermen," Danker added. All eyes were on Philips, waiting for an answer.

"And fishermen," he repeated, nodding. "So? I'll ask again. Who owns the waters?" Jan looked around. Then he said, "Everybody," he paused, and looked up at Philips. "And nobody?"

Philips nodded slowly. "Indeed," he confirmed, looking around the dim faces in the circle. All eyes were on him. "Everybody should be able to use it but nobody owns it." His companions all looked around and nodded. They liked that arrangement. Too many times had they suffered under the appropriations of so-called 'lords' – though 'thieves' was a more appropriate name.

The pot had been bubbling for a while and Maatje took it from the fire. It was cozy in the little house. There were no windows, only shutters, and they were closed. The only light came from a fish oil lamp on the rough hewn table the four men were seated around. Maatje put the pot next to the lamp and stuck the large wooden spoon in it. "You first, Father," she ordered. "Oh, thank you," Philips said. "Shall I bless our food?" All nodded. "Please, Father," Danker said. Philips folded his hands, paused, and closed his eyes. His companions followed his example.

"Dear Lord who art in heaven," he said softly. "Please accept our thanks for our daily bread. And, please hear our thanks for the friendship we received this day, bless the ship that carried us hither, and bless the house in which we found warm refuge. Please, oh Lord, bless our food and strengthen our resolve so we may continue our paths in health and in wisdom. May our hearts prosper and our stomachs be content. Amen."

Four more "amens" circled the table. Philips took the spoon and took a small scoop, brought it to his lips, and blew off steam. With all eyes on him, he slurped, chewed, widened his eyes in appreciation, and swallowed. "Delicious," he confirmed. A soft sigh went around the room. He passed the only spoon in the house to his left.

"We decided that nobody owns these waters," he continued. "Not even the Count or the Emperor." Nods went all around. "So, if the Count does not own it, can he then sell the rights for, say, a toll?" It was a rhetorical question and he heard several "no's". "Could he, or someone else, impose a fee or a tax on the fish you catch?" he asked Danker.

"No way," the little man said cheerfully. He was beginning to like the direction of the conversation.

"All right," Philips continued, "but what happens if someone like a lord or such charges you anyway? If nobody cares, who would stop him from doing so?" A silence followed. Danker's face had lost its smile. "You see," Philips went on, "the ultimate owner of everything is God." His audience had not expected this turn of reasoning but they liked it.

"Then you would have to protect us," Klaas concluded. Philips smiled.

"In a way," he admitted. "But I have no worldly power, no army, no courts, only moral conviction. So, no, it cannot be the Church." His companions looked disappointed. The spoon kept going around.

"There is one man in our empire who has the holy responsibility; who is the keeper of God's garden," Philips said. He waited. His four friends queried each other until Maatje exclaimed, "The Emperor! Of course!"

"The Emperor?" Jan said, "He is never here," and dismissed the notion.

"True," Philips conceded, "but he has a representative."

"Count William!" Maatje asserted. She felt vindicated.

"But why would he do anything?" Jan said. It was more a statement than a question.

"Several reasons," Philips said. "First, if all these little lords were putting up tolls it would be a terrible mess over which Count William has no control. These lords would start fighting over who owns what." He saw Danker's face light up again. "Fisheries and shipping would become expensive and slow and fewer folks would engage in them. Your fish would not go to the market in Steenbergen," he looked at Danker, "and you may be out of business. The harbors would be less busy. What would that mean for Count William?"

Klaas had the answer right away. He, after all frequented harbors and dealt with the authorities all the time. "Taxes," he said. "He would collect less."

Philips sat back and folded his arms. The pot was nearly empty and he was satisfied with both food and argument. "Indeed," he said. "It is a matter of order and income."

Klaas stood. Apparently he judged the discussion settled. "We sail at first light," he announced. Jan followed him out the door. The brothers would sleep onboard ship.

"It isn't much, Father, but you take our bed," Danker offered. Philips shook his head. "Absolutely not," he declared. "I would be happy with a small corner of your floor."

"I sometimes sleep on the floor, too, Father." Danker said with a faked plea in his voice.

"Oh? And why is that?"

"When she rolls over," he gestured at the large frame of Maatje, "That is where I end up!" ⊖

'sGravenhage, the Netherlands, 1355

We do not know how or when Philips first traveled to 'sGravenhage, but the speed with which William introduced some reforms indicates the young Count was familiar with Philips's theories even before he hired the jurist-cleric. He must have understood the merits quickly. The prospect of power was surely attractive. Today Philips's strategy strikes us as Machiavellian, but that philosopher would not appear until 150 years later. William's predecessors had substantially weakened the position of the Count by giving away rights and privileges in return for cash[108]. They had also borrowed large sums from Lombard financiers and sold annuities to investors in Flanders. The rights and privileges were in the hands of nobles and cities. They included toll collections, toll exemptions, fisheries, exploitation of peat and salt, proceeds from lands (agriculture), and perpetual use of estates that had not formally been made their property.

Philips regarded all of these a part of the public interest that a ruler could not alienate. The ruler therefore had the right and duty to revoke these ill-gotten rights. Almost immediately, Count William reclaimed many rights and privileges directly under his control.

He also made a start with another of Philips's ideas. Many of the nobles lived in castles or other fortifications. This was fine for the defense of the County's borders, but served no purpose in the interior other than the security of the noble himself, meaning independence from the Count. The nobles employed small armies to meet the requirement of putting them at the Count's disposal should he need them. But often these forces were used to settle disputes among the nobles themselves and, sometimes, cities. Philips's notion, that only the ruler could have an army and no one else (a monopoly on the legitimate use of force), was an easy sell to the young Count. William had all castles and fortifications in the interior dismantled. At Philips's advice he integrated all private armies into his own and made the nobles officers. In that way, the quarreling nobles and their armies were under his direct control. The concept was not entirely new. It had been practiced in parts of France previously and that is possibly where Philips learned of it.

The removal of privileges from nobles and cities probably raised some resentment. However, it also brought much needed stability and peace. Corrupt practices diminished. The power of the nobles weakened while an increase in trade and industry strengthened the power of the cities. The Count regularly conferred with representatives of the cities and appeared to govern with their approval.

Philips wrote the basics of his work before his employment with the Count. He continued to make small changes and kept adding to the tract throughout his life. No doubt new experiences in the employment of new masters introduced issues that demanded fresh views.

In 1357, Count William appointed Philips ambassador to the Pope in Avignon[109]. His travel there was surely dangerous. It could well be that he traveled through Germany and Switzerland in order to get around

Palace of the Popes in Avignon. Photo by J.M. Rosier

Flanders and Northern France where war and revolts traded places during the Hundred-Year War. The south of France was not much better. Private armies, unemployed during short-lived truces, roamed the country, raping and pillaging. The Pope sometimes bought them off, only to see them return for more. Philips's two years as a secular legal advisor to a worldly ruler, Count William V, must have given him perspectives that were useful to the other ambassadors he met in and outside the Pope's palace in Avignon. His success with the powerful Count of Holland had traveled ahead of him. He was back in his beloved France and he was relatively close to Montpelier and its progressive university. Philips renewed his acquaintance with old friends and made new ones such as Arnoud van Hoorn[110] who studied in Montpelier in 1361.

In 1358, one year after Philips's departure from Holland, a curious thing happened. The young Count William was declared insane. How, by whom, and why history does not tell. Throughout the times insanity was the cleaner tool to rid oneself of undesirable kings, queens, spouses, rich uncles, etc. (assassination being another). William's brother Albrecht replaced him but did not take his title. William remained Count while locked up in a castle in Hainault. It could be that some nobles and cities were unhappy with William and that scheming by Albrecht and his mother brought the coup about. But, if this were an old-fashioned power grab, why was William not killed? Maybe he was really insane. Perhaps William had annuities in his name, and payments to him (and the estate) would continue for as long as he lived?

Unfortunately, Albrecht revived disputes with his neighbors, the Bishopric of Utrecht in particular. Perhaps this contributed to Philips's decision not to remain in Holland after his return from Avignon in 1363. No doubt his French connections helped him land a position at the University of Paris, where he began teaching in 1365. Four years later, he received a promotion to *doctor decretorum* (doctor in Canon law).

Philips's absence from Holland apparently did not lead to a weakening of his espoused policies, since Count Albrecht revoked all toll exemptions in 1366. In 1371, Philips returned to Avignon on a mission for Albrecht. There he again met Arnoud van Hoorn who had just been appointed to become Bishop of Utrecht and who asked him to be his advisor. Apparently the problems with regard to governance in the bishopric were worse than those in Holland years earlier. Philips accepted the appointment but his remedies against the alienation of the public good ran into stiff opposition from the city fathers of Utrecht. The organization of the government of the city of Utrecht was different from that of Leyden. In Leyden, the wealthy merchants and industrialists formed the power base. In Utrecht the guilds of artisans controlled the city. Merchants and industrialists usually favored free trade while guilds were patently protectionist[111]. Because the government of Utrecht was made up of representatives of many guilds, and since the guilds were formed by many artisans, it was in fact more representative of a larger swath of the population than that of Leyden. This broader base made the citizens of Utrecht also more powerful in their position with the Bishop. Nevertheless, they did return some alienated rights to the ruler of Utrecht. When a fresh war erupted between Holland and Utrecht, Philips sided with his friend the Bishop, but blamed the citizens of Utrecht.

Eventually Philips retired to Leyden and spent the remaining years of his life working on his tract and tending his library in his house on the St. Pieterskerkgracht (St. Peter's church canal). Philips died in 1382. He had secured his legacy by donating his house and library to the church in 1372. True to form, he had attached the condition that his library be maintained and the house could not be alienated (sold)[112].

The 19th century Dutch historian Robert Fruin studied the work of Philips van Leyden and the impact it had on the institutions of government in the Netherlands, Holland in particular. His introduction is so insightful that instead of trying to distill his points it is better to translate the text.

> Every revolution in the state is accompanied by a change in definitions. With the new institutions a new system of jurisprudence arises. Small wonder: the moral human can have no peace with what becomes, unless he is convinced that it has the right to exist. Every fact, if it is to continue, has to be based on a right. The new state has to justify itself before it can settle in.
>
> Usually one thinks that the change in definitions has to precede the change in conditions and that the revolution is caused by the new insights. That is how the enemies of the French revolution award it to the teachings of philosophers and encyclopedists that shortly before arose; that the revolution was caused by atheism.
>
> But is that explanation correct? It is contrary to experience. The definitions do not change randomly but only under the pressure of changed circumstances and according to the demands of new needs. Law is eternal and unchangeable but all human principles of law are only relatively true and are kept true for as long as they fit the circumstances. If they change then the definitions and institutions of state change, too. Because the needs that belong to these new conditions demand satisfaction and that satisfaction is often in conflict with the recognized definitions of law as well as the existing institutions. The revolution therefore starts with the breaking of those laws. But can

they be rightful laws if they need to be denied and broken? That is unthinkable. As soon as one is convinced of the need for revolution then one is also convinced of its lawfulness. A new theory has to prove that law. It has to make lawful what has already taken place and that what necessarily still has to be done. It cannot be the cause of what is already fully in motion.

It is therefore not true that the theories of the philosophers and encyclopedists have defined the French revolution. It is not true that the words of Rousseau were realized by Robespierre[113]. Goethe's Faust is right: at the beginning was not the thought but the deed and the deed is born out of the need to do so. The large change of the last century[114] sprouted out of the needs that could not be satisfied under the old institutions. The intellectuals, who felt the needs as much as the masses, only pointed out the legal grounds on which to build the new conditions. Definitions and institutions thus move jointly and change together. None is causing a change in the other and the cause for change in both is the advancement of humanity.

Earlier, with Balthild, Landri, and Marculf in the 7th century, the need for institutional change was driven by the uncertainty of inconsistently applied laws. It affected all members of society. Although the nobles were the main beneficiaries of these inconsistencies, at times they were also victims, as were the Church, monasteries, and ordinary people. However, the people, and especially the slaves, suffered the most. Here the Church, as the traditional defender of the poor, was best positioned to bring change. It had been the retainer of Canon and Roman law and their conciliation with Frankish laws that had allowed the three collaborators of a previous chapter to establish a better delineation between the rights and duties of the respective participants in their society.

Philips had been faced with a different set of problems, but the fundamentals were the same: chaos brought on by inconsistent rules that placed conflicting incentives on competing interests in uncertain economic times. And he had the additional problem of an extremely powerful and corrupt church[115]. Society demanded a better approach with clear definitions of rights and duties anchored in better institutions. In both cases, the framers were unfamiliar with modern concepts such as democracy. Both were looking to the ruler to provide stability (remember the 7th century Frankish monasteries coming under the protection of the royals) and put their faith in a benign dictator.

But, where the Franks established rules or laws only, Philips went one very important step farther. He introduced the concept of making the Emperor (or Count) subservient to the public interest and, by doing so, in effect reintroduced the concept of "the State." It was an emperor's (or count's) duty to maintain and safeguard the public interest. Philips provided clear definitions of what was included. We may find some of the inclusions a bit odd and Philips probably worked until the end of his life to reconcile some of his opinions. Take, for instance, his assertion that the salt exploitation in Zeeland was a public interest. He applied two reasons for this of which the first one sounds arbitrary. Zeeland was the only place in Holland where salt was mined. Therefore it was a virtual monopoly. He was of the opinion that monopolies should not be in private hands (just like waterways, harbors, main roads, etc.) and should be controlled by the State, i.e. the Count. His second reason was directly public. The exploitation left much of the land damaged and prone to flooding. Just as in the later case of New Orleans in the United States, man's activity had weakened the coast and the protections it provided against the sea. Especially in 1375, Zeeland was suffering from loss of land and the agricultural goods it had produced.

In his thesis[116] Rijk Timmer provides an excellent analysis of the contents and importance of Philips' work. He categorizes Philips's public interest as follows:

1. Mining, Energy and Water.

We saw Philips agitating against the willy-nilly exploitation of peat and salt that caused a reduction in agricultural production. Since the Count (read State) received *tienden* (ten percent) of the proceeds, he was complicit in the harm to the public interest. In addition to peat and wood, wind was increasingly utilized as a source of energy. Philips asserted that windmills were a public interest and that only the Count could control them and then rent them to others. This may seem a bit odd until we realize that wind can be obstructed by woods and buildings. By making these mills a public interest they were protected from encroachment that would harm their performance. Albrecht, however, recognized the right to private ownership of the Waterland millers, whose mills were primarily positioned in rural areas and pumped water in order to keep low-lying land dry.

2. Traffic and Transport.

Waterways and roads were public. Only very small waterways and roads built on private land could be private and subject to private tolls. Harbors, ferries, and tolls were public and could be under the control of the Count only. The same held for the rights to fisheries and hunting. Access to public waterways also was public. Philips opposed the city of Leyden when it allowed a chapel to be built right on the Old Rhine. However, his advice was not always followed. Ferries in particular often fell into private hands and their owners often successfully opposed another public interest, the building of bridges. Some tolls were transferred to creditors as repayment of loans. Burghers of some cities were exempted from toll payments in return for loans or gifts.

Although ships were in private hands, they were subject to seizure if the Count needed them for emergencies such as warfare. This was a holdover from Frankish days when shippers were not Freemen. Under the Gerulfinger counts that had ruled Frisia (then roughly everything north of the big rivers) since 889, shippers were half-free. But these servants could pay the count for their freedom, as many did. Especially Count William IV tried to obtain ready cash this way. Burghers of cities were automatically free. Philips did not approve of this since it exempted them from mandatory public service.

3. Money and Taxes.

Only the Count had the right to issue coins and raise taxes. He was the protector of the currency and was responsible for the constancy of its value. He set the exchange rates. None of this could be privatized. The penalty for counterfeiting was severe (boiling). Counterfeiting weakened the whole currency since people would hoard the good coins while the bad ones remained in circulation. Devaluation caused monetary flight. The recently arrived Lombard financiers had a keen interest in currency stability since they expected to make a profit when a loan was repaid. Although Holland and Hainault had enjoyed a joint currency for a long time, monetary policy became so important that Count Albrecht separated Holland's from Hainault's. Notably, both William's and Albrecht's books show no distinction between personal and public expenses; the true accounting of public expenditures was still a long way off.

Of the taxes the Count collected the most important was the tribute, in particular the yearly tribute. Philips introduced the concept of including this tax in the regalia. Formally, individuals paid this tax on land. However, burghers did not pay the tax directly (the city paid it and collected from the burghers) and were less aware of it. An extraordinary tribute was levied in wartime. Although the Church and clergy were often exempted from this tribute, Philips insisted that they pay according to ability.

The Count received rental income from real estate such as land, farms and mills. Other income came from the 10% tax (*tienden*) on agricultural production, market levies, tolls, fisheries, hunting, and timber, and fines and confiscations.

When the Count was still short of funds, he could borrow from financiers. However, in the 14th century, loan interest was still against church dogma. A popular alternative was the annuity, which was a purchase and not a loan. Philips encouraged this form of financing but he did not realize the burden of accumulating payments. Under Albrecht, the debt became so large he had to borrow from his civil servants to service the annuities.

4. Administration, Justice, and Offices.

In the 14th century the public interest was expressed mainly by the internal and external peace and the legislating and administering of justice. As noted earlier, at Philips's advice, Count William V brought all castles and city walls under his control. He also took control of the armed forces and more or less reduced the nobles to army officers.

Philips insisted that the courts needed to become more professional under schooled judges. At the time judges were laymen who applied mostly Germanic common law. Their knowledge was sketchy because there was a shortage of written references. All this led to inconsistency and uncertainty. The Count decreed that only he could have prisons and carry out capital punishment and that lower nobles and cities could only impose fines.

A longstanding problem was the sale of offices. Even in our time, offices are sold for money or favors[117]. Philips recommended that public offices should not be bought with favors, loans, or other forms of payment and that all appointments had to be for a fixed term. Philips wanted to lower

Medieval baker

the temptation to sell offices by insisting that the ruler be very rich. He tried to separate the ruler's personal interest from that of the public's. He was a realist. He understood that self-interest governed public service. The best he could hope for was a benign dictator. Offices in the city of Leyden continued to be subject to purchase. This was the inevitable consequence of the practice that office holders were personally responsible for deficits and that these deficits had to be covered by any successor.

5. Cities, Guilds, Public Works, and Education.

Count William II and his successors issued many city charters that had, according to Philips, sold or given away rights that belonged in the public domain. These were therefore illegal and needed to be rescinded. This William V did with regard to tolls (levying and exemptions). Philips was no democrat. He railed against the city administrators and the concept of majority rule in the city councils which could come into conflict with the "public interest" beyond the city boundaries.

Like most medieval jurists, Philips was concerned about corporations. He felt that cities, guilds, and brotherhoods quickly became conspiracies against the incontestable power he wanted to instill in the ruler. As contrary to the public interest, he lamented the mutual price agreements of the guilds and the effective monopoly Leyden's weavers and wool combers enjoyed in a large area around the city. He therefore insisted that guilds could not participate in city government and blamed the war between Holland and Utrecht in 1374 on the guilds-run government of Utrecht.

Philips asserted that the maintenance of harbors, city walls, roads, etcetera, were the duty of everyone. Since most of these were in the cities, it was therefore the burghers who had the duty to maintain these public interests. If needed, the cities could force the wealthy to issue loans or pay taxes.

Having enjoyed an excellent education himself, Philips recognized its benefits to society as a whole. Previous counts had encouraged the founding of schools by issuing rights to educators. He insisted that teachers be paid well. Large cities had Latin schools that were partially financed by the city. This concept was not widespread in the rest of Germany (of which Holland was then a part).

Philips considered good health and access to doctors a public right. Presumably he based this on the public interest. A few sick people can make everyone sick. The plague that ravaged Europe during his lifetime and cut the population by half must have contributed strongly to this view.

In general, Philips was for order and against chaos. In his day, only a strong ruler could provide that. Cities and nobles formed rival powers that had to be weakened. Although the vast majority of his judicial peers lived and worked in the relative comfort and safety of academia, Philips operated in the real world and had to devise real solutions to real problems. He did not have the luxury of lofty theories. His was the task of making the "commonwealth of ruler and people" work.

Wherever the real power in a Government lies, there is the danger of oppression.
James Madison to Thomas Jefferson, October 17, 1788.

Chapter 4: Parliament Convenes

Timeline

Year	Event
1419-1467	Philip the Good Duke of Burgundy (b. 1396)
1461-1483	Louis XI King of France (b. 1423)
1467-1477	Charles the Bold Duke of Burgundy (b. 1433)
1477-1482	Mary the Rich Duchess of Burgundy (b. 1457)
1459-1519	Maximilian of Austria

One nation received more attention in Madison's notes than any other. This was no coincidence. The Dutch Republic had been a staunch ally during the fight for independence of the thirteen colonies on the Eastern Seaboard of North America. It had lent the fledgling nation large sums of money and it had supplied arms and ammunition through its small islands in the Caribbean, the rock of Saba in particular. In addition, its republican form of government provided a good point of reference for the revolutionaries, for better and for worse, since the Dutch experience had by no means been smooth sailing. And they had problems still. So, what else was there in their history that Madison needed to investigate?

Burgundy, 15th century

The forces of freedom continued to test those of feudalism and repression. In the 15th century, cities in the Netherlands (which then included present day Belgium) had gained substantial freedoms and functioned as virtual republics. Their governments were almost entirely formed and elected by property owners. In some these were the members of the guilds, the trade organizations, and in others these were the merchants and the new industrialists. Although they still received revenue, the executive powers of the sovereigns had diminished in matters of local governance and justice.

The territories of the Netherlands were not united. A number of counts with either French or German overlords ruled. To make matters more complicated, one noble could rule territories that lay in different empires.

This led to animosities that the citizens of those counties might otherwise not have felt. However, the various territories (counties, bishoprics, duchies, etc.) also enjoyed a measure of independence and their economic interests often led to strife. The sheer independence of the cities caused even more confusion. They used their riches to purchase rights from their rulers, often to provide economic protection from competing outside producers. The cities that were ruled by the guilds and the industrialists especially implemented such policies. This, of course, led to conflicts between cities. The lower nobility struggled to hold on to their old feudal rights of control and taxation, which in turn contributed to a continuous, mostly low level, conflict within the cities. Among these cities, Ghent, the capital of Flanders, stood out. It is still a magnificent city whose old stately buildings go back to its glory days in the 14th, 15th and 16th centuries. Fiercely independent, the Gantois[118] played a particularly important role in the struggle for freedoms and democracy. What happened in Ghent would reverberate in Holland. The burghers were quick to revolt, as were those of Amsterdam in Holland. As early as the 13th century, Ghent had become a major wool-producing center. It had four powerful guilds: weavers, fullers, shearers, and dyers for whom the majority of the population worked. The city saw frequent clashes between the workers and the rich bourgeoisie. Because of the insolence of its people, the city had gained independence and wealth, but it also put it at the receiving end of unrestrained, cruel wrath of any overlord.

Then add Burgundy. As if the picture was not already complicated, a new force had grown out of the chaos called France. Although the country's universities had sprouted some advanced thinkers and philosophers, its political system was still very much feudal. The king, ruler of all of France, could control the dukes, counts, and other nobility only through alliances with a number of them. In other words, he had to buy, cajole, or force them to do his will. Alliances shifted frequently through attrition and marriage and when a noble became particularly powerful, he could ignore the king and do as he pleased. That happened with Burgundy in northeastern France, causing a struggle for control between the kings of France and four generations of the house of Burgundy. Through marriages, inheritance, clever politics, and conquest, the Burgundians had steadily increased the territory under their control. Their ambition for a kingdom that stretched from the Mediterranean to the North Sea eventually gained them large tracts of northern and eastern France and nearly all of the Netherlands. Flanders came under Burgundian rule in 1384. One year later, the weavers of Ghent negotiated a separate peace with Philip the Bold. They retained their liberties and privileges, probably because their revolt, which had initially been successful, had not been against the French, but against their

General Assembly of Holland

own Count Louis II, who died that year. In order to bring some cohesion into the disparate Burgundian lands, the dukes started calling a general assembly in the various jurisdictions. Among the early ones were a meeting of representatives of the cities of Brabant and Flanders at Malines in 1424 and an assembly of the Estates of Brabant, Holland, and Zeeland in 1425.

Because of Burgundy's traditional hostilities with the French monarchs, it found a willing ally in England, whose conflicts with France were as old as the Norman conquest. However, in the 1430s, Philip (the Good) of Burgundy suddenly broke from England, entered into a treaty with France, and, in 1437, attacked the last remaining English foothold in Europe, Calais. Philip's armies were defeated and the English made a swift incursion into Flanders before retreating to Calais.

The Flemings were not happy with this war. They depended on a steady supply of high quality wool and it was cut off. They were traditional allies of the English and their overlord was waging war on their friends. To pay for the war, taxes had been imposed on the cities of Flanders. Indeed, some privileges had been received in return, but they were not worth much without production and trade. As was their custom, the burghers of Ghent and Bruges rioted. Fortunately the city fathers managed to prevent harm to the Duke's people and after mediation, Philip pardoned the burghers. But troubles continued. Apart from the internal strife between producers and workers, there was the continued upheaval caused by the return of the city militia from one campaign or another. They made their usual demands for provisions and money with a show of force, when necessary. Riots occurred throughout the 1430s, as did small wars between cities in Flanders. All these disturbances led to inflation, hunger, and disease, which spread north to Holland. Europe's richest and most densely populated area was in serious turmoil.

Philip the Good however worked patiently to unite his disparate territories and provide them with a common policy in economic and political matters[119]. In 1433, he summoned several Estates (provinces) in an attempt to set up an embargo of English textiles. After the introduction of a common currency, meetings of all the Estates, called the States General, increased significantly. In consulting the representatives of the power base in his territories, Philip gained a measure of their loyalty and took the edge off the intense competition among them. The States General grew in stature and, during Philip's absence on Crusade, were consulted in 1463-4 on the issues of governance. More significantly, to finance a looming war with France in 1465, Philip requested (!) a special tax. The duke was building on institutions that were part of the traditional fabric of governance in the Netherlands. The Estates had formalized assemblies of nobles and cities more than 200 years earlier and, in spite of the frequent violent conflicts between the parties, had found an important tool for consultation and mediation in these meetings.

This was not the case in France. Vaughn writes:

An important limitation to the influence and the status of the States General was the absence of representatives from the two Burgundies. Nor, it seems, was there any prospect of a comparable institution for the southern territories.

While limited, democratic institutions were developing and thriving in the Netherlands' territories. They were underdeveloped in feudal France.

Of the cities of Flanders, Ghent enjoyed the greatest degree of autonomy. Its burghers had the right to be tried only under the city's judicial system. This made them practically immune to the justice systems outside of the city and its immediate surroundings. Unique to Ghent, the city government was made up equally of the Duke's men and burgher representatives, but the deciding vote was with the burghers. Vaughn describes it thus:

..., for half of the eight electors were appointed annually ... by the outgoing echevins[120]. The other four echevins were appointed by the duke, but if this electoral college was divided equally on any particular nomination, one of the ducally appointed electors had to give way.

This arrangement saw to it that there were always four burgher electors. The seats in Ghent's government were divided according to formula between leading citizens, merchants, producers, and guilds[121]. Although not officially represented, the increasingly powerful workers found a voice through their employers. The government supposedly expressed the common will of the people but, as is still often the case, did the bidding of the rich and powerful.

It was no surprise that the Flemish governing traditions of consultation were directly opposed to the feudal traditions of their Burgundian overlords. Armed conflict was inevitable. Philip had been patient with his Flemish subjects. In 1447, he wanted to impose a salt tax on all his domains. If he could get it accepted in Ghent first, Flanders would follow and acceptance elsewhere would spread. As it was, Ghent refused. The dispute drew out and during negotiations in 1450 it became clear to the city that the duke was trying to undermine their privileges.

In 1451, Philip's supporters failed in a plot to take power in Ghent. The echevins were open to reason, but soon a full-fledged revolt of the burghers ensued. In spite of various military campaigns against the city, it wasn't until two years later, with the support of all other Burgundian territories, that Duke Philip was able to restore control of Ghent. His advisors urged that he destroy the city, but Philip supposedly replied, "Who would replace it if I ruin it?" He refrained from plundering or even occupying Ghent and merely deprived it of its special freedoms with regard to governance and justice. The cost of the war was high for both parties. Unlike his father, John the Fearless, who had made adequate accommodations with the unruly cities of Flanders, Philip had been dogged in his approach. Much of the economy was severely damaged, which reduced the burghers' wealth and, by extension, the ruler's tax revenues. But, for the first time in Burgundian history, the territories had united against an, albeit internal, common foe.

The decline in rights, freedoms, and other privileges in the Netherlands continued, but Philip also continued to call meetings of various Estates. Modern historians mark the assembly of the Burgundian Netherlands at Bruges in 1464 as the first States General. It was this very body that would play such an important role in the further development of democratic principles such as rule of law, justice, and civic consultation.

After Philip's death in 1467, his son Charles (the Bold) added ever-heavier taxes to the humiliation of the citizenry. Charles was just as ambitious for a Burgundian kingdom from Mediterranean to the North Sea as his predecessors. But he was impatient, rash, and impulsive. His favorite activity was the military campaign and he undertook many. After he ran through the wealth his father had accumulated, he depended on his subject Estates for funding. They, of course, protested but, finding themselves politically weak, ultimately complied.

Charles was equally rough with friends and foes outside his domains. After two marriages that had produced only one girl, he had the fortitude to marry Margaret of York, whose brother, Edward, became King of England. The alliance with England had potential, but Charles effectively severed it when King Edward crossed the Channel for a joint campaign to unseat King Louis XI of France, and Charles failed to show up with an army. Edward retreated and never helped again.

Margaret, however, was a well-educated and kind woman who was a caring stepmother to young Mary, Charles's daughter. They lived in the castle of *ten Walle,* where she was much liked by the people of Flanders and Ghent.

Mary was the unhappy ace in her father's game. As the heir to the richest lands in Europe, she was an irresistible prospect for current and potential allies against the main force that stood in the way of her father's ambitions,

Mary of Burgundy

namely France. Mary shed many a tear, especially when two successive suitors that she liked very much lost their lives in circumstances pointing at foul play. King Louis was sly as a fox, cunning as a coyote, and had the patience of a saint. But he was anything but a saint. He was ruthless, brutal, and utterly devoid of loyalty or honor. The struggle between these two powerful enemies lasted ten bloody years. It finally came to an end on a frozen battlefield.

Ghent, the Netherlands, 1477

Charles's death on January 5th brought chaos to much of Western Europe. Louis seized the opportunity to reduce the power of Burgundy once and for all. The Estates in the Netherlands saw a chance to restore their old rights and privileges. Various old suitors, which oddly enough included King Louis on behalf of his nine-year-old son, renewed their efforts to marry the heiress. All that stood between these men and their ambitions was one nineteen year old woman, Mary of Burgundy, Charles's heir.

To be born a woman of nobility was to be born a pawn. Princesses were the prime commodity in the trade for alliances. Their minds didn't count, their hearts were ignored, and their bodies were for sale to the highest bidder. With the many kingdoms, counties, and earldoms, and the sickly, warring, or otherwise perishable humans running them, the considerations for political, economic, or territorial advantage shifted constantly. Steady alliances were at a premium. A family bond was best. It provided an emotional bond but, more importantly, improved one's chances at territorial gain through inheritance. Since women usually went to live with their spouse's family, the bride was in any case a hostage and, as such, collateral against hostility from her family. The promise of marriage was a powerful lure. But once a princess or prince was actually married off, a ruler had one arrow fewer in his quiver. Marriages could not easily be undone. They required the permission of the Pope or the visiting of his wrath, both of which were very expensive.

The *ten Walle* Court in Ghent had been the residence of the counts of Flanders for a hundred years, and was therefore the residence of the dukes of Burgundy. It was luxurious by the standards of the times. The windows had glass to keep the weather out and some of the heat in. It stood at the north-west edge of the beautiful port city. Its towers provided a view of the busy city. Sitting alone in her quarters, Mary was forced to confront the consequences of her father's untimely death. Ever-restless, Charles the Bold had collected too many enemies and paid the price on a wintry battlefield near Nancy in France. Mary had no sisters to lean on or brothers to help her. She was an only child. Her mother had died when she was eight. Her father had remarried, but that union had not resulted in children. One of her relatives was a king, and her godfather, but, instead of helping her, Louis XI of France had moved in on her possessions[122] in Burgundy and the Picardy and was preparing to invade her entire inheritance of Artois, Luxemburg, Franche-Comté, and even the Netherlands. To make matters worse, her subjects in Burgundy, and especially in the Netherlands, had never liked her father, who had been considered a reckless and money-squandering warmonger. Charles the Bold had revoked many of the privileges and liberties that had helped bring the low-landers commerce and unprecedented wealth. But, by skimming that very wealth, Charles had been enabled to pursue his territorial ambitions. He had virtually formed a kingdom within the kingdom of France and thereby challenged its monarch, Louis. The king had no choice but to remove the greatest threat to his realm and take Mary's French possessions.

Mary of Burgundy, nicknamed the Rich, was faced with a seemingly hopeless situation. An almost identical one 40 years earlier had ended with the loss of titles and lands for the heiress of Burgundy, the equally orphaned and young Jacqueline of Burgundy. As in much of history, 15th century Europe considered women to be weak and poor rulers. Ironically,

Jacqueline had lost her possessions to Mary's grandfather. Like Jacqueline, Mary did not enjoy the protection of a powerful husband or suitor. Not that there had been a shortage of suitors, but all had given up after Mary's father had abused them with empty promises.

Mary was fastidious. She was energetic, high-spirited, and very well educated. She had high standards, but she was sensitive and had really liked three of her suitors, two of whom were already dead. However, after Charles's death, more had returned now that the pot of honey was there for the taking.

One was a boy of nine. Despite his youth, he was powerful. His name was Charles and he was the Dauphin of France, the crown prince, Louis's only son. The idea had its attractions. The marriage would make Mary the future queen of France and the age difference could make her influential over the youngster. More likely it could make her lose her young husband to the arms of younger mistresses and so relegate her into obscurity or worse. And there was Louis, dangerous and unpredictable, a most undesirable father-in-law. She shuddered at the thought of marrying the boy-child.

Ϙ Imagine Mary looking down at the splendid city from her high perch at the open window of her quarters and breathing the cold, still winter air, pondering the issues while the body of her dead father still lay frozen in France. The view was exquisite. The spires of the cathedral and multitude of churches poked the deep blue sky. Endless red tiled and grey slated rooftops stretched into a low hanging haze of smoke that emanated nearly horizontally from a hundred score chimneys. Below was the Lions Court[123] where the majestic beasts from Africa were kept. The road nearby was crowded with merchants bringing fuel and provisions and the palace square was bustling with people buying and selling goods and animals. These were her people, this was her city, and this was the country where she was born. To protect each other from the ruthless usurper, Louis, her people needed her as much as she needed them. Mary decided not to turn down the French overtures, not right away. Instead she would use them to buy time and tell Louis that, about such a momentous offer, she needed to consult with her council, the assembled nobility and representatives of cities of the Netherlands. ⊖

Mary had an advantage that Jacqueline hadn't had: the Dutch counties, whose people and leaders despised the French and their king even more than they had disliked her father. Under French sovereignty, the freedoms and wealth the Netherlands still did enjoy almost certainly would be curtailed further. That fact could rally the lowlanders around her. Then there was her stepmother, the highly educated, skilled, and respected Margaret of York, sister of King Edward IV of England.

Mary hastily appointed a Privy Council that included the Dowager Duchess, the Sire of Ravenstein, Chancellor Hugonnet, and the Earl of Imbercourt. They developed a two-pronged strategy. One was to buy time

SERENISSIMVS PRINCEPS WOLFANGVS WILHELMVS D.G.COMES PALATINVS RHENI. DVX BAVARIÆ. IVLIACI, CLIVLÆ ET MONTIVM:COMES VELDENTII, SPONHEMII MARCHIÆ, RAVENSBVRGI ET MOERSII.DOMINVS IN RAVENSTEIN. ETC.
D.A. van Dyck Eques Pinxit.   Ca.Privileg.   Karolflennan fculp.

Count Ravenstein

with Louis; the other was to assure the support of the Estates. In early February, she met in Ghent with the representatives of Flanders, Brabant, and Hainault and granted them unprecedented privileges. In late February, deputies from Holland, Zeeland and Friesland joined the assembly. The deputies formulated the privileges more carefully, added other stipulations, committed them to paper, and extended them to other territories of the Netherlands. Mary signed the document on March 14. The document's purpose had been short-term but the long-term effect was momentous. We will take a closer look at it later in this chapter.

With the goal of placating King Louis, Hugonnet and Imbercourt embarked on a mission to meet with him and discuss peace and marriage issues. To look sincere, the emissaries carried a letter for Louis, signed by Mary and her council, in which she offered considerations and concessions.

But her godfather, Louis, had not been idle[124]. Sensing the emotions of the Flemish people, he recruited his barber, Olivier le Daim. Louis had just elevated le Daim, who originally came from a village near Ghent, to be Count of Meulan. Le Daim was charged with fostering more disorder. The Flemings loathed nobles and foreigners and all those who had helped

Duke Charles suppress freedom. Ghent was in an uproar. Citizens killed several echevins and locked up others. Philippe de Commines[125], a player and witness, wrote in his memoirs[126]:

> They also put to death several substantial citizens besides, and others who had been friends and favourers of the duke's interest, of which number there were some in my time, who, in my presence, used their utmost endeavours to dissuade Duke Charles from destroying a great part of Ghent, which the duke otherwise would have done.

The conflicts of interest between parties and between people, and even within individual minds, were irreconcilable. The people hated the French, including Mary's two advisors, but they also hated the Burgundians. They hated Duke Charles but loved his daughter. They were upset with the English, who had ignored their duke's calls for help against Louis ever since the aborted expedition a few years earlier. They liked Dowager Duchess Margaret, stepmother of Mary. But they were afraid of her influence over Mary and the schemes she might devise in order to get Mary married to someone they didn't approve of. They wanted their freedoms back and their taxes lowered. But they also wanted the protection of a powerful overlord. It was too much.

As we will witness in the following pages, the situation became exceedingly complex. The events are still confusing to us now, and can only have been bewildering to the players and the people who experienced them. Yet, what emerged from the chaos can be better appreciated if we examine the chaos itself.

With Hugonnet and Imbercourt in France, the government of Ghent placed Mary under virtual house arrest and ordered Margaret to leave the Court. Except for Ravenstein, whom they allowed to remain, Mary was separated from her most important counsel. Margaret, too, was under house arrest, but she managed to continue her schemes. She requested aid from her brother, King Edward of England. He refused to get involved. She suggested to her younger brother that he wed Mary, but nothing came of it. And she contacted Maximilian of Austria, son of the emperor of the Holy Roman Empire[127], to whom Mary's father had made the last formal promise of marriage. The French king did everything in his power to frustrate these attempts.

Louis's ambassadors made it clear to the States of Flanders that for Mary to get married, she needed the permission of her sovereign, and that happened to be Louis himself (both the County and Duchy of Burgundy were part of France). They reminded the States that Charles had promised

Mary to Louis's son ten years earlier and that it was time to implement that promise. Although the States shuddered at the thought of becoming virtual slaves under the brutal king, they thought it better to engage in negotiations and try and prolong their precious privileges.

In the meantime, Mary's advisors, Hugonnet and Imbercourt, returned to Ghent to report on their negotiations with Louis. Ghent's own embassy to the King had hastened back as well and Mary was summoned to attend a meeting of the Council of Ghent. Almost immediately the gathering turned ugly when someone produced a copy of the letter Hugonnet and Imbercourt had carried, and another in which Louis expressed his gratitude to the people of Ghent for their approval and endorsement of the upcoming wedding between Mary and the dauphin. What had been intended as a ruse to buy time suddenly looked like a betrayal of Flanders. And the first letter carried the signatures of Mary and the two advisors.

Everyone was surprised and shocked, not least Hugonnet and Imbercourt, who had negotiated no such outcome. Amid cries of "treason!" the two understood the implications and in the ensuing uproar, they slipped from the room to find refuge in a monastery. The angry crowd caught up with them eventually. The delay may have spared them the usual summary justice of the Gantois – which might have been better. The people chose commissioners from among themselves and seated them as judges. The judges had already formed their opinions, so the investigation did not take long. Officially, the two were charged with having delivered the southern city of Arras to the king, having received money from a party in a lawsuit, and having contributed to a violation of the privileges of Ghent. Their main complaint, support for King Louis's design to have Mary wed the dauphin, was carefully left out since it was not a violation of law. Although the defense against the official accusations was simple, the accusers kept pressing other grievances. Mary of Burgundy spoke eloquently in the defense of her loyal servants, but the emotions and hatred trumped the love for her.

For six days Hugonnet and Imbercourt were cruelly tortured. They appealed their death sentences to the Council of Paris[128], which dismissed the appeal. They were given three hours to prepare for their executions while the noise from the erection of the scaffold echoed through their dungeon cells. When Mary heard of the sad news, she overcame her modest nature and escaped from her guards at the Court. In the midst of her enemies, she ran to the City Hall to confront the assembled people in the meeting room. "They are innocent," she impressed upon them. "They are faithful servants. I alone am guilty!" "Save them!" she finished.

The unexpected appearance of the young duchess stunned the judges for a moment. Then their dean replied that indeed they had been convicted without cause but that, "see all these people and their fury. They must be satisfied."

The condemned were taken from their prison in a cart[129]. Their tortured bodies were unable to walk. Mary ran to the Market Square and found an armed crowd and the fury of beating drums. She rushed to the feet of the bloodthirsty citizens, folded her hands, and begged them in tears. She appealed to the guards who had previously been responsible for her safety. The spectacle of this young woman, dressed in the black of mourning, clinging to their arms, her hair undone and wild, tears bathing

Mary pleads for the lives of her servants

her beautiful face, softened some souls. This was the daughter of a great prince before whom kings had once trembled. She was a desperate, noble orphan, abandoned, who appealed to the generosity of those who were in charge. A silence set in, then cries went up. "We must grant the princess her pleasure!" But quickly the death-wishers took control. Insults and threats were hurled at Mary and she was pushed toward the scaffold. She saw the ax hanging over the heads of Hugonnet and Imbercourt. She shouted thanks at them and fainted to the ground as the blood of her two loyal servants splashed onto her face.

If Louis had expected Mary to be compliant after this ploy, he miscalculated her resolve. The death of her friends as a consequence of the King's perfidy had confirmed Louis's despicable character, and any hope of an alliance was lost. But Mary was again returned to the Court and put under guard of the bourgeoisie. No one could enter without their consent and all correspondence was opened before it reached her. The remaining members of her Privy Council were removed from the Court for having signed the fateful letter.

While the country was in disarray, Louis moved on city after city and took them without much resistance. The nobles favored the King, but the people of the cities and countryside knew they had nothing to gain and everything to lose if he became their overlord. Freshly under French control, Arras went in full revolt and Louis was nearly killed in the fracas. While he regained Arras, news from Burgundy was not to his liking. Mary had written a letter to the Prince of Orange in which she protested the pretensions of the French king. Following the orders of his King, Orange had previously helped Louis take possession of the Duchy. But he grew increasingly disenchanted with the King's schemes. At the crucial moment, he chose Mary's side and joined the revolt. Possibly egged on by the Emperor of Germany, other territories took up arms. The Emperor, in turn, might have been encouraged by the dowager Duchess, Margaret, who reminded him in writing of the promised alliance of his son, Maximilian, with Mary.

A chaos of armies crisscrossing various territories, besieging cities, plundering them, and losing them again, lasted for several months. Eventually the English reappeared on the stage and entered into negotiations with Louis. The resulting agreement stipulated a marriage between the dauphin and the daughter of King Edward and included some territorial arrangements. It also promised a marriage between Duchess Mary and the Duke of Clarence, Edward and Margaret's younger brother. Presented with these prospects, Mary refused. It is not clear if Edward had really expected to see these agreements implemented or whether he, too, was playing for time. Clearly, a more powerful France was not in the English interest. Louis, too, may have engaged in these negotiations for fear of armed English opposition to his designs. After all, a Burgundy controlled by the brother of the King of England could not have appealed to him.

Louis's tactics of destruction in the conquered cities made the Netherlanders all the more determined to resist him. While various suitors renewed their suits for Mary, Margaret's efforts with the Emperor finally bore fruit. Time was of the essence and before anyone knew, a German delegation arrived in Brussels. It included the Duke of Bavaria, the Bishop of Metz, the Chancellor of the Duke of Austria, and several other German lords. Forces opposed to the German alliance tried to stop the delegation from coming to Ghent for a hearing with the Duchess, but found it impossible to justify the necessary violence. So the envoys were admitted to a large audience where they presented their credentials and explained with great respect the wishes of the Emperor for the alliance of Mary and his son Maximilian. They provided letters from Mary to Maximilian and asked, very humbly, if she would identify her signature and verify whether the documents reflected her intentions regarding the promises they contained. The gathering went silent and everyone anxiously awaited the words of the Duchess. Her Privy Council, which included some opponents of the alliance, had prepared a response for her but she chose her own. Mary of Burgundy, without a hint of indecision and in a strong voice, while resting her gaze on the envoys, spoke with dignity. "I understand that my lord my father, God rest his soul, agreed to and granted my marriage with Duke Maximilian. It is through his will and command that I sent the diamond and wrote these letters. I admit to the content and I am deliberate not to have another husband than the son of the Emperor." [130]

Despite attempts by Louis to deny the marriage by producing other such promises by Mary's father, Charles, a universal joy ran through Flanders. Knowing of the Emperor's financial troubles, the County immediately voted funds for the journey of the Emperor and his son to Ghent. Louis sent envoys to meet the Austrians at Frankfurt and Aachen to slow their progress. They failed and the procession of nobles arrived in Ghent with great pomp and to the great enthusiasm of the Flemish people. They received Maximilian as their liberator and shouted their dedication and loyalty to the young couple. After a stately dinner the young people found time to meet personally but neither spoke the language of the other. However, they read body language as well as the crowds did. They were drawn toward each other. Both were the same age, comely, and full of grace. It was clear to the people that the young orphan had put her sorrows aside and hoped for a brighter future. The engagement followed immediately and the wedding was fixed overnight.

On August 19, 1477, in the company of the Earl of Gruthuse and the Count of Chimay, Mary of Burgundy went to church where she was to declare her fealty to the Archduke Maximilian. They were followed by a few servants and women while two young children holding candles led the small procession. Mourning her father, Mary was dressed solemnly and the wedding of the richest heiress of the world took place without celebration.

The whole sordid affair of getting Mary wedded had been a reflection of the times when every noble plotted to acquire title to territories for himself or his offspring. The systemic problem of heritable titles and property, and with them economic and political power, had made it inevitable. The fact that these titles and properties included ordinary people who had to eke out a living was discounted.

However, the rise of the cities complicated matters. As sovereigns became dependant on the funds they could extract from them, they also became more sensitive to their demands. The shifts in the centers of power obviously also brought changes in the political dynamics. In France the kings resorted to harsh suppression of city power. In the Netherlands, the dukes found it better to accommodate them and profit from a good relationship. But accommodation did not guarantee tranquility. The cities proved to be capricious allies. They were not homogeneous – not as a group and not internally. They, too, learned over time that consultation was by far the cheaper way to resolve disputes, without and within. But, as we still witness today, disputes attract outside parties who will exploit them for their own benefit. Especially when one segment of the population is, for whatever reason, unable to participate fully in the consultative process, interested parties will attempt to mobilize that segment into actions that do make a difference: riots and revolt. An appeal to emotion is a tried and true tool to achieve that. King Louis understood it well and he exploited it in Ghent. But, emotions are fickle. As quickly as the Gantois had been riled up against the house of Burgundy, their anger was swept aside by the affection for a young, beautiful heiress who openly begged them for forgiveness, mercy, and support. Had their anger continued, Mary might well have died, with Flanders and the rest of the Netherlands falling into the hands of the feudal French. It was the turnaround of their emotions, not calculation, that forestalled doom. Crucial was the personality of Mary. Had she been as mean-spirited and loathsome as her godfather, Louis, had she not thrown herself at the feet of the Gantois, had she not been attractive and vulnerable, the course of history would have been very different.

The Great Privilege that resulted from all the turmoil is one of history's most important documents. It was almost lost in the intrigues and excitement of that fateful year. Without the continuity of Mary's rule it would have been null and void. Let's have a closer look.

Ghent, the Netherlands, February & March, 1477

The only way for Mary to get the Estates behind her was by restoring their privileges as they had been before her father and grandfather had curtailed them. Louis understood this, too, and he entered into negotiations with several cities offering the same. However, the burghers didn't trust him to honor such liberal agreements. As early as February 11, 1477, Mary called a meeting in Ghent of the representatives of the three most powerful counties of the southern Netherlands, Flanders, Hainault, and Brabant, plus that of Holland. On the occasion they formally recognized her as the heir to Charles. The representatives were keen to do that because it showed the determination of a united front against King Louis. But they demanded a clear understanding of their rights. They hashed out the fundamentals of the agreement in only one day and Mary signed the "Great Privilege"

Page one of the Great Privilege of 1477

without hesitation. Her ascension to the "throne" went into history as the "Joyous Entry." During the next four weeks, the document was further developed and made to include all of the Burgundian Netherlands.

Its very existence is remarkable. It was the first document that addressed, established, and confirmed the Netherlands as one nation. The language in which the *Groot Privilege* had been written was Dutch - not Burgundian French, nor northern French, and not Latin. For the first time in the history of the Netherlands, a document of such importance had been written in its own language. The Estates insisted that from then onwards, the language of State would be Dutch. That they, among themselves, could agree on which of the many dialects would prevail is remarkable in itself. They settled on the *Nederduitse Sprake* as spoken in the County of Holland. It was an indication of the growing importance of that northern county. The choice signifies three facts. The stature of Burgundy in Dutch affairs had been lowered irreversibly. The stature of the Church with Latin as the source of judicial learning had been replaced with secular jurisprudence. Most importantly, "the people" had at last found recognition of their interests and power.

In a modern MS Word printout the document is five pages long. The preamble lists Mary's many titles: Duchess of Burgundy, Lorrain, Brabant, Limburg, Luxemburg, and Gelderland; Countess of Flanders, Artois, Burgundy (there were two parts), Hainault, Holland, Zeeland, Namur and Zutphen; Mark-Countess of Rijks; Lady of Friesland, Salins, and Mechlin. The text identifies those present as deputies and commissioners of the Estates: Louis of Bourbon, the Bishop of Ludicke, the Duke of Bouillon, Adolf van Cleve Count of Loon, and Count Ravenstein. The last was recognized with titles that somewhat fit with our modern concept of prime minister: Stadholder General and Governor of all lands. Although afterwards nobles of high stature served in this position, and served their own interests to varying degrees, the construct was proto-republican, the significance and consequences of which will be explored in the coming chapters.

The text confirms the Dutch Estates as a nation. All territories have to come to its defense against foreign threats. Mary recognized the price the Estates paid for her father's wars and that their privileges had been taken away unjustifiably. She restored all "rights, privileges, customs, and usage for the maintenance of justice ... for the profit and prosperity all lands ..." A list of articles with specifics follow.

1. The organization of government. The article orders the formation of a large council headed by a chancellor who is required to master Latin, Walloon (French) and Dutch. The Estates will have the following

membership:
    Wallonia and Burgundy – 4
    Artois and Picardy – 2
    Hainault – 2
    Namur – 1
    German lands – 1
    Brabant – 4
    Flanders – 4
    Holland and Zeeland – 4
    Luxemburg – 2
    Limburg and Overmaas – 2
    Half of the representatives shall be nobles and the other half jurists[131] while Namur gets to have one more noble[132].

2. Mary and her successors will always seek consent from the Council and nothing will be kept from them. This is the principle of advice and consent. It implies that no law shall be enacted without the Council's consent. In practice, this is akin to "no taxation without representation[133]." Another requirement is that the members are all able to speak Walloon and Dutch.

3. The sovereign, the members of her private councils, and the members of the Great Council swear that they will, unconditionally, uphold all rights, privileges and customs of the lands and cities. This article elevates the document to the level of a constitution.

4. All cases that are brought before the "Great Council" shall be conducted in the language of the defendants.

5. All laws that infringe on the rights, privileges, and customs, already on the books or to be enacted, are and shall be null and void. This again points at a constitution.

6. All correspondence that emanates from the Great Council or its chambers shall be written in the language of the addressed parties.

7. All other parliaments are abolished and not to be instituted. The main reference is to Mechlin where Charles had seated a body modeled on the parliament of Paris. It was primarily a high court.

8. All unresolved cases shall be handled by local courts according to their customs. This implies States Rights.

9. Ditto for appeals.

10. Mary promises that neither she, nor her successors, shall declare war without informing the Great Council of the need and only after the Council unanimously approves the action. This effectively puts the responsibility for foreign affairs and defense in the hands of the Council – an unprecedented right. In the United States today this is

still an issue. Even though Congress has the sole power to declare war the executive can still effectively force the issue since it controls the armed forces.

11. If the Council decides to go to war, it has to publicize this intention in the cities and grant forty days to those who want to leave – including both persons and goods. They are not to be arrested. This article suggests recognition of the rights of individuals with regard to life and liberty. It was probably included to accommodate the many foreign financiers and to give merchants the opportunity to get out before their possessions (e.g. ships) could be confiscated for purposes of war, as had happened often in the past.

12. If there is to be war then vassals, or feudatories, will be at the service of the armed forces of the country at their expense but no farther than the borders of the country, whenever the States order it. For the first time the word "States" is used in the context of a unity of purpose.

13. All other ordinances regarding feudal lands will be nullified. In effect, all privileges will be suspended. This harks back to the "Public Interest" and inalienability of rights that Philips van Leyden had addressed a century earlier.

14. Neither Mary nor her successors will put anything in the way of the States to pursue their commercial interests and pass ordinances to that end. In other words, States and Cities can pass their own laws without interference from, or consent of, the sovereign. This stresses States' Rights.

15. The same for the cities.

16. People are subject only to the laws of their domicile and cannot be tried in another jurisdiction. Again the rights of the individual are protected from arbitrary judgment in alien territory. The consequence of this article is a gradual development of universal rights in the Netherlands.

17. Judicial courts cannot be "rented out." This rule curtailed the power of the nobles and firmly places the courts under the, mostly local, authorities, effectively the State.

18. No merchants or their vessels shall be restricted from entering fellow States.

19. The same for officials and dignitaries.

20. No new tolls shall be set up. Again Philips van Leyden's concept shines through.

A number of clarifications, guarantees, and safeguards follow. Then Mary commits herself and her successors to the articles and abdicates all rights to recall the rights and privileges. The document carries the signatures of Mary and the aforementioned representatives of the States.

Unlike previous documents, such as the Frankish codes or even Magna Carta, the document uniquely addresses the issues of governance of a sovereign state. It dictates the rights and duties of the branches of government and the relation between the States under their newly defined union. It does not dictate civic or penal law other than that it confirms that the States and the Cities have the right to address those with the provision that individuals are subject only to the laws of their own state of residence. The document was the most advanced of its time and served as a "Basic Law" to which all other laws were subjected and by which all conforming laws were protected. The historian Thomas E. May[134] observes:

> All the privileges of the cities were confirmed: they appointed their own magistrates, had their own municipal courts, and were not to contribute to taxes which they had not voted. Similar privileges were granted to Flanders and other provinces; and thus a constitution was obtained for the Netherlands, which recognised, to an unexampled extent, all the rights of a free people under a constitutional monarchy.

History does not tell us whether Mary of Burgundy championed, or even understood, the significance of the articles of the Great Privilege. However, the excellent education she received and the place where she grew up – the rich port city of Ghent – had exposed her to sophisticated thinking. She was aware of the workings and importance of commerce and good governance. She must have been aware of her own limitations and was wise to surround herself with quality advisors. The formation of the Great Council and the powers it was given assured not only continuity of her rule but, by giving the people a large stake in its success, gave that rule purpose and legitimacy in the eyes of her subjects. Governing had become a partnership.

The Union under Siege, 1480s

Despite Mary's union with Maximilian, the war with France continued, even after the latter's great victory near Guinegate in Artois in 1479. However, the Netherlands themselves were tranquil. The new nation prospered in its newly established union and governmental and commercial freedoms. Mary bore a son, Philip (1478), and a daughter, Margaret (1480). The people adored the young duchess and her two children and, enjoying the competence of her Privy Council and the Great Council, she found more time for herself and her family. All was well as long as kindhearted Mary was the sovereign. She spent much time riding her horses. Particularly the falcon hunt had her intrigued. Shortly after the infant death of her third child in the spring of 1482, she visited Hainault and received the same adulation as elsewhere in her domains. On returning to Bruges with her husband, she wanted to get away from the pomp and circumstance of her duties. They retreated to the castle of Wijnendaal (Wine dale) where, on a bright sunny day in March, Maximilian organized a large bird hunting party.

Mary's horse fell

⊕ Mary really enjoyed herself[135]. Followed by a large entourage, she rode to the falcon launch point. She wasted no time and took off the falcon's hood, launched it, immediately spurred her horse, and rode after the fast moving bird. Keeping her eyes on the falcon she relied on her horse to negotiate any obstacles. But the horse galloped against a tree, lost its footing, and toppled over. Mary fell on a piece of deadwood and her horse landed on top of her. Her servants came rushing and found her unconscious with the horse standing nearby. They wailed at her limp body. Mary came to but felt a severe pain in her side. She did not want to raise any alarm and slowly got to her feet. Once in her quarters at Wijnendaal, she found a large wound in her right abdomen. Determined not to let anyone know, she treated it herself. But her condition got worse and soon all knew that their beloved sovereign was seriously ill. The Court encouraged the crowds to pray in the churches, and processions with the holy sacraments were held in Bruges. All was to no avail. Mary of Burgundy, holding Maximilian's hand, with the Knights of the Golden Fleece standing around them, uttered the names of her most loyal men, and exhaled her last breath on March 27, 1482. Maximilian was inconsolable with the loss of his spirited soul mate and cried for a long time after whenever he heard her name. She was laid to rest next to her father in a mausoleum in Bruges. ⊖

It goes without saying that King Louis was delighted at this news. Events had gone well for him in the previous two years. By attrition in France, he had inherited Maine, Anjou, and Provence. And the Flemings made a move that was useful to him. In accordance with an agreement made before Mary's marriage, Maximilian had lost his authority over the Netherlands upon Mary's death. Maximilian's only claim rested on his parenthood of their children. The Flemish city of Ghent quickly formed a council of regency over the two children[136]. Flanders had no choice but to defend its interests alone. French armies were advancing and its industry and commerce suffered. Holland and Zeeland had already accepted Maximilian's regency. Utrecht opposed Maximilian and drove out its Burgundian bishop. The Hook party in Holland allied itself with Utrecht and occupied Leyden with an armed force[137]. Arnhem in Gelderland was about to revolt, and, evidenced by history, the Union could not expect help from the Germans or the English. In reaction, Maximilian tried to seize and hang some opponents in Ghent. Hoping to find peace of any kind, the Flemings, under the leadership of Ghent, turned to, of all people, King Louis of France. With the prospect of gaining peacefully what he could not get by force, Louis was eager to assist[138].

The States General of the Netherlands met at Alost in November of 1482 and formalized the negotiations with Louis that already had been secretly underway. They offered little Margaret in marriage to Louis' son. As Dower, she would bring the duchy of Burgundy and its French territories back into France. The States General didn't leave it there and offered the counties of Burgundy and Artois too. Of course none of these lands were theirs to give away, but Maximilian was powerless to stop it. And, if that weren't enough, they settled that young Philip should pay homage to Louis for Flanders. This in effect would restore the old system of vassalage. It provided a fresh pretext for French intervention. The Flemings were prepared to go at any length to revive their commerce by restoring free trade with France.

Flanders's envoys traveled to the French fortress of Plessis-les-Tours. It was a gloomy place with iron portcullises, iron gates, drawbridges, towers, and soldiers. Once inside they were led into a small, dimly lit chamber where they met with Louis XI. The monarch was but a shadow of his former self. Nearing 60, he suffered from cerebral arteriosclerosis and confined himself to the fortress[139]. He was almost completely concealed in rich furs and he barely moved. Louis was dying. In his effort to cling to life and power, he was more suspicious and harsh than ever. He ordered a Bible so he could swear an oath. When the time came he said, "If I swear with my left hand, you will excuse it; my right is a little weak." Aware that an oath

Maximilian by Dürer

with the left hand could be annulled, he touched the Bible with his right elbow. The treaty of Arras was concluded in December, 1482.

Confronted with additional problems in southern Germany, there wasn't much Maximilian could do. His annual pension from the Union was denied him until he accepted the terms of the treaty. He did so in March of 1483[140]. The situation grew still worse for him. The ancient Knights of the Golden Fleece, a left-over from the days of noble power, declared that Maximilian was no longer the head of their order. Bruges refused him entry if accompanied by more than a dozen people.

Just as Maximilian's outlook was bleakest he received a momentous break in the death of King Louis. With this formidable, scheming adversary out of the way he no longer had to worry about external threats and could move freely to face the national challenges head on. In September, he put down the revolt in Utrecht and subsequently moved on Flanders. In January of 1485, he defeated Ghent's forces at Oudenaarde but failed to take the city. Instead a French army entered Ghent. The French soldiers behaved so badly that the city forced them out again. It proved a turning point when Maximilian's allies in both Bruges and Ghent regained control and eventually allowed the cities to completely submit to the Austrian. His son was returned to him.

Maximilian showed restraint when he declared a general amnesty and executed only thirty-three ringleaders of the French faction. Meanwhile, in Germany, he was elected Roman Emperor and he quickly returned there to be crowned. In the summer of 1486, Emperor Maximilian went back to the Netherlands, where he was well received. However, turmoil in the lowlands continued. The confusion was much like before and involved all the aforementioned actors: France, the various Flemish cities, and a number of powerful individuals. It wouldn't be until May of 1493 that peace returned to the Netherlands.

The events show the difficulties that the republican forces of the cities faced in the 15th century. The power of republican systems rested on their commercial strengths. But, as such, the cities functioned much as entities unto themselves. Even within these small quasi-republics, various factions (nobles, merchants, and workers) struggled to gain or maintain power. In the pursuit of competing commercial interests, these cities found frequent conflict with each other. The Balkanization of power also transferred to the Estate (County, Bishopric, etc.), where representatives of the cities and nobility made up the Council. In turn, representatives of those councils formed the Great Council or States General.

It is easy to understand that, in the absence of a compelling common cause, such as a strong leader and/or a strong enemy, the resulting union was weak. Since so many layers of government needed to be consulted, the Union was slow to react[141]. This explains the chaos in the Netherlands, the ability of Maximilian to restore his power, and a return to civic order under his strong leadership. Through her marriage, Mary had saved the Netherlands from an oppressive French king, but at the cost of making the country subservient to another monarch. As we shall witness, the confederate arrangement would continue to compel the republic to look for strong central leadership in monarchs, counts, earls, or other traditional rulers.

The teachings of Philips van Leyden still held true[142]. And, as we shall see in these pages, one ocean away, at a fateful constitutional convention three hundred years later, the above events would provide ample argument both for those who opposed the formation of a republican form of government, and those who favored a strong republican central government.

The independent-minded and rebel-rousing Dutch did not relent in their quest for freedom. But they had yet to find the discipline, the format of national government, or the common cause strong enough to hold them together. However, the adversarial environment in which they had to survive forced them to hone their laws and institutions. Their governance slowly inched toward ever more inclusiveness. Increased participation brought increased acceptance of the rule of law and of consultation and negotiation as a means of settling differences. As the slow integration of their economies increased their interdependency, a hint of nationalism entered the collective of Dutch cities and lands. The republican experiment needed more time. Would it get it?

*When men exercise their reason coolly and freely, on a variety of distinct
questions, they inevitably fall into different opinions on some of them. When
they are governed by a common passion, their opinions, if they are so to be
called, will be the same.*
James Madison in The Federalist No. 50.

Chapter 5: *The Revolutionaries*

Timeline

Year	Event
1477	Great Privilege (of the Netherlands)
1500	Charles V Emperor of the Holy Roman Empire
1509	Henry VIII King of England
1517	Martin Luther nailed his theses on a church door
1533	William of Nassau born
1547	John of Barneveld born
1555	Philip II King of Spain
1558	Elizabeth I Queen of England and Ireland
1568	Dutch Revolt
1584	William of Orange-Nassau assassinated
1603	James I King of England

Mary of Burgundy gave the Netherlands its *de facto* constitution. The
document acknowledged and guaranteed the rights of the States and their
people. Although Mary did not have the rank of a queen, the Great Privilege
gave the country the world's first constitutional monarchy. Unfortunately,
her life was too short for contemporary powers to get used to the novel
arrangement of governance. In spite of the republican tendencies of the
cities and estates, the country wasn't altogether ready for it. Much less were
the power-brokers ready for a full-fledged republic. Mary's marriage to
Maximilian made her untimely death even more significant. The country
became the property of a conservative monarchy, Austria. Compared to
the other monarchs of the times, Maximilian was benevolent. But, again by
the arbitrary workings of royal attrition and inheritance, the Netherlands
eventually became a territory of Spain, perhaps the most conservative
monarchy in Europe. Serious conflict was inevitable.

The Reformation, which effectively started with Martin Luther's verbal assault on the Church of Rome, added a powerful emotional element to the independent minded people of the Netherlands. Organizationally, the Protestant churches were not hierarchical. They answered to no one but their congregates. Their governance was participatory, democratic even. A religious dogma, different from that of the traditional church, added fervor and righteousness. The events around one extraordinary family will help us understand the forces at play in the complicated chess game that played out in Western Europe.

Dillenburg, Germany, 1535

Φ The Nassau family gathered in the chapel of the castle to celebrate the baptism of their newborn son, John. Just two years earlier, they'd met here for the naming of their first-born son, William. The large double doors were facing west. Late sunlight skirted the defensive walls, streaming through the high stained-glass windows and bathing the apse in a bright, multi-colored mosaic — the perfect setting for a baptism. Many of the Nassaus were present. They celebrated a traditional Mass, but the ceremony had fewer of the traditional elements of the Church of Rome than two years earlier. A scant eighteen years after the monk Martin Luther had nailed his protestations on a church door, Germany was changing. Luther's objections against the corruption in the old church had also opened the doors for scrutiny of dogma and liturgy. A theological revolution was sweeping over Western Europe. The elder William of Nassau had been moving away from Rome and made his long-planned official step toward Protestantism. He would reject membership of the prestigious Order of the Golden Fleece, too[143]. ⊖

By the year 1542, the family counted two more boys and one girl, Louis, Adolf and Elizabeth. The children grew up in a learned environment. The library was well stocked and, in accordance with the times, much time was given to matters of religion. Considering his father's adoption of Protestantism around the time of John's birth, we may assume that the finer points of governance and dogma in the new church entered the young children's brains. Their mother, Juliana of Stolberg, had established a school that was highly prized among neighboring castles who enrolled many of their youths.

While religious strife reigned in Germany, various localities handled the practical implications differently. Places that went entirely Protestant took over all churches, while those with a large Catholic majority often did not allow any Protestant worship within their boundaries. However, many sought to compromise by allocating churches by means of some formula or by assigning time-slots for services in a jointly run church[144]. Emperor Charles V, the heir to Maximilian of Austria, who was also King of Spain, was a Catholic. He was inclined to support the Church's interests, but found he could not forcibly repress Protestantism without destroying the Empire. Moreover, Charles depended on the taxes he raised in the wealthiest part of his domains, the Netherlands. And, he loved Brussels. The Emperor chose tolerance.

The older William of Nassau followed an equally moderate policy and so a measure of tolerance toward religious preference became part of the Empire's fabric.

Breda, the Netherlands, 1544

When young William was eleven years old, his cousin, Prince René of Orange, died and William inherited the principality of Orange in southern France. There was a downside to the new wealth and prestige: a condition

Young William of Orange (before inheriting the title Count of Nassau)

was that the young prince be raised and, from that point forward, educated in accordance with the Church of Rome. He was to be placed in the care of Charles V's sister, Marie. Although she was the widowed Queen of Hungary, she lived in Brussels as Regent of the Netherlands – then part of the Empire. Young William moved to the city of Breda in 1545, leaving his younger brother, John, the eldest at their ancestral home. William shared his house and education with the young Counts of Westerburg and Isenburg, and learned to speak, read, and write German, French, Flemish (Dutch), Spanish, and some Latin. William's life was good. He often traveled to the Regent's Court at Brussels. Queen Marie looked after her ward with warm care. Both she and her brother, a frequent resident, were fond of the soft-spoken, intelligent young man. At Court, he found a remarkable harmony among the Catholic and Protestant staff. Although many followed the teachings of Erasmus[145], neither they nor the adherents to the ancient church made an issue of it. Despite the fact that repression of free thought was enshrined in very strict laws, it was rarely enforced. The authorities were hesitant to impose severe punishment. In addition, Charles's frequent opposition to papal politics made him almost an ally of the Protestants. Even the fierce reformer John Calvin praised the Emperor for his moderation.

Amersfoort, the Netherlands, 1547

The old city of Amersfoort, in the province of Utrecht, was the home of two families, one prominent and the other dubious. The family that shared its name with the city had contributed a long line of knights and nobles to its government and the deliberative body of its province. The other was named van Oldenbarnevelt. According to a revisionist account by its ablest member, the family had contributed to the causes of the citizenry for generations. The account told of how the two families were joined by marriage that resulted in the birth of a healthy boy. Much of the world would know him as John of Barneveld who later wrote this account of himself:

"I was born in the city of Amersfoort," he said, "by the father's side an Oldenbarnevelt; an old and noble race, from generation to generation steadfast and true; who have been duly summoned for many hundred years to the assembly of the nobles of their province as they are to this day. By my mother's side I am sprung from the ancient and knightly family of Amersfoort, which for three or four hundred years has been known as foremost among the nobles of Utrecht in all state affairs and as landed proprietors."[146]

Brussels, the Netherlands, 1550

William's character did not escape notice in the Empire. At age seventeen, he received a proposition of marriage to the sole heir to the Count of Buren, Anna of Egmond. Because of his minority, a governor was appointed and the preparations for the final settlement took a while. During that time, the prospective heir to Charles's throne received his introduction to the Empire. The teenaged *Infante* Philip traveled around the Netherlands and spent a festive few days at William's house in Breda. However, their characters and appearance differed greatly and the seeds of contention were probably planted there. William was handsome, inquisitive, and deliberative. Philip was homely at best, narrow-minded, and scheming. One observer[147] wrote overhearing William: "… the Prince of Spain, without any apparent cause, cannot endure me and it is impossible for me to please him. I am unable to discover the reason for his animosity, being unconscious of having offended him."

William and Anna were married in the summer of the following year. With the marriage came the official recognition of his majority and he graduated out of his wardship. The sudden elevation to a position of great power would have tempted any eighteen year old into arrogance and abuse. Not so William. In the mean time, the relationship with his father had grown, in spite of the geographic distance between them — not least because of the interference each received from the same sources. Their friendship and common cause would prove important to William's future designs. Later that year, he received his commission as Captain in the cavalry under the immediate command of the Regent of the Netherlands, Marie. Frequent military threats from France kept the Prince away from his young wife. But they also introduced a new element into Netherlands' society. In defense of his northwest territories, Charles V sent around nine thousand Spanish troops, officers, and nobles into the country. Their presence would have serious, unexpected, long-term consequences.

Brussels, the Netherlands, 1555

William's rise through the ranks was stellar. In 1554, just before turning twenty-one, the Emperor promoted him to the rank of General-in-Chief of the Dutch Forces during the absence of the Duke of Savoy. As happened often, the remuneration was less than the expenses such a position brought. Fortunately, his young, wealthy wife was happy to supply his financial needs. William was now closer to the Emperor than ever and soon he became a member of the *Raad van State*, the highest political advisory council in the Netherlands. However, Charles V was getting on in years and felt it time to transfer power to younger men. He decided to abdicate all his titles in a splendid ceremony, not in Madrid, but in Brussels, his beloved city. His son Philip would become King of Spain, Duke of Burgundy, and Lord of the Netherlands. The office of Holy Roman Emperor with its attached titles did not convey. It was not hereditary[148]. Charles appointed William to the organizing committee for the abdication ceremony. As the Prince shuttled between Brussels and his soggy military camp, insufficient funds hampered preparations. However, they managed to put together a magnificent event[149].

During the ceremony, Charles rose to his feet to address the States General and all other dignitaries present. He summoned the same young man on whose arm he had entered the great hall of the palace. William, tall and handsome, immediately came to his master's side. Dark and chiseled, his appearance was more Spanish than German. His intelligent brown eyes and short dark brown hair were accentuated by a deep tan, due to long exposure in the field. Despite his 22 years, lines already engraved his high forehead. He had a moustache and a pointed beard. His magnificent apparel, however, was decidedly Dutch. With the great Emperor's hand on his shoulder, he moved forward. Charles's other hand leaned on a crutch, and held a closely written brief from which he addressed the assembly. He spoke of his many military campaigns and the love for his diverse subjects. Then he addressed his son. He advised Philip to look out for the interests of the provinces and that their welfare would insure his own. He implored him to rule wisely, to live in fear of God, and to maintain law, justice, and the Catholic religion. Turning to the States he entreated them, as a nation, to obey their new prince, to maintain concord, and to preserve the Catholic faith.

The words were a warning. Charles understood the Netherlands and its people. Even though he had ruthlessly put down a rebellion in Ghent, he had not destroyed the city. Rather, he had earned its citizens' respect by maintaining some of their privileges, albeit on his terms. Now he told the people they would continue to prosper if they stayed faithful to throne and church. He admonished his son to be firm, but understanding and apply the carrot and the stick thoughtfully. The fact that Charles, out of all the splendid cities in his realm, had chosen Brussels as his residence and the venue for his abdication shows how highly he regarded the Netherlands. The country was a major contributor to the financing of his rule and could only be so if its people were allowed privileges and freedoms that supported their industry. Not that he had been overly generous. He had applied the minimum of freedom necessary for a maximum of revenue. Charles may well have anticipated the problems that were to come.

Once again, the people of the Netherlands found themselves transferred to a different power – one with a vastly different culture this time. While the Netherlanders were industrious, the Spanish hidalgo (nobility) looked down on work as the purview of peasants[150]. Spain was then Europe's mightiest power and engaged in the wholesale rape and pillage of the South American continent. Isabella of Portugal had raised Philip in Spain and the new King was in all respects a Spaniard. The young Lord installed himself in Brussels with many Spanish nobles in his entourage and Spanish troops still stationed in the provinces. He almost immediately reactivated the Religious Inquisition and started an active persecution of Protestants in his dominions. The period of effective tolerance was over. The terror had begun.

Brussels, the Netherlands, 1559

William's wife, Anna, had died the previous year. Philip did not allow the widower any leave because his diplomatic skills were needed in peace negotiations with France. While he was at the Court in Paris, the Catholic King Henry II divulged secret negotiations with Philip's representative, the Duke of Alva, about the eradication of all heretics in Europe. William was horrified at the prospect of having numerous good citizens end up on the pyre. His dislike of the unimaginative King of Spain had quickly grown into disgust. Meanwhile, Philip had enough of the recalcitrant people of the Netherlands. He wanted to go home to Spain. To rule the Netherlands on his behalf, he appointed Margaret of Parma, his half-sister, Governor. Apparently still trusting William in military affairs, he appointed the Prince to the post of Stadholder (military commander) of four provinces, Holland, Zeeland, Utrecht, and Burgundy. The first three were powerful mercantile centers. Significantly, a fanatic church official, the Cardinal Granvelle, became prime minister, and persecution of heretics became government policy.

William's new position put him in close contact with the provincial and city councils, whose members wasted no time informing him of their needs – needs that were quite contrary to the highly centralized and dictatorial government. Irritation mounted with the Spanish troops, the almost complete takeover of government by the Spanish, and the

Council of Troubles

harsh persecution by the Inquisition. Joined by the Counts of Hoorn and Egmont, William was soon one of the most prominent members of the opposition in the *Raad van State*. The States General voted to fill two vacant positions at the *Raad* with nobles not of Philip's liking. Modeled on the Great Privilege of 80 years earlier, they voted to refuse funds to the King unless the Spanish troops left the Netherlands. Philip was livid and accused William of scheming. But the King was powerless to effect a change in the secular institutions of government, at least up to that point. Instead, he reorganized the Church and brought hitherto independent monasteries under the control of newly reorganized dioceses, effectively nullifying Queen Balthild's nine-hundred-year-old work. The power to appoint bishops he held to himself and thus he increased his, and the Church's, hold on the country.

Dillenburg, Germany, October 1559

On October 6, the old William of Nassau died. Young William became head of the family. However, since he'd left his family home, his brother John had taken on the duties of an oldest son. Increasingly, John had taken over the management of the estate and with it the negotiations with the various creditors and political allies. Disputes with would-be heirs and claimants had severely depleted the coffers of the Nassaus and left them deep in debt. John conducted these tasks with competence and a measure of success. The brothers decided to continue the arrangement.

John of Nassau

The death of William's loving and supportive wife was painful but, as is often the case with big changes, it also presented an opportunity. In those days family connections created powerful alliances. John set to work and opened negotiations with Elector Maurice of Saxony. His granddaughter, Anna, was a strong headed, physically deformed seventeen-year old. But the northern German state was rich and powerful. Nassau was in need of funds. Anna was a prize. But she was a Protestant and her father objected to the prospect of having her marry a Catholic. It took lengthy negotiations, during which John no doubt mentioned his brother's increasing disgust with the Catholic Spanish-controlled government in the Netherlands and his sympathies for their Protestant subjects. Eventually John and Maurice reached an agreement in which Anna was to remain a Protestant. The marriage took place in Leipzig in 1561, after which the couple settled in Brussels.

Brussels, the Netherlands, 1561 – 1564

Philip's new government in Brussels increasingly ignored the institutes of state Charles V had maintained or created. Only unimportant business was referred to the *Raad van State* or the States General while all decisions were made by Cardinal Granvelle's close circle. Even Margaret's role was reduced to that of a figurehead. Philip had designed this arrangement. If his underlings were at loggerheads they would have to come to him for a decision. The regime was piqued with William's Protestant wife and the frequent hosting of Protestant Germans at his house. Originally, Granvelle and William had been friends. Their outward congeniality ended as well.

In 1563, after eighteen years of intermittent deliberations, the Council of Trent, a body of Roman Church officials burdened with the task of formulating acceptable theology, pronounced that orthodoxy was infallible. They made no concessions to the Protestants. Granvelle, at the behest of Philip, intensified the work of the Inquisition. The Dutch nobles were angry at the regime's policies and deceit, aggravated by Granvelle's pomp, arrogance, and self-indulgence. In 1564, the nobles sent the Baron Montigny to Spain to inform Philip of the state of public opinion and urge the King to come back north.

Finding no result, Orange, Egmont, and Hoorn wrote a polite but forceful remonstrance to Philip. They explained that Granvelle's mismanagement was alienating the people from their King and asked to be dismissed from the *Raad van State* if the King thought that they acted in their own interest. Granvelle cleverly sent a letter of his own that supported the nobles' assertion of dysfunction and suggested the nobles be transferred to positions far away from the Netherlands. Margaret then wrote to Philip that she could not entrust Orange and Egmont with state secrets.

The arguments found fertile ground in Philip's distrustful mind. All the while, Philip's ally in Rome, the Pope, kept haranguing William about the increasing heresies in his principality of Orange. As if that were not enough, the financial troubles of his family estates in Germany kept haunting him. But a point of light appeared in an unexpected corner. Margaret, caught in the middle and unhappy with everything, identified as the main problem that she was being used as a front for Granvelle's policies. The State was near bankruptcy and needed the goodwill of the Estates (provinces) to get the necessary funds. The situation reflected badly on her and she had lost confidence in her prime minister. But King Philip had already decided to recall the Cardinal in his position of prime minister. In order not to encourage the Dutch nobles, he wrote to Granvelle that it was time to visit his mother. No one was fooled and the nobles celebrated a victory.

Around the same time John of Barneveld took up studies at the Latin School in the ancient capital of Holland. His ambition was to attend law school and become a jurist.

Brussels, the Netherlands, 1565 – 1567

William's youngest brother, Louis, joined a large group of lesser nobles in the formation of the Confederacy of Noblemen. They petitioned Margaret to end the persecution of Protestants. The country witnessed a number of uprisings and riots. Between August and October of 1566, a wave of iconoclasm[151] swept the Netherlands. Margaret needed to find the tools to quell the unrest. She saw Granvelle's recall as a nod from Philip to make accommodations. She granted the wishes of the Confederacy if they would help restore order. She allowed William and other prominent noblemen to work with her.

As was often the case in those days, the younger sons in the Nassau family pursued a military career. Being a subject of the Holy Roman Empire, Adolf of Nassau joined its army and participated in the campaign of 1566 against the Turks who were making progress in Europe.

Meanwhile, John of Barneveld completed his studies at 'sGravenhage and signed up at the University of Leuven near Brussels. Leuven was a haven for enlightened academics. Among its scholars and professors were luminaries such as Adriaan Florenszoon Boeyens (the later Pope Adrian VI), Desiderius Erasmus, and Gerardus Mercator. However, the southern Netherlands was too chaotic and violent for John and he probably already had Protestant leanings. He moved to Bourges in France. He chose the Humanist School, which aimed to study and borrow from Roman law for the improvement of French law and judicial administration[152]. The university of Bourges became the main centre of the *mos gallicus*[153], owing principally to Jaques Cujas (d. 1590). He was the most outstanding exponent of humanism, and he taught at Bourges (with a few interruptions) from 1555 to 150[154].

There can be little doubt that the young Barneveld was interested in and influenced by Humanist teachings. Many were inspired by the philosophy of the Huguenots, the French Protestants. He may have met the young theologian de la Boétie who espoused the right of every man to satisfy his natural desire for freedom. His teaching encouraged, "resisting a sovereign who impoverished his people and enslaved their consciences[155]." De la Boétie was talking about the kings of France, but John of Barneveld could easily substitute King Philip of Spain.

The Netherlands, 1567

In order to quell unrest in Amsterdam in January, William made an accord with the citizens that allowed the Protestants to hold their assemblies in the city until they could build an auditorium outside the city walls in the spring. He chose a pragmatic solution that showed his tolerance of religious preference. Margaret was not happy, but consented.

Philip was now completely distrustful of the Dutch nobles and directed that all government functionaries sign an oath of allegiance. He ordered Margaret to apply this test to the troops and specified that anyone who refused would be declared a traitor. William responded that it would not be convenient for him to take this oath in person. Earlier, he had already expressed his lack of confidence in the King by stating that he would rather resign than be held responsible for the harsh policies. In March, he received the formula of his oath for his signature. Instead, he offered Margaret his resignation, which she refused. Some of the lesser nobles of the Confederacy launched a small revolt in Brabant that was put down quickly. Calvinists in Antwerp wanted to come to the aid of the defeated force, but were held back by William. With the help of the merchants, William was able to control the uprising and avoid certain death not only for Catholics, but also Lutherans and Anabaptists

Cardinal Granvelle
Detail of a painting by Titian

who were all considered enemies by the Calvinists. As a consequence, the latter now viewed William as a two-faced papist.

On April 10, William sent his letter of resignation to Philip and explained the reasons for his transition from loyalty to rebellion: He recognized Philip's sovereignty but disapproved of the policies of his local government. The next day he traveled to Breda and ten days later retreated, followed by a growing train of fugitives, to Germany. William went to his ancestral home of Dillenburg.

One month later, the Duke of Alva left Cartagena for the Netherlands at the head of an army. With Alva, the King had replaced the Cardinal Granvelle with someone much more ruthless. The nobles had celebrated too soon. In August, Alva formed the Council of Troubles (also known as the Council of Blood). That body summoned some ten thousand people whom it suspected of involvement in the various rebellions. William was one, but refused to appear. The Council declared him an outlaw and confiscated his properties in the Netherlands.

France, 1567

In September, the so-called Armed Peace between Catholics and Huguenots ended when troops loyal to the latter attempted to capture the weak French King and his mother. When Catholics in Nîmes were massacred, war broke out again. France became unsafe for the young students and they quickly moved east into German controlled territory. John of Barneveld was in Montbéliard[156] where an important Protestant college was located. After a short stay, he traveled on to Cologne and continued his studies. Eventually, he signed up at the University of Heidelberg for, in his words, "law study and the right fundamentals of the true Christian religion, to better understand it reformed of the tyranny, Godly elevation, and heresies of the Popery." He was on a clear course of rejection of the Church of Rome.

The Netherlands, 1568

For the Dutch, the only course of action left was armed resistance. William asked his brother John to collect funds and sell off property in Germany. John forged an alliance with German Protestants while their brother Louis did the same in France. William assembled an army of mercenaries. He supported the *Watergeuzen* (Protestant corsairs) who raided Dutch coastal cities and, much to the irritation of the Spanish, found refuge in English ports with Queen Elizabeth's passive approval. Adolf and

On leaving the Netherlands in 1559, King Philip II accused Prince William of Orange-Nassau of treason

Louis invaded the northern Netherlands in May. During the battle, Adolf's horse bolted, carrying him straight into the Spanish lines, where the young man swiftly met his death. However, the invaders surrounded and defeated the Spanish army. The Duke of Alva was furious and responded with the rapid trying and killing of prominent nobles in his prisons[157]. In July, Louis met with defeat, but managed to escape. These hostilities heralded the beginning of the Eighty Year War between the emerging Republic and its waning proprietor, Spain. This conflict, and all the others that emerged between the various religious denominations, led to the most deadly period in the written history of European humankind. For more see Pinker[158].

William invaded the southern Netherlands with a large army. Alva avoided significant engagement, anticipating that time would be an enemy of the mercenary army and make it fall apart. The sly general was correct and, before losing the remainder of his army, William quickly retreated into Germany.

In November, the Prince came to the aid of the Huguenots in France. However, King Charles chose to pay William off. Once again short of funds, William gladly accepted.

William was very highly regarded in the Netherlands. He had large quantities of pamphlets printed and distributed among the people and they proved quite effective. However, none of the incursions he undertook had led to the popular uprising he hoped for. Over the next four years, the Prince kept trying to find the financial and material support needed to keep a large army in the field. But, in the absence of significant military successes, support was hard to find, while without support, military success was out of the question. In the meantime, William's wife, Anna, had left Dillenburg and set up a household in Cologne. She complained bitterly that William's cause was wasteful and futile and that it was the reason for her poverty. She appealed to King Philip to return the Dutch properties to her, stating, "… the Prince of Orange had suffered civil death under Netherlands law, I am therefore a widow under that law, and that the estates are mine." The response from Spain declared that she had aided and abetted her husband and was thus a culprit too.

The correspondence[159] between John, William, and Louis shows John's unwavering and competent handling of matters ranging from the reconstruction efforts at the castle of Dillenburg to the solicitation of funds and the organization of troops in support of his brothers and the Dutch Revolt. He convinced Protestant rulers in Germany that the Dutch cause was also their own and that King Philip of Spain was a threat to the religious stability that so painstakingly had been established in many of the German States.

William's marriage to Anna of Saxony continued to deteriorate. Eventually she moved to Dillenburg, but hated it there. She frequently traveled to Cologne, where she started an affair with Albrecht Dürer, the famous artist. On William's behalf, John negotiated with Anna and Anna's grandfather, the Elector at Leipzig. Unable to defend his granddaughter's behavior, the Elector consented that her two children be placed in John's household while Anna be removed to Leipzig in his care. Raving mad, she died there in 1577 at age 32. Ever conscientious, John cared well for the young Prince Maurice and his sister Anna.

Heidelberg, Germany, 1568-9

Although Heidelberg was regarded an international center of "the new religion"[160], it was also one of the many religiously divided German cities where the factions had made accommodations by distributing the church buildings among them. The Calvinist congregation there was relatively tolerant of the others[161] and not as dogmatic as some churches in the Netherlands. Barneveld's religious beliefs did not unduly dominate his view of life. He was a theoretician who saw faults in Catholic explanations of scripture, but was unwilling to accept Calvinism's ultimate conclusions. However, at Heidelberg, John of Barneveld denounced the Vatican and became a Protestant.

Not all was peaceful in the university city. A vicious dispute erupted over the issue of state power over the church. One heretic was burned at the stake. Barneveld's views were in line with those of the philosopher, Professor Erastus[162], who advanced a complete separation between Church and State, albeit with the provision that eventually the State had the final word[163]. However, most theologians were more interested in spiritual welfare than politics. Barneveld found solace in the teachings and company of professor Bocquinus, a conscientious man. But Barneveld found it impossible to accept two of Calvinism's main tenets, predestination and damnation. When he shared his concern and the consequences for his salvation, Bocquinus and a colleague reassured him[164].

Religion was perhaps the most important force in the lives of people at the time. Barneveld could not escape religion either. But, as a great intellect, he had a need to understand and he found that his critical thinking about religious issues caused him more anxiety than he could handle. He decided not to torment himself further with too much investigation and not to endanger his faith by too much research.

Padua, Italy, 1569-70

In 1569, Barneveld traveled to Padua to continue his studies. The university had been founded in 1222 as a school of law. There he was briefly joined by Adriaen Junius and Arminius, both of whom would play important roles in the Netherlands. Junius had a high regard for Barneveld and called him, "kind, helpful, level-headed and tactful, not one to form hasty opinions." At Padua, he certainly must have studied the philosophies of Professor Pendassio. Pendassio studied Aristotle's writings and advocated the immortality of the human soul[165]. Another professor, Panciroli, taught Roman law and civil law at Padua until 1570. Panciroli demonstrated his broad interests with his book *The History of Many Memorable Things Lost*, which describes just about everything from fruits to buildings, materials to garments, and funeral rites to military customs. If anything, Barneveld's horizons would have widened considerably.

The Netherlands, 1570

Loaded with new ideas and concepts, the young jurist traveled back home to fill the position of attorney for the Court of Holland. He was only twenty-three years of age. By 1572, he had a reputation for integrity.

On April 1, 1572, an unexpected event took place. The Dutch corsairs took the city of Brielle on the Zeeland coast and, instead of their usual sacking, declared it for the Prince. It was the signal for open revolt against the Spanish. City after city declared allegiance to the Prince and his cause. All Protestants chose for the Prince and cities welcomed his army with opened gates. The whole country was now the scene of fierce battles. The Spanish response was cruel. Of the cities they recaptured, most were sacked and some saw their citizens massacred. William had counted on the help of the Huguenots, but France again was engaged in civil war after the St. Bartholomew's Day Massacre[166].

Most officials in Rotterdam decided to move to the free city of Utrecht. Barneveld was one of the three attorneys who were the first to join the newly formed government of Prince William. By the fall of 1572, the Prince was called the Father of his Country while the "Wilhelmus"[167] was the rebels' song.

In February 1573, Barneveld moved to the free city of Delft in Holland. He joined a group of volunteers to help Haarlem, which was under siege of the Spaniards. He funded his part of the operation himself. Near Haarlem, Spanish troops almost captured him. He escaped, but with a serious wound. He moved to Rotterdam and the following year volunteered again, this time with the breaching of dikes near Leyden to frustrate the Spanish siege there. However, he fell ill and missed the actual liberation of the old university city. One year after his marriage, he became the chief advisor to the Council of Rotterdam. He appeared regularly in meetings of the States of Holland and those of the States General. Often he traveled to Antwerp, Utrecht, and Zeeland.

Utrecht, the Netherlands, 1579

In March, 1578, John of Nassau had been elected Stadholder of Gelderland. He, like his oldest brother William, had devoted his heart and soul to the cause of the Netherlands' freedom, but his Calvinism was more pronounced than his brother's. From the moment of his acceptance of the position of Stadholder he set to work to effect a close

Spanish Netherlands in 1579. Union of Utrecht, dark grey. Union of Arras, lighter grey. Disputed land light grey. Map by Moyogo and Siebrand

union between Holland, Zeeland and Utrecht with Gelderland and the adjoining districts that lay around the *Zuyder Zee*[168]. It was a difficult task, since the eastern provinces were afraid (and not unjustly) that Holland, with its much greater wealth, would give that State predominance in the proposed confederation. The areas of control were fairly well established. The rebels held the territories north of the Rhine and some to the south. Barneveld was now Grand-Pensionary[169] of Rotterdam and was able to negotiate disputes between Catholics and Protestants in his city and keep the peace. He spent much time in the States General as a member of the Holland delegation. He understood that the Provinces needed a stronger bond than just the one provided by a common enemy. He believed that it needed to be formalized.

The Act of Union was authored by John of Nassau and signed at Utrecht on January 29, 1579. Signatories were representatives of Holland, Zeeland, the town and district (*sticht*) of Utrecht, Gelderland and Zutphen. They agreed to defend their rights and liberties and to resist all foreign intervention in their affairs by common action as if they were one country. They established, and would maintain, freedom of conscience and worship within their boundaries. The document had a strong resemblance to the Great Privilege of 100 years earlier. At first, William did not seem to have been altogether satisfied with his brother's handiwork. He still hoped that a confederation on a much wider scale might be formed, comprising the greater part of those who had

appended their signatures to the Pacification of Ghent. It was not until some months had passed, after he saw that his dreams of a larger union could not be realized, that he signed the Act of Union. Other provinces and cities followed suit. By this time, William was well aware that Philip's new Governor General, the Duke of Parma, had succeeded in winning over Catholic nobles in the south of the Netherlands with promises of peace and a return of their rights. And, in any case, the nobles were not very sympathetic to the cities and their independent burghers. The French-speaking provinces then concluded the Union of Arras.

Balthazar Gerards kills William of Orange-Nassau

A majority of cities in the two most important of the southern provinces, Brabant and Flanders, joined the northern union, among them the ever-assertive Flemish city of Ghent. The war had been fought to a stalemate and hostilities were now limited to skirmishes and occasional revolts by mercenary troops. The relative stability thus created allowed Philip to withdraw most of his troops from his provinces in 1581. That same year, the northern Netherlands declared their independence in the Act of Abjuration. Written by John of Barneveld, it stated that Philip II of Spain had forfeited his rights to the Netherlands by murdering its citizens.

'sGravenhage, the Netherlands, 1584

An attempt at the assassination of William of Orange-Nassau failed in March of 1581. The second attempt succeeded. Under a ruse of friendship, the spy Balthazar Gerard managed to gain entry to William's house and shoot him while the leader walked down the stairs to greet his visitor. It left the country without a clear leader. Parma proved a wily adversary. By deceit and treachery, and helped by the confusion following the assassination, Parma took advantage of infighting among the ever restless people of Ghent. The Spaniards managed to retake Ghent and other wayward cities by 1584.

Barneveld, then Advocate of Holland, understood why the assassination of the Prince created such a problem. It was embedded in their system of governance. The Union had a States General where the representatives conferred and legislated, but it did not have an official executive branch. Unofficially, those tasks had been given to William of Orange-Nassau, in his capacity as Stadholder of most States.

Barneveld, on the strength of his skills as a lawyer and his success in negotiations with foreign states, and in keeping with Philips van Leyden's teachings of 200 years earlier, pushed for the elevation of Orange's eldest son, Prince Maurice, to fill the void and provide that strong leadership. The man was young and brash, but as a general he had earned the respect and admiration of friend and foe alike. Barneveld made the proposition to the States and the young general was elected Stadholder of most States in quick succession. After the shock of the assassination the country regained its confidence and the following twenty years were relatively successful. However, as the Executive branch had still been left officially ambiguous, it was only a matter of time until this deficiency resurfaced.

Tyranny has perhaps oftener grown out of the assumptions of power, called for, on pressing exigencies, by a defective constitution, than out of the full exercise of the largest constitutional authorities.
James Madison in The Federalist No. 20.

Chapter 6: *The Commoner Statesman*

Timeline

Year	Event
1477	Great Privilege (of the Netherlands)
1500	Charles V Emperor of the Holy Roman Empire
1509	Henry VII King of England
1517	Martin Luther nails his theses on a church door
1533	William of Orange born
1547	John of Barneveld born
1555	Philip II King of Spain
1558	Elizabeth I Queen of England and Ireland
1568	Dutch Revolt
1584	William of Orange assassinated
1603	James I King of England
1609	Truce between Spain and Netherlands
1619	Execution of John of Barneveld

Soon after the Articles of Confederation were put in effect by the Continental Congress in North America, it became clear there was no mechanism to address conflicts between the newly united states. It took over three years (late 1777 to early 1781) for all the states to ratify them. The Continental Congress was the only central government structure. There was no central executive and no central court.

The Dutch Republic had a similar structure. There the central void had been, and still was, a constant cause for strife between powerful men who tried to fill it. The princes of Orange claimed military leadership in the provinces and so gained central power. Advocates of Holland, the most powerful province by far, assumed central power in service of the States General, the equivalent of the Continental Congress. During periods of absence of the princes of Orange they rose to the title of Grand Pensionary and thus formed an executive branch. But in Madison's day the Oranges had reclaimed their hegemony and even returned some members of the nobility to power. Madison understood that America needed a central government – one strong enough to avoid the plight that befell one of Europe's greatest statesmen.

'sGravenhage, the Netherlands, 1618

"Many who had been promoted by him to high places," said a contemporary, "and were wont to worship him as a god, in hope that he would lift them up still higher, now deserted him, and ridiculed him, and joined the rest of the world in heaping dirt upon him."

John of Barneveld

Thus, John Lothrop Motley relates the comments in his well-researched volumes *The Life and Death of John of Barneveld*[170]. Barneveld was a hero of the Dutch Revolt against Spain, a founder of the Dutch Republic, pre-eminent statesman, *de facto* prime minister of the United States of the Netherlands, and prime mover of events in Europe for over 40 years. This is a long period of time; long enough to make many friends, and acquire many enemies.

Democracy was not yet a system of government in Europe, but some countries were moving in its direction even if they did not know it. As more commoners (i.e. not of noble descent) gained economic clout, their political influence grew as well. A participatory form of government became inevitable.

In previous chapters, we saw the growth of both in the Netherlands. It is no surprise then to see the people of that country among the first to revolt against absolute rule. Out of their municipal structures, they created a consultative national government around which to unite in order to find protection for their provincial and municipal rights and freedoms. The concept of having a say[171] suited the tolerant[172], but opinionated Dutch well. When people can express their ideas and feelings, can test each other's words, the discourse is usually calm and reasoned, leading to positive results.

However, participatory government can be untidy. It sounds familiar to us, with our impassioned commentators, newspapers, blogs, campaigns, and congressional speeches. Monarchs and dictators destroyed their opponents with impunity — usually hidden from the public view. Even if they allowed the public to witness the results of intrigue, it was powerless to affect them. In a democracy, ruthless opponents wield a different tool, mass psychology. They achieve this with propaganda designed to stir up the lowest emotions in human evolutionary heritage – blind hate – by which the forces of reason are shut out and silenced. In our day, specialists hone these tools applying technology to find language that is most effective on the most receptive audience – the targeted message. The messengers of the 17th century were equally devious and mean-spirited. Motley goes on,

> The unsigned publication of the States-General, with its dark allusions to horrible discoveries and promised revelations which were never made, but which reduced themselves at last to the gibberish of a pot-house bully, the ingenious libels, the powerfully concocted and poisonous calumnies, caricatures, and lampoons, had done their work.

Since the withdrawal of the Romans from Western Europe, every powerful ruler had been a warlord, or "noble" descended from one. Some had claims going back a thousand years, others were counts with royal aspirations. The most famous of the latter was Charles the Bold of Burgundy[173]. He pursued his ambitions of empire with particular zeal, and, as was often the case, met with unintended consequences that influenced the development of Europe. He helped unite the Swiss cantons (against him). He helped create an independent Savoy in the south of France, which would become an ally of the Venetian republic against Catholic and feudal forces.

But, most importantly, he united the provinces of the Netherlands. Although the provinces enjoyed a common culture, they had never been part of one country before. Charles's father gave them their States General in January of 1464, the institution that acquired the essential powers of government from Charles's daughter Mary in January of 1477. This institution would proclaim independence from Spain and would prove indispensable to the survival of that new concept of governance, the confederate republic. Without this republic, Protestant Europe would not have survived and the liberal environment, in which important humanist values could thrive, would not have been created. However, those 150 years were anything but smooth or easy. Feudalism ruled Europe; ruthless royals executed their schemes; rulers hurled whole territories, including their hapless inhabitants, between arbitrarily delineated countries; too many innocents lost their liberties, their possessions, and their lives.

Meantime, Barneveld sat closely guarded in the apartments of the Stadholder while the country, and very soon all of Europe, was ringing with the news of his downfall, imprisonment, and disgrace.

So, what led to Barneveld's imprisonment?

The Netherlands, 1547 - 1573

John of Barneveld was born in 1547 in Amersfoort in the province of Utrecht in the Netherlands. His family had a bad reputation[174]. His father, Gerrit, had a long rap sheet that listed frequent public drunkenness, assault, even murder. Apparently, the burghers of the city recognized his mental deficiencies and nicknamed him "Simple Gerrit." John's mother was illegitimate. His siblings did not turn out well. He had a brother in the army with a reputation for "shameful behavior". One of his four sisters had a child whose father was "unknown". Another sister married a "soldier of fortune" from Hamburg, Germany. His third sister married a "simple glass painter" from Utrecht.

Not surprisingly, John of Barneveld deemed it wise keep as far as possible from these characters. Eventually, he invented a lofty heritage and, while he was respected, no one would challenge it. However, he kept in touch with his sister Odilia who lived in his castle Gunthersteyn near Breukelen[175]. His background made his success in public life all the more remarkable. At the time, family status was just about the only vehicle to a good education and public office. There is no direct evidence of this, but, considering his employment and later schooling, he likely attended the Latin School in Amersfoort. Someone may have recognized his intellect and paid the dues. His family certainly did not. As his career shows, John of Barneveld was a very effective networker who made friends among the powerful wherever he could. This, no doubt, helped him find a job at a law firm in 'sGravenhage, the seat of government of the important State of Holland. He was only seventeen years old. It is unimaginable that, young as he was, he would not have forged contacts with jurists, legislators, and nobility. Where did he find the funds to study in Leuven, Heidelberg, and Padua? It could have been the same unknown benefactor. Upon his return to Holland, he became a lawyer for the Court of Holland in 'sGravenhage. Unlike under today's separation of powers, the Court dealt with jurisprudence, but also had a function in the executive branch of government.

Risk and Rise, 1573 – 1586

Much had changed during the years of his absence from 'sGravenhage. When he left, King Philip ruled the County. Upon his return, it had revolted and was at war with the King. In 1573, while living in Delft, he lived across the street from Maritgen van Uytrecht, the daughter of a wealthy family. The order of events is uncertain, but he successfully pleaded her legal case in a dispute over her inheritance. They got married and the documents mention him as her sole heir.

Barneveld joined a civil militia assigned to relieve the city of Haarlem from a Spanish siege. Few details of this adventure survive, but having no military experience, he and his compatriots ran into trouble. Barneveld sustained a serious wound, but managed to escape capture. This bad experience did not keep him from participating in the successful relief of Leyden one year later.

In 1576, Barneveld became Pensionary of Rotterdam. The position included official membership of the States of Holland, which frequently carried him to 'sGravenhage. The city was now not only the seat of the States of Holland, but also that of the States General, the governing body of the free Netherlands. This gave him exposure to the powerful institutions and their leaders and the prominent families of the day.

Although he was not its author – that was John of Nassau, William of Orange's brother – Barneveld strongly endorsed the articles of the Union of Utrecht that formally united the free provinces into a confederation in 1579. It is inconceivable that he and Nassau were not communicating about this. More likely, they collaborated. Following the signing of the Union by the various States, Barneveld proposed that the States adopt the abjuration of Phillip II, King of Spain. He wrote the *Plakkaat van Verlatinghe*[176], which was eventually ratified by all provinces in 1581. Essentially, it was a declaration of independence. To fill the now empty seat of Count of Holland, he helped draft and pass the act that created the post of Stadholder with William of Orange in office.

The Dutch Republic was a confederation. There was a general assembly made up of representatives of all the States. In the absence of a Governor

General or a King, there was no formal executive branch. Yet someone needed to execute the collective will. Because of the competence that the Advocate of Holland displayed, the States General allocated many tasks to him. Barneveld became responsible for the Foreign Service and the connections with foreign heads of state. King Henry IV of France treated him as a friend and made him a confidant. Queen Elizabeth of England had great respect for him and sought his advice. Rulers in Germany did likewise. Barneveld quickly became Europe's foremost statesman. In spite of being a commoner, many, if not most, of Europe's monarchs regarded and treated him as an equal[177]. This was most unusual. A lesser man would have let it go to his head. Several aspects of Barneveld's character stood in the way of that. He had a strong sense of duty and felt an unwavering responsibility towards the States and their people.

Still, the States of Holland recognized a void in the governing arrangement that, in the limited views of the day, only nobles could supply. They polled several foreigners to see if they would be interested in becoming Count of Holland or even sovereign of the Union. Some turned out to be unsuitable while others refused. With Barneveld's support, they solicited William of Orange. Negotiations were ongoing when an assassin's bullet ended William's life in 1584. After the assassination, Barneveld had done his best to secure for his son Maurice the sovereign position of which murder had so suddenly deprived the father.

As we saw, the appointment of Prince Maurice to the position of Stadholder in many States restored a measure of cohesion and continuity to the Republic. But Barneveld understood that, unlike his father, Maurice was not a statesman, just a very good general. They needed a sovereign. The States General decided to ask their foremost ally, Queen Elizabeth of England.

The following year Barneveld and several representatives sailed to Brielle in Zeeland, where they assembled a small flotilla to escort them to London. After 16 days on the water, they arrived July 4. Significantly, neither the English nor the Dutch attempted secrecy. Elizabeth's representatives treated the delegation to a warm reception around the community table of a public restaurant[178]. On July 9, delegate Menin met with Elizabeth and made the formal proposition. Apparently, Her Majesty delighted in the offer, but she had already made up her mind. The next day the Dutch delegation met with Elizabeth's advisors, who conveyed their sovereign's response:

".... that Her Majesty, having heard the remonstrance and request, also having examined the articles with regard to the States General of the Dutch Provinces, approved, as did her counselors, and thanked the delegates for the honor aforementioned States had bestowed on her by sending such a delegation and by requesting and presenting same Majesty with the aforementioned remonstrance. But considering that Her Majesty in no part was subject to any ambition, neither is ambitious to attract any foreign lands ...."[179]

Elizabeth was probably reluctant to become involved. The enterprise was uncertain. She likely also figured that being a sovereign of such independent-minded people would be more trouble than it was worth. Instead, she offered the States protection from the Spanish. By offering help she bound the Dutch to her more than sovereignty could have. After all, as opposed to a sovereign, an ally could pull out. It is hard to know whether the Dutch delegates were disappointed or whether they feigned it. If the offer of sovereignty had been a ploy, then the outcome was successful. During the month-long negotiations that followed, Elizabeth put deeds by her words by promising English troops for the relief of Antwerp and the defense of a number of Dutch towns. Furthermore, she specified that these troops would be the best she had, and be led by her favorite, the Earl of Leicester.

Queen Elizabeth I of England

By August 23, Barneveld and most delegates were back in the Republic. The States General was delighted with the results of the mission. Instead of having to deal with a new sovereign, the country maintained full independence while enjoying substantial protection. The nation's advocate continued to conduct the republic's business with equal success. From his friend, King Henry, he obtained loans and troops. He negotiated moneys and troops from Germany, Sweden, and Switzerland. The man who had started his life as the child of a simpleton and a bastard was now quite possibly the most powerful man in Europe.

However, there was one major problem with the construct of his position. He was not a prime minister, not a president, and not a prince. He was merely in the employ of the States General as their Advocate. His power was the result of his skills, no more. In the absence of clear instructions, his actions often were his own. But, as his success increased, so did his visibility. Envious people became aware of the weakness of his office and tried to undermine him. It was only a matter of time until they would find and exploit his Achilles' heel.

'sGravenhage, the Netherlands, 1609

The truce between the kingdom of Spain and its former possessions, now the United States of the Netherlands, was signed in 1609. It was an admission of defeat. Two people were responsible for bringing Spain to its knees. Prince Maurice of Orange had proved himself a brilliant innovator in the art of war and had become Europe's eminent strategist[180]. Barneveld had earned the respect and friendship of Europe's foremost monarchs and nobles. Elizabeth I of England and Henry IV of France became the young republic's indispensable allies and protectors. The success of both Dutchmen had saved the country and it was only natural each wanted to finish the job, as he knew best. Maurice advocated continued war and break from Spain forever. Barneveld feared a decline in foreign support and advocated diplomacy and peace with international guarantees. Queen Elizabeth's successor, James I, was advocating peace most fervently. In France, King Henry was getting on in age and Barneveld was certain that the succession would put the throne in Catholic hands. He won the argument, but the ensuing peace left Maurice with little else to do but reflect on his political defeat. Barneveld's assessment regarding France proved correct when the following year Henry was assassinated. The Catholic Queen Marie de Medici assumed the regency for her underage son, Louis.

'sGravenhage, the Netherlands,
Wednesday, August 29, 1618

A man of action, Prince Maurice became increasingly irritated at being sidelined. To him, diplomacy was a dirty and uncertain business. Warfare was clean and straightforward. He was also annoyed with Barneveld. The man had assumed far more power than his station warranted.

Maurice found him arrogant – which he probably was – and was jealous of his intellect. The truce allowed the Republic to become introspective. Particularly, the issue of what should be the correct Protestant theology caused much infighting. Years back, Barneveld had decided to stay out of issues of dogma. He felt individuals needed to determine these things for themselves. Dictation was neither needed nor desired. So he advocated churches and States work it out for themselves. The Prince, who coveted order, saw it differently. To him, the Republic was about to fall apart over dogma. Only a strong hand could keep it together, and his was it. In the end, the weakness of Barneveld's office became his downfall.

After his arrest, Barneveld was imprisoned in the quarters of Prince Maurice. The orders for his arrest were highly irregular. They were issued by the States General, but, under the Act of Union[181], that national body had no jurisdiction in the province of Holland. In addition, it was signed by only six of its members and was not the result of a vote. It looked like a coup. Probably to preempt the perception that he was its leader, Maurice ordered the prisoner to be moved from his house and across the Binnenhof[182] to a recent structure behind the ancient hall of the Counts of Holland. The new location was convenient since it had a courtroom and was the seat of the chief tribunals of justice of Holland. The spacious rooms on the second floor also provided reasonably comfortable quarters for the still highly respected, and probably in some quarters, feared old statesman. It was customary in those times to throw prisoners in a dungeon and feed them no more than water and bread.

> There in the opposite building were the windows of the beautiful " Hall of Truce," with its sumptuous carvings and gildings, its sculptures and portraits, where he had negotiated with the representatives of all the great powers of Christendom the famous Treaty which had suspended the war of forty years, and where he was wont almost daily to give audience to the envoys of the greatest sovereigns or the least significant states of Europe and Asia, all of whom had been ever solicitous of his approbation and support[183].

With Barneveld imprisoned, Maurice wasted no time. He trekked with his army through the provinces and deposed hostile city governments, replacing them with his supporters. He dissolved the municipal militias and posted army units in the cities. These actions again lacked legality. The Act of Union clearly left the responsibility of order and justice to the cities and their States. But, said Maurice, "The quiet of the land requires it. It is necessary to have unanimous resolutions in the States-General at 'sGravenhage. This cannot be accomplished without these preliminary changes. I believe that you had good intentions and have been faithful servants of the Fatherland. But this time it must be so." The coup was complete and Barneveld had no allies left in the halls of power.

So, who were his opponents, who had found their champion in the Prince? Barneveld had good reason to vie for peace while the country was still strong. After the death of Henry IV in 1610, France was in turmoil. The Crown Prince was very young and the Court was under control of his mother's Catholic boyfriend. Although Barneveld managed to hold the Court to the old treaty with Henry, who kept a contingent of French forces in the Netherlands, the alliance was fragile. Maurice had favored active support for a coup by Protestant nobles in France, with which he was related by marriage. In England, James I, a proud man of little intellect who regarded himself the ultimate theologian and the savior of the "True Religion", the Protestant Church, had succeeded the Virgin Queen,

Prince Maurice of Orange-Nassau

Elizabeth[184] in 1603. James was capricious and proud. He also insisted in meddling in Dutch political and religious affairs.

The truce allowed the Netherlands to look inwardly. Differing opinions on the finer points of divine philosophy expanded into life and death issues, and James was all too happy to provide his illuminating guidance in these matters[185]. Barneveld had always been a moderate and a mediator. While the war still raged, he was able to defuse various standoffs in the Republic. He also managed to contain James and even feed the self-declared theologian some lines that contradicted his earlier utterances. The truce made James less beholden to the alliance. The growing resentment the King felt for the superior intellect of Barneveld began to show in his correspondence with the States. Maurice stayed out of the religious disputes, saying that he had no knowledge of such fine points. However, the increasing sectarian conflict in the country went against the grain of his character, and, in any case, it further weakened the already weak confederation. While Barneveld preached toleration, the Prince came under the influence of a militant faction. Expecting it to bring back order, Maurice supported a call for a national synod where a unifying theology could be settled upon. In accordance with the Act of Union, whose first article gave each province the sole right to deal with issues of religion, Barneveld favored provincial synods before a potentially divisive national synod would take place. King James, of course, supported Maurice.

The difference in character of the two most powerful people in the Republic could not be starker. Maurice favored discipline. Barneveld valued process and moderation. Against Maurice's decisiveness, the Advocate appeared plodding. But, against Barneveld's knowledge and intellect, the Prince looked boorish.

The French ambassadors, who had been unwearied in their endeavor to restore harmony to the distracted Republic before the arrest of the prisoners, now exerted themselves to throw the shield of their sovereign's friendship around the illustrious statesman and his fellow-sufferers.

Unlike the English ambassador, the French were still highly sympathetic to the Advocate. Barneveld's counsel had been and still was instrumental in the internal peace of France. Queen Elizabeth's old ambassador had been another friend, but James had replaced him with a veritable enemy. The Republic's Ambassadors to the Courts of France and England were Barneveld's men, but the previous ambassador to France, Aerssens, was a protégée-turned-enemy. Upon his return to Holland, Aerssens tirelessly endeavored to get the ear of influential men and fill them with slander and lies concerning bribes and corruption. Barneveld had provided his opponents with ample ammunition because he, as was customary in his day, had sometimes sought personal advantage while conducting official duties[186]. The French delegation tried their best before the States General to instill reason into the Dutch factions and protect Barneveld. The Republic's governing body had a much different composition after the replacements made by Maurice. The eloquent language of the French envoys sounded much weaker coming from representatives of a country that was no more than a shadow of its powerful past. Their intervention failed.

He now informed the nobles that they must receive into their body Francis Aerssens, who had lately purchased the barony of Sommelsdyk, and Daniel de Hartaing, Seignior of Marquette.

We recognize the name of the former Dutch Ambassador to France. The body in question was the Order of Knights of Holland. This ancient holdover still wielded great influence in large matters on which it got to vote before any assembly and thus set precedent. Although there was no proof of this, Maurice probably feared that the nobles' leaning toward Barneveld might become a problem. There had been rumors that the election of Maurice's younger brother to the order had been part of a scheme to replace Maurice in his post.

It all went back to the problem of a head of state. Some, including Barneveld, saw the necessity for a stronger union and there were suggestions to elevate Maurice to the level of sovereign. It probably flattered Maurice and he may have recognized a duty in this regard. Nevertheless, he did not advocate it in public. Barneveld set in motion a legal process to this end, but may have discouraged it privately. The lack of structure left the political process short of a means to handle crises of state. The confederation did not have the legal instruments to settle national political differences. The Act of Union did not define a central government. Barneveld was in the service of Holland as Advocate and executed the wishes of the States of Holland. By the wealth, population (over half of that of the union), and power of Holland, he was the *de facto* prime-minister of the Union, but could as such not be deposed or voted out. Only the States of Holland could do that. Prince Maurice's position was equally unsettled. As Stadholder of a majority of the provinces, he was the head of the armed forces of the Union and acted accordingly. Legally, however, he was subject to the commands of each of the States. This situation was workable as long as the confederacy was facing a life-threatening common foe. The truce of 1609 changed all that.

The Synod, held at Dordrecht, came to its inevitable pronouncements. It was settled that one portion of the Netherlanders and of the rest of the human race had been expressly created by the Deity to be forever damned, and another portion to be eternally blessed.

The enemies of religious tolerance won. The ideals of Maurice's father, William of Orange, founding father of the Republic, were defeated. Barneveld's efforts at mediation borne of tolerance were now deemed bordering on the heretical. All the powerful forces in the country had united, against the Advocate.

Thursday, March 7, 1619

... the trial of the great Advocate began. He had sat in prison since the 29th of the preceding August. For nearly seven months he had been deprived of all communication with the outward world save such atoms of intelligence as could be secretly conveyed to him in the inside of a quill concealed in a pear and by other devices. The man who had governed one of the most important commonwealths of the world for nearly a generation— during the same period almost controlling the politics of Europe — had now been kept in ignorance of the most insignificant everyday events.[187]

The preparations for the trial, if it could be called that, were audible in Barneveld's prison above the large chamber. After six months of almost complete isolation, which included the gloomy winter, it was a relief for the old man to face his accusers at last. The odd thing was, he still did not know of what he had been accused. Although pamphlets exclaiming his treason had circulated for months, there were no formal charges brought. This was in violation of the ancient provision in Holland's law that charges had to be brought within six weeks of the arrest. Failing that, the prisoner had to be released. However, this was a minor point after the violation the arrest itself constituted. The States General of the United Provinces of the Netherlands[188] had no jurisdiction in Holland. It could not bring charges against an individual of any province. Moreover, as a high functionary of Holland on official duty (at the time of his arrest he was on his way to the High Council of Holland) he was protected on two more counts. The violations did not end there. He was imprisoned, and now tried, on the soil of Holland, in buildings that housed the Assembly and the Courts of that State, by the States General, who, as a guest, had no jurisdiction whatsoever. His arrest had come without a lawful warrant while he was answering an invitation by Maurice to attend a meeting. Since the country was at peace and not under martial law, the military arrest had clearly been an entrapment.

Barneveld must have felt energized now that at last he was to enter the arena in which he excelled. After fifty years of study and practice, he knew the law better than anyone.

His military guards led him from his room and down the narrow circular stairs of the turret to the hall below – a journey he would make hundreds of times more. The hall was packed to the gills. Comfortably seated behind a great table were 24 commissioners. He recognized several fierce enemies among them. Leaning on his staff, he looked at each of the officials with the same haughty command to which they had been accustomed. Some shrank with shame while others rose to their feet and uncovered their heads. Initially, the judges had intended to treat him as a common criminal by making him stand throughout the proceedings. But they now made room and saluted as the Advocate passed among them to the warmth of the fireplace, where they offered him a chair. A lifetime of respect and habit was not easily undone. As he surveyed the judges, Barneveld must have sensed this was not going to be an ordinary trial. Many of them were personal enemies. Most had little knowledge of the law. Few understood the Latin in which most law was still written.

The composition of the court was entirely the result of political wrangling. At the insistence of Holland, there were 12 members from Holland and two each from the other provinces. There was no foundation in law for this since, again, the States General had no jurisdiction. Of the three prosecuting officers, one was an archenemy of Barneveld's who had designs on, and was to become, the successor to his offices. It appears that there were some attempts to cover the proceedings with legality. The States General had no criminal courts and could therefore not appoint judges for such. Instead, they appointed a commission with the power to demand, from the individual's province, punishment if it proved an individual guilty of an offense.

The great table carried stacks of documents – record of a lifetime of service to the nation – from which the accusations against him were to be divined. In any case, Barneveld was still in the dark about his supposed crimes. There was no indictment, no arraignment, and he had no counsel. There were no articles of impeachment. He asked to hear a list of charges. The judges refused. Even if they had wanted to grant the request, they probably could not because they had not figured out exactly what to charge him with. Barneveld then asked if he could have access to his documents. That, too, was refused, presumably out of fear that the Advocate would find ample evidence in his defense. Instead, the old man had to rely on memories spanning two generations.

That memory and brain were capacious and powerful enough for the task. It was well for the judges that they had bound themselves, at the outset, by an oath never to make known what passed in the courtroom, but to bury all the proceedings in profound secrecy forever.

The nearly seven months of malicious propaganda through pamphleteering and sermons from the pulpit had done their work. The majority of the population was against the Advocate. But the politicians and commissioners knew that the weakness of their case and the eloquence of the Advocate would eventually turn against them, should the proceedings become public. After all, Barneveld had built the ship of state and sailed it through stormy and rocky seas out of the grasp of the reviled Spaniard. The people had become accustomed to, and appreciative of, the rule of law, the institutions of government, and all the liberties that they protected. In the irregularity of the proceedings, the public would have recognized the tyranny that they had so recently escaped and they would have rejected it in customary Dutch fashion; popular protest and riots in the streets.

Spring, 1619

During the three-month proceedings, the tribunal asked questions and listened to answers, but even then the members made no accusations. The sheer mass of documents provided no more than a jumbled collection of hearsay or insinuations and extrapolations from regular events. Witnesses added gossip and invention to the crimes thus invoked.

The attacks against Barneveld mainly covered the following. He had allowed Arminius and Vorstius, two prominent theologians, to work at the University of Leyden. The two theologians denied

Barneveld in his prison

predestination, one of the defining tenets of Calvinism, and were now considered heretics. He had opposed the National Synod. He had asked King James to recommend religious toleration and had failed to do anything against pamphlets that insulted the King in his self-appointed position of chief theologian. He had recommended (as a strong advocate of states' rights) that the municipalities and States exercise their right to form militias strictly under their control. By extension, these States controlled their heads of the armed forces, the Stadholders. For most States, that was Prince Maurice. The accused had warned against Maurice's intention to disband these forces and control these lands himself with the Union's army without the right to do so. At various occasions, he had damaged the character of the Prince by insinuating that he aspired to the sovereignty of the country. He had received gifts from foreign potentates. He had opposed the formation of the West-India Company because its main goal was piracy. Many years earlier, he had remarked that the Provinces had better return to Spain (the intention was to scare them into better cooperation, which succeeded). Taken all together, his actions had exposed the States to a potential bloodbath.

In their zeal to condemn the Advocate, some of his accusers actually indicted themselves. It was customary in those days to reward mediators for their efforts. The Dutch participants in the negotiations for a truce between Spain and its former dominion received money from Spain. Understanding the conflict of interest, Barneveld suggested that the recipients transfer these funds to the State. Others preferred to keep the money – Ambassador Aerssens among them. During his testimony, Aerssens admitted to keeping the reward and, by extension and without proof, implicated the Advocate as having done the same.

The victorious sect of the Protestant Church accused Barneveld of supporting Catholics and, by extension, Spain. After all, they argued, the war of independence had been waged to further the Protestant religion. The Advocate reminded them that this had never been the stated reason. Instead, the first proclamations about the war declared that freedom of conscience was the reason so that the citizens could support any of the Protestant doctors of divinity, and that even the Catholics enjoyed such protections[189].

With regard to the West-India Company, he had opposed its formation because the partners were mostly a ragtag of buccaneers who preyed on Spanish and Portuguese ships. Now that there was a truce, this was no longer appropriate and a threat to the peace. Moreover, he detested the monopoly the company would obtain. It would be a danger to the free trade that was so beneficial to all citizens.

The unlawful proceedings lasted for three frustrating months, during which the Advocate appeared about sixty times before the commission. At times Barneveld struggled to control his impatience with, and disdain for, the tribunal's members. At length, the Advocate had explained the illegality of the court. He had reminded them of the States' rights in religious, judicial, and military affairs. He had explained and refuted every accusation. Every one of his official actions had been by the explicit or implicit order of the States of Holland and the States General. If he was guilty, surely these two bodies were guilty as well. If any of the commissioners had understood the many legal points, it still probably would not have mattered. They had made up their minds before the proceedings started.

Some of Barneveld's supporters either were under arrest or kept a low profile. His family, who like the great man himself had always honored the Prince, was convinced that the outcome of the trial would amount to a removal from office. If, at all, the verdict demanded continued imprisonment, then surely the Prince would grant a commutation for the old man. These expectations probably contributed to a cavalier attitude that brought some irritation to Maurice, who feared that his creation was not taken seriously.

"It is a bitter folk," said Barneveld to his servant as he went to bed. "I have nothing good to expect of them."

His assessment proved correct. On May 1, he had the last of the arduous sessions with the commission. Ten days later, he heard that the sentence was ready.

4 pm, Sunday, May 12

It was Sunday. The door of Barneveld's prison opened. The provost marshal, chief prosecutor van Leeuwen, and prosecutor Sylla entered. They ordered Barneveld's servant, John, to leave. Hearing the voices, Barneveld appeared from his dressing room. His long furred gown was draped over his shoulders. The old man greeted the visitors courteously and took position behind his chair. He rested firm hands on its back. Van Leeuwen said, "We have information from the judges." As Barneveld just stared at him quietly, the chief prosecutor continued, "Would you not rather sit down?" Barneveld shook his head.

Despite the corner they had driven the Advocate into, van Leeuwen was still uncomfortable in the Advocate's formidable presence. He said bluntly, "Tomorrow you are to appear before the judges to hear your sentence of death." The three prosecutors held their breath.

"Sentence of death?" Barneveld exclaimed, without moving. "Sentence of death! A sentence of death!" He was astonished rather than horrified. This was a turn of events he had not expected. The court proceedings had not run their course. As an experienced lawyer, he knew the trial could not formally be over. He was baffled and spoke hastily. "I never expected that! I thought they were going to hear my defense again. I had intended to make some change in my previous statements, having set some things down when beside myself with choler."

Barneveld referred to his long service to the country. Van Leeuwen nodded and acknowledged them. Perhaps the prosecutor regretted the harsh way he had brought the news to the old man. He said, "I am sorry that his lordship took my message ill of me."

"I do not take it ill of you," Barneveld responded. Anger welled up and found its way into his voice. "But let them see how they will answer it before God. Are they thus to deal with a true patriot? Let me have pen, ink, and paper, that for the last time I may write farewell to my wife." Barneveld's words were filled with accusation and contained a dismissal of the prosecutor. It was the typical way with which he disapproved of perceived incompetence and a flouting of long-standing jurisprudence.

Van Leeuwen felt the sting. He nodded and looked down at his shoes. "I will go ask permission of the judges," Van Leeuwen said, "and I cannot think that my lord's request will be refused." Without looking again at Barneveld, the chief prosecutor turned and left.

Barneveld was not done. Looking at one of the remaining prosecutors, the Advocate said, "Oh, Sylla, Sylla, if your father could only have seen to what uses they would put you!" Sylla also appeared to study his shoes and was silent.

5 pm, Sunday, May 12

Van Leeuwen returned with pen, paper, and ink and the permission from the president of the commission to write the letter. Barneveld sat down and calmly started writing.

Van Leeuwen and Sylla remained standing. After a short while, Sylla warned sternly, "Beware, my lord, what you write, lest you put down something which may furnish cause for not delivering the letter." Barneveld stopped writing. Slowly he took the glasses from his face and turned to face Sylla. Looking him in the eyes he said calmly, "Well, Sylla, will you in these my last moments lay down the law to me as to what I shall write to my wife?" While Sylla was weighing a response Barneveld continued, "Well, what is expected of me?" Van Leeuwen intervened. "We have no commission whatever to lay down the law," he said. "Your worship will write whatever you like."

After a short while, someone was heard treading up the circular stairs and a preacher entered the room. Barneveld did not know him and asked what he came for. The preacher said, "I am not without commission. I come to console my lord in his tribulations."

The Advocate looked at him briefly, turned back to his letter and said, "I am a man, have come to my present age, and I know how to console myself. I must write, and I have now other things to do." The preacher nodded and said he would return later. "Do as you like," the condemned man said as he calmly continued his letter. When he finished his message, it immediately went to the judges for inspection. They forwarded it right away to the nearby Barneveld family mansion.

5:30 pm, Sunday, May 12

In his quarters, Maurice was uncomfortable. In his heart, the verdict was not what he wanted. However, it was what the situation in the country demanded. He was the only one with the strength and fortitude to restore peace and tranquility to a nation that might otherwise well fall apart.

But the life of Barneveld was a steep price to pay. The old man had stood at his father's side. His sharp mind and political cunning had provided the framework for the nation that Prince William had liberated. Maurice was neither a politician nor an intellectual and he knew it. But Barneveld had been wrong about the truce with Spain. Not only had it given the Spaniard air to breathe and opportunity to scheme anew, it had also given the people of the Netherlands the time to examine their own differences. The religious disputes had grown more violent. King James' interference was unhelpful, but he was a key ally and needed to be maintained.

Barneveld's answer to the divisions and violence was to have the cities hire mercenaries. These strangers had no social ties and would be respected more. But this would increase divisions and, perhaps more importantly, the balkanized forces would make national control very difficult. And that directly affected the responsibilities of the Stadholder in his function of military commander.

Barneveld had been too strong. The Advocate had outmaneuvered Maurice every time. His argumentation, his experience, his dignity, and his self-assured attitude were no match for any man. Maurice tried to recall the man of thirty years ago. He had been a family friend, a constant presence, an uncle almost. After the death of Prince William, the Advocate had trusted the young Maurice enough to sponsor his elevation to Stadholder of five States. And each with his own weapons, they had beaten the Spaniard together. If only Barneveld would admit his guilt and beg for forgiveness! Maurice did not like this kind of pondering. He was a man of action. This waiting had lasted long enough. He wished for a quick resolution.

6 pm, Sunday, May 12

A servant immediately carried Barneveld's letter to his wife. Rumors had been circulating and the family had already gathered in the parlor. Barneveld's oldest son read,

Very dearly beloved wife, children, sons-in-law, and grandchildren, I greet you altogether most affectionately. I receive at this moment the very heavy and sorrowful tidings that I, an old man, for all my services done well and faithfully to the Fatherland for so many years (after having performed all respectful and friendly offices to his Excellency the Prince with upright affection so far as my official duty and vocation would permit, shown friendship to many people of all sorts, and wittingly injured no man), must prepare myself to die to-morrow.

I console myself in God the Lord, who knows all hearts, and who will judge all men. I beg you all together to do the same. I have steadily and faithfully served My Lords the States of Holland and their nobles and cities. To the States of Utrecht as sovereigns of my own Fatherland I have imparted at their request upright and faithful counsel, in order to save them from tumults of the populace, and from the bloodshed with which they had so long been threatened. I had the same views for the cities of Holland in order that every one might be protected and no one injured.

Live together in love and peace. Pray for me to Almighty God, who will graciously hold us all in His holy keeping.

From my chamber of sorrow, the 12th May 1619.

Your very dear husband, father, father-in-law, and grandfather,

John of Barneveld

Perhaps the judges did not read the letter. Perhaps they knew that what it said was true enough but irrelevant to what was coming. Barneveld had once more laid out his innocence with clear arguments and in clear language. However, the difference was that this time his audience went beyond the secrecy of the proceedings and that in a few hours his family, friends, and possibly the public, would know of it.

The effect on his family was emotional. Throughout the ordeal, they had believed in the benevolence of the Prince and expected a mild sentence or pardon. Seeing Barneveld's acknowledgement of his impending death in his own writing brought a rude shock. Until this moment, only people directly involved with the trial knew what exactly the Advocate had been accused of. Now that the family read of the conviction, they also had a fine synopsis of the three-month proceedings.

8:30 pm, Sunday, May 12

The preacher had been waiting patiently and he soon returned to Barneveld's room. When the Advocate learned that the man was Antonius Wallaeus (Anton van Wale), a professor at Middelburg and deputy to the Synod of Dordrecht, he apologized for his somewhat terse greeting earlier, and invited both the preacher and the provost marshal for supper. They accepted.

Anton van Wale

The convict displayed no anguish. He ate in his normal way, with appetite. He talked cheerfully about a number of subjects and toasted each of his guests with a glass of beer.

After the provost marshal left, Barneveld's servant, John, returned looking gloomy. He had only just heard from the guards that his master would be executed. The judges had increased the number of guards and they instructed John that he should speak in a loud voice to Barneveld so that they could not exchange secrets. A student of man, Barneveld noticed his servant's mood and asked what was on his mind. At first John probably shrugged as he was not able to convey the news in a loud voice. As soon as he had a chance, John whispered the instructions in Barneveld's ear. Barneveld berated the soldiers. Many had spent the last months with the old statesman and held him in high regard. They asked him not to take it personally. They had to obey orders.

The old man turned back to his dim oil lamp lit room and sat on his elaborately ornamented Spanish chair. Shadows danced on the walls at the rhythm of the flames. He pondered for a moment, looked up at Wallaeus, and came to a decision. "Reverend," he said, "I am a prisoner and cannot travel. Would you be willing to go to Prince Maurice on my behalf?" Wallaeus nodded slowly. "Tell his Excellency," Barneveld explained, "that I have always served him with upright affection so far as my office, duties, and principles permitted. If I, in the discharge of my oath and official functions, have ever done anything contrary to his views, I hope that he will forgive it, and that he will hold my children in his gracious favor."

The preacher must have noticed that there was no apology in the old man's words. Perhaps disappointed, he affirmed the request with another nod and turned toward the stairs. He walked across the dark courtyard that separated the courthouse from the Prince's apartments. After he identified himself, he was let in right away.

10 pm, Sunday, May 12

Maurice received the verbal message with tears in his eyes. He told Wallaeus how deeply he felt for the Advocate's misfortunes. He said how much affection he had for him and that he had often warned him against his mistaken actions. Particularly devious had been his accusation that Maurice aspired to be sovereign. In addition, Barneveld's actions had placed him in such danger in Utrecht (when the advocate encouraged the city to stand up for its rights). But, in spite of all that, he forgave him. After a pause, Maurice added that as far as his sons were concerned, they could rely on his favor as long as they behaved. Wallaeus nodded. The content and tone of the last sentence indicated the audience was over and the preacher moved to take his leave. Maurice, however, called him back and asked with some eagerness, "Did he say anything of a pardon?"

"My Lord," Wallaeus replied to the Prince, "I cannot with truth say that I understood him to make any allusion to it." Maurice nodded silently and gestured the preacher to be on his way. Wallaeus turned, looked down, and shook his head. In their own limited way, the two most powerful men in the Republic had looked for a way out. Their pride and stubbornness now led them onto a path from which there was no turning. The cleric left the mansion with head hung low.

During Wallaeus' absence, two preachers arrived at the prison, Jean la Motte and a clergyman from 'sGravenhage. La Motte wept on seeing the Advocate. The other was more collected. They wished to console Barneveld with religion. Barneveld acknowledged their good intentions. He was calm as usual and seemed undaunted at the fate so suddenly and unexpectedly opening before his eyes. But he was indignant at what he deemed the ignorance, injustice, and stupidity of the sentence to be pronounced against him. "I am ready enough to die," he said to the preachers, "but I cannot comprehend why I am to die. I have done nothing except in obedience of the laws and privileges of the land and according to my oath, honor, and conscience." He went on, "These judges come in a time where other maxims prevail in the State than in my day. They have no right therefore to sit in judgment upon me." The preachers replied that the twenty-four judges who had tried the case were no children and were conscientious men. "It is no small matter to condemn a man and they would have to answer it before the Supreme Judge of all," la Motte added.

Barneveld nodded. "I console myself in the Lord my God, who knows all hearts and shall judge all men. God is just." Then he continued, "They have not dealt with me as according to law and justice they were bound to deal. They have taken away from me my own sovereign lords and masters and deposed them. To them alone I was responsible. In their place they have put many of my enemies who were never before in the government, and almost all of whom are young men who have not seen much or read much. I have seen and read much, and know that from such examples no good can follow. After my death, they will learn for the first time what governing means. The twenty-four judges are nearly all of them my enemies. What they have reproached me with, I have been obliged to hear. I have appealed against these judges, but it has been of no avail. They have examined me in piecemeal, not in statesmanlike fashion. The proceedings against me have been much too hard. I have frequently requested to see the notes of my examination as it proceeded, and to confer upon it with aid and counsel of friends, as would be the case in all lands governed by law. The request was refused. During this long and wearisome affliction and misery, I was not once allowed to speak to my wife and children. These are indecent proceedings against a man seventy-two years of age, who has served his country faithfully for three-and-forty years. I bore arms with the volunteers at my own charges at the siege of Haarlem and barely escaped with life." The preachers listened in silence and then admitted that they did not know much of such affairs. They had come to call the Advocate to repentance for his open and his hidden sins and to offer the consolations of religion.

"I know that very well," Barneveld said, "but I too have something to say notwithstanding. I have never been able to believe in the matter of high predestination. I have left it in the hands of God the Lord. I hold that a good Christian man must believe that he, through God's grace and by the expiation of his sin through our Redeemer Jesus Christ, is predestined to be saved, and that this belief in his salvation, founded alone on God's grace and the merits of our Redeemer Jesus Christ, comes to him through the same grace of God. And if he falls into great sins, his firm hope and confidence must be that the Lord God will not allow him to continue in them, but that, through prayer for grace and repentance, he will be converted from evil and remain in the faith to the end of his life. These feelings I have expressed fifty-two years before to three eminent professors of theology in whom I confided, and they had assured me that I might tranquilly continue in such

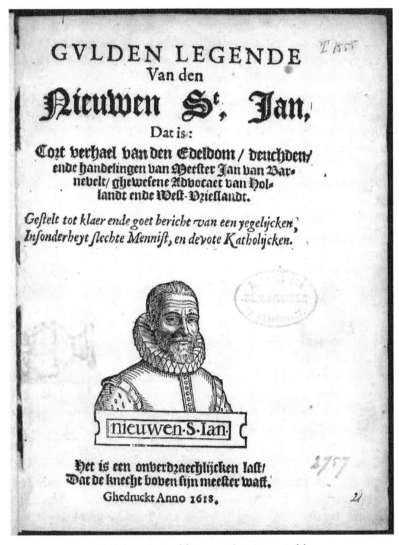

A vicious pamphlet accusing Barneveld

belief without examining farther[190]. And this has always been my creed," he finished.

Bringing up the issue of predestination caused the preachers to start arguing with each other. Barneveld intervened with eloquence and earnestness and his philosophical arguments held them spellbound for a time. When he asked about the Synod they told him its decrees had not been promulgated, but that the heretics had been condemned.

"It is a pity," Barneveld said. "One is trying to act on the old Papal system, but it will never do. Things have gone too far. As to the Synod, if My Lords the States of Holland had been heeded, there would have been first a provincial synod and then a national one. But," he added, looking the preachers in the face, "had you been gentler with each other, matters would not have taken so high a turn. But you have been too fierce one against the other, too full of bitter party spirit."

The preachers said that they could not act against their conscience and the supreme authority. They asked him if there was nothing that troubled him in his conscience in the matters for which he must die; nothing for which he repented and sorrowed, and for which he would call upon God for mercy.

"This I know well," Barneveld replied, "that I have never willingly done wrong to any man. People have been ransacking my letters to Caron[191] — confidential ones written several years ago to an old friend when I was troubled and seeking for counsel and consolation. It is hard that matter of impeachment against me to-day should be sought for thus." Then he fell into political discourse again on the subject of the mercenaries and State rights, and the villainous pasquils[192] and libels that had circulated so long through the country. "I have sometimes spoken hastily, I confess," he said; "but that was when I was stung by the daily swarm of infamous and loathsome pamphlets, especially those directed against my sovereign masters, the States of Holland. That I could not bear. Old men cannot well brush such things aside. All that was directly aimed at me in particular I endeavored to overcome with such patience as I could muster. The disunion and mutual enmity in the country have wounded me to the heart. I have made use of all means in my power to accommodate matters, to effect with all gentleness a mutual reconciliation. I have always felt a fear lest the enemy should make use of our internal dissensions to strike a blow against us. I can say with perfect truth that ever since the year '77 I have been as resolutely and unchangeably opposed to the Spaniards and their adherents, and their pretensions over these Provinces, as any man in the world, no one excepted, and as ready to sacrifice property and shed my blood in defense of the Fatherland. I have been so devoted to the service of the country that I have not been able to take the necessary care of my own private affairs."

10:30 pm, Sunday, May 12

Walking slowly, Wallaeus crossed the square to the courthouse and walked up the stairs. There he found Barneveld in a lively discussion with two colleagues he recognized. The three looked up as Wallaeus came in. Barneveld asked how it had gone. "Not well," Wallaeus responded. Barneveld asked for particulars but the preacher was reluctant to divulge the Prince's words. As Barneveld pressed, Wallaeus related the whole conversation.

"His Excellency has been deceived in regard to the Utrecht business," said Barneveld, "especially as to one point. But it is true that I had fear and apprehension that he aspired to the sovereignty or to more authority in the country. Ever since the year 1600 I have felt this fear and have tried that these apprehensions might be rightly understood."

A bell sounded eleven o'clock. Barneveld asked if one of the preachers could say an evening prayer. La Motte led them. Afterward Barneveld asked if they could return by three or four o'clock in the morning. They said that they had been directed to stay with him all night. The Advocate told them that was not necessary. The three preachers left. Next, John helped the old man undress and he went to bed. There he took off his signet ring and handed it to John. "For my eldest son," he said. Suspecting secret communication, the soldiers ordered the servant to sit at the other side of the room.

11:30 pm, Sunday, May 12

The grief that the letter had brought to the family at the Voorhout, just a stone's throw from the court and prison, was paralyzing. Barneveld's wife, Maria van Utrecht, was joined by her sons and daughters and their children. All personnel down to the humblest servant of the house attended to her every need. They all revered and loved the austere statesman who was to them the simple and benign father, master, or husband. Over the last three months, they had solicited the help of learned counsel who had prepared elaborate and argumentative petitions. In name of the family, three of these had been submitted to the judges. There had been no response. The family did not know of the simple reasons that the points were difficult to answer and that the accused should have no counsel. However, at last the family decided to try one more time and write a letter to the Prince as well as the judges: "The afflicted wife and children of M. van Barneveld humbly show that having heard the sorrowful tidings of his coming execution, they humbly beg that it may be granted them to see and speak to him for the last time." If the reasoning of Barneveld's letter to the family regarding his innocence at all occurred to them, they did not act on it.

1 am, Monday, May 13

Barneveld asked his servant to read from the Prayer Book. He could not sleep. The sentry heard the biblical texts and decided to call in a clergyman. As soon as the preacher entered, he went to sit at the bed of the old man. They acknowledged each other in silence and the preacher started reading softly from the Consolations of the Sick. However, the churchman could not help himself and started making pronouncements about the text. If it had been his intention to arouse the Advocate, he succeeded. A lively discussion ensued. Barneveld expressed himself with great fervor and eloquence. Where the preacher invoked narrow points of dogma, Barneveld countered with alternative explanations and the goodness and tolerance of his Creator. Everyone in the room listened and the preacher was mute for half an hour. At the open door, the sentry winked at the servant. "Had there been ten clergymen," he whispered, "your master would have enough to say to all of them." To Barneveld, the disputes over Scripture amounted to no more than the question of how many angels could dance on the head of a pin.

Eventually Barneveld asked where the place of his death had been prepared. The preacher answered, "In front of the great hall, as I understand, but I don't know the localities well, having lived here but little"

"Have you heard whether my Grotius[193] is to die, and Hoogerbeets also?" Barneveld asked and the preacher said that he did not know. "I should most deeply grieve for those two gentlemen," said Barneveld, "if that were the case. They may yet live to do the land great service." He took a deep breath. "That great rising light, de Groot, is still young, but a very wise and learned gentleman, devoted to his Fatherland with all zeal, heart, and soul, and ready to stand up for her privileges, laws, and rights. As for me, I am an old and worn-out man. I can do no more. I have already done more than I was really able to do. I have worked so zealously in public matters that I have neglected my private business. I had expressly ordered my house at Loosduinen to be got ready, that I might establish myself there and put my affairs in order. I have repeatedly asked the States of Holland for my discharge, but could never obtain it. It seems that the Almighty had otherwise disposed of me." Then he announced he would try to get some sleep. He was probably bored with the clergyman. The latter was probably uncomfortable in the presence of such a superior mind and took his leave.

2 am, Monday, May 13

Barneveld asked for his French Psalm book and read for a while. After a while, two more clergymen entered. They asked the Advocate if he had slept, if he hoped to meet Christ, and if there was anything that troubled his conscience. "I have not slept, but am perfectly tranquil," he replied. "I am ready to die, but cannot comprehend why I must die. I wish from my heart that, through my death and my blood, all disunion and discord in this land may cease." He bade them to carry his last greetings to his fellow prisoners. "Say farewell for me to my good Grotius," he said, "and tell him that I must die." The preachers left him saying they would be back between five and six o'clock.

Hugo Grotius (de Groot)

4 am, Monday, May 13

Far away, the rumble of drums pulled Barneveld from his thoughts. The sound came and went in the rhythms of the wind until it grew stronger, along with the tramp of soldiers.

Not far from his bed, his two sons were on a mission in the cool night air. They carried their laboriously crafted petition. Getting the words right and having everyone agree to them had been difficult. When they finally got underway, they had first delivered one copy to the Prince. They had waited for a response but none came. Nervous and disappointed, they crossed the familiar square to the courthouse. They found a number of people already there. Among them was de Voogd, the president of the commission of judges, and they handed the letter to him. De Voogd dutifully presented the letter to other present members of the commission. No one took it upon himself to inform Barneveld of the request.

Another, better connected, person was also awake and busy that night. Louise de Coligny, widow of the late William the Silent and stepmother of Maurice, had at a late hour heard of the sentence. She knew Barneveld well and was keenly aware of how much he and her husband had meant to each other, what great things they had accomplished, and how the Advocate had helped Maurice learn the affairs of state. She was horrified and determined to do what she could to avert this disaster. She requested an interview with the Stadholder, but was informed he was asleep and could not be disturbed. It was heart-wrenching. She had no influence. And at last, she received the message that all intervention was useless.

5 am, Monday, May 13

Finally, there was the indefatigable French ambassador, du Maurrier. He had already gone beyond the reasonable in his efforts to save the life of the great man. He had just heard of the sentence and would now make a last appeal. Before five o'clock, he made an urgent application to be heard before the Assembly of the States General as ambassador of a friendly sovereign who took the deepest interest in the welfare of the Republic and the fate of its illustrious statesman. They refused. As a last resort, he drew up an earnest and eloquent letter to the States General, urging clemency in the name of King Henry. The appeal was refused out of hand. There was nothing more to be done.

7 am, Monday, May 13

During the night, the Advocate decided he could not trust that the preacher La Motte had delivered his letter to his family. He asked a soldier to ask the judges if he could send another. Captain van der Meulen returned with permission, but said he would wait to take it to the judges for their inspection. "Must they do this, too? Why, it is only a line in favor of John," Barneveld said. He sat down and wrote quietly:

> Very dear wife and children, it is going to an end with me. I am, through the grace of God, very tranquil. I hope that you are equally so, and that you may by mutual love, union, and peace help each other to overcome all things, which I pray to the Omnipotent as my last request. John Franken has served me faithfully for many years and throughout all these my afflictions, and is to remain with me to the end. He deserves to be recommended to you and to be furthered to good employments with you or with others. I request you herewith to see to this.
> I have requested his Princely Excellency to hold my sons and children in his favor, to which he has answered that so long as you conduct yourselves well this shall be the case. I recommend this to you in the best form and give you all into God's holy keeping. Kiss each other and

all my grandchildren, for the last time in my name, and fare you well.
Out of the chamber of sorrow, 13th May 1619.
Your dear husband and father,
John Of Barneveld.
P.S. You will make John Franken a present in memory of me.

8:30 am, Monday, May 13

Wallaeus entered the Advocate's prison saying he had a message from the judges. "The High commissioners think it is beginning," he said. "Will my Lord please prepare himself?" Barneveld, ever in control, said, "Very well, very well. Shall we go at once?" Wallaeus suggested a prayer first, which they did. Then Barneveld offered his hand to the provost marshal and the two soldiers. They shook. He bade them adieu, and the group walked down the stairs. When they neared the chamber of the judges, they were told there had been a misunderstanding. "Would they please wait a little?" They all went back upstairs where Barneveld sat down in his chair and started reading in his French psalm book.

9 am, Monday, May 13

The provost marshal and Captain van der Meulen entered Barneveld's room to escort him back down the narrow staircase. As they went, Barneveld said, "Mr. Provost, I have always been a good friend to you." The provost acknowledged, "It is true, and most deeply do I grieve to see you in this affliction." They walked to the judges' chamber but were told the sentence would be read in the Great Hall. Were all these delays and changes an indication of nervous discombobulation on part of the commission?

The small group turned and went down another narrow flight of stairs and entered the oldest part of the buildings, the Great Hall of the Counts of Holland. Its cedar ceilings were high and vaulted. At the center stood a long table at which the twenty-four commissioned judges and the three prosecutors were seated. All were in the sober black caps and gowns of their office. Soldiers lined the room and a crowd of spectators, who had waited all night, thronged to get a better view. Someone brought a chair for Barneveld, who sat. At once, the clerk stood and nervously proceeded to read the sentence. It was a long, rambling, and tedious missive. During it all, Barneveld moved in his seat and at times seemed to want to interrupt the clerk. But despite the preposterous accusations he controlled himself and let the clerk reach the conclusion.

Then he spoke. "The judges have put down many things which they had no right to draw from my confession. Let this protest be added." He went on, "I thought too that My Lords the States General would have had enough in my life and blood, and that my wife and children might keep what belongs to them[194]. Is this my recompense for forty-three years' service to these Provinces?" By the haste with which the judges had started the proceedings and read the sentence it was clear they would not pause for anything. Reason was the Advocate's domain, not theirs.

President de Voogd stood. "Your sentence has been pronounced," he said. "Away! Away!" He pointed to one of the large windows that had been converted to a door. Barneveld got up as well and strode to the temporary exit, his valet and the provost marshal by his side. Soldiers escorted them outside where a mob of spectators poured out of every door. On the square, in front of the opening, stood a hastily patched-together platform of rude planks. The makeshift scaffold had been built the night before. It had a rickety railing to keep out the crowd. A heap of sand sat toward the middle. To the side two soldiers were playing with dice on top of a smelly, dirty wooden box of unfinished boards. It had been intended for the body of a condemned criminal who had received a pardon from the Prince a long time ago. The wager between the soldiers was whether the Lord or the Devil would get Barneveld's soul and it was the subject of loud jeering by the spectators nearby. Seven months of relentless pamphleteering had succeeded in poisoning the minds of many.

Leaning on his staff, the old statesman walked out onto the makeshift platform and calmly looked around. He stared into the eager faces of the three-thousand people that filled the square. Then he looked up and murmured, "Oh God, what does man come to?" Then he said bitterly to no one in particular, "This then is the reward of forty years' service to the State."

La Motte, who attended him, said fervently, "It is no longer time to think of this. Let us prepare your coming before God." Barneveld looked around. "Is there no cushion or stool to kneel upon?" La Motte said he would send for one but the Advocate had already knelt on the planks. John, his servant, waited on his master calmly as if they were at dinner. Both were stoic Hollanders and shed not a tear on the scaffold. La Motte led a prayer that lasted 15 minutes. Barneveld stayed on his knees. Then he got up and said to his servant, "See that he does not come near me," pointing at the executioner who stood at a distance holding a long, double handed sword. Barneveld quickly unbuttoned his doublet and John helped take it off. "Make haste, make haste," Barneveld said.

Barneveld's execution at the Binnenhof in The Hague

In his shirtsleeves, he walked forward to face the people. The square grew silent. Then he said in a loud, firm voice, "Men, do not believe that I am a traitor to the country. I have ever acted uprightly and loyally as a good patriot, and as such I shall die." He turned and took his cap from John and pulled it close above his eyes. Walking toward the sand he said, "Christ shall be my guide. 0 Lord, my heavenly Father, receive my spirit." He was preparing to kneel when La Motte said, "My Lord will be pleased to move to the other side, not where the sun is in his face." The old man moved around the sand pile and knelt to face his own house. John said a farewell and Barneveld said to the executioner, "Be quick about it, be quick." The executioner swung and severed the neck in one blow.

Maurice's cousin and fellow Stadholder, William Louis, had questioned the wisdom of the trial and execution of the Advocate. Maurice felt he owed him a report on the proceedings and resulting execution.

After the judges have been busy here with the sentence against the Advocate Barneveld for several days, at last it has been pronounced, and this morning, between nine o'clock and half past, carried into execution with the sword, in the Binnenhof before the great hall.
The reasons they had for this you will see from the sentence, which will doubtless be printed, and which I will send you.
The wife of the aforesaid Barneveld and also some of his sons and sons-in-law or other friends have never presented any supplication for his pardon, but till now have vehemently demanded that law and justice

should be done to him, and have daily let the report run through the people that he would soon come out. They also planted a maypole before their house adorned with garlands and ribbands, and practiced other jollities and impertinences, while they ought to have conducted themselves in a humble and lowly fashion. This is no proper manner of behaving, and moreover not a practical one to move the judges to any favor even if they had been thereto inclined.

With the letter, Maurice at the same time sought to justify himself and abdicated responsibility for the proceedings of the commissioners, an institution for whose creation he had pushed. In addition, he used the legal defense as a reason not to grant a pardon. This behavior was reminiscent of that of a slighted monarch. If Prince Maurice ever had aspirations to the sovereignty of the country, they were now difficult to pursue. He had denied it so many times and he had let Barneveld die for the accusation. However, with the military power at his disposal and the support of the victorious Contra-Remonstrant[195] movement, he could have forced the issue. Whether he declined the temptation out of pride, honor, or duty, we will never know. Perhaps he considered it superfluous. He held the position of Stadholder in all States but one (his cousin was Stadholder of Friesland). With the elimination of Barneveld, he had permanently reduced the position of Advocate. By trampling on States' Rights, he had given the country a stronger sense of cohesion, with himself as the unifying force. He had strengthened the confederation without the need to create a federation. Is it cynical to think that with the Advocate's death Maurice had given the nation new life? Had the end justified the means?

The Advocate's body and head were hurled into the squalid box on which the soldiers had rolled their dice. The entry for that day in the register of the States of Holland read,

Monday, 13th May 1619. To-day was executed with the sword here in 'sGravenhage, on a scaffold thereto erected in the Binnenhof before the steps of the great hall, Mr. John of Barneveld, in his life Knight, Lord of Berkel, Rodenrys, &c., Advocate of Holland and West Friesland, for reasons expressed in the sentence and otherwise, with confiscation of his property, after he had served the State thirty-three years two months and five days since 8th March 1586 ; a man of great activity, business, memory, and wisdom — yes, extraordinary in every respect. He that stands let him see that he does not fall, and may God be merciful to his soul. Amen!

Conscience is the most sacred of all property.
James Madison in an Essay on Property, March 29, 1792.

Chapter 7: The Congregationalists

Timeline

Year	Event
1477	Great Privilege (of the Netherlands)
1500	Charles V Emperor of the Holy Roman Empire
1509	Henry VII King of England
1517	Martin Luther nails his theses on a church door
1533	William of Orange born
1547	John of Barneveld born
1555	Philip II King of Spain
1558	Elizabeth I Queen of England and Ireland
1568	Dutch Revolt
1584	William of Orange assassinated
1603	James I King of England
1607	First "Pilgrims" arrived in Holland
1607	Truce between Spain and the Netherlands
1619	Execution of John of Barneveld "Pilgrims" sail for America; *Mayflower* Compact

Hierarchy Challenged

While the Netherlands were struggling with their issues, developments in England would have important consequences both for the Netherlands and for the colonization of North America. To understand what developed we will go back in time a bit and examine the sequence of events.

When the people of the Netherlands won unprecedented concessions in 1477, they found refuge from the French military threats in Maximilian of Austria. They didn't treat their protector very well, especially when he tried to assert his sovereignty. But they were not united in purpose either. Internal economic and political disputes between the municipal republics caused many to look for support from bigger powers –England, Austria,

Spain, even France. That only amplified their differences and eventually hurt their liberal gains. Again they were subjected to the arbitrary territorial switches that birth, marriage, and death of royal families brought about. Charles V, Holy Roman Emperor and already King of Spain, became their ruler in 1519. Because of its high level of development and great wealth, the Netherlands was his treasury's milk cow. As we saw, the provinces and their cities had thus far enjoyed relative autonomy of taxation and government. By introducing a more centralized governmental structure, Charles removed the tax middleman and curbed local government. Obviously the cities and their people were chagrined.

King Henry VIII of England

Charles ascended the Empire's throne two years after Martin Luther nailed his Ninety-five Theses on a German church door. The objections that Protestants had against the Church of Rome were primarily about church governance. The sale of indulgences[196] was just another excess of widespread corruption. The hierarchy tolerated no input from the flock. Since the people had no instrument with which to change church governance, it was only logical some would reject the organization itself. Once that schism was established, other (e.g. theological) reasons were identified, too.

Various break-away groups adopted a congregational[197] form of organization – from the bottom up. The most influential were the Anabaptists, who had the members of the church decide church matters. This included the selection of a preacher and the oversight of funds. Church governance was following the examples of civic innovations with a patently democratic form of governance. No wonder many of the burghers of the municipalities in the Netherlands found it appealing.

It did not appeal to Charles V, however. As Holy Roman Emperor, he had to protect the interests of Rome. He forbade the heretical, independent churches and persecuted, though mildly, its members. The quest for freedom now included that of religion. Many of the oppressed wanted to leave the Netherlands.

Meanwhile in England, King Henry VIII displayed particular zealotry in opposing Luther, which earned him the title of "Defender of the Faith." However, England was rather isolated from the Reformation. At age 43, Henry was worried he still had no male heir.

When the Pope refused to grant him a divorce from his Spanish wife of twenty-four years, he declared England's church independent, with himself at its head. With the Act of Supremacy in 1534, he created the Church of England, proceeded to divorce his wife, then married a succession of wives, during which he finally begot a son. Freed from the worries of succession, marriage, and religion, he found time to consider other questions.

One of those was the state of the wool industry in his country[198]. The Flemish manufacturers in particular used advanced techniques and produced high quality cloth. Now that a good number of them wanted to leave the Netherlands, Henry was all too happy to provide them with a home. As early as 1536, he had allowed one group to settle in Norwich under the protection of the Crown. However, many, if not most, of the immigrants were Anabaptists. In addition to their deviant religious convictions, the foreign believers advocated a separation between Church and State[199]. When the immigrants started to express their beliefs openly and converted English subjects, Henry persecuted them and his own wayward subjects with horrific zeal. Illustratively, Henry's men strangled and burned William Tyndale that same year for having the audacity to translate the bible into English[200].

Under Henry's successor, his minor son, Edward VI, there was a brief respite. Edward died young and was succeeded by Henry's daughter, Mary. A devout Catholic, Mary outdid her father and earned the name Bloody Mary when she had three-hundred "objectionable personages" put to death merely because they were Protestants. Fortunately for the wayward, Mary didn't live long. Henry's youngest daughter, Elizabeth, was a Protestant. She revived the Church of England and expediently gave it its odd mixture of aspects: Catholic symbolism, Protestant theology, Episcopalian organization[201]. This arrangement satisfied both the clergy, who retained their positions, and the flock, who retained their Protestant beliefs. The congregational Protestants, whose churches were independent and appointed their own priests, were therefore still a threat. However, like her father before her, she invited Dutch refugees to settle in England for economic reasons. Many went to Colchester in 1570[202], but most chose to settle in Norwich. By 1586, Norwich had a majority of Anabaptists and many were English converts. The fifth column was firmly installed and doing its subversive work.

Indeed, all the English Free Churches were indebted to the Anabaptists[203].

By some estimates, the number of community churches around the country grew to 20,000 by 1592[204]. Critics that stayed within the Church of England called themselves Puritans; the ones that left, Separatists, of which the followers of John Brown[205], called Brownists, were the first.

Cambridge, England, mid 16th century

In 1533 a young man named Edwin Sandys (pronounced Sands) registered at St. John's College in Cambridge[206]. He was attracted to the church and studied to be a priest. King Henry's Act of Supremacy a year later opened the door for many to examine the Reformation more closely. Edwin was an early convert to the Church of England. In 1542, he became Rector of the University and Master of Catharine Hall in 1547. By 1553 he was Vice Chancellor. When England had a succession crisis with the death of the child-king Edward VI, Sandys advocated in public that a remote

Archbishop Edwin Sandys

cousin and a Protestant, Lady Jane Grey[207], be crowned. This put him on the wrong side of the outcome and the court of Queen Mary ordered him imprisoned at the Tower of London. Fortunately they moved him to Marshalsea Prison, from whence Sir Thomas Holcroft, a knight marshal, allowed him to escape.

Sandys sailed to Antwerp in the Flemish Netherlands and traveled through Western Europe before settling in Strasbourg, Germany. The city was a hotbed of Calvinists. He married and had a child. The boy died in 1557 and his wife the following year, probably from plague. Sandys moved to Zurich in Switzerland and lived with the venerable Peter Martyr Vermigli, a noble from Florence and early reformer. After Queen Mary's death and with Elizabeth firmly in control, Sandys returned to England in 1558, where he met his second wife, the much younger Cecily Wilford. In late 1559 he was made Bishop of Worcester, in 1570 Bishop of London, and in 1576 Archbishop of York. Their ten children grew up with the lessons of their father's nuanced civic and religious convictions, enriched by his European experience.

As we witnessed in the previous chapters, King Philip succeeded Charles in Spain and inherited the Netherlands. Philip loathed Protestants and after a few years' stay in Brussels, vacated to Madrid, never to return. He unleashed the fury of the Spanish Inquisition. Thousands of citizens were burned at the stake, drowned, quartered, or otherwise murdered, all in the name of the merciful Church of Rome. Eventually the Dutch had enough. In 1566, they raided churches[208] and staged a full revolt in 1568 with William of Orange in the lead.

Queen Elizabeth of England, a staunch Protestant, was a strong supporter of the Dutch cause. She committed English troops to the Netherlands. England was at war with Spain.

Virginia, America, late 16th century

With the Spanish war in full force, English privateers were looking for a base from which to attack Spanish ships laden with treasure from the American conquest. It had to be close to Spanish shipping lanes, but not too close to their settlements in Florida. The Outer Banks of the Carolinas were ideal. Sir Walter Raleigh received a charter from Queen Elizabeth and, after an exploratory expedition, sent out ships with veterans from the English-Irish war to establish a colony[209]. While they were plying up and down the coast, looking for a place to put the settlement, they got into trouble with the Indians. They destroyed one village and burned its chief at the stake. In spite of the enemies they had made, and with most of their supplies spoiled, they left some seventy-five men at the northern end of Roanoke Island with the task of building a fort. It was August of 1585 and the ships were to return April next. However, no relief had arrived by the time Sir Francis Drake stopped over in June of 1586 from a raid in the Caribbean. When he offered to take the colonists back to England, they accepted. Shortly thereafter the relief ships did arrive, but found the colony abandoned. The relief party left a small force of fifteen men behind and returned to England.

In 1587 a group of 117 colonists crossed the Atlantic with instructions to pick up the fifteen men at Roanoke and go north to establish a colony in the Chesapeake Bay area. They found only the bones of one man. Instead of moving on as instructed, they decided to stay and renew relations with the local Indians, which largely failed. When Indians killed a colonist, the others feared the same fate as that of the previous settlers. While the colonists set up camp, they sent the ships back to England to ask for reinforcements.

The war got in the way. In 1588, the Spanish sent their entire fleet to the English Channel. Bad weather and the clever tactics of the English and

Dutch captains largely destroyed the Spanish Armada. But greed among the merchants added more delays and ships only returned to Roanoke in 1590. There was not a trace of the colonists. Clues indicated that they had moved to Croatoan Island where a friendly tribe lived. There are some accounts of a later date that a few survivors were in Indian captivity[210]. Others may have lived free among the mainland Tuscarora, to which the Croatoans belonged, but there is no solid evidence. Three attempts at colonization had failed.

Scrooby, England, late 16th century

Along the highway from London to Edinburgh, between Lincoln and York, still lies the old village of Scrooby. In those days, it was no more than a collection of farms and an old, decaying manor house. The Church of England owned the properties and held them under the administration of the Bishopric of York. In addition to Postmaster for the Crown, William Brewster was Receiver and Bailiff for the church-owned manor. In 1580, his son, also William, attended college at the great Puritan University of England in Cambridge. "He there became inoculated with radical religious ideas, and was first seasoned with the seeds of grace and virtue.[211]" In the fall of 1583, the young Brewster served in the household of William Davidson, who was working at the Court of Queen Elizabeth in "positions of consequence". Brewster was probably a confidential attendant to Davidson. He accompanied his master on various diplomatic missions to the Netherlands. One anecdote recalls a long ride across the eastern counties on the way back from Holland when Davidson placed a gold chain around Brewster's neck. The States General had given it to the ambassador and he asked his companion to wear it as they entered London. Brewster was still with Davidson in 1587, but in 1588, he returned to Scrooby to take care of his ill father and family affairs.

After his father's death in 1590, he became Receiver, Bailiff, and Postmaster of Scrooby. He married in 1591/2 and had a son in 1593. Brewster was acquainted with one Richard Clifton, a minister in the nearby village of Babworth around 1595. Clifton was known for his radical ideas. Another minister, John Smyth of nearby Gainsborough, had even more extreme notions about government and doctrine. Possibly following their example, Brewster formed a small group of villagers who met regularly on Sunday afternoons in the old Manor House. They discussed doctrine and worshipped together, but did not officially separate from the established church. They invited nearby ministers and villagers, asked traveling ministers to attend, and continued their meetings for another ten years.

Scrooby, England

London, England, late 16th century

Edwin Sandys Junior was born in 1561 in Worcestershire in central England[212]. He was the second son of an up and coming official of the Church of England. The record does not explicitly state this, but most likely young Edwin would have heard of the reasons of his father's exile on the continent and learned about the injustices of intolerance and hatred. In 1571, while his father was Bishop of London, he entered the Merchant Taylor's School[213] then went on to Oxford's Corpus Christi College, where he was joined by a close friend, George Cranmer. Edwin's father had arranged for the boys the tutelage of one Richard Hooker.

Izaac Walton described Hooker[214] as making, "the subtlety of all the arts easy and familiar to him, and useful for the discovery of such learnings as lay hid from common searchers. So that by these, added to his great reason, and his restless industry added to both, he did not only know more of causes and effects; but what he knew, he knew better than other men." Hooker would have exposed his two pupils to the dogmas of the reformer John Calvin in Geneva[215]. The fresh traumas inflicted on Oxford by the Church of Rome and Queen Mary instilled a desire for religious tolerance.

The three became close friends. Edwin graduated with a bachelor's degree in the Arts in 1579. Meanwhile, his father was Archbishop of York. The young Sandys obtained his Master's degree in 1583. Hooker had married and all but disappeared from the academic scene. Both Edwin and George looked him up and found him completely under the thumb of his rather unpleasant wife. Feeling sorry for Hooker, Edwin wrote a recommendation and request to his father. Soon after, Hooker was appointed Master of the Society of the Temple[216]. Here Hooker embarked on his important work, "The Laws of Ecclesiastical Polity", which stated clear religious principles, but at the same time opposed the elevation of the Church above the State.

These important principles could not have escaped Edwin. The young Sandys became Bachelor of Civil Law in 1589. He had always harbored a curiosity about law and politics and how they could advance the interests of the public. He was elected to represent Andover in parliament in 1586 until that body was dissolved the following year. His father had often spoken of Europe and young Edwin wanted to visit it and understand its religious strife. In 1593 he traveled with his friend, George Cranmer, to the continent. The Dutch Republic was then in the success years of its war of independence from Spain. Its liberal policies and declaration of religious tolerance made it the refuge of Protestants from all over Europe. Germany, where the two traveled extensively, had a mixed record. The north was primarily Protestant, but some were Lutheran and others Calvinist. The south was mostly Catholic. Many cities had made accommodations for the allocation, or even the sharing, of churches between the various religious groups[217]. In most cases, this managed to save the peace.

After Cranmer returned to England in 1596, Sandys spent time in Venice, Italy with the religious philosopher Paolo Sarpi, who inspired or urged him to write a treatise on State and Religion. He traveled to Geneva and studied the democratic form of government there. In 1598, King Henry IV declared his acceptance of and protections for Protestants in mostly Catholic France. The religious divisions were tearing the country apart and through the issuing of the Edict of Nantes he hoped to still the deadly unrest. Somewhat emboldened, Edwin Sandys moved to Paris and started work on his treatise, *Europae Speculum*, the following year. In the document, he cautioned against intolerance and showed sympathy for all religions, including Catholics. Between the lines, he weighed the separation of Church and State. Apparently he did not seek publication, probably because of the controversial nature of the subject matter.

In 1599 he returned to England. He made up his mind about what religion to adhere to and, in 1603, traveled to Scotland to join the Court of King James VI. James was a Calvinist and next in line to succeed Elizabeth

I in England. As if Sandys was clairvoyant, Elizabeth died the same year. After James was crowned King James I of England, Sandys was among the first to be knighted. He was elected Member of Parliament for Stockbridge, Hampshire, the same area he had represented when M.P. for Andover. James appointed him ambassador to the Netherlands. But then suddenly, in 1605, printed copies of his treatise[218] began to circulate. Because of the potentially damaging ideas regarding the separation of church and state (James I was both King of England and head of the Church of England), he denounced the publication as pirated and unauthorized. He arranged for all known copies to be bought and burned. King James approved.

Around this time it is possible that Edwin Sandys was married for a fourth time, having lost his first three wives in death. His first and third wife each bore him daughters[219].

Scrooby, England, 1606

In the fall of 1606 the congregation in Scrooby, more than fifty members strong, decided to separate from the Church of England, the "Anti-Christ", and formalize their own church. Around that time two important men joined them. William Bradford was a teenager and John Robinson a man of about thirty. The latter had two degrees from Cambridge where he had been a fellow at Corpus Christi College. Around 1603, he was appointed preaching Elder of St. Andrews in Norwich, the Anabaptist stronghold. Their independence proved irresistible. The city was home to the strongest bodies of radical Protestants in England. Robinson struggled with doubts and misgivings during his four-year stay. During a visit to Cambridge, he decided to leave the Church of England. He started drifting. Via Norwich and Lincoln, he eventually made his way to Scrooby, where he joined the fresh separatist congregation. Young Bradford came from a family with a long history of reformed sympathies. There is evidence[220] that the reformed martyr John Bradford (†1555) was William's great-uncle.

Queen Elizabeth had died in 1603. Her successor, James, saw himself as shepherd of his flock with the duty to educate and guide them through the maze of religious uncertainty. A Calvinist, he was the self-appointed savior of the Reformed church. He was intolerant of anyone who doubted his theological pronouncements, whether they were contradictory or not. But a Protestant church as such did not exist. Already Protestantism was diverging in many different directions of dogma, scripture, governance, and ritualism. This did not discourage James. Rather, it reaffirmed his quest.

Persecution of the little congregation began almost immediately, and from an unexpected corner. Friends and relatives of the congregation accused them of treason; that by their separation they had abandoned the Protestant cause against the Catholic majority in northern England. And, the holier-than-thou attitude of the little group didn't solicit any sympathy.

Was this William Brewster, to whom they had so long paid their rents, and whose orders they had so long accepted, who had grown up among them from a child, to be rated then as a prophet and wiser than the learned in London, Oxford, and Cambridge? Was this pale and puny youngster, William Bradford, who in truth declared himself too weak and too proud to hold the plow, like his honest father and grandfather, now to stand forth as instructor and leader in the deepest experiences men can have?[221]

The nagging, scoffing, and deriding became daily events. Silent spying, prying, and watching were possibly even more unbearable. The previously tolerant Anglican authorities in York received complaints and reports of hostilities in and around Scrooby, and launched an investigation. The High Commissioners started proceedings against several members of the new church but, unlike elsewhere in England, the punishment of the separatists was mild for those who appeared and the ones who chose not to show up were not actively pursued. By contrast, contemporaries in London were executed.

Nevertheless, the congregation decided it was time to leave England, to go on a pilgrimage to the Promised Land, and embark on a crusade for righteousness. England was not clean and, if they stayed, they would be vulnerable to philosophical pollution and religious contamination. They condemned the Established Church and, for giving in, the Puritans in the south. They decided to go to the Netherlands, where Smyth's congregation had settled two years earlier. The success of that group made the prospect of living in that tolerant country favorable. They made their final decision in the late spring or early summer of 1607 and started preparations. The few who owned land sold it quickly. Most were tenants and could move fast. All would bring household goods, clothing, and books. However, the permanent export of such goods for the purpose of emigration was practically unknown in those days, and permission nearly impossible to obtain. They would have to steal out.

London, England, 1607

On March 19, 1607, "James, by the grace of God, &c." issued an Ordinance and Constitution enlarging the number of the King's Council of Virginia, "and augmenting their authority, for the better directing and ordering of such things as shall concerne the two several Colonies."[222] Two appointees stood out: Oliver Cromwell, uncle of the later Lord Protector, and Edwin Sandys.

Even though the Virginia Company was a private enterprise, the colony was a royal dominion under the jurisdiction of the Crown. Sandys was already an investor and the appointment put him in a good position to further his interests. It is likely that those were not entirely financial. In the preceding pages we saw how his travels had acquainted him with modern thinkers and exposed him to republican forms, particularly in the Netherlands, Switzerland, and Germany. Perhaps such governments could find fertile ground in the new settlements of America?

Boston, England, 1607

Quietly the congregation traveled to the port of Boston in Lincolnshire and made arrangements with a shipmaster to take them and their possessions to the Netherlands. To avoid detection by the authorities, they agreed to meet somewhere up the coast. During the second night, the ship appeared and took them on board. All seemed well until, to their dismay, customs officers in small boats suddenly appeared out of nowhere. They were soon surrounded. The shipmaster had betrayed them.

The constables conducted bodily searches, ordered them into the boats, and rowed them ashore. In a nearby town, the fugitives were paraded in the marketplace. After that, the local authorities treated them courteously.

Holland "Fluyt" courtesy 17thCenturyWarships

They enjoyed "honorable confinement", probably in the houses of some townspeople. When the Privy Council declared their case unimportant, they were sent home. Brewster and six other leaders were held a little longer, but also came to no harm. In the fall of 1607 a number of this group reached the Dutch Republic. Their success prompted the rest of the congregation to try again that November.

Brewster made arrangements with a Dutch captain to pick them up at a deserted, shelving place on the coast south of the Humber. The men walked while the women, children, and all baggage were loaded in boats. They sailed down the Idle to the Trent and from there into the Humber, and finally down the coast. The waters were stormy but they arrived a day early. Many became seasick in the boats, so they took shelter in a small creek nearby.

The next day the storm subsided. The men arrived on the beach and the ship moored nearby. However, low tide stranded the boats in the creek. The captain launched a boat to take the men on board while waiting for the tide to turn. When the first load reached the ship, a large crowd arrived on the shore in the distance. Some were on horseback, most were on foot. Some had muskets and other weapons. The captain was not about to wait for the obvious to unfold. He weighed anchor, raised his sails, and took off, leaving most of the men on shore and the women, children, and possessions stranded in the creek. The men on board had nothing but the clothes they wore, and could do nothing but worry about their families. Was the whole pilgrimage doomed?

Brewster and the other leaders were still on shore. They sent the majority of the men away to escape arrest while the leaders went to take care of the women and children. Many of the latter were crying for their husbands. They tried to comfort their children who were cold and afraid. They feared arrest. The pursuers took them to the local authorities, but they did not know what to do with such a large group. There was no jail big enough. So, they went around the various houses and eventually found enough residents willing to put up the women and children.

The next day, the constables brought the refugees before a justice of the peace. He, however, found that no crime had been committed. The local authorities found different judges, but judge after judge came to the same verdict. The locals realized that the best way to make the problem go away was to help the Pilgrims[223] leave. Since no higher authorities told them to do otherwise, they let them escape. Brewster and Bradford stayed to the last so they could help the weak and the poor make the journey. Eventually all emigrants arrived safely in Amsterdam, the Netherlands.

Holland, the Netherlands, 1608

Conditions in the Netherlands were good. The country was rich, making economic progress relatively easy. Refugees from many parts of Europe proved it. The country was at war with Spain but, oddly enough, appeared to make money off it. The capture of Spanish gold and silver made huge profits. The war also united the people. Religious tolerance was the consequence. The plethora of beliefs was so great that Bradford described it thus, "The Fair of all the Sects where all the Pedlars of

Leyden from Town Hall

Religion have leave to vend their Toyes." They found themselves among Anabaptists, Socicians, Jews, Arians, and Unitarians. All were heretics, beyond salvation, and more corrupting than even Papists or Episcopalians. Religious freedom is what they had sought, but religious contamination is what they got. Amsterdam was the wrong place. The search was on, again.

As a result of the 1585 Treaty of Nonsuch, Elizabeth I sent troops to assist the Dutch against the Spanish in the Eighty Year War. Under the terms of the Treaty, the Dutch provided garrison churches and permitted English services to be held for the troops. These centers of worship were also open to other English-speaking residents and one of the seventeen cities where the original garrison churches were founded was Leyden[224]. The city was home to Europe's most liberal university, nearly half its population was foreign born, and tolerance for culture and religious practice was unmatched.

They chose Leyden and, as with all Dutch cities, they had to put in a residency application. The city fathers accepted it in May of 1609. The city was still suffering from the decimation of its population brought on by the extended Spanish siege of a generation earlier. The administration was still working to refill under populated neighborhoods. The absence of "bad" religious sects, the famous university, the booming economy, and the job opportunities in the cloth industry all were attractive to the immigrants.

They packed up and made the move. Robinson, who had now caught up with them, also made the journey south. At the time that they bought a large house for their meetings, they were around two-hundred strong. Robinson, chosen to be their minister, lived upstairs. From the scant knowledge of their personal lives, we know that William Bradford was married to Dorothy May on December 10, 1613. She was sixteen. After having run through his savings in 1616, William Brewster became a partner in a printing shop with one Thomas Brewer, whom he met in Leyden. They printed in English only since their sole customers were in England. However, their books were not welcome with the English authorities. In 1619, the English ambassador complained to the Dutch authorities that the printers were breaking English law. The Republic enjoyed freedom of the press, but the authorities did not want to upset King James. Forced to close shop, Brewster took his family back to, ironically, England.

London, England, 1609

AND we do also GRANT and confirm to the said Treasurer and Company, and their Successors, as also to all and every such Governor, or other Officers, and Ministers, as by our said Council shall be appointed to have Power and Authority of Government and Command in and over the said Colony and Plantation;[225]

In his quest to acquire one or more Spanish princesses for his sons, King James had been pressuring the Dutch to accept a truce with that country. Prince Maurice preferred to fight on while the Advocate, Barneveld, thought it better to placate James and continue England's friendship. Spanish designs could be frustrated by other means. The truce would also suspend the officially sanctioned English piracy on Spanish ships.

Sandys saw an opening. The Virginia Company proposed that James sign the territory of Virginia over to them so that it would no longer be the responsibility of the Crown. Should any hostilities against Spain continue from that quarter, James could not be blamed. The truce, and the princesses, would not be in danger. James accepted the argument and the Second Charter for Virginia, written by Sir Edwin Sandys, was signed in 1609. It gave the company total control over the territory and government of Virginia. Because of seasonal and shipping delays, a new governor and Sandys's instructions for the formation of a more democratic government arrived only the next year.

Edwin Sandys's work in Parliament increasingly put him at odds with King James. As a leader in the Patriot[226] Party, he had expressed his belief kings did not rule by divine right. In addition to this break with orthodoxy, he advocated a constitutional monarchy where Parliament's decisions were binding. At some point, James let it be known he did not want to meet with Sandys, but he could not disqualify a man whose standing with the power brokers had, if anything, strengthened. We may well assume that Sandys' ploy to wrest control of the Virginia colony away from the King and his haste to populate it, and to have other colonies founded in America, was partially intended to undermine the monarchy. Where Sandys had failed in the English parliament, he would succeed in America by creating little republics whose influence would eventually extend to England's governance itself. Obviously, he was not choosy about the kind of people who went over. Christians wanting to escape other Christians would do, and, with the vicious persecutions in much of Europe, candidates were a-plenty.

Leyden, the Netherlands, 1616

The members of the Separatists did not find life in the Netherlands as easy as expected. Their problems can be summed up thus:

- The Guilds. As non-citizens, they were disallowed membership of the trade organizations. That effectively precluded them from owning any sort of business. Being in the service of someone else was their only option. The work they knew best, farming, was not available in the urban environment. As unskilled labor, they could find only low paying. hard-labor employment. The only way to escape poverty was to become Dutch citizens, learn the Dutch language, adopt Dutch customs, join a Dutch church, and lose their heritage and newfound religion forever.

- The university. At first it had appeared an innocuous institution, an attractive center of learning, even. But the simple farmers and villagers had no idea what a place of higher learning was about, and this was the most liberal in all of Europe. Some of Europe's most famous scholars resided there: Junius, Snellius, Donellus, Raphaelengius, Descartes, Bronckhorst, Baudius, Molineus, de Groot, Gomarus, Heinsius, Arminius, and Vorstius, to name some[227]. The university was radiating intelligent discourse, which naturally attracted some curious Separatists. The multitude of new ideas posed a serious threat to the Pilgrims' unquestioned dogma.

- Sexual attraction. Inevitably young men and women formed liaisons with young people outside the group. This led not only to inter-faith marriages but also to the mixing of nationalities. Beliefs and culture were increasingly contaminated.

- Religious strife. The truce with Spain had opened a window of introspection in the Netherlands. Disagreements of dogma rose to the level of hatred and destruction, the effects of which we saw in the previous chapter. The Separatists no longer felt safe.

Taken together, the forces around them were tearing them apart, and they had no power to thwart them. Their concept of religion could not survive in Holland; the only answer lay in complete isolation from the corrupting influence of the World.

The leadership could not force the decision to uproot again. During their stay as an isolated community in the Republic, they were exposed to the mechanisms of governance of the guilds, the municipality, the State, and the Nation. They had adjusted their ways of consultation, participation, and elected office accordingly. They were not just a congregation of believers but, as a community in an alien country, they were also a mini-republic. Bradford wrote that they never used the magistrates of the city. The members took all decisions by vote of majority and the elected officers implemented them. They were unusual in that sense. Other English congregations followed their traditional system of elected officers who made the decisions. And by this time most of those were in trouble as well. Many dissolved. Robinson had keenly understood this and pressed Brewster and Bradford to stick with their direct rule. This form of democracy, however, did not yield quick decisions. Over a period of many weeks in the winter of 1616-17, they met at the great house and discussed shipping out to the New World. It was a terrifying prospect for many, only one decade after Captain Henry Hudson's voyage of discovery on the Dutch ship the *Halve Maan*[228]. Stories abounded of shipwrecks, filthy ships, famine, nakedness, diseases, and Indian cruelties. How would they pay for the voyage and the equipment needed to survive there? And, if they were barely able to scrape out a living in the Netherlands, how could they expect to carve one out among Indians and Spaniards? Had not the English of Roanoke been massacred, those of Jamestown decimated, and the French Huguenots[229] in Florida wiped out?

Bradford later wrote[230],

It was answered, that all great and honourable actions are accompanied with great difficulties, and must be both enterprised and overcome with answerable courages. It was granted the dangers were great, but not desperate; the difficulties were many, but not invincible. For though their were many of them likly, yet they were not cartaine; it might be sundrie of the things feared might never befale; others by providente care & the use of good means, might in a great measure be prevented; and all of them, through the help of God, by fortitude and patience, might either be borne, or overcome. True it was, that such atempts were not to be made and undertaken without good ground & reason; not rashly or lightly as many have done for curiositie or hope of gaine, &c. But their condition was not ordinarie; their ends were good and honourable; their calling lawfull, & urgente; and therfore they might expecte the blessing of God in their preceding. Yea, though they should loose their lives in this action, yet might they have comforte in the same, and their endeavors would be honourable. They lived hear but as men in exile, & in a poore condition; and as great miseries might possibly befale them in this place, for ye 12. years of truce were now out, & ther was nothing but beating of drumes, and preparing for warr, the events wherof are allway uncertaine. The Spaniard might prove as cruell as the salvages of America, and the famine and pestelence as sore hear as ther, & their libertie less to looke out for remedie.

In spite of the uncertainties, a majority voted in favor and the focus shifted to identifying a suitable location. They rejected Guiana because of the Spaniards, and Virginia because of the English Episcopal settlements. However, there were isolated parts of the Virginia Company's (V.C.) territories. They would enjoy its protection and, by extension, England's, but they would be remote enough to escape the control of the Crown and her Church. There was a problem though. Surely they would need the permission of the Company and the Crown. They could not just go and expect their presence to remain a secret. The risks of confiscation and repatriation were very real.

Leyden, the Netherlands, 1617

There was, however, a small chance they might get permission to go. While still in Scrooby, the Brewsters had been acquainted with the Archbishop Sandys, whose son Edwin was now Sir Edwin Sandys, an important man in the London branch of the Virginia Company.

In the middle of 1617, Deacon John Carver and Robert Cushman traveled to London for negotiations with the Company. They agreed on the business aspects fairly quickly. The settlers would fish and trade for the benefit of the company and grow crops for subsistence. Although a commercial enterprise, the Virginia Company was subject to King James's notions of acceptable theology.

The Pilgrims understood that religion would be an issue. They had prepared seven articles that were probably the result of a compromise after considerable discussion. On the one hand, they placed conditions on the King's supremacy in religious matters, church organization, and theology. On the other hand, they would subscribe to the Thirty-nine Articles[231] in the same sense in which the "Reformed Churches where we live and also elsewhere" accepted them. Since there was a wide range of Reformed churches, this provided freedom through ambiguity. More important was the clause addressing the King's power, "in all things obedience is due unto him either active, if the thing commanded be not against God's Word, or passive if it be, except pardon can be obtained." This way they could decide whether the King had ecclesiastical authority or not.

Sir Edwin Sandys

Oddly, Sir Edwin Sandys didn't object and expected these statements to pass muster with the King and his Bishops. When the company wrote a letter of encouragement to Brewster and Bradford in Leyden, they responded with more specifics: their industry and frugality, their preparedness for hardship, and above all their commitment to Separatism and each other's welfare, and by extension, the company's. Their forthrightness proved detrimental. In a letter of January, 1618 to the Virginia Company, Robinson and Brewster backpedaled from their earlier enthusiastic encouragements. The Privy Council had raised concerns with Sandys about the institution of Bishops, the Sacraments, and the condition under which the petitioners accepted the supremacy of the King. The whole process of wriggling their way out of this self-dug hole took the better part of that year. In April of 1619, Cushman and Brewster talked to the Company, but it now was struggling with internal divisions over funding. However, shortly after Sir Edwin Sandys was elected treasurer, the Pilgrims were awarded their patent[232]. Curiously, it was issued to an individual, a Mr. John

Wincob, "a religious gentleman belonging to the Countess of Lincoln." This way the Pilgrims, and their seditious ideas, were separated from the patent, and presumably invisible, although plenty of people must have known of the arrangement. It was June and preparations commenced. In the fall, they learned of the fate of another expedition. Old friends from Amsterdam had returned from a failed journey to America. Many crew and voyagers had died from lack of fresh water, proper food, and overcrowding. It was a timely warning. They would need a larger ship and more supplies. Both were beyond their resources. There was no other alternative than to attract commercial interests. To serve that end, their expedition had to be a profitable venture.

In January of 1620, they received an offer from Dutch investors to take them across the Atlantic. They could scarcely refuse this generous and definitive deal. Surely Sandys got wind of the Dutch offer. The Virginia Company didn't want a Dutch-controlled settlement on the Virginia coast. Anxious to get the Hudson River settled, Sandys hastily sent a business relation to Leyden with the assignment to make an offer.

He sent Thomas Weston, a London merchant who was a Puritan with strong Separatist sympathies. Several Pilgrims knew him. He had contracted with the Virginia Company in 1616 to sell lottery tickets for the financing of the Virginia colony. He was also engaged in fisheries off Nova Scotia[233] and familiar with the northern American coasts. Weston proposed a seven-year partnership of adventurers[234] and colonists, with no formal incorporation. Weston told them his group already had a patent under which the enterprise would operate. The arrangement would make the Pilgrims entirely invisible to the Crown. It was perfect.

The agreement included:

Establish a permanent trading post where they live and operate from.
Fish on the Grand Banks.
Cut lumber and collect valuable roots.
Trade with Indians for fur.
Build houses, till the soil, and ensure permanence.

Every colonist sixteen and over would be rated at one share of common stock of £10. Adventurers would finance the enterprise and receive stock accordingly. Proceeds from sale of goods in England would benefit the partnership. Colonists worked four days a week for the partnership and two days for themselves. After the seven years the colony, the houses, and improved lands, became the property of the colonists. Unimproved land would be divided between the adventurers and the planters, each to dispose of its share as best it could, and the profits be distributed proportionately to the shares contributed by each. The officers of the church and Weston signed the document and they agreed on a date by which the Pilgrims were to deliver the money and goods they had committed.

Detailed discussions on logistics commenced in April. The Pilgrims realized that they were too numerous and could not all go. They had to decide how many should go and who; which leaders would accompany the settlers, what they would bring, and what the group that stayed behind was supposed to do. As usual, they put everything to a vote. Eventually they decided that: slightly under half would go (those that voted for going) with Brewster and Bradford as leaders. Robinson would stay. If the settlers were successful, the rest would follow. If the settlers failed, they would return. During their time of separation the two groups would have churches unto themselves.

While preparations in Leyden proceeded with speed, Weston ran into resistance from the adventurers in London. The potential profits did not reflect the risks. The entire efforts of the colonists had to be part of the venture. This included all land and houses and all labor, not just four days per week. Cushman, who was still in London, eventually had to agree to these terms. The adventurers elected a president, a treasurer, and committed money and goods. The treasurer, Christopher Martin, would go to America to represent his partners.

Upon hearing this, the Pilgrims in Leyden were furious. Cushman had committed them to serfdom[235] at worst and indentured servitude[236] at best. They were not common laborers. They must land as free men. Also, they must own the improved land and buildings that resulted from their labor. Some decided not to go. Some wanted their money back. Some declared Cushman's concessions invalid since he had no authority to act on their behalf. They wrote to Cushman and Weston accordingly. But they were really at a point of no return. They had purchased a ship, the *Speedwell,* and equipped it. They had sold their possessions.

In London, by contrast, almost nothing had been accomplished. The company had underestimated the expense and difficulty of the venture. They could not handle such a large group and the goods and food to maintain them. The large ship that was supposed to carry the majority of the colonists had not been procured, much less outfitted and supplied. The plan to have two ships sail forthwith from Southampton to escape the scrutiny of the authorities was in jeopardy. Summer was approaching and the window for sailing and settlement might be lost. Urgent letters from Leyden spurred Weston into action. On June 10th, he and Cushman found a ship of 120 tons, but that same weekend one of the adventurers offered them a larger ship. The 180-ton *Mayflower* was ready to sail by the middle of July with Captain Jones in command and a John Clarke as pilot[237].

Late July, after a long day of praying, singing, fasting, discussing, and feasting, the colonists left Leyden in canal boats. They boarded the *Speedwell* in Delftshaven and the next day were seen off by friends from Leyden and Amsterdam. Bradford described Robinson,

> … falling downe on his knees, (and they all with him), with watrie cheeks commended them with most fervente praiers to the Lord and his blessing. And then with mutuall imbrases and many tears, they tooke their leaves one of an other; which proved to be the last leave to many of them.

James Towne, 1619

On April 28, 1619, the investors of the Virginia Company elected their new Treasurer, Sir Edwin Sandys. Sandys became the equivalent of a modern CEO charged with day-to-day operations and planning. Since most of the

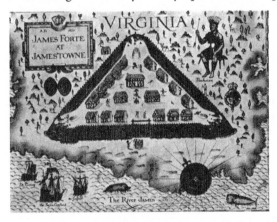

Jamestown, 1607

assets were across the Atlantic in America, he was essentially running Virginia; its commerce, properties, and government. Founded as a military outpost with limited freedoms, the colony was not doing well.

Sandys and his allies believed that a greater ownership stake would encourage colonists to work harder. At last he had the opportunity to implement his republican ideas. In May, he had a committee codify the regulations of the company, select a form of government, appoint magistrates and officers, and define their functions and duties. Sandys wrote the articles of government himself. He was careful to include all the provisions necessary to please the King and his Council. These addressed the "maintenance of the Church of England," the supremacy of the Crown[238], and that land tenure and the penal code were as in "the mother country." The governing Council was to be appointed by the Virginia Company in

CAPTAIN JOHN SMITH.

John Smith

England, but the members would elect a President from among themselves. Sandys empowered this body to enact its own laws and ordinances, but added the provision that they were subject to the approval of the Company or the Crown.

With the wording of this clause, Sandys put Company and Crown on an equal footing. Then he added a sentence that in a subtle way, limited the power of the Crown: "... provided always that [the ordinances] be such as might stand with and be consonant to the laws of England and the equity thereof." In effect it made the King subject to Common law. Given the distance from the mother country, it would take many months before a law or ordinance could be repudiated. This made the colony independent indeed. Other articles provided for a treasurer and storage and trade rules. One article was perhaps typical of Sandys's character. It told the colonists "to show kindness to the savages and heathen people in those parts, and use all proper means to draw them to the true knowledge and service of God."

Around the time of Sandys's appointment, the newly appointed Governor arrived in Virginia with fresh orders, sometimes referred to as the Great Charter. Governor Yeardley was a former mercenary in the Dutch armed forces. On instructions from Sandys, he organized the formation and election of the House of Burgesses, the legislative body of representatives. The House first met on July 30, 1619. Its first action was to approve the articles of government, which made Virginia practically an independent republic.

Southampton, England, 1619

After four days sailing, *Speedwell* and its colonists met *Mayflower* in Southampton[239]. There they were approached by Captain John Smith, of Jamestown fame[240], who offered advice, and possibly his services. However, Smith was in His Majesty's service and they dared not trust him. The Pilgrims turned down his advances. Cushman and Weston insisted that the group sign the agreement and a fierce argument ensued with both parties digging in their heels. Eventually Weston left, saying angrily that they were on their own. Since he hadn't paid the port dues, he had knowingly or unknowingly forced the issue. The Pilgrims feared scrutiny. They quickly sold some supplies and paid the dues. They wrote a letter to the adventurers defending their refusal to sign and offering to add a clause that extended the seven years should large profits not materialize. Luckily the offer was not accepted, for it would have committed the colonists to servitude indefinitely.

The group gathered to decide on allocations of people, goods, and supplies. When that was done, Bradford produced a letter that their preacher, Robinson, had given him at their farewell in Delftshaven in Holland. The young leader read it aloud so that all present could hear.

> ... you are many of you strangers, as to ye persons, so to ye infirmities one of another, & so stand in neede of more watchfullnes this way, least when shuch things fall out in men & women as you suspected not, you be inordinatly affected with them; which doth require at your hands much wisdome & charitie for ye covering & preventing of incident offences that way. And lastly, your intended course of civill comunitie will minister continuall occasion of offence, & will be as fuell for that fire, excepte you dilligently quench it with brotherly forbearance.

Robinson reminded his friends of what they had already experienced in Amsterdam and Leyden with their international populations and diverse cultures and religions. Holland was, in Robinson's mind, what America would become.

He went on:

> A thing ther is carfully to be provided for, to witte, that with your comone imployments you joyne comone affections truly bente upon ye generall good, avoyding as a deadly plague of your both comone & spetiall comfort all retirednes of minde for proper advantage, and all singularly affected any maner of way; let every man represe in him selfe & y whol body in each person, as so many rebels against ye comone good, all private respects of mens selves, not sorting with ye generall conveniencie. And as men are carfull not to have a new house shaken with any violence before it be well setled & ye parts firmly knite, so be you, I beseech you, brethren, much more carfull, ye the house of God which you are, and are to be, be not shaken with unnecessarie novelties or other oppositions at ye first setling therof.

Here Robinson urged them to put the community before the individual and to stick with their tried and true methods while the colony was working towards a firm footing.

Then he laid out how the new settlement should govern itself.

Lastly, wheras you are become a body politik, using amongst your selves civill govermente, and are not furnished with any persons of spetiall eminencie above ye rest, to be chosen by you into office of goverment, let your wisdome & godlines appeare, not only in chusing shuch persons as doe entirely love and will promote ye comone good, but also in yeelding unto them all due honour & obedience in their lawfull administrations; not beholding in them ye ordinarinesse of their persons, but Gods ordinance for your good, not being like ye foolish multitud who more honour ye gay coate, then either ye vertuous minde of ye man, or glorious ordinance of ye Lord. But you know better things, & that ye image of ye Lords power & authoritie which ye magistrate beareth, is honourable, in how meane persons soever. And this dutie you both may ye more willingly and ought ye more conscionably to performe, because you are at least for ye present to have only them for your ordinarie governours, which your selves shall make choyse of for that worke.

Their wise old preacher urged Bradford and the congregation to adopt a government for the people, by the people. His model was their church. But he extended the principles to the secular community, knowing that the congregation would inevitably absorb people from the outside. Or, if it was absorbed in turn, it might influence governance by its example. Democracy would be the best guarantee against tyranny from within or without. The community was on its way to become the first true democracy in America.

Both ships sailed from Southampton in early August. *Speedwell* immediately started leaking and put into Dartmouth for repairs. When it leaked again, they went to Plymouth where they disembarked. A more careful examination found repairs would take too long and be too costly. They sent it back to London with a number of discouraged Pilgrims. The rest transferred to *Mayflower*. In early September, 102 colonists finally left Plymouth. Among them only Brewster and Bradford originally came from Scrooby. Thirty-three others were from the Leyden congregation, which would prove, with men like Carver, Winslow, and Allerton, the backbone of the colony. Although males were the large majority, compared to previous voyages the number of females and children was large. There were nineteen adult females and thirty-nine children. Unlike the Jamestown expedition, this one carried no military men. *Mayflower* was about ninety feet long, twenty-four feet wide, had three masts, high fore- and aft decks, a broad, low middle deck, and low 'tween-decks. The crew counted between fifteen and twenty under the leadership of Captain Jones[241]. Small farm animals were penned in the front near the crew quarters while the passengers had cabins and bunks in the rear. They brought no furniture. For food, they carried bacon, hard tack, salted beef, smoked herring, cheese, ale in caskets,

The Mayflower in the storm

and gin. There was butter, vinegar, mustard, lemons to avoid scurvy, and prunes for the stool. They lived in tight quarters and must have had limited opportunities for washing or laundry. In spite of the fair weather, a number suffered seasickness.

The Jamestown settlers had sailed to America using the southern route via the West Indies to avoid storms farther north. But it took them more than four months to reach Virginia, where they arrived weakened. The captain of *Mayflower* opted for the direct route across the North Atlantic and headed straight for the Hudson River. They encountered storms halfway through the crossing, which caused a main beam in the ship's hull to crack and snap out of place. Captain Jones called a meeting to discuss the situation. Some wanted to return to England. As it was, they needed to repair the damage and had to do it right there. The crew took a great iron jack from the hold and began the careful job of forcing the mast back into place. They eventually succeeded and positioned a number of wood braces to keep the beam in place. The officers assured the wary colonists that the ship was sound below the waterline and that the journey back was just as long as the one to America. To help convince the concerned colonists they promised to be extra careful and that there would be no real danger.

… upon the ninth of November following, by break of day we spied land which we deemed to be Cape Cod, and so afterward it proved. And the appearance of it much comforted us, especially seeing so goodly a land, and wooded to the brink of the sea. It caused us to rejoice together, and praise God that had given us once again to see land. And thus we made our course south-south-west, purposing to go to a river ten leagues to the south of the Cape, but at night the wind being contrary, we put round again for the bay of Cape Cod. And on the 11th of November we came to an anchor in the bay, ...[242]

The anonymous journal sounds rather cheerful. The sighting of land was of course a relief, but the account does not mention they were close to 100 leagues east of northeast from their intended destination, the Hudson River. It was therefore not written by any of the leaders of the expedition. Originally, they had accepted the Hudson because it fell under the charter of the Virginia Company, was far from other English settlements, i.e. Jamestown, and was controlled by the Dutch, who were trading there and who had earlier invited the Pilgrims to settle there.

Why they so quickly abandoned the surety of their patent for the uncertainty of Cape Cod Bay is still the subject of speculation. It is not inconceivable that Weston wanted them near Cape Cod. Probably unbeknownst to the Pilgrims, he had not obtained a patent for the Hudson River. He already ran substantial fisheries (and probably fur trading) in New England and was well familiar with the conditions. As primary investor, he had no obvious interest in placing *his colony* on the Hudson, where the Dutch already had posts that would offer competition in the Indian trade. Massachusetts, Maine, or Nova Scotia were better for a permanent settlement in support of his enterprises. He also must have known of the failed attempts at settling in more northern parts. Cape Cod was a safer bet (In 1622, Weston was the sole investor in the Weymouth colony just north of Plimoth). Instead of abandoning the Pilgrims, as he had told them on the quay in Plymouth, he had instructed Captain Jones to take them north. Presumably unaware of Weston's designs, Sandys called the diversion "pilot error;" an error that left the Hudson River area open for others. Indeed the Dutch started a permanent settlement there in 1624.

What is certain is that they grounded in the shallows around the Cape. They managed to free themselves and deemed it better to find relative shelter in the bay. Captain Jones pressed that they should land and establish a settlement as soon as possible so they could prepare for the approaching winter. It may well be that the Pilgrims liked the remoteness. The nearest permanent settlement was far to the south in Jamestown, Virginia, and Dutch traders plied most of the coast in between. It was a good buffer. One possible problem was that Cape Cod was outside the Virginia Company's charter. However, they had heard that other companies might be formed with charters for the Massachusetts area, that they surely would welcome settlers, and allow them to negotiate better terms than with the London adventurers. It could be that Captain Jones told them this to help them decide.

No matter why they got there, they decided to stay near the Cape. Immediately a number of the colonists from London said that, now that the patent was abandoned, they were free from any agreement and could pursue their own interests. There were heated discussions, but the leadership reminded all that success and survival could only be achieved with cooperation. They drew up a document, known as The Mayflower Compact. All but three of the men signed it.

> ... to plant ye first colonie in ye northern parts of Virginia, doe by these present solemnly and mutually in ye presence of God, and one of another, covenant & combine ourselves together into civill body politick, for our better ordering and preservation & furtherance of ye ends aforesaid; and by virtue hearof to enact, constitute, and frame such just & equall lawes, ordinances, acts, constitutions, & offices, from time to time, as shall be thought most meete & convenient for ye generall good or ye Colonie, unto which we promise all due submission and obedience.

With this document, they had followed Robinson's farewell advice to the letter and founded a small republic. Although the Compact had the appropriate references to King James in onset and ending, nowhere does it declare subservience to England, its laws, or its monarch. Author Jeremy Bangs, a notable expert on Dutch Renaissance history, thinks that all Pilgrims who had lived in Leyden were strongly influenced by its institutions and life-styles[243]. Robinson's letter and the Compact that followed would bear this out.

Now they could concentrate on finding a suitable location. It had to be fertile so they could grow the seeds they had brought: onion, turnip, parsnip, and cabbage. It had to be close enough to the Indians so they could buy corn seed for eating and the first planting, and trade for furs, etc. And it had to be close to prime fishing areas. They reassembled their shallop[244], which had been stored in the hold. The work met with some difficulty and it would be two weeks before they could use it. That hampered exploration because they feared running into hostile Indians on long walks. But, since they encountered nobody and saw no signs of habitation the first several days, their excursions extended inland. On the first such excursion, they found the soil sandy and the land covered with small ponds and brackish gullies. They concluded that this location was unsuitable. They found game tracks and discovered evidence of Indian and European presence, although old. Importantly, they found several caches of corn that they took with them. Careful not to make enemies, they later returned to leave valuables in exchange. On November 27, the shallop was finally seaworthy and they explored the Pamet River. A wintry weather accompanied them and ice from the driving spray and sleet covered the rowers. But they found more corn to take back. The urgency of finding a permanent settlement was clear. On December 6, the shallop set out with sixteen men for a trip of several days to explore many miles south. The weather was worse than before. Along the way, they discovered a number of abandoned Indian dwellings, more corn, and in the distance saw some people whom they assumed to be Indians. That night they made camp near the shore and barricaded themselves. With the help of an entry in *Mourt's Relations*, we can reconstruct what happened.

They had divided their camp into two groups. A number of men stayed to guard the shallop at the water's edge while another group barricaded themselves a little higher on the beach. They had the advantage of a fire to keep them warm. Around midnight, in the light of the full moon[245], this group was awaked by a loud cry of a sort they had not heard before. The two men who had watch duty immediately called out, "Arm. Arm!" The gloom of their fire lit activity all around. Everyone was up now and trained their muskets in the direction of the noise. Two or three men fired into the silvery night. Except for the surf of the waves on the beach the silence returned. "What was that?" a soft voice asked. Another man answered, "Could have been wolves or foxes. I've heard them when we were up in Newfoundland." That seemed to calm everyone down. Someone added logs to the fire and, except for the guards, all slowly went back to sleep.

Around five in the morning an identical cry woke them up. It was followed by similar cries but of different pitches. Against the brightness of the low moon, the silhouette of one of their own came running. "They are men! Indians! Indians!" he screamed as he dived behind their barricade. No sooner had he reached safety then a barrage of arrows flew into their camp. Some of the men quickly retrieved their guns. Captain Standish had his snaphance[246] at the ready and fired a shot in the dark. He probably intended to scare off the attackers or draw a response that would give the defenders a better idea of where the attackers were. "Hold your fire," he instructed the others, "until we can see what we are shooting at." Only four of the men were armed with muskets. The others had left them outside the barricade. They called out to the men at the shallop to see how they fared. A few shots came from that corner and then a voice shouted that they needed a fire-brand to light their matches. Immediately one of men in the barricade took a log from the fire and ran toward the shallop. Curiously, the unexpected run with a brightly sparking torch distracted the attackers and gave the unarmed men an opportunity to run out and recover their arms. The armed men took position at the opening in the barricade, determined to ward off any attempt at taking the makeshift fort. The hesitation of the attackers ended and, with loud shrieks and cries, they assaulted the men who had just retrieved their arms. A robust native with a lot of courage stood behind a tree no more than half a musket shot away. He had a bow and shot a quick volley of three arrows at the men. One man ducked and avoided his projectile while the other arrows missed their targets entirely. When they aimed muskets at the native, he uttered another loud and frightful cry and followed his raiding party into the woods.

Thus ended the first encounter with the local population. But they were not discouraged and, fortunately, interactions with a different tribe proved beneficial to their survival.

The next few days they sailed along the shore and steered towards the mountain of Manomet and a known safe harbor. In their haste, they broke the mast and rigging, but entered the harbor under the power of oars. The sea was rough until they found shelter in the lee of a small island on which they stayed two nights. Having seen no evidence of natives, they crossed over to the mainland. The tide was high and carried them to a sandy shore. The weather was mild and sunny. There was no snow and

The Pilgrims landed

the ground was not frozen. The group, which included Bradford, Standish, Carver, and Winslow, explored at length. A small stream tumbled from a high embankment to wind through a grassy meadow to the beach. There were previously cleared fields nearby, but no sign of current habitation. Next they sounded[247] the harbor and found it deep enough for ships to dock. The date was Tuesday, December 12 when they all agreed; they had found their new home.

Author's note: For the definitive history of the Pilgrims read the 894 page tome *Strangers and Pilgrims, Travelers and Sojourners*[248]. Jeremy Bangs's exhaustive research of the Pilgrim families and their lives in England, Holland, and America forms a breathtaking picture of who they were, what forces influenced them, and, in turn, what their influence was on America. Without explicitly acknowledging it, Bangs' work makes a strong case for the thesis that the city of Leyden, with its multinational population, of which many immigrated to the various American colonies, can be regarded the proto-American city.

*The interest of the man must be connected with the constitutional rights of
the place. It may be a reflection on human nature, that such devices should
be necessary to control the abuses of Government. But what is Government
itself, but the greatest of all reflections on human nature?*
James Madison in The Federalist No. 51.

Chapter 8: The Atlantic Republics

Timeline

Year	Event
1603	James I King of England
1607	Virginia founded
1607	First "Pilgrims" arrived in Holland
1609	Truce between Spain and the Netherlands
1618	Adriaen van der Donck born
1619	Barneveld executed Virginia Articles of Government passed.
1620	Plimoth Plantation founded
1621	Spanish-Dutch War resumed
1624	New Netherlands founded
1624	Virginia a Royal colony
1629	New Hampshire and Maine founded
1630	Massachusetts founded
1633	First school in America in New Amsterdam
1634	Maryland founded
1635	Connecticut founded
1636	Rhode Island founded
1638	Delaware founded
1643	United Colonies of New England
1647	Rhode Island constitution allowed separation of Church and State
1648	80 and 30 Year Wars ended

1649	King Charles I executed
	Petition of the Commonality of New Netherlands
	Remonstrance of New Netherlands
1649	Toleration Act in Maryland
1653	Cromwell Lord Protector of England
1653	Municipal Charter for New Netherlands
1653	North Carolina founded
1657	Flushing Remonstrance
1660	English monarchy reinstated, Charles II King
1663	South Carolina founded
1664	British take New Netherlands, New York Founded
1664	New Jersey founded
1676	Bacon's rebellion in Virginia
1682	Pennsylvania founded
1732	Georgia founded

Three circumstances were responsible for the growth of the British colonies. The first was the bundling of short-term commercial adventures in long-term arrangements called corporations, designed to encourage would-be colonists and finance large-scale operations. The second was religious intolerance in Europe that forced people to look for freer environments. The third was that in Britain, the oldest son inherited the entire estate. Younger siblings had to fend for themselves. For the women, this meant either find a husband or join a convent. The men often had no option but to leave their homes to find a place with opportunities. The population of the Dutch colony grew for the same first two reasons. However, many, if not most, settlers were not Dutch, but rather religious refugees from all over Western Europe, England included. Much exaggerated narratives of easy pickings and riches from returning sailors attracted many men, and women, to the new lands. Naturally the corporations stimulated the migration so their business could expand and their profits grow.

Birth of the Corporation, 1602

They were emphatically special jurisdictions, and their founders and inhabitants exhibited all the love for corporate liberty which characterizes the history of such jurisdictions.[249]

Prior to 1602, international trade and attempts at settlement had been conducted by individual adventurers. Although some did work together, the "company[250]" only lasted as long as the single trip. Typically there were no enduring arrangements. Various European governments claimed jurisdiction over territories well beyond their actual control. The indigenous people who lived there were often referred to as savages and therefore had no rights. Governments issued patents or charters to individuals for permission to trade or settle at loosely defined territories. It was all a bit messy and there was no continuity.

The States General of the Dutch Republic introduced something entirely new.

After the unification of Portugal and Spain in 1580, the Portuguese trading destinations in Asia became legitimate targets for the rebelling provinces of the Netherlands. Dutch adventurers conducted successful voyages to Java and beyond, during which they took Spanish and Portuguese ships and established trading relations in the Far East. However, the various Dutch adventures and joint ventures were not all successful and sometimes found themselves operating in competition with each other.

The States General wanted to see a stronger unity of purpose and eliminate the randomness of success and failure of individual adventurers. To do so, the States General dictated a consolidation of all East-Indian ventures into one company. The Dutch East-India Company was founded in 1602. Its organization and governance were modeled on those of the Republic itself. It was the ultimate commercial innovation. It was the birth of the corporation with an indefinite length of life[251]. An added innovation was the ownership model of publicly tradable stock. And thus the stock market was born, too. Other nations, such as England and France, followed this example shortly thereafter and founded their own companies on a similar model.

American Diplomacy

The participation of commoners in government was practiced in a few places only. In the proto-industrial world, the concept was young. It had barely gained a foothold in Europe. However, in its infancy, the movement managed to make the leap across the Atlantic Ocean to just three places on the coast of North America. The immigrants who carried the concept were separated from their mother countries by four months of sailing on an unpredictable ocean. The colonies were much closer to each other than to their home lands. Inevitably, they interacted, traded, and became dependent on each other. Their interaction was similar to those their home countries had enjoyed across the Narrow Sea. The people were English and Northern and Southern Dutch. They had a common culture that included a preference for making decisions after extensive deliberations. Each colony practiced a level of consultative or participatory government. It is no surprise that the earliest official meeting between leaders of two colonies turned out to be so indicative of what was to come. However, the reason for the meeting and the way in which it was conducted is also indicative of what went before.

Plimoth Plantation, Monday, October 4, 1627

Isaack de Rasiere was an official of the Dutch West-India Company. He was on a company ship sailing north from New Amsterdam to honor an invitation for a visit with those of Plimoth Plantation. He described his approach,

> [252].....Coming out of the river Nassau[253], you sail east-and-by-north for about fourteen leagues, along the coast, a half league from the shore, and you then come to "Frenchman's Point" a small river where those of Patuxet[254] have a house made of hewn oak planks, called Aptucxet, where they keep two men, winter and summer, in order to maintain the trade and possession. Here also they have built a shallop, in order to go and look after the trade in sewan[255], in Sloup's Bay[256] and thereabouts, because they are afraid to pass Cape Malabar[257],.....

To Europeans, the east coast of North America was a vast, unknown, and undeveloped country inhabited by wild and alien savages. There were just three firmly established colonial settlements. James Towne and Plimoth Plantation were British, and New Netherlands was Dutch. Their isolation from the parent countries was nearly complete. The colonies were virtually independent entities. Under these conditions, a unique meeting between leaders of two settlements was to take place. The length at which these men later wrote about the encounter showed that they thought it a hugely important engagement[258]. Using their accounts and adding a granule of imagination let us witness the events.

> ☦ A small sailboat negotiates the shallow waters near a long, sandy land tongue. The shallop rounds the sand dune at the tip and turns its bow south toward the only sign of habitation on the wild coast, a small shabby town on a steep rise above the shore. A British flag flies from the masthead above a sprit rigging. The boat

and its crew are British but the passengers are not. They are visitors from farther down the coast and they look ruffled and tired from their long journey. Their anticipation is high now that the risky trip by ship, on foot, and in the small boat is finally reaching its destination. The long awaited embassy[259] of New Amsterdam to Plimoth Plantation was going to take place.

Unexpectedly, a few of the Dutchmen bend down to reach into their bags and pull out trumpets. At a signal of their leader they put the mouthpieces to their lips and start playing. The unusual swelling sound carries across the water and up the hillock of Plimoth. In the silence of the town, every burgher hears the eerie but pleasing sound. People abandon their chores to come from their houses, stores, and fields to investigate. Seeing the spectacle on the water below and wanting a closer look, they negotiate the slope down to the narrow beach. As the boat draws nearer, the townspeople take in the multicolored dress of the dozen or so visitors. They have not seen a cheerful display of colorful clothing in years. The visitors' stockings are bright; their leather boots are high and have a wide, folded top with shiny buckles adorning the foot. Their short, puffy pants are striped with multiple colors. They wear tailored vests over laced white shirts and their hats have large rims and ostrich feathers on top dance with every move of their heads and flutter with every puff of air. Some townspeople smile as they look down at their own simple, humble, and practical clothes. They remember the places whose decadence they had escaped to live in accordance with their religious beliefs of humility. Their own clothing is of wool or linen. It is not dyed and has the natural colors of beige, gray, and an occasional brown. Apart from the local Indians, the crews of a few ships, and the survivors of a failed colony, the people have not seen much else in the seven years since their arrival. The foreign scene is a novel treat.

When the boat lands on the beach, the motley group of colorful characters jumps off the bow while the trumpeters keep playing as best they can. The most flamboyantly dressed man waits at the gunnels. He is also the largest and most rotund. A rich mustachio hides his upper lip while a large brimmed hat with a white ostrich feather sits over his free flowing wavy brown hair. The group of men wades to the gunnels and, with considerable effort, lifts the large man from the boat and carries his bulk over the lapping water. With deference, they lower him onto the light-colored sand of the beach. The large man adjusts his tunic and turns to face the

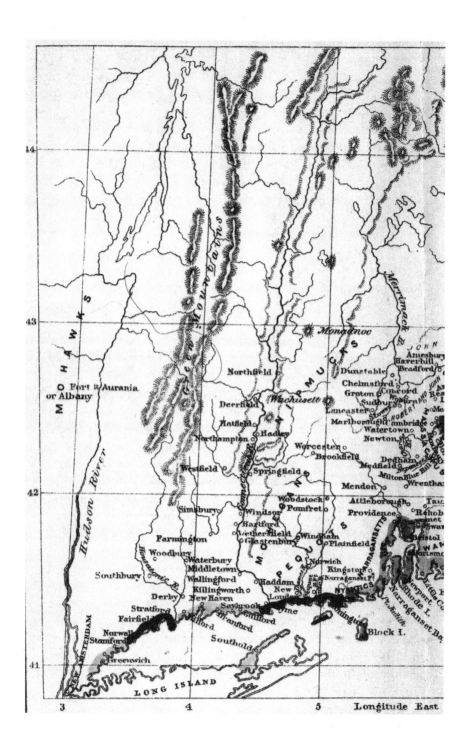

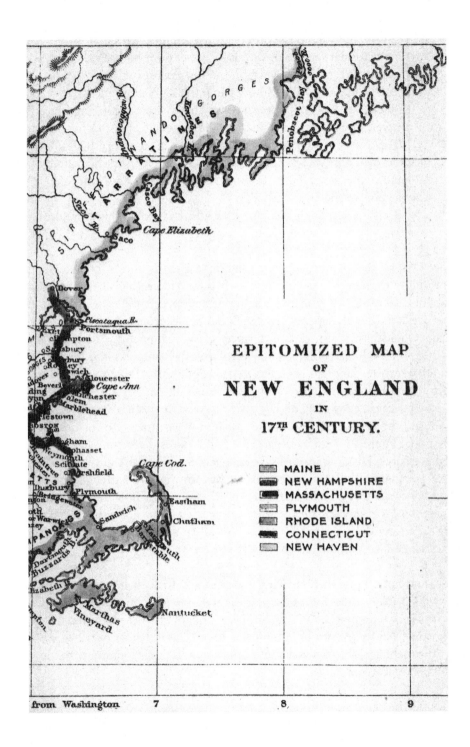

EPITOMIZED MAP
OF
NEW ENGLAND
IN
17ᵀᴴ CENTURY.

MAINE
NEW HAMPSHIRE
MASSACHUSETTS
PLYMOUTH
RHODE ISLAND
CONNECTICUT
NEW HAVEN

land. He searches among the townsfolk to identify a leading figure. He can see nothing in the dress of the bland burghers that would distinguish their leader. However, he notices one whose collected demeanor and steady gaze indicate authority. Dressed as drably as the rest, he appears to be waiting patiently to greet his guest.

"Isaack de Rasiere, at your service," the visitor says in English. His accent speaks of a French/Dutch heritage. He offers his hand.

The townsman replies, "William Bradford." Bradford had not lost his own Yorkshire accent despite his twelve years in the Dutch Republic and seven years in America. "Welcome to Plimoth. I hope your journey was agreeable."

As if they had enjoyed a long friendship, the two shake hands warmly. ⊖

Despite this being their first meeting, a lengthy correspondence had preceded the encounter, during which they had learned a fair amount about each other. They shared one important experience: Each had found refuge in the Dutch Republic from religious persecution in his own country. This would have given each a measure of sympathy and respect for the other. The exchange of letters between Plimoth Plantation and the Dutch at New Amsterdam had been businesslike, but cordial. Being so far away from their homelands, each colony was vulnerable and had an incentive to settle peacefully any dispute they might have with another. However, each was also under pressure from their distant governments to further their national interests. Bradford especially had to consider a complicated mix of pressures. His king wanted him to assert British sovereignty over all of New England. This was an impossible task for the tiny settlement, whose influence spread no more than thirty miles in any direction and whose area of control was smaller still. But, he was expected to persuade the Dutch not to trade anywhere near the trading post at Aptucxet[260]. In his writings he acknowledged that the Dutch were familiar with it.

> They came up with their bark to Manomet, to their house there, in which came their Secretary, Rasiere, who was accompanied with a noise of trumpeters and some other attendants, and desired that they would send a boat for him, for he could not travel that far overland. So they sent a boat to Scusset and brought him to the Plantation with the chief of his company.

At the same time Bradford could not complain too much about the Dutch for fear that the English Crown might decide to send a military governor, which would cost his little colony its independence. Then there were the shareholders of the Plymouth Company, both back in England and on location, who wanted a profit after years of losses. He had to look for more and better trading opportunities. Recently arrived adventurers, who did not regard Bradford very highly anyway, and who were causing civil disturbances, demanded a more business-like approach, too. These adventurers were not especially religious and did not fit well with the more disciplined Separatists. And lastly, what weighed most heavily on his heart, there were his own fellow religionists who were unable to pay off their debts to the Company and lived in abject poverty.

De Rasiere's task was seemingly simpler. He had to keep the status quo. The Dutch knew they were operating a clandestine pelt trade with the Indians in territory claimed by Charles, King of England and Scotland. They also knew that, as long as they did not cause any disturbance, the British monarch, who was an ally of the Dutch Republic, would do no more than grumble. De Rasiere wanted to keep the pelt trade a secret as long as possible. As a matter of fact, the Dutch had trading posts all along the coast of modern day Rhode Island, Connecticut, New York, New Jersey, and Delaware. The Dutchman was under pressure from his government to not create any hostilities. The Dutch-English alliance against Spain was of mortal importance. Yet his employer, the Dutch West-India Company, had instructed him not to give up any trading grounds. This meant he had to hold on to the trade near Aptucxet, right in Bradford's back yard. Somehow he had to reconcile the interests of his country with those of his company and his own.

Both men knew that, despite a degree of competition, there was a large measure of interdependence. Both conducted trade with the native tribes and with their respective home countries. But they also traded extensively with each other. Plimoth depended a great deal on the Dutch merchant ships delivering goods the colony needed, such as agricultural implements, cloth, and coveted foods like cheese. Obviously the Dutch wanted to continue that profitable trade, too. That left little to negotiate. De Rasiere expected though that he would have to give up something to placate the English Crown and make Bradford look good. He, too, did not want a British military governor in Plimoth.

Bradford invited the visitors up to the town on the hill. It consisted of a collection of small houses neatly laid out in perpendicular streets. The roofs were thatched with long reeds harvested from nearby lakes. Some were made of a timber frame covered with boards, while others were put together with wattle and mud. All had roughly hewn plank doors and shuttered windows. Houses had no glass to let in the light while keeping the wind out. The town was young and poor, very poor. Nevertheless, the residents had built a church which did double duty as their meeting hall. Some of Bradford's people accompanied the visitors inside, where they found simple sustenance and entertainment. We can imagine the leaders exchanging pleasantries about the country in which each had found refuge. They probably spoke a fair amount of Dutch to each other. They had common ground in Amsterdam, their lives in the Netherlands, and the tolerance that their religious beliefs had found in the enlightened country.

However, despite the commonalities each man had a very different history. Who were these two leaders and what did each man bring in

Fort and meeting house at Plimoth Plantation.
Photo by Swampyank at en.wikipedia

terms of personality and religious and political convictions? What were the differences in culture that could possibly hamper the negotiations? Conversely, what were the fundamental commonalities that could help forge a positive outcome?

Bradford was born in 1590 in the village of Austerfield near Duncaster, Yorkshire, and was drawn to a small church in Scrooby, another village in the area. He became an orphan at an early age and attended services there when very young. There the boy had attracted the attention of a member of the congregation, one William Brewster.

At age twelve Bradford was living with the Brewster family. Their church was unusual in that it adhered to a new sect that had broken entirely from the Church of England. Like the Puritans, its followers rejected the riches and hierarchy of the official church but, unlike the Puritans, judged it beyond redemption. So they formed themselves as the "Separatists." Dismissing the traditional hierarchy, the congregation ran the church in a democratic way. This was not unlike the civic organization of towns and cities where leaders were elected by taxpaying burghers. It amounted to a stakeholder membership. The established Church of England with the Crown at its head perceived these churches a threat to its control of religious life and to the Crown itself. The official Church and the Crown persecuted the followers of Separatist churches vigorously. Bradford's group was refused permission to leave for the Netherlands, but managed to escape in 1608. They first settled in Amsterdam and moved to Leyden a year later. They continued to worship according to their beliefs, governed their church in the same democratic fashion, and found themselves in cities with governing councils elected by the taxpayers. They were living in a country without a monarchy, a country where the cities elected the State's representatives who in turn elected the members of the States General, the Republic's parliament.

Isaack de Rasiere was born in Middelburg, Zeeland, in the Netherlands in 1595, the son of religious refugees from the southern Netherlands. Many Huguenots from Wallonia escaped the Spanish Inquisition and certain death. The Dutch Republic enjoyed freedom of religion and it offered excellent economic opportunities for enterprising people. Little is known about Isaack's youth, but, since he grew up in the Republic, it is certain he spoke fluent Dutch (or the local dialect thereof). His father was a merchant in Middelburg, Zeeland. The city had a lively harbor and was an important trading center for Dutch, English, and German merchants. In 1613, his step-mother's father married into a family of large merchants such as the van Rensselaers (who in 1629, would found, and become the patroon[261] of, Fort Orange colony, near what is now Albany, NY, as we shall see later).

The exposure to his father's trade and the big Amsterdam trading families steered de Rasiere into commerce. In the mid 1620s he was in Amsterdam. After the Spanish had largely destroyed Antwerp and the Dutch blockaded it, Amsterdam had quickly replaced the old commercial center as the largest port in Europe, if not the world. There de Rasiere became a protégé of Samuel Blommaert, a merchant and shareholder of the Dutch West-India Company (and who partnered with van Rensselaer in 1629). There are no records of his church-going. However, he did grow up in an increasingly liberal environment (with the end of the Truce with Spain in

1621 religious strife calmed down). All Dutch towns and cities were home ruled. They had, just like some of their English counterparts, a governing council elected by the taxpayers, i.e. the merchants and manufacturers. Amsterdam was the first to introduce a second tier electorate by allowing ordinary citizens to purchase the right to vote. That drew in many of the artisans and craftsmen, who belonged to the guilds. Thus Isaack de Rasiere was well acquainted with the concepts of democracy and the governing by committee with its inevitable negotiations and compromises among competing interests. When he started work for Blommaert, he encountered the same concept in shareholder meetings of the Dutch West-India Company, where everything was decided by majority vote.

The Dutch West-India Company operated many trading posts along the coast from Rhode Island, and not far from Aptuxcet, in the north to Delaware in the south. The English King, James I, had claimed the coast from the "French Bay" (the St. Laurence estuary) to Florida as his sovereign domain and had granted charters to two English companies for their exclusive trade and settlement. In addition to territories that were uniquely allocated to each company, there was a large area in the middle, between Connecticut and the Delaware River, where both companies could settle as long as each kept a distance of 50 miles or more from the other. Wanting to avoid friction and with plenty of coast to work with, the two companies left the overlapping territory unoccupied. Always on the lookout for opportunity, the Dutch quickly filled the void with a string of trading posts. In 1624, they created a permanent settlement on a small island now known as Governors Island and founded Fort Orange near present day Albany, New York. Soon after, they moved onto Manhattan.

Bradford and his band of Separatists initially planned to settle along the Chesapeake Bay or at the mouth of the Hudson River. Both locations were then part of Virginia, which, in those days, was defined as all points between Long Island and Florida. Eventually they had decided on the Hudson River. However, in late November, 1620, an alleged diversion and a storm helped push *Mayflower* past Cape Cod and into the quieter waters of Cape Cod Bay. There was not much time for the would-be colonists to establish a foothold and get to the business of surviving a winter that had already started.

Whether de Rasiere knew of the alleged diversion[262] or not, he had reason to be wary of the Plimoth settlers. Although he could expect a degree of friendship from Bradford, not all settlers were Pilgrims. A good number were rough and tumble men from an ill-prepared and failed colony up the coast. The Plymouth Company had taken them there so as to settle, spread out, and increase production and profit. There were also new settlers straight from England. The unexpected newcomers burdened the Pilgrims with their care and survival. Their motives were material and they considered the Pilgrims dim-witted and lazy. Who would come all this way and accept such hardships only to grow food, raise families, and pray? Being primarily interested in trade and a speedy profit, these men were the ones most concerned with the Dutch competition. Bradford had to take their interests into account, as well as those of the investors who had brought all of them here.

So, what exactly took place at the negotiating table? What deals were made that neither wanted to write about? It probably went like this.

⊕ Two sets of three men were seated on rough-hewn backless benches around an equally rough table. The location served as both a fort and a meeting house. During religious services the table was used for an altar. A south facing window with hand-blown glass helped a standing oil lamp at the opposite end of the table illuminate the meeting place. The double doors at the north end of the space were closed and there were no other people inside. A large wooden bowl on the table offered apples, hard sausages, and hunks of bread. A water bucket made of staves and hoops stood next to it. A wooden ladle was added to fill the pewter mugs standing nearby.

Bradford told of the settlers' great debt to the investors and that the colony was in danger of insolvency. He had decided that the Dutch had to throw King Charles a bone and that the cold truth would be the best way to get it. Bradford demanded that the Dutch give up any trading with the natives near the Aptuxcet trading post that the men from Plimoth had built there in 1626[263]. He explained that the small concession would satisfy the Crown and get King Charles off both their backs. Of course the opportunities would help the shareholders back home and the adventurers in his colony, while the post would yield some extra income for his own people. It was the ideal solution.

But Bradford was no merchant; de Rasiere was. The latter knew Bradford was under pressure to find more trade. The Pilgrims had recently discovered a small shiny shell called wampunpeag was of value to the natives. They had not yet discovered how sought after it really was, much less that the Dutch were using it to trade for furs. If the Plimoth traders should find out, the Dutch trade would suffer. De Rassiere decided that buying the shell from the Indians would divert the native currency away from Plimoth while they could use it to purchase more furs. ⊖

De Rasiere later wrote[264]:

….. and in order to avoid the length of the way[265]; which I have prevented for this year by selling them fifty fathoms of sewan[266], because the seeking after sewan by them is prejudicial to us, inasmuch as they would, by doing so, discover the trade in furs; which if they were to find out, it would be a great trouble for us to maintain, for they already dare to threaten that if we will not leave off dealing with that people, they will be obliged to use other means. If they do that now, while yet ignorant how the case stands, what will they do when they get a notion of it?

Aptuxcet trading post.
Photo by Kevin Rutherford, CC-License

Bradford wrote[267]:

For they now bought about £50 worth of it of them, and they told them how vendible it was at their fort Orania…..

ⴲ De Rasiere understood that a concession could help smooth the way ,even if it was only a perceived one. So he made his offer. To help their finances, he was willing to buy all their wampunpeag and purchase more when they had it. He added that he understood the political implications with regard to territory and proposed that any trade with the natives in the Mamomet area be left to

Plimoth Plantation, but that Dutch ships might visit the trading post to take in fresh water.

Bradford recognized that this would suffice, but he could not be sure about the wampunpeag de Rasiere spoke of. So he made a counter offer. He accepted the Aptuxcet arrangement for the length of two years. During that time the Plantation would see how much the wampunpeag would yield. If it proved as lucrative as de Rasiere suggested, then the small trading post would remain open to Dutch visits.

With the trading post accessible, de Rasiere would gain an opportunity to spy on their activities. Eventually his company would have to make concessions, but for now, he had bought valuable time, time to conduct more trade and make more profit. De Rasiere had got what he wanted at little cost. He extended his hand and Bradford took it. They had a deal. ⊖

Plimoth Plantation, October 5-onward, 1627

Both men must have been relieved the negotiations concluded positively. Each had achieved his goals and each could report back to the various interested parties with a sense of accomplishment. No doubt there was a little celebration, perhaps with the aid of some Dutch *brandewijn* (brandy) or *jenever* (wheat and juniper liquor). As they relaxed, the two had time to discuss other issues such as daily life and politics. As a result de Rasiere was able to give a detailed description of Plimoth Plantation:

New Plymouth lies in a large bay to the north of Cape Cod, or Malabar, east and west from the said point of the cape, which can be easily seen in clear weather. Directly before the commenced town lays a sand-bank, about twenty paces broad, whereon the sea breaks violently with an easterly and east-northeasterly wind. ... They apportion their land according as each has means to contribute to the eighteen thousand guilders which they have promised to those who had sent them out; whereby they have their freedom without rendering an account to anyone. [268]

He continued to explain the short time it took the townspeople to catch the abundant fish in the bay, enough to feed the fifty or so families for a day. In fact there was so much fish they used thousands of small ones to fertilize their maize fields! He continued:

New Plymouth lies on the slope of a hill stretching east towards the sea-coast, with a broad street about a cannon shot of 800 feet long, leading down the hill; with a crossing in the middle, northwards to the rivulet and southwards to the land. The houses are constructed of clapboards, with gardens also enclosed behind and at the sides with clapboards, so that their houses and courtyards are arranged in very good order, with a stockade against sudden attack; and at the ends of the streets there are three wooden gates. In the center, on the cross street, stands the Governor's house, before which is a square stockade upon which four patereros are mounted, so as to enfilade the streets. Upon the hill they have a large square house, with a flat roof, built of thick sawn planks stayed with oak beams, upon the top of which they have six cannon, which shoot iron balls of four and five pounds, and command the surrounding country.

De Rasiere clearly spent time walking through the town, for his observations are detailed. Undoubtedly he made notes as he went. This shows Bradford or the townsfolk gave the Dutchman complete freedom of movement or, perhaps, even encouraged it. De Rasiere noted that the religious practices contained information on security alertness.

The lower part they use for their church, where they preach on Sundays and the usual holidays. They assemble by beat of drum, each with his musket or firelock, in front of the captain's door; they have their cloaks on, and place themselves in order, three abreast, and are led by a sergeant without beat of drum. Behind comes the Governor, in a long robe; beside him on the right hand, comes the preacher with his cloak on, and on the left hand, the captain with his side-arms and cloak on, and with a small cane in his hand; and so they march in good order, and each sets his arms down near him. Thus they are constantly on their guard night and day.

The description indicates that the visitors were treated as friends who had full access to any part of the town. That they were allowed to examine the military arrangements shows that Bradford believed there was nothing to fear from the Dutch. The two also discussed the local form of government. De Rasiere's account is:

Their government is after the English form. The Governor has his Council, which is chosen every year by the entire community, by election and prolongation of term.

The form of government, as Bradford explained it to his guest, differed somewhat from that of the Dutch colony, but it was one de Rasiere was familiar with. The latter writes that it "is in the English form". Perhaps he meant that the right of each and every adult male colonist to vote in Council elections is unique to this English colony, which was correct. Democracy in the Dutch colony was very limited. Unlike that in the Dutch Republic, where all taxpayers could vote, New Amsterdam was a company town governed by a Secretary General in the employ of, and responsible to, the West-India Company. The office-holder was also in the service of the Dutch government as Governor of the Province. Obviously this arrangement held a major conflict of interest with, as we shall see, severe consequences for the colony. Although there were occasional Councils, the Secretary General wielded absolute power.

Back in the Netherlands, both Pilgrims and Walloons had frequently participated in discussions about secular and religious rights. Leyden, like all cities in the Dutch Republic, was governed by a council elected by the burghers. The judiciary was fairly independent and its rulings gave the confidence necessary for a merchant society to flourish and people to feel safe. There is every reason to believe both groups adopted some of the concepts that had given them refuge in Holland and that they subsequently transported these across the Atlantic to their new settlements. It is true that the Pilgrims already decided church affairs by majority vote of the whole congregation. But extending this democratic principle to the governance of Plimoth Plantation was new. It was also smart. People who have a say in the affairs of their common enterprise, are stakeholders in the well-being of the entire community, will feel greater ownership and with it, greater responsibility.

Undoubtedly many of the two groups of refugees knew each other or knew of each other. The fact that the Pilgrims left the Republic in pursuit of greater security appealed to the Walloons. An old neighbor[269] of the Pilgrims in Leyden, Jesse de Forest, had been instrumental in convincing the Walloons and the Dutch government to set up permanent colonies around the Hudson estuary. It was only three years after the founding of Plimoth that the first Walloons settled on *Nooten Eilandt*, what is now Governor's Island, New York.

Even though there was an inevitable rivalry between the colonies, their relations were good as is witnessed by their correspondence. So wrote Bradford in Dutch to the governor of New Amsterdam:

.... our very loving friends and Christian neighbors
....
Acknowledging ourselves tied in strict obligation into your country
and state, for the good entertainment and free liberty we had, and our
brethren and countrymen yet there have, and enjoy under your most
honorable Lords and States ..... for which we are bound to be thankful
and our children after us.

From their negotiations and discourse, we have to wonder what the
existential nature of the embassy was. Was it between sovereign nations
in Europe, or between two nominally independent nations in America?
Of course each man was a citizen of his respective country. But, more
importantly, each was also a representative of a local entity with uniquely
local interests far from the protection and supervision of their European
overlords. The embassy was foremost a negotiation between two companies
on behalf of their stakeholders, companies that, for all practical purposes,
had founded practically independent *American* nations. Bradford's
admission that "if the King should choose to send a governor-general, they
would be obliged to acknowledge him as sovereign overlord," shows how
independent he thought they were at the time. It also shows his trepidations
about a possible reining in of that independence (and how right he turned
out to be some years later).

Both men must have liked each other. Bradford wrote that de Rasiere
was "a man of genteel behavior". But neither wrote much about the
commercial substance of their encounter, which would indicate that the
accepted outcome was pretty much the status quo. It is certain that the
Dutch trading posts in the vicinity of Aptucxet played a role in the exchange,
not only of goods, but also of ideas. As we shall see in subsequent pages,
with their shared and their unique heritages, these two company territories
would maintain good relations, first as trading partners, sometimes against
hostile Indians, and later against the overbearing British Crown. The
correspondence between Bradford and de Rasiere was quite forward and
open. So wrote Bradford on March 19, 1627, to de Rasiere,

... we are but one particular colony ... there being divers others beside,
unto whom it hath pleased his Majesty's Council for New England, to
grant the like commission and ample priviliges to them (as to us) for
their better profit and subsistence; namely to expulse, or make prize
of any, either strangers or other English which shall attempt, either to
trade, or plant within their limits...[270]

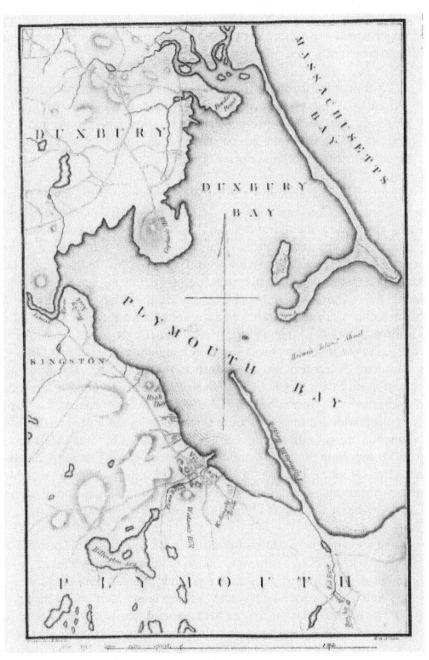

Plimoth Plantation and environs

The passage is a clear warning to the Dutch while the rest of the letter is filled with friendly words. Bradford's letter of August 14, 1627, has even stronger words of warning for the repercussions British ships not from Plimoth may bring on trespassers.

> ... We cannot likewise omit (out of love and good affection toward you and the trust you repose in us) to give warning of the danger that may befall you, that you may prevent it; for if you light either in the hands of those of Virginia or the fishing ships, which come to New England, peradventure thay will make prize of you...[271]

Thus the two companies, through their representatives, maintained open channels of correspondence and trade which would play a major role in the economic and political future of the North American continent.

After an apparently pleasant stay, de Rasiere returned to New Amsterdam to report to the Governor. He shared his findings with the stakeholders and traders of his company, his friends in the colony and at home, and the minister of his church, the congregation, and the settlers of the colony. His assessment of the economics of the location and its resources contrasts with his descriptions of Indian customs and culture. He referred to the Indians as savages and, although he had a few good things to say about their way of life, he wrote that, "the men ... are very inveterate against those whom they hate; cruel by nature, and so inclined to freedom they cannot by any means be brought to work." He observed that, "they are very much addicted to promiscuous intercourse," and judges married life among the Indians rather primitive. His observations of Indian ways were detailed and, from the way he wrote, gave the impression that he tried to be objective. Of course a person can only assess other people's culture with his own as a starting point and can do no more than explain it from what he considers the standard. It is a limitation all of us live with. He went on,

> When a woman here addicts herself to fornication, and the husband comes to know of it, he thrashes her soundly, and if he wishes to get rid of her, he summons the Sackima with her friends before he accuses her. And if she be found guilty, the Sackima commands one to cut off her hair in order that she may be held up before the world as a whore, which they call poerochque, and then the husband takes from her everything that she has, and drives her out of the house..... And when a man is unfaithful, the wife accuses him before the Sackima, which most frequently happens when the wife has a preference for another man. The husband being found guilty, the wife is permitted to draw

off his right shoe and left stocking…; she then tears off the lappet that covers his private parts, gives him a kick behind, and so drives him out of the house; and then "Adam" scampers off.

The lengthy descriptions show that he was reporting customs that were alien to him and that he expected his reader to find them equally strange.

Although both colonies traded with the Indians, the level of trust the English and Dutch enjoyed did not extend to the "savages." Thirty thousand years or more separated the cultures of Europeans and Native Americans. The customs, rules of behavior, and institutions of the natives were unfamiliar. Interactions between the groups were guarded and trade was carried through immediate exchange rather than promise. The natives had no written language, so contracts were verbal and easily misinterpreted. Often the trust broke down and, following misunderstanding and panic, deadly violence would follow.

Both Bradford and de Rasiere were governed by rules. They had to protect the interests of their shareholders. They were subject to the wishes of their respective governments and the laws of their respective countries. They each had a similar understanding of those rules and the repercussions for not honoring them. They had been raised and educated in similar societies and so had the values of trust imbedded in their psyches. And, they each benefited from the trade between them.

From their writings, we can conclude that Bradford and de Rasiere both accepted some form of democracy. They also appeared to be content with the concepts of free trade — it benefitted both. The companies they worked for were owned, financed, and ruled collectively by investors whose stock was tradable. Bradford and de Rasiere may or may not have discussed religion. There is no record of it. But, at a minimum they must have respected each other's presumed beliefs. In his description of the church at Plimoth Plantation de Rasiere mentioned its democratic form of governance.

The influence of the Pilgrims' ten year domicile in Leyden was substantial. They instituted secular marriage, religious tolerance, and a separation between church and state. For all three there was precedence in the Dutch Republic but not in Britain[272]. In 1643 the colonies of Plimoth, Massachusetts Bay, Connecticut, and New Haven concluded the Union of the United Colonies. It was an arrangement that was unknown in Britain. As Bangs observed, "the primary precedent was the Union of Utrecht, signed on February 1, 1579, by which the Netherlandish provinces in revolt against …. Spain combined in order to regulate a common foreign policy respecting their war of independence, to settle jurisdictional disputes among each other, and to regulate taxation for covering the ongoing expenses of the war." Years later John Quincy Adams said that, "the New England confederacy of 1643 was the model and prototype of the North American confederacy of 1774." One of the prime instigators of the New England confederacy was Edward Winslow of Plimoth.

Massachusetts, 1630s

During the time that Sir Edwin Sandys conspired to have the Pilgrims go to America, he was engaged in a struggle with Sir Ferdinand Gorges over the founding of a new corporation with a new charter. Until then the Virginia Company controlled all of the east coast from the Carolinas to Massachusetts. Gorges asked King James for a charter for the "Council established at Plymouth in the County of Devon for the Planting, Ruling, and Governing of New England in America", or New England Council for short. It wanted far more rights than Sandys's Virginia Company was willing to relinquish.

However, Sandys lost his case before the Crown and the new corporation set about its business of granting settlement rights to various groups. Under James II, England was hostile to Puritans and Separatists and starting a life free from religious oppression appealed to many. The first attempts at settlement under the new charter was that of Puritans through the Plimoth colony, while others outside of Plimoth were not successful until John Winthrop and the Massachusetts Bay Company[273] arrived[274]. As happened at Plimoth Plantation, the Native Indians had no defense against the diseases the Europeans brought. The local Neponset tribe dwindled and left behind large cornfields. As had the Pilgrims before them, on May 30, 1630, a group of sixty families took advantage of the abandoned fields and settled nearby. They called their town Dorchester. The land was divided in lots of fifty to one hundred acres per family. Its government was the same as that of its church, which had been formed in England before setting sail to America. Apparently the town was well organized. Official records go back to 1632 and are the oldest in Massachusetts. In 1633 the government was vested in the form of a town with "selectmen" elected by all the males, a form soon copied by other settlements. The town pursued commercial and fishing interests with great success. It quickly became the largest and most influential settlement in the colony. It did not take long for news of the bustling colony to travel back to England.

Frank Francis

As we have seen, the colonies were separated from their mother countries by months of travel. Having to fend for themselves in a wilderness, they acted as independent republics that treated with each other as necessity dictated. One peripatetic named Francis Doughty moved through the majority of them. His journey began in England.

Old church at Sodbury

Soppanbyrig was the Saxon name for an Iron Age fort that was used by the Romans, the Saxons, and the English under Edward IV[275]. The church of Old Sodbury, as the town is known today, dates from the 13th century. In 1634 the pastor was Francis Doughty, the son of a Bristol brewer[276]. With his wife, Bridget, and their three children he lived in a nearby town. He was among those in the Anglican Church who abhorred its Catholic symbolism and called themselves Puritans. It was but a few years before he was noticed by the Anglican authorities and relieved of his position. In 1638, like many before and after, Francis pulled up stakes and took his family across the Atlantic[277]. Others have it that he settled in Holland first and moved on to Plimoth Plantation in 1633[278].

Their ship anchored in Boston harbor, at Dorchester, where they took up temporary residence[279]. Being a minister, Francis probably helped out in the local church. But trouble followed from England in the form of his married sister, Elizabeth Cole[280]. She was the executrix of their father's estate and claimed he owed her a considerable amount. She sued him in Boston, but there was no quick decision. Instead the case dragged on. After a year in Dorchester, Francis was rewarded with a congregation of his own in the town of Cohasset[281], where they were registered under the last name of Doubtyes[282]. Cohasset's location, some twenty miles inland from Plimoth Plantation, shows the speed with which native peoples retreated (through illness, death, or otherwise) and the colonists spread. The town was founded in 1637 by a group of Puritans who gave it the name First Parish. The Doughtys were now six strong, the fourth child having been born recently. Francis was probably a stubborn man who harbored strong preferences regarding religious doctrine that was more Presbyterian. Shortly after his appointment, a Master Hooke and Master Stout arrived from Boston, one a pastor, the other a teacher. Whether they were sent to check on Francis we do not know. However, trouble came quickly when Francis asserted that the children of the baptized also should be baptized[283]. Apparently that belief did not go over well with the Puritan visitors. They told him that hence forward he had to conform to Puritan views. Francis refused. After all, he had been preaching this way from the beginning. The Boston ministers believed they were in the right and appealed to the local magistrate to intervene and rule in their favor. The magistrate, who was officially a secular official, ordered the constable, also a secular official, to arrest the offending minister, Master Doughty. Apparently the constable chose to do this during a church assembly and Francis was dragged out. If that was not enough, he was then ordered to leave the town. In the mean time, suits and counter suits continued with his sister. Francis wrote to John Winthrop, then governor of the colony.

S" — My service rem to yo' worship, may it please you, hearing my sister Cole hathe petitioned against me, I make bold to intreat you doe me the fauor to let me vnderstand theffect of her pceedings & whether I shall need to attend the next Co', & w' you guesse she will doe then, & when the Cort is. I pray God increase yo' honour & ppetuate yo' happinesse, resting, till you command. - Fr: Doughty.

Eventually that case was decided in his favor. The Cohasset ruling however could not be undone. Probably he already had a name as a troublemaker. Earlier in March, 1640, he had been fined for selling gunpowder to the natives, while his servant was set in the stocks for "swearing profanely." Again, with a few followers this time, the family packed up and left for a more hopeful place.

The situation thus described was fairly typical for Massachusetts. The colonists were primarily Puritans of the strictest kind. These were the people who couldn't stand living in England among the corrupting high church Anglicans and others. So wrote a contemporary, "One may live there from year to year, and not see a drunkard, hear an oath, or meet a beggar.[284]" And another, "As Ireland will not brook venomous beasts, so will not that land vile persons and loose livers.[285]" The lawyer Thomas Letchford wrote, "Profane swearing, drunkenness, and beggars are but rare in the compass of this patent.[286]" The Reverend Nathaniel Ward of Ipswich wrote,

> I thank God I have lived in a Colony of many thousand English almost these twelve years, am held a very sociable man, and I may considerately say, I never heard but one oath sworn, nor ever saw one man drunk, nor ever heard of three women adulteresses, in all this time that I can call to mind.[287]

Others observed how New Englanders slept while their doors were kept unlocked. Because of the uniformity of the colonist population, strict rules and behaviors were quite acceptable, and even desired. Even the intrusion of the church into the arms of government was acceptable.

The magistrate who, for all practical purposes, banned Doughty from Cohasset was acting as an arm of the church that had a firm grip on the judiciary. The intolerance of other beliefs and life philosophies and the fear of aberrations would have severe consequences for those that were accused of being different or of committing witchcraft. We see examples of those outcomes in places like Pakistan today, where a charge of blasphemy is used to get rid of an enemy. Quakers were banned from the colony from the start. Some arrived anyway. Even supposedly intelligent people like John Winthrop stooped to primitive superstition when, in March, 1638, he ordered the deformed body of a stillborn and buried baby exhumed. The mother was guilty of heresy. Winthrop described it:

> It was of ordinary bigness; it had a face, but no head, and the ears stood upon the shoulders and were like an ape's; it had no forehead, but over the eyes four horns, hard and sharp; two of them were above one inch long, the other two shorter; the eyes standing out, and the mouth also; the nose hooked upward; all over the breast and back full of sharp pricks and scales, like a thornback [i.e., a skate or ray], the navel and all the belly, with the distinction of the sex, were where the back should

be, and the back and hips before, where the belly should have been; behind, between the shoulders, it had two mouths, and in each of them a piece of red flesh sticking out; it had arms and legs as other children; but, instead of toes, it had on each foot three claws, like a young fowl, with sharp talons.

To us it sounds like utter nonsense but this was serious business. Eventually the mother became a Quaker. In Massachusetts that was a crime punishable by death. Like others before her, she was hanged in June 1660.

In 1692/3, the charge of witchcraft led to the execution of twenty women and men in Salem Village after a number of adolescent girls developed mass hysteria[288]. In fact, long-standing disputes between neighbors were at the root of the animosity. The marriage of Church and State, a situation they had loathed and had escaped from in England, was instituted in Massachusetts. Anyone with beliefs different from the Puritan was in danger. The amount of local control over law and order was stronger than in other colonies where colonists did not necessarily have the rights of self-government. There, everything was dictated from three different sources above them: their magistrates (appointed by the company leadership), the company, and ultimately the King. Every enterprise and plantation was under the control of a corporation or single proprietor whose interests were primarily financial. As a rule, these new corporations were chartered in England.

Massachusetts was different. When John Winthrop had obtained the Royal charter for the Massachusetts Bay Colony, he had been able to leave the location of the company ambiguous. In 1630 he moved the company and all its proceedings to Massachusetts. With him came the Governor, the deputy Governor, assistants, and enough patentees to form a quorum. In the next several years they resolved to give voting rights to church members and freemen for the election of magistrates and legislators. In essence the government of the corporation had merged into the colony as a whole so that the colony was in fact an open corporation. Winthrop explained it thus, "When the patent was granted, the number of freemen was supposed to be so few, as they might well join in making laws; but now they were grown to so great a body, as it was not possible for them to make or execute laws, but they must choose others for that purpose." The colony's government had not grown out of municipal structures but out of corporate governance (with a strong role for the prevailing Puritan church). Eventually a legislature of two chambers was created. One was formed by proportional representation and the other by geographic representation.

The whole design gave the colonists the feeling that they were independent and the colony was virtually a republic. Inevitably, friction between the colony and the homeland increased over time. Britain imposed taxes without giving the colonies any say in how the money was to be used (taxation without representation) and it forbade the colonies to trade directly with the Caribbean. All goods had to be shipped via Britain, where they were subject to a tax.

Rhode Island, 1630s

Having been banned from Massachusetts, Francis Doughty, his wife Bridget, and their four children traveled south, possibly with the intention to go to the colony of Connecticut[289]. Traveling by way of the Rhode Island Plantation, they landed in a new settlement founded by religious dissidents[290]. Newport seemed a perfect fit. The family probably arrived in late 1640, shortly after the town voted, "that one hundred acres should be laid forth and appropriated for a school, for the encouragement of the poorer sort, to train up their youth in learning.[291]" The town had been founded in 1639 on the principals of civil liberty, social order, and religious freedom. After Portsmouth, it was the second truly democratic town in Rhode Island[292]. Portsmouth and Newport were then called Rhode

View of NEWPORT from Brenton's Cove.

Island Plantation and a royal charter for the whole area was not obtained until 1663. But as long as the area was British territory and subject to the ever-changing religious and political winds in the home country, religious tolerance would be elusive. With a group of people Francis developed a plan to settle in the New Netherlands where the Dutch Republic guaranteed freedom of religion.

The charter of 1663 united the Rhode Island Plantation with Providence and others into the colony of Rhode Island. The charter stipulated a democratic form of government. Also here the colony was corporate and also here the owners lived and worked in the colony. Rhode Island remained the most tolerant regarding religion of all colonies. It became a haven for the much maligned Quakers. However, being a corporation explains why commercial interests trumped moral ones. Newport and Bristol became the largest slave markets in the colonies[293]. The colony had a questionable distinction of being the only one in New England where slaves were both made to work and traded. Not surprisingly, it had the highest ratio of blacks to whites in New England. It was not until after the Revolution in 1784 that the legislature started a process of emancipation.

Adroit Adriaen

Some say a man inherits most traits from his maternal grandfather. It is quite possible that the genius of Captain Adriaen van Bergen was passed on that way as well. Made a military officer under the Dutch Prince Maurice[294], he was the owner-operator of a peat boat that supplied the Dutch fortress city of Breda. The city had changed hands a couple of times and was again occupied by Spanish troops. The Dutch Revolt had been going on for 22 years with many of the battles fought in and around the province of Brabant. The Dutch wanted to free the city and Captain van Bergen had a plan. On February 25th, 1590, two of his nephews poled their heavily laden peat boat through the canal to the gates of the walled city[295]. The winter was cold, the peat was stacked high. Spanish soldiers knew the brothers well and inspected the load only perfunctorily. Seeing nothing untoward, they ordered the gate opened and the boys slowly poled the boat inside the city. As many as sixty eight Dutch soldiers appeared from under the peat, seized the gates, and let in the bulk of the army. Breda was freed and with it the large swath of land under its control.

Adriaen van Bergen's daughter married Cornelis van der Donck. In 1618, she bore a son named Adriaen, after his maternal grandfather. Children from well-to-do families usually went to school around age five or six. It is unclear what happened to the family when, in 1625, the city was retaken by the Spanish. The family was committed to the Protestant religion and they were fierce patriots. It is hard to believe they stayed put. More likely they left for a place where the children could grow up in safety and receive a good education.

Breda again fell into Dutch control in 1637 and records show that Adriaen's parents were in Breda in the 1650s just before they left for America. There are no known records of the parents' whereabouts in the intervening years. It is certain, however, that Adriaen went to a Latin school. The Latin coursework was a prerequisite for admission to Law School. The early 17th century brought a philosophical, scientific, political, and educational revolution to the young Republic. Names such as Decartes, Huygens, Snellius, Grotius, and Stevin were found in new schools of higher education and universities. In the 1630s, many so-called *"Illustre Scholen"*[296] were established throughout the Dutch Republic. It was one of those schools that Adriaen would have attended and it had to be in such an environment that his interests in justice and the human condition were kindled.

In 1638, Adriaen entered the University of Leyden to study law[297]. The school was then the center of enlightened thinking in Europe. In the Republic, it was the center of religious freedom and the city enjoyed complete freedom of expression and the press. A major influence on Adriaen's thinking were likely the philosophies of Grotius[298], often described as the father of modern international law[299]. Descartes, who taught at Leyden, published his *Discourse on Method* there in 1637. Even Isaac Newton chose to publish his *Discourses and Mathematical Demonstrations Concerning Two Sciences* at Leyden in 1638.

Descartes's thinking was revolutionary. Traditionally churches, of all denominations, and monarchs dictated how and what the people had to believe. Descartes declared thinking was the purview of the individual and could not be dictated by authority. At Leyden, great advances were made in Science, Mathematics, Medicine, Philosophy, Law, and related fields. Despite his exile[300], Hugo Grotius's philosophies on "Natural Law" were highly popular at the university. Grotius suggested that the determination of right and wrong could be made through the application of human reasoning rather than biblical citations. The Age of the Individual was awakening.

In this environment, Adriaen received his education. An authority on Roman-Dutch law, he graduated in 1641 and would have done well for himself in the booming economy of the rich Republic. However, he wanted to do something more exciting and go to the colony in America, the New Netherlands. Through family connections, he got in touch with

Samuel Blommaert[301] in Amsterdam. Blommaert was one of the directors of the Dutch West-India Company. However, Adriaen found the Dutch West-India Company, which ran the colony, too regimented. During his inquiries, he spoke with another of the company's directors, Kiliaen van Rensselaer. Oddly, this Amsterdam diamond merchant privately owned several thousand acres of land up the Hudson River, purchased from the Mohicans, and eighty miles from the nearest Dutch settlement. His fief was eleven years old and populated with farmers, carpenters, bricklayers, smiths, and all kinds of other specialists. The rapid development and success of the up-country colony contrasted with the economic stagnation at New Amsterdam that suffered under the stifling rules of the Dutch West-India Company (DWIC). Also oddly, van Rensselaer managed his affairs from Amsterdam and had never visited America. The success of his enterprise led to a logical problem: the settlement was without a government to provide it with the leadership, law, and order a growing community required. The young lawyer knocked on the director's door at exactly the right time.

New Netherlands, 1640s [302]

At the south side of Manhattan, the new Schout[303] of Van Rensselaerswyck disembarked from the *Compagnieschip Den Eickenboom*[304] into a sloop[305]. Adriaen must have been elated that the long ocean journey had come to an end and his adventure in America was about to start. The Dutch were a seafaring people, but life aboard ship was usually Spartan. Against a backdrop of islands and waterways and undulating forests, the small town appearance of New Amsterdam would have been a delight for the eye. There were probably a number of ships and boats in *De Baai*[306], as the harbor was then known. Once on land, Adriaen would have encountered a rich hustle and bustle. All this activity was quite new. In response to the over-regulation and subsequent stagnation in the colony, the DWIC had just relinquished its trade monopoly and declared the whole province a free trade zone. Instead of smugglers and pirates, the town now attracted merchants, farmers, and tradesmen. In addition to the numerous transients, there were about four hundred permanent residents of many nationalities and religions.

Adriaen walked to the fort and delivered a letter of introduction to the Governor of the New Netherlands, Willem Kieft. After a brief, formal meeting, Adriaen left to make arrangements for his journey north.

As early as 1540, French traders had built a fort on Castle Island in the Hudson River just south of present day Albany[307]. It washed away, but the Dutchman Adrian Block built a few huts and rebuilt the fort in 1614. It too

Adriaen van der Donck

flooded and the DWIC built Fort Orange on the shore in 1624. The land on both sides of the river and surrounding the fort was in the hands of Adriaen's new employer. Rensselaerswyck had around one hundred permanent residents. The Dutch outpost was a mere speck in the endless wilderness. But it was flourishing. The manager provided him with a small house on a small island and all looked well.

In late 1641 or early 1642, Francis Doughty set out for a visit to New Amsterdam. The Dutch had an active policy for the settling of Nassau (present day Long Island, NY) and English refugees from New England would do just fine. Francis knew that, as a colony of the Dutch Republic, it enjoyed freedom of religion. He wanted to speak with Governor Kieft to see if he could acquire land for a settlement. To his delight, the visit was a success and he was granted a patent on March 28, 1642 for 13,333 acres of land on the island of Nassau[308]. He received manorial privileges as "patroon"[309] and absolute power to do as he pleased in his domain. Once again, the family moved on and they made their home at Mespacht[310]. Perhaps right away or shortly afterwards, they were joined by a Richard Smith and a number of other friends from Massachusetts and Rhode Island. They built houses and set out to work the land. Francis and Bridget's children were growing up fast. Their oldest, Mary, was now fourteen years old and labored alongside her parents.

While the Doughtys were developing their settlement, an unfortunate incident near New Amsterdam involving an old fur trader and a young Wickquasgeck[311] ended with the old man's head being cut off. For the young man, it was a simple act of revenge for a massacre committed against his family some fifteen years earlier. As happens so often when two cultures fail to understand each other, the reaction was all out of proportion. Governor Kieft nursed tyrannical tendencies and during his tenure, he had been hard on the native tribesmen. The result had been that many tribes, who normally disliked each other, now formed an alliance against the common enemy. True to form, Kieft sent out a force to avenge the old fur trader's death and inevitably a number of innocent natives were killed. Equally inevitably, the full fury of the tribes landed on the colonists in the outposts. Although Francis's relationship with the locals was good, they attacked the small settlement of Mespacht in September 1643[312]. Some of the men were killed, their cattle were stolen or killed, and all their houses and barns were burned. The survivors were lucky to escape with their lives to the safety of New Amsterdam. Francis Doughty and his family and friends had again lost their livelihoods and their homes. One source has it that Francis' wife, Bridget, died that year[313]. It is possible she was among the murdered.

Adriaen van der Donck chose to ignore some of his employer's instructions. He did make many sorties into the wilderness and on occasion caught an inattentive smuggler or two. But mostly he used the time to study the natural environment and the culture of the local tribes, whom he learned to respect. He had a strong sense of justice and developed empathy for the people who were under contract with van Rensselaer. Instead of punishing them for non-performance, he tried to improve the conditions of their work environment. His employer's correspondence became more heated. Van Rensselaer accused Adriaen of behaving like a manager rather than a policeman. It became clear that his job would come to an end. Largely thanks to Adriaen's peaceful interaction with the locals, Rensselaerswyck did not suffer the fate of its southern counterparts. But headquarters was micromanaging without the benefit of local knowledge. Using his contacts with the Mohawks, Adriaen tried to purchase land of his own. Upon hearing about his lawman's apparent defection, van Rensselaer quickly instructed his manager to preempt the purchase by buying it himself[314]. Eventually, van Rensselaer's health failed him and he died in 1643[315] before the terms of Adriaen's contract expired. In 1644 the heirs did not renew them. Adriaen had enough of the job anyway. The stubborn young man packed up and located to New Amsterdam.

Francis Doughty and his family were reasonably content with their lives in New Amsterdam. Francis had first become an acting minister to the English. Being very independent, it wasn't long before he founded his own church. It was the very first Presbyterian Church in the Americas. But he had not given up on his settlement at Mespacht. Together with other similarly displaced colonists, he strongly opposed Governor Kieft's policy regarding the natives. But the colonists did not know how to counter the dictatorial Kieft. Since 1623, the colony was officially a full-fledged province of the Dutch Republic[316]. All Dutch laws applied. Among the rights that they had been denied were the rights of assembly and elected government. The colonists did organize themselves, and wrote petitions to the DWIC's directors in Amsterdam. They also understood that the directors had only a commercial interest in the colony. So they wrote to the States General in 'sGravenhage. But without knowledge of the law and its proper language they were floundering.

A young, recently unemployed lawyer walked into town. News traveled fast in the small colony. Adriaen must have been well aware of the troubles between the Governor and the colonists. In October 1643, Adriaen attended a clandestine meeting of the activists[317]. They had learned to go underground after Governor Kieft started to arrest opponents at will. Adriaen was tickled with the prospect of taking on this interesting case. The colony was subject to a glaring conflict of interest. While it was a part of the Netherlands and subject to Dutch law, it was also the property of a large commercial concern, the DWIC. This marriage of interests was concentrated in the office of Governor, who was also the company's Director for North America. The conflict of interest extended all the way to the Republic. Many representatives in the States General, or their clients, also held financial interests in the company. Furthermore, the company had been brought to life by that same States General. The Republic's government had no court of law[318] in which to bring the case against either the company or the States General. In fact, the States General had appointed itself as the appropriate court of national and international law. The Republic was a confederation in which the States were responsible for their own legal affairs. Everything regarding their union was handled by the States General.

The meeting produced a sharply worded petition that outlined Governor Kieft's dictatorial behavior and policy failings. The document was smuggled out of the colony and taken to the DWIC directors in Amsterdam. Unaware of the petition, Kieft now insisted that the Long Island settlers return to their land. With his usual directness, Francis Doughty told Kieft that if he thought it was safe he should camp out there himself[319]. Equally hot-headed, the Governor rescinded the land grant at Mespacht and had the minister locked up for a day.

On another front, the Governor did understand that he needed a better relationship with the native tribes. When a conflict broke out between colonists and natives near Fort Orange, he knew just the person to help. A group of soldiers accompanied Governor Kieft, a council member from New Amsterdam, and advisor Adriaen van der Donck on their journey north to Fort Orange near Rensselaerswyck. Kieft did not know of Adriaen's involvement with the angry colonists and the lawyer was not about to enlighten him. The mission was in the interest of all parties. After some difficulties due to Kieft's unpreparedness, Adriaen managed the negotiations to a good conclusion. The Governor was grateful and so were the colonists.

In June 1645 Francis Doughty was suing a man for singing a slanderous song about his daughter Mary[320]. It so happened that Adriaen was in court that day, too. Perhaps he was Francis's lawyer. In the small community, it is hard to imagine this would have been the first meeting between Adriaen and Mary. A romance developed. In July that year Kieft's gratitude towards Adriaen materialized in the form of a large land grant adjacent to Manhattan. With Francis as one of the signatories, a peace with the native tribes was concluded in August. Adriaen and Mary wasted no time. They married in October, started the development of their land, and moved there permanently in 1646[321]. Today only the name Yonkers remains. It was derived from the Dutch title *Jonkheer*, meaning young lord, by which Adriaen was known.

All was well except that in England, Cromwell had defeated King Charles and that all the British colonies were in turmoil. At the same time, the colonists of New Netherlands intensified their opposition to the DWIC and their director, Kieft. Behind the scenes, Adriaen had helped the opposition. The colonists understood that it had been van der Donck who had brought peace with the natives. Furthermore, they found that, with the lawyer a wealthy and important man, they were well positioned to carry the fight for a free land all the way to the Republic's government, the States General.

As a result of their petitions, Kieft was recalled. Finally, in 1647, he awaited the ship that brought his replacement and that would take him back to Holland. The mood in town was festive. The new Governor and Director was a successful naval officer whose legacy had traveled ahead of him. He was missing one leg and his name was Pieter Stuyvesant. He arrived with strict orders: keep the colonists in line. The colonists had jumped from the frying pan into the fire.

Stuyvesant had read the entire file on the colony. He knew the issues and he knew the players. His upbringing on the farm and his military training had made him a creature of orders, given and received. The colonists were trained in self-reliance. They had survived and enjoyed the freedoms that come with seafaring, trading, and life on the frontier. Perhaps without even knowing of the great philosophers, they were living the ideals of Descartes and Grotius. They were in charge of themselves. So, while the new Governor settled in, the colonists were working on a plan for representative government. In their belief, it was a universal right and under Dutch law it was their right. Van der Donck shaped the fiery arguments into legal argument and trusted them to paper. However, he kept his role hidden from Stuyvesant and tried to win his friendship. Stuyvesant also perceived advantage in a good relationship with the powerful lawyer. The fact that Stuyvensant's wife and Adriaen both hailed from Breda probably helped forge a bond. Extensive meetings and correspondences ensued between the Governor, the colonists, and the DWIC in Amsterdam. Kieft had wanted two colonists tried in Holland on a charge of sedition. Instead, the colonists demanded that the two be heard locally as patriots[322]. Stuyvesant quickly approved this course of action. With the British colonies in turmoil after Cromwell defeated King Charles in England, he had more important matters to attend to.

And so Kieft and his opponents boarded for the Republic. When their ship wrecked on the rocks of Wales, that part of the dispute died along with the disputants.

The civil war in England caused the British colonies to rely more than ever on Manhattan as their trading hub. Winthrop in Massachusetts recognized this as much as Stuyvesant did. Fortune had it that the four New England colonies had just attended a meeting in Boston when the Dutch envoy arrived. Winthrop soon sent Stuyvesant a joint letter declaring, "*hoping all the English colonies shall enjoy within your limits all the fruites of a neighbourly and friendly correspondency in a free concourse,*" and signed the letter with, "*Your loving Friends the Commissioners of the vnited Colonies.*[323]" This correspondence amounted to a memorandum of understanding between five North American territories that behaved very much like independent republics.

Stuyvesant could now look south and address the Swedish colony that had been established ten years earlier under, ironically, two Dutch ministers. Slowly but surely, the Dutch took repossession of the territories in present day New Jersey, Delaware, and Pennsylvania.

Meanwhile, Francis Doughty had moved to Vlissingen (present day Flushing on Long Island) where he was again a minister and active in local affairs. The colonists were still clamoring for some form of democratic government. What ultimately swayed Stuyvesant was what had swayed rulers in the past: funding. By granting some form of participation in government, he would be able to tax the colonists and raise more funds for important projects, such as defenses for New Amsterdam. The Governor agreed that the towns should elect eighteen representatives. Stuyvesant would select nine of them to serve on his council. Adriaen was not among them, but some of his close friends were. He probably calculated that his influence would be greater if he remained friends with the Governor while coaching his own acquaintances behind the scenes.

Peter Stuyvesant

Stuyvesant did make good use of Adriaen's services. When an Englishman arrived in the Dutch towns of Long Island and declared he had been made governor, Adriaen was sent to reassure the populace. The usurper was eventually put in irons and shipped off to Holland. Adriaen advised Stuyvesant in matters concerning the Mohawks (whom he knew so well) and the virtual republic of Rensselaerswyck up on the Hudson (where he had worked). The Governor tried to subjugate the fiefdom, but the manager was a fierce opponent. Stuyvesant and Adriaen van de Donck traveled north and the lawyer made their case in the local court in 1648. The outcome is uncertain, but events make clear that the Governor and his legal advisor made a good team. Stuyvesant was delighted when, in December, Adriaen was elected to New Amsterdam's governing Board and he wasted no time in appointing his valuable friend to the Board of Nine. The colonists were equally delighted and the Board gave him the title

"President of the Commonality." Unlike the Council, which was a company body, the Board was representative of the people. At first the Governor approved of the Board's actions and collaboration with him but, as is the case with most new representative bodies, it soon started to lead a life of its own.

In January 1649, Stuyvesant received a letter informing him that the Board intended to send one or more members to 'sGravenhage with an appeal to the Dutch government to take over the colony from the DWIC. Stuyvesant was understandably furious, especially since his friend and legal advisor was leading the Board. However, the letter was not so much intended as a vote of no confidence in the Governor, but more a reflection of changing conditions. The Peace of Westphalia in 1648 had ended the 80 Year War and the 30 Year War in Europe. Raids and piracy, the main reason for the founding of the DWIC, were no longer part of the income stream in America. Adriaen and the Board held extensive consultations with traders and manufacturers and concluded that Manhattan's large natural harbor and its location on the east coast of America made it the preeminent trading center. This was all the more so while England remained in a state of civil war. A proper civic government modeled on that of the Republic was required to take full advantage.

That same month a ship arrived from Holland. To everyone's amazement, it carried a survivor of the ship that had wrecked on the rocks of Wales. It was one of the two disputants with Kieft and he carried a stack of official papers from the government in 'sGravenhage. The gist was that Kieft had been wrong in just about everything, that Stuyvesant had been wrong in his sentencing of disputants, that both Kieft and Stuyvesant had hampered the representatives of the people, and that Stuyvesant or his representative had to travel home to explain his conduct. To put a big fat exclamation mark on it, the documents included a letter from Prince William of Orange admonishing the Governor to obey the States General's resolutions and respect the population's freedoms of life, limb, and property.

The Board needed no further prodding. Its members divided the streets of New Amsterdam among themselves and started to knock on doors and collect opinions. These were compiled in a dossier. Adriaen took on the task of distilling the essence into a single document. Stuyvesant confronted Adriaen with what he considered a betrayal. When his onetime friend neither backed down nor apologized, the Governor broke off personal ties. However, the two needed each other. Tensions were rising between the Republic and England, which, ironically, had just overthrown its King and was functioning like a republic under Cromwell. Adriaen understood that Stuyvesant was a great military leader and Stuyvesant knew that he needed the population to stand behind his efforts to save the colony from conquest by the English. The population was very international with the Dutch and the English making up the largest groups. Adriaen knew that the people required a firm stake in the affairs of the colony and that only self-government could bring that about. Without it the colony would dissolve from within.

Unfortunately Stuyvesant could not reconcile himself with what he called rabble-rousing liars, usurers, and spendthrifts. He imprisoned Adriaen and another board member and called an emergency meeting of his Council and a few members of the Board. After much maneuvering, and on the verge of a popular uprising, the Governor eventually had to stand down and recognize the power of the people and their board, which had been unequivocally confirmed by the government of the Republic. Even his erstwhile supporters and some underlings were now against him. Adriaen van der Donck was a free man. He was banned from the Board, but had gained the admiration of the people. Stuyvesant had attached a condition for his release – that Adriaen would review the survey and prove his conclusions or recant. The lawyer was delighted since he had been given license to continue his reform work. Adriaen put all issues on paper with the intention of making his case in front of the States General in 'sGravenhage. In May, Stuyvesant accused Adriaen of having obtained unlawful and unverifiable "depositions from private persons", but it didn't stop the lawyer. By the end of June, the "Remonstrance of New Netherland" was complete. The eighty-four pages included a compilation of the opinions of the people, a history of Dutch discovery and development, the legitimacy of the Dutch claims to its American territory, and his vision for the future.

Stuyvesant could not stop his opponents from going to 'sGravenhage. Being involved in delicate negotiations with the New England colonies, he could not go himself. He sent his very partisan assistant instead. The Board of Nine chose Adriaen and two others and, at the end of July, a former pirate vessel took the opposing parties across the ocean.

In the ten years that separated Adriaen from his country both had changed. Having brought its enemies to their knees, the Republic was at the pinnacle of its power and was the wealthiest nation in the world. Adriaen had grown up into a man with unusual experiences and an unusual vision. He and his friends had become Americans – a word that he was the first to apply to the people living in America, including colonists, and that recurred frequently in his writings as a concept of identity[324].

Adriaen van der Donck and his friends received their opportunity to address a special committee of the States General on October 13, 1649. He presented his arguments for a democratic government free from the oppression of the DWIC with great flourish. He submitted a large map of the American east coast showing the extent of the colony and Manhattan's central position as a trading hub. He showed the gathering a beautiful colored pen drawing of New Amsterdam. He painted the dire economic and political conditions under the DWIC, but outlined the colony's potential wealth and emphasized his point with a display of pelts, fruits, corn, and other products. Many of the representatives were impressed, but the outcome was uncertain at best. The DWIC was very powerful. The delegates' hopes for a swift resolution were dashed by two outside events that distracted the States General.

In 1649, Cromwell had King Charles beheaded. The execution of a monarch added support to the argument of Republicans in the Netherlands that a monarchy is not god given, but rather a gift of the people. And that gift could be taken away by the people. The Republic had its own noble family, the Orange-Nassaus. Its current Prince William was the head of the armed forces and had the title of Stadholder. His son, also William, was married to King Charles' daughter, Mary Stuart[325]. It followed that a rising number of voices in the Netherlands called for the abolition of the office of Stadholder. The war with Spain over, the States General's voted to draw down the army. Prince William did not help his position when he applied military force in response. With the memory of Prince Maurice of Orange fresh in their minds, the States General acted swiftly and abolished the office of Stadholder in November 1650.

Adriaen and his fellow Americans did not sit still. They found a publisher to print the Remonstrance, which became a best-seller and enticed many to want to emigrate. The first ship had to turn away hundreds, so more ships followed. Even Adriaen's mother and siblings sold their belongings and prepared to go. The DWIC now faced a conflict. But even as they were fighting the obnoxious lawyer, they also benefited from his salesmanship. By April, 1650, the States General found time to rule on the dispute under the title, "Provisional Order respecting the Government, Preservation, and Peopling of New Netherland." The verdict put the blame on the officials of the DWIC and they called Stuyvesant home to report. New Amsterdam was to have an elected council, but the DWIC would remain. The Americans got nearly all they had clamored for. Adriaen hastily composed a letter to a respected figure in the colony who had previously been neutral, and invited him to join the new government. He stayed on in 'sGravenhage to be sure that the States General would carry out the special committee's recommendations and used the time to work out the format of the new government. He wanted the colony to become the eighth State of the Dutch Union.

During these exciting years, Francis Doughty and his son Elias led a seemingly quiet life in Flushing. Occasionally he received written word from the court of law in Boston about the dogged pursuits of his sister Elizabeth Cole[326]. She continued her quest for compensation for her brother's alleged theft of their inheritance. It may have been a hefty estate since their father had been a well to do merchant and brewer in Bristol, England. She had moved to New Hampshire in 1644, but after her husband died, she returned to Boston to reopen the case in May 1647. She obtained a court order for a letter to be sent to her brother. It gave Francis six months to produce a copy of the disputed deed, in the absence of which the Court would decide the best it could. Francis ignored it. In October 1648, Elizabeth Cole again went to the Court, which tiredly ruled that they would summon her brother provided she put up a security for charges and damages. Apparently meeting no success, she again petitioned in May 1649 and again in May 1650. She must have been in a desperate state of mind and failing in health. The Massachusetts Colonial Records state: 10 October, 1650, "being visited with longe & sore sicknes, & bailing spent all her estate," she petitioned for help and the government granted £20. On 14 October, 1651, John Lewes petitioned for fifty shillings expended for her "mayntenance"

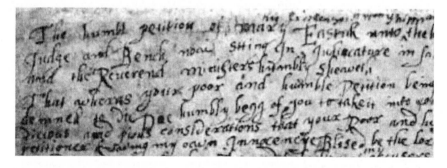

and it was granted, "it beinge the last the country is like to pay for her, whose extremity was such as deserued pitty". The last court action came in May, 1652, in the form of a grant to pay a final "phyeician's" bill.

Back in New Amsterdam, Stuyvesant felt beleaguered from all sides. Adriaen's volleys kept coming in the form of a stream of correspondence and the directors of the DWIC were angry with him about his erstwhile friendliness with their nemesis van der Donck. Stuyvesant's vice-director had earlier chosen to side with the colonists and now had to pay for it by being thrown in prison. Meanwhile, in spite of all those distractions, the Governor kept up his successful diplomacy with the British colonies. Stuyvesant impressed his neighbors to the north with brazen assertiveness when he had a Dutch smuggler ship in New Haven boarded and taken to

New Amsterdam. He countered the protests from the British colony with a reminder that New Haven was in Dutch territory[327] and that he had every right to take a Dutch offender. He also sent respectful and conciliatory letters to the new Governor of Massachusetts while reminding him of the might of the Dutch Navy. The result was that the New England governors and Stuyvesant agreed to work out their disputes in a meeting at Hartford. Although the town was inhabited by English, it was an historic claim of the Dutch who maintained a small fort nearby. For all intents and purposes, the meeting was that between heads of state of their respective republics. There was no involvement of the colonial masters in Europe. The final agreement established a permanent boundary between the territories. Stuyvesant gave up Hartford and Connecticut, which were already entirely settled by the English, and eastern Long Island, the boundary being that between present day Nassau and Suffolk Counties.

The Netherlands, 1650s

In 1651, Mary Doughty crossed the Atlantic to join her husband Adriaen, who still was in 'sGravenhage. They had been apart for two years. Stuyvesant's assistant was fighting the accusations Adriaen had brought against him in the States General. The lawyer found unexpected help from an age-old human weakness when the Director's assistant had found himself engaged with a young woman and maintained a room for that purpose. He had failed to share with her that he had a wife and children in America. When the affair came to light, he was arrested, fined, and put on a ship together with his amour.

With his opponent out of the way, Adriaen appeared before the entire governing body of the Republic on February 10, 1652. He made the same case as before, but added the many dispatches he had received from the colony since his last appearance. The High Mightiness, as they were known, understood that the community of Manhattan had advanced from a ragtag collection of fur traders, soldiers, and whores to one of respectable citizens for whom martial law was no longer appropriate. Eventually Adriaen's victory was crowned with a letter he was to present to Stuyvesant in person. In it, the States General called the Governor back home. Adriaen was to resume his position of President of the Commonalities.

With this indisputable victory in his pocket, he started to make preparations to return to New Amsterdam. His estate had been neglected during his three-year absence and both Mary and he hired new personnel in the Republic. There was no shortage of applicants. They purchased equipment and supplies and in May, Adriaen requested permission from the government to leave. Finally, in July 1652, the ship carrying Adriaen's mother, other family members, his wife Mary, their new hires, and all their supplies pushed off and sailed to America. But Adriaen was not on board.

Fourteen years earlier, another ship had left for America without a booked passenger. That ship had left from London and the man was Oliver Cromwell[328]. The reason both were left behind was a refusal by the governing authorities to let them depart. Cromwell went on to lead a parliamentary revolt, had King Charles beheaded in 1649, and eventually became England's Lord Protector. One of his ambitions was to see England become the primary maritime power, which put him in direct conflict with the Republic.

England passed the first Navigation Act in 1650. It declared that only British ships could bring goods from British colonies to British ports. Dutch merchants did not comply. The colonies did not either, since the Act put them at the mercy of English merchants who had been given a monopoly. More by accident than by design, a sea battle broke out in the English Channel and the two nations were heading toward war. As a consequence, the DWIC, which had been weakened by the peace of 1648 as well as Adriaen's assaults, came back with a vengeance. The States General needed their powerful navy. The States rescinded their order for Stuyvesant to come home, rescinded their orders for the Governor to hand over government to the Board and the people, rescinded permission for Adriaen to sail, and ordered him to hand back the letter he was carrying for Stuyvesant. A hero only a few weeks earlier, Adriaen had become a dangerous subversive. It was a grave mistake and might have caused the colony to fall to the British sooner than it did, if it would have fallen at all. The Anglo-Dutch war was a turning point for the two nations as well. Separated by the sliver of water once called the "Narrow Sea", the two peoples were more alike and akin than any other two nations in Europe. Of course there had been occasional quarrels as happens between close relatives. Cromwell had energetically built up his navy while the Dutch had weakened theirs in part to weaken the monarchical ambitions of the Prince of Orange. The war was fought entirely at sea – another novelty.

But, it left Adriaen stranded. Instead of being listless, he frantically traveled between 'sGravenhage, Amsterdam, Leyden, and Breda to further his cause[329]. In Leyden, he obtained a law degree that allowed him to appear before the highest court. In Amsterdam, he gained a meeting with officials of the DWIC, only to be called a "notorious ringleader ... of a lawless and mutinous rabble." In 'sGravenhage he appealed to the government, but found no sympathy. Always a fighter, he started writing about the colony and its huge potential. It was eventually published in 1655 under the name, *A Description of New Netherland*. As if clairvoyant, he described how, modeled on the Republic, America would become a haven for refugees from "eastern Europe, Germany, Westphalia, Scandinavia, Wallonia, etc." and how they could find opportunity in the Dutch system; a system that was free, capitalist, tolerant, and social all at once. His ideals proved so remote that late in 1653, his quest had been thoroughly crushed and the government deemed it safe to give Adriaen permission to return home. It may sound familiar to us that in a nation at war, the corporate powers and commercial interests win out over the power of the people. Adriaen promised to refrain from all public engagement and obey the Company[330]. Then he went on to hire a number of artisans in Amsterdam to work on his estate, and eventually sailed back to Manhattan in the winter of 1653/54.

Manhattan, New Netherlands, 1650s

Stuyvesant made sure not to be burned again by the wily lawyer. He refused him access to the archives (presumably for research for his upcoming book about New Netherland) and banned him from practicing law, knowing that no one in the colony could match Adriaen's knowledge and cunning. Adriaen was busy anyway. His estate had suffered during

New Amsterdam, 1641

his absence. He had much planning to do and put to work the artisans he brought back with him. And then he had to help settle the relatives that had come over.

But politics would not leave him alone. To the colonists and their representatives, he was still a hero and they sought his advice. New arrivals from both the Republic and New England swelled the population of the towns near Manhattan and inevitably attracted thieves and pirates[331]. One notorious fellow specialized in stealing horses up and down the north coast of Nassau[332]. Several leaders, which no doubt included Francis Doughty in Flushing, demanded action from the DWIC, failing which they would not pay their taxes. Stuyvesant accused them of siding with England in the war. It is true that most were of English descent, but they preferred relatively free Dutch rule over invigorated Puritan rule of the English.

In 1653, the people of seven towns presented Stuyvesant with a petition[333] that was written in English but followed Dutch legal forms. It was similar in tone to Adriaen's earlier writings and complained of the "arbitrary government" of Stuyvesant's. They wanted what New Amsterdam had — a municipal government – and that city supported their demand. Stuyvesant suspected Adriaen's hand, but there was no proof. More likely, the colonists had by now learned enough from their friend and from books shipped from the Republic to make compelling arguments themselves. All that Adriaen was guilty of was that he had started a movement that still was alive and well. Nevertheless, Stuyvesant rejected the petition. In June 1654 the first Anglo-Dutch War came to an end.

New Amsterdam again prospered. Foreigners flocked in, streets were paved, and new neighborhoods went up. But the city remained very Dutch in appearance[334]. It was clean, well kept, and organized.

After the publication of his book about the colony in 1655, there are few references to Adriaen. He probably concluded that he had done all that could be done. He had failed and he had succeeded. He must have spent more time at home, away from the limelight in the City. In September 1655 there was a raid by natives[335] on his *boerderij*[336]. He was killed or mortally wounded. His wife, Mary, survived.

Maryland and Virginia, 1650s

Francis Doughty was called upon by Stuyvesant to help resolve a problem with newly arrived Quaker refugees from New England. Dutch Protestant ministers had complained about them. Since the Quakers had more or less settled in Francis' town, Flushing, Stuyvesant wanted him to become their minister[337]. The Quakers, who have no ministers in their church, refused. Some say that Francis joined them, which is hard to believe considering his theology.

In any case, Francis was on the move shortly thereafter. Perhaps it was the death of his son-in-law, Adriaen, perhaps it was his fellow minister in the City, Samuel Diisius, who told him of an offer for a parish of his own. Perhaps it was many reasons combined, but in late 1655, he was preaching in the border area of Maryland and Virginia[338]. The latter was the oldest of the North American colonies, but had become early on, unlike the others, a royal colony with a governor appointed by the King. That fact, however, had not erased the sense of independence that the republican constitution of Edwin Sandys had instilled and confirmed[339].

Edwin's brother, George, had been Virginia's treasurer from 1621 to 1628,[340] during which time its ownership was transferred from a company to the Crown. However, the House of Burgesses, Virginia's version of popular representation, was still in place. As would be the case in New Netherland, conflict between an authoritarian owner and the colonists could not be avoided. As early as 1624, Virginia's Assembly passed a resolution denying the King the right of taxation. The Assembly asserted that only it could do that. The conflict continued at varying levels of intensity. In 1651, one year after Charles's beheading and when England was ruled by Parliament, that body passed a second Navigation Act to bring the rebellious colony into submission. In January of the following year, an expeditionary fleet arrived.

The governor at the time was sympathetic to the colonists. His response was most interesting. He ordered his 1,200 man strong militia into position and asked visiting Dutch vessels to arm themselves for resistance. Being at risk of confiscation under the new act, the Dutchmen needed little persuasion. For all intents and purposes, Virginia acted like an independent nation and called on another to come to its aid.

As it was, no shots were fired. The commander of the British fleet asked to be allowed on shore and negotiations got underway. The Dutch ships slipped away. Knowing that they ultimately could not resist the home country, the colonists gave in and signed the Act of Surrender. Curiously, the name implied the surrender of one jurisdiction to another. Certainly a colony did not fit that description. More curiously, the agreement was not a surrender at all. The articles were those of a treaty[341]. The General Assembly would govern Virginia, England recognized the colony's rights given in past and present Royal charters, and Virginia should have free trade while only the Grand Assembly of the Governor could approve or impose taxes. All this did not end the wrangling between Crown and colony and it continued through the reign of Oliver Cromwell.

Maryland and Virginia, 1660s

Francis Doughty found a rich land populated with rich people. There were thirteen counties, most along the James and York Rivers, some 20,000 non-native people of whom 6,000 were indentured servants, and

500 African slaves[342]. He settled in Northampton County, on Virginia's Eastern Shore, where he became rector of an Episcopal church[343]. As ever, he was controversial. Some parishioners loved him (he was mentioned in a will), and others loathed him. In 1658 he married Ann Eaton, the widow of his predecessor (who also had been the brother of a former governor of Maryland[344]). Apparently he was in Maryland sometime in 1659. His daughter (Adriaen van der Donck's widow, Mary) had followed him to Maryland. She was childless[345] and only around thirty years of age. She met and married a Captain Hugh O'Neal there[346]. He may have been a chaplain[347]. Francis was preaching for a short time at Patuxent, where he was visited by Dutch Commissioners who were trying to resolve a boundary dispute with Maryland. In 1662, the couple showed up in the records of Rappahannock County[348] where Francis was rector of two parishes on opposite sides of the river. Virginia was entering a period of repression similar to that in England where King Charles II embarked on a policy of ignoring Parliament. Virginia's governor likewise ignored the House of Burgesses. On issues of economics and trade, the governor was a strong defender of the colony's rights and treatment by the Crown, but at a local level he was reactionary. "...I thank God," he wrote, "there are no free schools nor printing, and I hope we shall not have these in a hundred years. For learning has brought disobedience and heresy, and sects into the world, and printing has divulged them, and libels against the best government.[349]" Of course he had conveniently forgotten how his own Protestant religion had come about. The Puritans in Massachusetts and some Protestants in New Netherlands suffered from the same amnesia.

In 1662 Francis and Ann Eaton[350] bought 200 acres of land[351]. It is remarkable that real trouble between Francis and his parishioners took six years to develop, but in 1668 an argument with two prominent members ended up before the County Commissioners. Apparently "he denied the supremacy of the King contrary to the canons of the Church of England.[352]" – no surprise there. Having been fired from Sittingbourne parish, he made preparations to leave. He placed his farm under trustees for the benefit of his wife, declaring that he would go, "to some other country that may prove more favorable to my aged, infirm and decayed body than where I now reside." He sounded like a man whose good intentions were routinely misconstrued. Maybe his wife misconstrued them, too. She decided to stay with her kindred. That same day Francis had a deed drawn up that stipulated the reversion of his property to his youngest son, Enoch, who lived with his family in Maryland.

Maryland was founded in 1634 by Lord Baltimore, a Catholic, when Catholics were suffering from persecutions in England as badly, or worse, than other minority religions. It was a proprietary colony where its owner, Baltimore, held absolute power. To his representatives and first settlers he gave the strict instruction that, "to preserve peace and unity and avoid all occasion of offense, that all Protestants be treated with as much mildness and favor as justice will permit, and that all Roman Catholics abstain from public discourse concerning matters of religion and perform all their religious acts as privately as circumstances would permit," and proclaimed in 1638 that, "disputes tending to the opening of a faction in religion, shall

A Settler's Log Cabin

From a drawing based upon contemporary sources

be suppressed. " His intentions were good, but it was imposed from above and had not come from the colonists themselves. As elsewhere, the colonists resented their lack of influence. There was an assembly of the people, but under the Charter only Baltimore had the right to propose and approve laws. It came to a head as quickly as 1637 when the Assembly asserted its will by first voting down all of Baltimore's proposals and then approving their own. The Assembly's proposals were not very different from the lord's. Baltimore accepted the process and, by doing so, transferred the power of legislating to the

Assembly[353]. The structure of government was improved in 1639 and again in 1650. Maryland then adopted an Upper and a Lower House of Assembly; the Governor, his Council, and people summoned by special writ forming the first and the second elected by the freemen (people with property). As in other colonies, people who had found freedom for their own religion were intolerant of others'. In spite of the Toleration Act of 1649 and 1650[354] in Maryland, this led to several "civil wars" which the Crown attempted to settle in 1689 by making it a Royal Colony and declaring the Church of England the church of the Province.

Francis's daughter, Mary, stayed in Maryland, as did his son Enoch. His sons Francis and Elias remained in Flushing, where Elias was involved in a protest about religious tolerance. After Francis unsuccessfully intervened on the behest of Governor Stuyvesant in a problem concerning newly arrived

Quakers, Stuyvesant banned all Quaker meetings. Of course they were held anyway and, in 1657, a respected resident of Flushing was fined and banished. A number of townspeople protested their Governor's intolerance and drew up a document dated December 27, 1657 and known as the Flushing Remonstrance. It was signed by people of different denominations and was America's first popular appeal for religious tolerance. Unfortunately Stuyvesant continued his policy. He also continued to suppress the people's participation in government. When the English fleet arrived in 1664, the people had little enthusiasm to defend their limited freedoms and refused to take up arms and defend their colony. Stuyvesant had no choice other than to surrender the colony to the British.

English rule proved a disappointment since the Duke of York, the later King James who later was deposed by William of Orange, was an autocratic proprietary ruler. But the people had not forgotten Adriaen van der Donck's ideals. Dutch-Roman law would survive in the laws of New York.

One source stated that Francis Doughty moved back to Maryland and died there[355]. The Doughty DNA Project[356] states that he died in Maryland on March 2, 1682, but this author has not been able to confirm this. In every colony he visited he experienced the birth, infancy, or growing pains of virtual republics and saw the development of the rule of law and democracy. He suffered the small-mindedness of religious intolerance in Massachusetts, lived among the free in Rhode Island, learned about the powers and limitations, of the people in New Netherland, and witnessed the evolution of participatory government in both Virginia and Maryland. Mostly he followed the footsteps of others, but in New Netherland he was, briefly, a pioneer. He mixed with the movers and shakers and quite literally lived the beginnings of what would become the American Nation.

*If justice, good faith, honor, gratitude & all the other Qualities which enoble
the character of a nation, and fulfil the ends of Government, be the fruits
of our establishments, the cause of liberty will acquire a dignity and lustre,
which it has never yet enjoyed; and an example will be set which can not
but have the most favorable influence on the rights of mankind.*
James Madison in Report on Address to the States by Congress, 25 April,
1783.

Chapter 9: The Dutch Invasion

Timeline

Year	Event
300-500CE	Saxons and Angles crossed over to Albion (Britain)
1066	William of Normandy defeated Saxon King Harold of England
1215	Magna Carta
1270	Flemish wool cloth workers settle in England
14th & 15th Cty	Specialist weavers from Flanders and Brabant settle in England
1570s-1700s	British forces in the Netherlands
1630s-1650s	Dutch engineers drain the Fens in Lincolnshire, England
1650	Dutch Republic abolished the position of Stadholder
1672	Dutch at war with most of Europe William of Orange appointed Captain General
1688	Dutch invade England. Glorious Revolution
1689	William and Mary crowned King and Queen of England, Scotland, and Ireland Bill of Rights Permanent Parliament Act of Toleration
1695	Queen Mary died
1703	King William died

The Narrow Sea

Our species has always been peripatetic. From our origins in Africa we spread across the world over tens of thousands of years. An isotopic analysis of the teeth of a man found near Stonehenge in England in 2002 concluded that he had spent his childhood in Central Europe[357]. In today's world that would be no surprise, but this man lived more than four thousand years ago. Scientists speculate that Stonehenge may then have been known as a place of healing and that he may have traveled there in search of a cure for his severely infected knee wound. A stone tool and fine strands of gold found in his grave indicate he was a metalworker – the first known in the British Islands. Whatever his reasons, the long journey exposed him to lethal danger from people and animals alike. But, people moved around anyway.

In the middle ages, the body of water that separated South-East England from the Netherlands was known as the Narrow Sea. The very name implies that it did not form much of a barrier. This is where in the early centuries of the common era (CE) the Saxons and Angles crossed to visit, and later settle, parts of Albion and gave it names such as Sussex (South Saxon), Essex (East Saxon), Wessex (West Saxon), and East Anglia. Although over time different dialects developed, coastal people maintained contact through trade and naturally conversed in one or another dialect. The Anglo-Saxons in England and the Saxons in the Netherlands maintained and developed their participatory forms of government while outside forces exerted often-destructive influences. England's Saxon rule came to an end when elected King Harold was killed on the battlefield near Hastings in 1066 and the French-Norman Count William of Normandy conquered the country to install his feudal reign. This setback would see the beginnings of a remedy only after 170 years with the drafting of Magna Carta in 1215, which King John II signed but then repudiated.

During the centuries that followed, contacts between the two coasts continued while a long series of wars between England and France hindered the development of relations between those nations. In 1270, King Henry III invited Flemish wool workers to settle in England and, in 1331, Edward III did the same[358]. The immigration of Flemish, Zeelanders, and Hollanders continued throughout the 14th and 15th centuries. Henry VII brought over specialist weavers from Flanders and Brabant. Goudhurst[359] in Kent, England, and many neighboring villages, still have weavers' cottages of this period. Inevitably, these skilled workers brought their customs, preferences, and ideas with them and, equally inevitably, some of their culture rubbed off. Many of

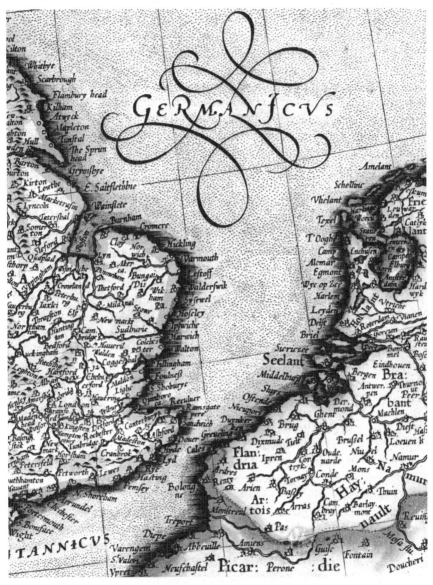

**The Narrow Sea. Detail of the Map Anglia, Scotia, Hibernia in the Hondius
Atlas of 1623**

these immigrants changed their names to English ones so as to blend in more easily. These were the early stages of the prolonged Dutch invasion of England.

Earlier in these pages we saw how Henry VIII invited Anabaptist Flemish craftsmen[360] to help strengthen his textile industry. His daughter Elizabeth I, in a further attempt to modernize her country, embarked on an aggressive policy to bring Dutch know-how to her shores. The fact she was a Protestant made England a natural ally of the emerging Dutch Republic, whose birth was forged out of the need to escape the vicious Spanish religious persecution. Thousands of Protestant refugees from the still occupied Southern Netherlands settled in the free Northern Netherlands and England while thousands of English and Scottish soldiers were stationed in the Republic. Many more Dutch immigrants took on English names to facilitate their integration[361]. Many British soldiers married Dutch women. After completing their tour of duty, some would stay, others would take their families home. King James continued the policy of importing Dutch know-how and so did King Charles I after him.

The seventeenth century was called the Golden Age in the Netherlands. For a while, the Republic was the wealthiest, most densely populated, and powerful nation in the world. Its ships plied the oceans carrying goods far and wide. The country practically functioned as a large free trade enterprise and Amsterdam saw the first stock exchange in the world. The formation of the world's first corporation, the Dutch East-India Company, in 1602 was emulated in England in 1606 with the creation of the Virginia Company. Dutch painters were at the top of their field and prized among the connoisseurs of Europe. Many of their works found their way to England, as did a number of the master painters[362]. At the direction of the Earl of Bedford and King Charles I, Dutch engineer Cornelius Vermuyden and his Dutch workers drained the 680,000 acre Great Level of the Fens to create England's richest agricultural region[363]. Member of Parliament and later Lord Protector, Oliver Cromwell's staunch opposition to the project earned him the name "Lord of the Fens." [364]

Dutch and English scientists exchanged theories and experimental results. Many worked together. One such collaboration yielded a clock that kept time while on the turbulent ocean, making navigation more reliable. Politically, the two countries were tied more than either was willing to admit. From the reign of Elizabeth I through that of Cromwell, there had been numerous attempts to unite into one nation. In short, the nations were very much intertwined and the westward move of enlightened ideas and the institutions it created could not be stopped. Two men played a crucial role in the establishment of a truly constitutional monarchy in England.

'sGravenhage, the Netherlands, 1650-1668

If there was one association between humans as remarkable in its harmony, effectiveness, and importance in the historic course of the modern West, it was that between Hans Bentinck[365] and William[366] of Orange. Let us examine the journey of these two people and the two countries whose very survival they effected.

The name William of Orange is familiar from previous pages. Born in 1650, this William was the great-grandson of the revolutionary namesake who, some seventy years earlier, liberated the Dutch from the oppression and persecutions of Spain. The other, Hans Bentinck, was born in 1649[367]. He was the fifth child of relatively minor nobility in the eastern province of Gelderland in the Dutch Republic. Hans' father was the representative of the Bishop of Utrecht in the city of Deventer. It appears his childhood was a happy one and he received a good education. However, as third son, he did not have any prospects for inheritance and would have to find his own way. Most likely he received a measure of military training, as was often the case with younger sons. As longtime supporters of the Orangist party, the family found its fortunes linked to that of the Orange family. Dutch sentiments for the princely family were at a low point when, following the death of stadholder William II in 1650, the Dutch Republic entered a period of purer Republicanism. Five of the seven provinces, including Holland, abolished the position of stadholder, the top military job that traditionally had been held by the princely Orange family.

Nevertheless, the Bentincks demonstrated their commitment when Hans became a page at the court of the young prince William III of Orange in 'sGravenhage in 1664. The transplant must have been quite a change for the young man. Although he surely had spent time in the small commercial city of Deventer, his short life had mainly taken place in the comfort and freedom of the mansion in the country and in the company of his seven siblings. He was apparently very close to his oldest sister, Eleonora. 'sGravenhage was a very different place. It was, and still is, the seat of two important governments; that of the province of Holland, whose population counted for more than half of the Republic as a whole, and that of the Republic itself. The city's beautiful buildings and boulevards were teeming with the rich and the influential, who displayed their importance with richly decorated clothing, the number and outfit of their entourage, and the splendor of their transportation. Numerous embassies housed the cream of European diplomacy. If Hans felt sad about the loss of his family or the eccentricity of his new surroundings, he would soon find unexpected comfort in the distressed circumstances of an unlikely person.

Young William was born at an absolute low point in the fortunes of both his parents and their families. William's father had died of smallpox only a few days earlier and was still unburied[368]. His mother had been miserable in the Netherlands to begin with and was now surrounded only by people with whom she had little more in common than mutual detestation. Internally, the Republic was divided by the disputes between Orangists and Republicans. That was nothing new, but this time a powerful external force tilted the scale decisively away from the princely family. Young William's father, William II, was married to Princess Mary Stuart of England. At the time of the marriage it had seemed a good political choice, but no longer. The landscape had changed in England. Oliver Cromwell, Lord Protector of England, was now in power and he had beheaded Mary's brother, King Charles I. England was a virtual republic. In 1654, the English and Dutch signed a secret agreement in which the Dutch accepted that no Orange would ever again hold the position of stadholder[369]. In addition, the relationship between the two women in young William's life, his mother, Mary Stuart, and his Dutch grandmother, Amalia van Solms, had deteriorated beyond repair. Already in 1651 William had been placed under the protection of the State to be raised and educated by strangers. His isolation got worse after the death of his mother in 1660. Courts were and are centers of power where people necessarily position themselves to outdo others, a stage for continuous intrigue. His isolation, his loneliness, and the jockeying of those around him influenced the young prince profoundly. As a child, he was solemn and serious, taciturn even. He was suspicious of people's motives and was forced to rely on himself.

Hans was fifteen when he was employed at the Court and met his fourteen-year-old master, William. Hans was the junior page of three at the Court and was likely assigned unobtrusive tasks. In the intimacy of isolation, the two boys would have found opportunity to get acquainted and discover the comfort of empathic and compatible minds. Very soon after, Hans was a member of the Prince's entourage at the funeral of the Frisian stadholder. William was attracted to the stories of family life that Hans related – not unusual for an orphan. William suffered from bouts of depression and was sometimes fainthearted. Hans was less complicated, uninventive, and steady. The two boys drew closer after the Dutch republican government affected a major purge of Stuart sympathizers at the Court[370]. Many of William's caregivers and confidants were removed. Considered a harmless youth, Hans was allowed to stay. In their isolation during their teenage years, they grew dependent on each other and developed a strong friendship.

But, would the purge of the English Stuarts signal an end to the historically strong relations between England and the Netherlands?

Betrayal, 1668-1672

The two boys' four years together formed the most continuous relationship in William's life. It showed in a letter William wrote to Hans's parents, in which he pledged to take care of their son's future. The Prince also visited Hans's parents in Diepenheim. Upon the death of the elder Bentinck in August of 1668, William wrote an extraordinarily warm condolence to his friend that translates something like this: "I can assure you truthfully that what has afflicted your house hurts me as it does you for I am your friend. Whatever happens to you is as if it happens to me."

Prince William III of Orange-Nassau

William's seclusion came to an abrupt end. Increasing unhappiness with the conduct and performance of the Grand Pensionary during the stadholderless period had, by 1668, changed the political climate in the Republic in favor of the Orangists. The family relations between King Charles of England and William of Orange helped warm-up relations. William was now of age and, through various political maneuvers, was hurled into positions of power. Organized events took the Prince all over the country with Hans in attendance. Undoubtedly as a way to raise Hans's stature and experience, Hans was appointed cornet[371] in a battalion in May. The two were in Middelburg in September, where William took his seat in the States of Zeeland. In these political events, William relied mainly on his older cousins and Hans's role was minor.

Unbeknownst to them, King Louis XIV of France was taking advantage of a dispute concerning the succession to the Spanish throne. The Spanish Netherlands (roughly what is now Belgium) was partially French speaking. Louis claimed rights over them through his wife and had his army invade in 1667. A weakened Spain didn't resist and France took all of the territory the next year[372]. The English and the Dutch arranged a "Triple Alliance" with Sweden to defend "Protestantism and Liberty against Catholic aggression." Later that year, France had to relinquish most of its conquests in a treaty with Spain. Louis was furious. He especially loathed the Dutch. Mere traders and republicans – they dared comment on, and ridicule, his actions. Rather than sulk, Louis devised a new plan. He needed the cooperation of England. French envoys had already started negotiations with Charles II as early as 1668. Only a small inner circle at the Court in London knew about it.

In the autumn of 1670, William took his cousins and Hans to visit King Charles II. They traveled around the country and Hans received honorary degrees from Oxford and Cambridge universities. While in London, they lodged at Whitehall. Inevitably, Hans must have seen a great deal of life at the English Court. Interesting as these experiences were, the mission did not accomplish much.

The French achieved much more with their endeavors. As a result of the secret negotiations, an agreement was reached in May of 1670 and the Treaty of Dover[373] was signed. It contained the following text:

The King of England will make a public profession of the Catholic faith, and will receive the sum of two millions of crowns, to aid him in this project, from the Most Christian King, in the course of the next six months, ...
The two Kings will declare war against the United Provinces. The King of France will attack them by land, and will receive the help of 6000 men from England. The King of England will send 50 men-of-war to sea, and the King of France 30; the combined fleets will be under the Duke of York's command. His Britannic Majesty will be content to receive Walcheren, the mouth of the Scheldt, and the isle of Cadzand, as his share of the conquered provinces. Separate articles will provide for the interests of the Prince of Orange.[374]

It was so secret that England's ambassador in 'sGravenhage was not aware of it and the full text did not see daylight until 1830[375]. Louis would get his Spanish Netherlands. Charles had been bought at a price of two million Crowns. He even declared his allegiance to the Catholic faith, which absolved him from Protestant commitments. Curiously, as if feeling guilty about earlier disfavors to his nephew, William of Orange, and the latter's powerless position in the Netherlands, Charles insisted that a substantial portion be left and William made sovereign. History does not record whether any words regarding this arrangement were exchanged between Charles and William during their meeting of 1670.

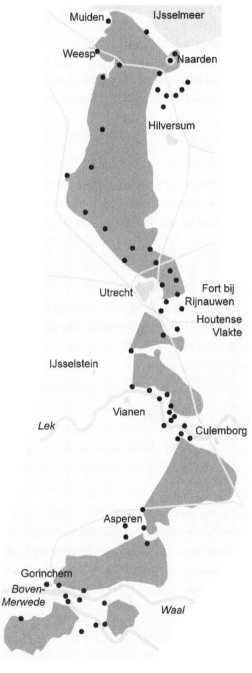

"Waterlinie" defense system of flooded lowlands. Map by Niels Bosboom, CC-License

Increased French military movements and threats indicated that something was afoot. Having earlier abolished the position of Stadholder, the provinces of Gelderland and Holland appointed William Captain-General in January 1672, much against the will of the Grand Pensionary[376]. The joint French-English attack followed in March[377], upon which Holland reinstated the Stadholderate and appointed William in July. These were desperate moves. Although the fleet held its own with victories against the English, the ground forces were overrun by the French, who advanced across the rivers Rhine and IJssel in June. Only a swath of hastily flooded lowlands lay between the coastal provinces and their enemies.

How could a young and inexperienced Prince save the country? At first William's military advisors were few. But by June 1672, the Prince had surrounded himself with experienced advisors who all were his senior by a decade or more. He entered into negotiations with the English envoy. This man knew nothing of the Dover treaty and had been betrayed by his King as much as the Dutch. Negotiations went nowhere. A most curious war broke out, in which the Republic was up against England, France, and parts of Germany, whose armies quickly took most of the country. However, the coastal provinces of Holland, Zeeland, and Friesland were taken over by the Orangists and resisted the invaders. Curiously, the Holy Roman Empire and Spain sided with the Dutch, but contributed no armed forces.

William had Hans by his side but, although now an officer, Hans's experience was limited. However, Hans had a quality few others could match. He was unconditionally loyal and trustworthy, he understood William completely, and he would carry out his friend's orders to the letter. A contemporary writing under the name Monsieur de B. described him thus: "his mind was limited, easy to influence, but very difficult to change once made up.[378]" Hans devoted himself to the military and climbed quickly through the ranks. From Captain of the infantry, he was elevated in April to Captain of the cavalry. Monsieur de B. went on, "He had endeavored to retain the affection of his master with an attendance bordering on slavery, having all the hours he was working to devote to conversation. It was a rare constancy that he had upheld by four or five years." The chronicler de B. clearly had a rather low opinion of Hans Bentinck, but he was an exception.

That same month Hans was promoted to be his friend's chamberlain.

The Ascent, 1673-1676

In July 1673, Hans held a high enough rank to be ordering battle plans and reporting on the strengths and positions of armies. He became a colonel the following year and started to take care of the logistical aspects of campaigns. His aides issued daily marching orders.

A Dutch army invaded Germany and took the city of Bonn, forcing the French to retreat. England sued for peace in 1674. A document from 1676 shows Hans actively engaged in planning such as the supply of troops and weaponry and the various tactical options regarding a major attack.

The young man's connections and lightning ascent did not go unnoticed and sometimes earned him the envy of fellow officers. After Hans had attempted to find favor for a cousin, his commanding officer summoned him and told him, "A chamberlain should restrict his activities to fetching the slippers of the Prince!"

William fell seriously ill with smallpox in 1675. At the time, doctors believed that the company of a healthy body would encourage the drawing out and breathing of the pox and thus the healing of the afflicted one.

William's doctors suggested Hans would be suitable[379]. Hans agreed. He cared for William for sixteen days and nights. He administered food and drink, as much as the Prince was able to take. He helped with bodily functions and kept him clean. And he shared the bed whenever he was not up and about. William later said, "I don't know if he slept or not while I was ill since during those sixteen days and nights I never had to call him. He was always there[380]." When William was well enough, Hans was exhausted and ill. He requested to be allowed to go home to his parents where his own bout with smallpox took its course. In his memoirs, English envoy Temple related the remarkable episode:

> I cannot here forbear to give Monsieur Bentinck the character due to him, of the best servant I have ever known in Prince's or private family. He tended his master, during the whole course of his disease, both night and day; nothing he took was given him, nor he ever removed in his bed, by any other hand; and the Prince told me, that whether he slept or not he could not tell, but, in sixteen days and nights, he never called once that he was not answered by Monsieur Bentinck, as if he had been awake. The first time the Prince was well enough to have his head opened and combed, Monsieur Bentinck, as soon as it was done, begged of his master to give him leave to go home, for he was able to hold up no longer: he did so, and fell immediately sick of the same disease and in great extremity; but recovered just soon enough to attend his master into the field, where he was ever next his person.

The very intimate two weeks together resulting in William's healing cemented any possible gap there might still have been between them. Hans remained the Prince's foremost confidant until death did them part. Hans shook off his illness and attended to his military duties soon after.

A year earlier, Hans had been appointed Drost[381], Bailiff, and Deputy Stadholder of Breda. Now he was also Drost of Lingen. The following year William granted Hans the estate of Drimmelen for one purpose only. It made him eligible for a seat on the Council of Knights of Holland which, in turn, allowed him to sit in the States of Holland, the center of power in the Dutch Republic. With the help of Holland's Pensionary, Hans was admitted as one of only ten knightly members. He was twenty-five years old.

Mouthpiece, 1676 – 1685

Monsr. Benthem[382], they consider as the man the Prince most confides in, and to who he unbosomes his private thoughts, his feares and his pleasures, and who will never contradict him in any thing.[383]

The clergyman Gilbert Burnet, who spent time at the Court in 'sGravenhage, described Hans as most intimately involved in all the Prince's affairs, public and private. He ascribes to the young man "great probity, sincerity," and adds that Hans remained modest, "and has nothing of the haughtiness that seems to belong to all favourites." Let us listen to Burnet:

> He is a virtuous and religious man, and I have heard instances of this that are very extraordinary, chiefly in a courtier. He has all the passion of a friend for the prince's person, as well as the fidelity of a minister in his affairs, and makes up the defects of his education in a great application to business; and as he has a true and clear judgement, so the probity of his temper appears in all his counsels, which are just and moderate; and this is so well known, that though commonwealths can very ill bear inequality of favour that is lodged in one person, yet I never heard any that are in the government of the towns of Holland complain of him; nor does he make those advantages of his favour which were ordinarily made by these that have access to princes, by employing it for those who pay them best, I do not know him well enough to say much concerning him; but though I naturally hate favourites, because all those whom I have known hitherto have made a very ill use of their greatness, yet by all I could ever discern, the prince has shewed a very true judgement of persons in placing so much of his confidence in him.

Now that Hans was greatly involved with William's public duties and frequently conveyed the orders, he also became the catch-all for criticism and envy. William was often suspicious of other people's motives and played his cards close to the chest – probably a leftover from his traumatic childhood. He had few confidants and made sure each one endorsed his views and did not contradict or overrule him. Only of Hans he could be absolutely certain and only his friend was involved in all aspects of government. For the three main parts of his government, military, local politics, and foreign affairs, he relied on respectively the German Prince of Waldeck, Grand Pensionary Fagel, and Everard van Weede van Dijkveld.

Under pressure of Parliament, Charles II of England had ended hostilities against the Netherlands in 1676. The threat from France was by no means over. Protestant forces in England convinced Charles an alliance with the Republic was more beneficial to the country. Following the ancient tradition of sealing such relationships with marriage, it was thought a liaison between William and Charles's niece, Mary, would do.

Hans arrived in London on June 14th, 1677, with the task of exploring

the proffered peace and wedding. It was his first mission abroad. He bypassed the Dutch ambassador and went straight to see King Charles and his brother James, Duke of York and Mary's father. He was warmly received, but his initial optimism was somewhat dampened by the complex political situation in England and the conflicted messages it generated. Although his mission yielded nothing much concrete, it had opened the channels and established a common ground between Charles and his Dutch nephew, William. Soon after Hans's return to the Netherlands, an English envoy followed to continue negotiations. Finally, in October of

King Charles II

that year, William and Hans and an entourage crossed the Narrow Sea for William to formally ask for Princess Mary's hand. Hans meanwhile had acquainted himself with Mary's lady-in-waiting, Anne Villiers, and a few weeks later both couples were married. It seemed hardly possible, but the relationship between the two friends had tightened even more.

The mission had proved Hans's worth as an emissary and would be the beginning of a new responsibility in addition to all the others. He was not to negotiate, though, but only communicate or execute strict instructions. He did not know it then, but the contacts he established with powerful individuals in England would play a major part in future years. In addition he had gained much knowledge of the English court and its intricacies.

In 1678 Anne bore Hans a daughter, whom they named Mary (and in 1681 a son whom they named William – what else?). The war with France ended with the Peace of Nijmegen. German involvement forced Louis XIV to seek accommodation in 1678, although the conditions of the peace were favorable to France. It also left some important issues unsettled, such as the borders in the Spanish Netherlands.

Hans continued his military secretarial duties.

> The great attachment he had had to the Prince since his earliest youth, had deprived him of the means to acquire knowledge other than the routine business that his master communicated to him. He was ignorant about anything else.[384]

Some people were not convinced of Hans's competence. In diplomatic matters, he was naïve and unprepared for intrigues and sudden changes of fortune. William recognized this weakness and so did Hans himself. But a report to the States General stated that Charles II had "expressed particular confidence in a gentleman who enjoys the intimate favour of His Highness." As a result, Hans was now permanently engaged with matters in England, where they were going from crisis to crisis.

Charles II had no legitimate sons, so his brother James was first in line to the succession. But James was an outspoken Catholic. Between 1678 and 1681, the Protestants in Parliament tried to enact the Exclusion Bill[385]. All attempts failed, which caused consternation in both England and the Republic. William was in a bind. He was James's nephew through his mother, and son-in-law through his wife. But if he supported James, he would in effect support a Catholic and potential enemy. If he supported the English Protestants, he risked alienating a future King of England. So he muddled through. It made him no enemies, but gained him no respect from either party.

The next crisis came when a conspiracy to assassinate both Charles and James was discovered, the Rye House Plot of 1683. Many of the suspects fled to the Netherlands and again William found himself in an untenable position. He sent Hans to England to defuse the tension. Hans conveyed his friend's congratulations for their good fortune. William wanted to make clear he had nothing to do with the plot and would do his utmost to pursue the conspirators.

He also needed to know what the King's thoughts were on foreign affairs, particularly with regard to France. Louis XIV was employing ancient charters to claim the Spanish territories in the Netherlands and again threatened force if he would not get his way. Hans tried to convince Charles that England's support was desperately needed, if only because of England's own interests. In addition, the German emperor was preoccupied with the Turks who threatened Vienna.

Despite all these valid arguments, Hans got nowhere. As his frustration mounted, he frequently lost his temper during the discussions. His badgering was unsuccessful and his cajoling incompetent. Wholly dissatisfied, Hans left for home, where affairs weren't much better. France had laid siege to Luxemburg. The most powerful city, Amsterdam, of the most powerful province of the Dutch Republic, Holland, declined to send troops for the defense of the country. Instead, Amsterdam sent signals that it was not an enemy of France. The city fathers had decided that, with England uninterested, Germany preoccupied, and Spain impotent, a take-over of the Southern Netherlands by France was inevitable. William was furious. The defense line in the Spanish Netherlands was the cornerstone of the defense of the country. William and Hans traveled to Amsterdam, but were unsuccessful in changing the city's position. In 'sGravenhage, they tried to force the States General to order troops, but were opposed by two more provinces. Since the Act of Union compelled each State to defend all, the country was faced with a constitutional crisis. In the mean time, the English ambassador was discussing a French offer for a truce with Amsterdam. Luxembourg fell to the French in July of 1684.

As if that were not enough to sour the mood of the Orangists, King Charles II of England died in February of 1685. The avowed Catholic James II was king. Alarmed, Hans wrote to his friend Sidney, "our loss is large enough to occupy all our thoughts, and to fill our minds of fears for the Protestant Religion." Charles's illegitimate son, the Duke of Monmouth, who had been suggested as successor in Protestant quarters, was already in 'sGravenhage, where he had been warmly received and lavishly feted by William. Both William and Hans had extensive discussions with the Duke, but when Charles died, they deemed it better for the Duke to be quartered outside the city so as to not give the impression of support. That proved wise when many Protestant English and Scottish refugees joined the Duke and convinced him to champion their cause. However, the Duke and Hans, and by extension William, stayed in close contact as was evidenced by the sighting of the Duke's page in 'sGravenhage.

Confronted with the potential consequences of the uncertain situation in England, William hatched a daring plan. To counter French designs he needed England to stay neutral or, better yet, become an ally against France. He figured that he could win James over with the dispatch of an Anglo-Dutch army in the King's support. Knowing full well that the Dutch Republic was hostile to the Catholic King, as was the Protestant majority of the English people, William sent Hans to the States General to discuss the idea. To add drama to his ploy, Hans pulled a piece of paper from his pocket and announced that it contained James's personal request. Shock and consternation surrounded him. Never had been such a weighty request made through such an unnatural channel. Expecting, and probably hoping, the States would not honor the request, Hans reported to the English Lord Treasurer that he had served the King's interests. Meanwhile, William promised he would have Monmouth arrested and put tabs on the British refugees.

Not surprisingly, Monmouth was allowed to escape. Three refugee-sponsored ships, headed for Scotland, failed to garner the attention of the Dutch authorities. Obviously the mood at the English Court hovered between suspicious and hostile. To placate James, William gave in to two demands: appoint new officers for the Anglo-Dutch brigades that were still serving in the Netherlands and abandon Monmouth. A third demand, "support my policies", he kept under advisement. Hans wrote to his English alley, "His Highness assuredly will do all that the King can expect of him. Except in religion, I believe that you know enough to know that he does not usually do things by halves."

James II

Unfortunately, James received news that Monmouth and his rebels had set sail for England and Scotland. Hans was hastily sent to talk to James. It was not without risk. The French envoy wrote, "His British Majesty is confident that Bentinck is his personnel enemy who always had dealings with Monmouth. Without any advance notice from the King of England he was not the right and proper man to be sent." William hoped that his permanent envoy would be able to quell the notion that he had supported Monmouth and thus pave the way for Hans. A truce between England and France had to be avoided at all cost. At the same time, he demanded the removal of the English ambassador who had interfered in Amsterdam.

The outcome of William's derring-do was better than might be expected. James reprimanded two representatives from Amsterdam for not stopping Monmouth. Next, Hans conveyed William's offer to lead a force of Anglo-Scottish mercenaries into England, which James of course turned down. The Catholic King did not need more Protestant forces in his country if commanded by his son-in-law, another Protestant. But he had to acknowledge William's loyalty, and accepted Scottish and English troops with their native commanders. Finally, Hans was to find out whether James would rely on the King of France or the States General as his most reliable ally. He tried to convince James that the French were behind the rebellion. Despite all the difficulties, the Dutch envoys slowly but surely made progress and, while James was trying to extricate himself from the French sphere of influence, they managed to see all existing Dutch treaties with England renewed. During the summer of 1685 Dutch treaties with Spain and Brandenburg were either renewed or newly made. At last, French diplomacy was in retreat.

Number One, 1685-1686

In late 1684, Hans Bentinck had been on a mission to Friesland with the goal of winning over that State's Stadholder and William's cousin, Hendrik Casimir II, who had an alliance with Amsterdam in the Peace Party. This was just after the Frisian Stadholder had visited Amsterdam to deny any reconciliation with William and confirm his support for the city's policies regarding the withholding of troops to fight the French. Hans's mission had been utterly unsuccessful. The following spring, Hans heated up the debates over the troops in the States General. Now, however, he was beginning to make some headway. The increasingly aggressive voices of Catholics in both France and England caused Amsterdam and Friesland to rethink their refusals for troops. The Republicans[386] in Holland[387] weakened to the benefit of the Orangists.

Through his dealings in the States of Holland, Hans was getting interested in affairs of state, and started to play a growing supporting role, albeit not a leading one. He also started to acquire some diplomatic skills and learned to control his outward emotions and apply them strategically. He attended debates that concerned William's interests as Stadholder and Captain General. He therefore sparred regularly with representatives from Amsterdam and other cities, which were footing most of the bill for state finance. In 1686, Hans participated in deliberations about the augmentation of army and navy forces. With hopes of getting funding in July, he furiously fought a motion to have the inconclusive session of the Holland legislature suspended. Trying other channels after his failure, he stayed in 'sGravenhage until September.

However, eventually Amsterdam approved the war budget[388] while reconciliation between William and cousin Hendrik Casimir was bought with the latter's right to appoint officers in the Frisian and Groninger regiments of the national army. In December, Hans was actively involved in an ongoing dispute with the city of Dordrecht and in March of 1687, he was in 'sGravenhage for debates on ways and means. Although William had many "favorites" working for him, they each handled a specific task or were responsible for one of the aspects of governance: diplomacy, military, or internal affairs. Hans Bentinck was now involved in all of them, which placed him in a unique position. All these experiences prepared him well for what was to come.

Smiley's People[389], 1687-1688

During his visits to England, Bentinck had made contact with leading Protestants. Over the years, relationships solidified and were further strengthened through his friendships with people like Sidney, an English envoy to the Republic. Other confidants of William's had established excellent rapports with English envoys as well. With the rise of Catholic influence in England, Protestant power brokers were looking for help from the Dutch with increased urgency. These developments provided the opportunity to expand the network of sympathizers and informers in England. Sidney, although not part of the inner circles anymore, played an important role utilizing his good connections.

Together they set up what amounted to a secret service on the island nation. The sophisticated network communicated orally, used letters that contained passages in invisible ink, and documents that were encrypted[390]. Many were sent to undercover addresses in both London and 'sGravenhage. A prolonged correspondence started in December 1687 between Hans Bentinck and the Scottish noble James Johnstone. What on the outside appeared to be a business exchange was really a dissemination of useful intelligence. One of the correspondents joked, "Gardeners as we all are, when we speak of plants and flowers probing people would expect to find mystery." Sidney spread this kind of correspondence among various people in William and Hans's circle so as not to attract attention. Most of these eventually became personal aides to Hans. All provided William with a constant stream of information about the goings-on in England. Of course the Dutch ambassador also sent reports on English affairs, but the contents of those were about official policy. In addition, that correspondence was likely checked and not reliably secret. Many of the intelligence recruits in and outside England were clergy. Considering the religious nature of the rising conflict in England, this is no surprise. Hans also kept close tabs on the growing number of English religious refugees in the Republic – he had served with English Huguenot[391] soldiers while in the military and knew them well. Some provided useful information and many would later join the invasion army.

All the intelligence thus gathered informed William and helped fine-tune his policies. However, It was impossible to keep the steady stream of English visitors at the Court at 'sGravenhage in the summer of 1687 a secret.

Diplomatic maneuvering between William and James continued, but yielded nothing more than time. The situation became more stressed when suddenly there was a potential Catholic heir to the throne. James's queen was pregnant. Tensions in England were rising following James' repressive policies. Relations with the Dutch also got worse. One correspondent wrote to Hans, "… they believe things near their crisis, and … that a stricter Alliance being lately made, between us and France; it is believed the Dutch may next summer find the effects of it."

James Johnstone. Courtesy Wellcome Images by the Wellcome Trust

Thus far William and Hans had been planning military options that concerned the West Indies only, but decided to reconsider that option. They needed to find out whether there was a chance Parliament would bend James's way. Frantic feelers went out to the spies in England and news came back that even the Court itself was divided and that it was unlikely that James would be able to form a loyal Parliament. James employed stronger measures and started a buildup of forces, but Hans learned that James did not have the resources for a large buildup. The Dutch were therefore not alarmed, but mobilized some of their own forces nonetheless.

A major conflict between James and the Anglican bishops got so far out of hand that James had many tried for sedition and locked up in the Tower in June 1687. James was emboldened when the Queen bore him a son on the 20th of that month. Initially William ordered Hans to go to England to congratulate James. However, Hans's wife, Anne, was seriously ill and he could not go. Meanwhile in England, rumors turned up that

Queen Mary had miscarried and that the child was a switch. Likely English Protestants had come up with the story to plant doubts. It worked among the Protestants and Hans was intent to take advantage of it. Soon after the arrival of a dispatch from spies in London criticizing a mission of homage, William hastily called a meeting with his closest allies. All public celebrations for the birth were suspended. Hans refused to lend trumpeters to the English ambassador for their celebrations.

Planner in Chief, 1688

The French ambassador to England promised James troops and warships should he need them. Meanwhile, a dispute about the religious consequences of a succession in one of the German states came to a head when a French army moved on Cologne.

In May 1688, Hans traveled to Berlin in Brandenburg. This Protestant German state was still lukewarm to the possibility of military involvement in Cologne. Pro Dutch and pro French factions were divided fairly equally, despite the fact that Prince Frederick of Brandenburg was a strong Calvinist. William sent Hans for three reasons. Frederick held him in high esteem; having Hans there showed Frederick the urgency of the mission; and showed the French the seriousness and potential outcome. William worried that the Holy Roman Emperor, Leopold, and various German princes would not be able, or did not care, to defend the freedoms German Protestants had enjoyed for so many generations. Hans scoured the Protestant parts of Germany and eventually established a defense alliance with a number of important states. He had learned a lot in the last years and this time he returned home, completely successful, in August. Brandenburg's forces moved south to the vicinity of Cologne.

With German support in place, the French halted their advance. But as long as England's position was uncertain, the threat remained. A new plan had hatched at the Dutch court: intervention in England. It is uncertain exactly when the right circumstances for such a bold plan were in place. No doubt the possibility of intervention had been discussed, and rejected, over the last few years. In any case, there is no mention of it in any of the correspondence prior to July 1688, when an English courier arrived with an "invitation to intervene" signed by seven leading Protestant politicians. The pretext was there but, as Hans noted, could only be acted upon if a strong army would protect the Republic while its forces were occupied in England. Only Brandenburg could field such strength. It is therefore entirely logical that Hans discussed the matter with Frederick in Berlin and received the Prince's unequivocal commitment. Two other princes, of

Saxony and Hannover, pledged to defend the Empire against the French and thus defend Brandenburg. Hans wrote to a friend that the affairs in England, "... would burst into extremities, in which case we cannot sit still, but have to do our best, or the Republic and Religion is lost."

In England meanwhile, James thought he had the law on his side. In 1661, Parliament had enacted the so-called Corporation Act of the Clarendon Code. Its intention was to strengthen the position of the Anglican Church and it demanded that nonconformists be excluded from public office. Towns were organized in corporations and through these members of Parliament were elected. The corporations were, however, sanctioned by the King by means of a charter. The law regarding royal charters could equally be applied in reverse. Uncooperative Anglican or Protestant M.P.s could be gotten rid of. No charter, no corporation, and thus no representation. That is how James resolved to fix his problem and have a more loyal Parliament seated by the winter of 1688[92].

Having secured the defense of the Republic, Hans now needed to convince the Dutch of the merits of an invasion of England. Soon after his return from Germany, he dispatched to Amsterdam. Military preparations for the adventure were already underway. But the leaders in Amsterdam, as usual, were skeptical. In September, German allies occupied Cologne. Of course the scale of the preparations made it impossible to keep it a secret. However, the organizers came up with a ruse. Algerian pirates in the Mediterranean had been a problem for commercial shipping there and the Dutch let it leak that they were preparing an expeditionary fleet to deal with the pirates once and for all[393]. The French, eager for a fight in Germany, marched their army away from the Dutch border and into the German Rhineland, where they would be occupied for many months. William ordered his troops at Nijmegen to march to Hellevoetsluis to join the fleet there.

Parallel to the invasion plans, Hans developed a propaganda campaign. Central stood the slogan, *"pro religion et libertate,"*[394] as part of the "Declaration of Reasons." It argued that James sought absolute power in defiance of constitutional tradition. The paper would assure the support of all Protestants, Dutch and foreign, and would encourage English Protestants to be sympathetic to a foreign invasion. Stacks of the Declaration were printed, but kept under wraps in Hans's private apartment. More copies were to be printed in England where distribution was to coincide with the invasion. Hans had a hand in the drafting of the text. Early copies in his archive were annotated in his handwriting[395]. He later wrote to William it had been, "in service to God, for the defense of the law of England, and the freedom of this State and the interest of all of Europe."

Two important spies from England arrived in the Republic with the unfortunate news that communication with allies overseas had broken down. Hans hastily sent his personal secretary, who arrived in London September 11. The courier secretly contacted two of the signatories of the "invitation." Later that month he returned with intelligence about naval movements, fortifications, military strategies, garrison strengths in the ports, and advice on where to make the landings.

Armed with these, Hans received the Dutch admirals at his residence to hammer out naval strategy. They decided not to engage the English fleet if at all possible. The resulting plan showed 196 Dutch ships divided in nine groups with one warship each and one group of ten ships. Thirty-nine Dutch warships would surround this fleet.

In early October, twenty thousand (!) troops embarked at Hellevoetsluis under Hans's personal supervision. A week later they were ready to set sail. William spoke at length with his wife and took an emotional farewell of the States General in the 'sGravenhage. He declared that he, "always had the country's best at heart[396]". He appointed a head of the armed forces during his absence, and ordered that, "in case something human may befall him," they care for the Princess. He implored them to be united in the difficult days ahead. He addressed the States of Holland in warmer terms than usual and moved many sturdy men to tears.

It must have been a difficult time for Hans. His wife was again seriously ill and he wanted to be with her. With the whole enterprise at a crucial stage, he just could not get away.

William joined the fleet October 27 and stationed himself on the warship *Zeven Provincien*[397]. Amazingly, the planning and implementation of the largest military enterprise of the 17th century had taken half a dozen men less than two months. Keeping the planning group small helped keep the real purpose of the enterprise a secret. Had the French known of the planned invasion, they would surely have withdrawn from Germany and attacked the Dutch Republic.

With the cooperation of Amsterdam, the entire fleet had grown to over 400 ships[398]. It must have been a magnificent sight. There were forty men of war, of which thirteen had sixty or more cannon, seven had more than fifty, eleven had over forty, and twelve had around thirty. There were four light frigates with twenty-two pieces each, ten fire ships[399], seven advice yachts, and some 340 galleons, flutes, and other troop transports. Nearly one thousand masts pointed up to the cloudy sky. In addition to the Dutch tri-color, most flew long orange vanes in honor of the House of Orange and its leader William. The fleet was four times the size of the Spanish Armada one hundred years earlier. It carried fourteen thousand mercenaries and seven thousand other soldiers, with among them Huguenot, English and Scottish volunteers.

On October 30, in a strong south-westerly wind, the fleet sailed west into the North Sea. Their aim was northern England or Scotland. Almost immediately they ran into severe weather that forced them back to Hellevoetsluis. Disappointment was everywhere. The leaders feared that the setback would take away the element of surprise. If James found out, he might mobilize a strong resistance. Equally, the French might abandon their foray into Germany and attack the Republic. Hans appeared unemotional and remarked, "It appears the good lord would not want it yet."

With no change in the winds in sight, William dispatched a letter to Princess Mary inviting her to meet him in Brielle. He made the trip from Hellevoetsluis over a very bad road on the back of a horse drawn cart[400]. Hans traveled to 'sGravenhage on November 9to be with Anne. The wind changed to the east that same day. The planners decided that there could be advantage in the wind since it would keep the English fleet locked up in the Thames while that same wind could carry them to the southwest of England. On November 12 the fleet put to sea. An urgent letter of that date from William to Hans indicates that Hans may not yet have returned. However, on November 14, the two friends were reunited and Hans advised William to sail for Torbay in Devonshire, expecting that James surely would not have a force there. Presumably he was relying on information from his spy network. They sailed west, passed under the coast of Dover and, at Hans's suggestion, reached Torbay the next day. As expected, the English fleet was nowhere to be seen. From high on a bluff, the two friends watched the rapid disembarkation of the troops. November usually being a month of heavy storms, the army marched in heavy downpours toward Exeter. Artillery pieces had to be pulled through thick mud. Hans's intelligence proved correct in that there was no English army anywhere near. Eventually they reached Exeter, where their reception was unexpectedly cool. Perhaps the memory of the earlier failed invasion of the Duke of Monmouth dampened enthusiasm for the latest invaders. Probably with some trepidation, the Mayor declared his loyalty to James. William was disappointed. Hans observed, "it appears that fear of the scaffold has more effect on their spirits than their zeal for religion."

Some historians suggest that William stayed in Exeter for a while out of disappointment. More likely it was a combination of bad weather and strategy. Hans expected that it would not be long for gentry from outside Devon to come flocking — as indeed they did. During the twelve days, they regrouped their battalions. They worked with the English officials who had come to Exeter to meet them and set up a council of influential gentry. In the absence of a sitting parliament, and therefore the absence of a means to raise revenue, they worked to create a revenue system.

When news of the landing reached James, he marched his army into the Salisbury plain, but then appeared to think better of it. On December 17, he sent his commissioners to Hungerford to meet with William with an offer to convene a "free" parliament. This meant that he would not manipulate charters in order to affect a "loyal" parliament. William invited the commissioners into a room, together with a delegation of William's English supporters. After the door closed, William was the only outsider present. Whether he intended to be a mere arbiter or sought to drive home his English credentials, history does not tell. In any case, William ignored the proposals by the commissioners and presented a list of demands that were entirely in line with the interests of his English supporters, a free parliament. The demands in hand, the commissioners left.

In the night of 22-23 December, Hans received a letter from the commissioners with unexpected news. During the last few days, James had judged the situation highly unfavorable. He would face a hostile parliament, his resources and thus his troops were limited and, perhaps, not as loyal as required, and he would have lost his freedom of action entirely. The

Council at Torbay

King decided to leave the country and fight another day. The Dutch were delighted and happy to help James into exile. However, before Dutch troops could get there, English forces arrested James and took him to Rochester.

The House of Lords, assembled at Guildhall, had temporarily taken over the administration. In their indecision, they had James escorted back to London, where he was allowed to settle in St. James's palace. William was livid. The action had prevented James's departure from the country and with it the argument of voluntary abdication. Post haste, he dispatched his men to move James to Ham House, ostensibly for his safety, but really in the hope he would try to flee again. As Hans was preparing to put pressure on James to do so, the King asked to be allowed to go back to Rochester. Hans gladly granted the request and once there, and under "a blind eye" of the Dutch guards, James boarded a ship for France.

During the march to London Hans received the news of Anne's death. It was not unexpected – she had been ill for a long time. He probably felt guilt for not having given her more attention than his frantic duties allowed. In a letter he wrote about his, "great sorrow for the death of my wife."

As early as August, William had known English politicians could be indecisive. With the King absent, they would be even more so. William had to take the lead if he wanted to get the English into the Dutch war with France in time. French troops were advancing and their preoccupation in Germany would not last forever. Another option had entered his mind. What if he sought to replace James with Mary, or even himself? The idea was probably not entirely new. However, until that very moment, there absolutely had been nothing in his words, writings, or actions to indicate such an ambition. He had adhered strictly to the Declaration of Reasons.

Advocate, 1689

William was effectively in control of the country. The English had asked him to oversee the administration until a convention could be held. However, he felt it prudent not to overplay his hand. He was used to the deliberative process in the Republic and not familiar enough with political gamesmanship in England. But he was also in a hurry and did what many a military leader had before. He swarmed the streets of London with his troops. Sir John Reresby noted that[401],

"the streets were filled with ill lookeing and ill habited Dutch and other strangers of the Prince's army. And yet the Citty was soe pleased with their diliverers that they did not or would not perceave their deformity nor the oppression they laid under, which was much greater then what they felt from the English army."

Hans made it clear that interference with the Dutch army would not be tolerated. The spectacle impressed upon the English who was in control. However, when the convention commenced, William withdrew some of his troops from the city. The point had been made.

The second part of the strategy was propaganda and the Dutch were good at it. It rang loudest from the pulpits proclaiming the Prince as the deliverer for the Protestant cause. On the 10th of February, when the Lords were engaged in a hot debate on William's position, his supporters organized a national day of thanksgiving. Reresby wrote that,

> "The lords that were for conferring the crown immediately upon the Prince, fearing the contrary interest of makeing him only regent, or crowning him in right of his wife, might prevaile, sent some instruments to stirr up the mobile [mob] who came in a tumultuous manner with a petition, offering it both to the Lords and Commons this purpas: to crown both the Prince and Princess of Orang, to take speedy care of religion and property, and for the defence of Ireland."

All these activities certainly put pressure on the Lords, but it would not have been enough if they hadn't been convinced by the potential merits. James had systematically chiseled away at the powers of Parliament. With William, who came from a country with more democratic traditions, they were in a better position to see some, if not all, of their wishes implemented. Hans was not about to leave affairs to chance either. He must have found his friend and master, William, somewhat indecisive, weak perhaps. Even though he was in total control, William had left the initiative mostly to the English. But they in turn were indecisive, too.

Until now William had given no indication of interest in the British throne. He had come as an arbiter of British affairs with the ultimate goal of securing the British alliance in the war against France. Hans was more forceful. He believed that goal was most reliably achieved with William on the throne[402]. Although the English were increasingly annoyed with Hans's assertive involvement, his detractors could do little while the Dutch were in control and while their propaganda machine was putting pressure on the parliamentary convention taking place. Hans's strategy was two-fold. On the one hand, he assured the skeptics that William had no ambitions to the throne. At the same time, he encouraged the Williamites to make their case for William's ascension most strenuously. Among the latter he narrowed the discussion on the issue of a single monarch, William, or a joint reign of William and his wife Mary. Negotiations were not easy. There were different opinions in parliament. Some did not want a foreigner on their throne. Also, hostilities between England and the Republic had not been forgotten. The idea of a Dutchman as king was somewhat painful. Realizing that they had to give the liberator something, they offered William the regency, no more. Others wanted Mary to be sole Queen. After all, she was the rightful heir. Hans had gauged the mood well and eventually the joint reign option prevailed in the convention. In April 1689, William and Mary were crowned King and Queen of England, Scotland, and Ireland.

King William III and Queen Mary II

The success of Hans's diplomacy was rewarded in two important ways. He received several new offices and grants in England. He was given the country house of Theobalds; made Keeper of the Privy Purse, Groom of the Stole, First Gentleman of the Bedchamber, and Superintendent of all the gardens of the royal palaces; he was allocated apartments in Kensington, Hampton Court, and Whitehall; and, last but not least, was made First Earl of Portland, which landed him a seat in the Lords. The lavish bestowments on a foreigner caused jealousy among the English, and there would be more.

In addition to the three Kingdoms, William was still the Eminent Head of the Dutch Republic. He had always preferred to manage his affairs closely but, to his dismay, that was now impossible. He needed to delegate his duties to others. In the British Isles, he called upon his closest confidant, Hans, to direct the affairs of government. Hans had already shown his skills and interest in British politics. Even though the position did not yet exist, he functioned somewhat like a prime minister who operated not from Parliament, but from the palace.

The installation of a King, who in his native Holland was familiar with, and appreciative of, deliberative and participatory government, was a godsend to the British. Throughout its history, Parliament had been at odds with its monarch over the powers of each. The new king allowed both to work toward a common purpose. The result was the passing of important legislation in the first year of his reign. The Bill of Rights established new rights for Parliament, some of which echo the Great Privilege of 1477 in the Netherlands. Its provisions included the sole right to levy money, including that for a standing army in peace time, the right of subjects to petition, the right of electors to freely choose their representatives, the right of Parliament to freedom of debate, and the necessity to meet regularly. With that last provision, the permanent Parliament was established for the first time.

William signed the Act into law and with it Britain became a constitutional monarchy. That same year, the Act of Toleration passed. To some extent it was modeled on an article in the Union of Utrecht (Netherlands, 1579) which stipulated freedom of religion. The Act of Toleration did not go as far as Dutch law, which was, perhaps, an indication of English realism since the Dutch never lived up to its letter. The English act stopped persecution of Protestant dissenters or Catholics, although they could still be discriminated against. However, a measure of toleration was politically and economically expedient, as it had been in the Dutch Republic. It weakened Catholic support for the exiled aspirant-king, James III, and allowed full commercial participation by religious minorities. In 1695, another important act established freedom of the press, opening the way for the free expression of political and religious ideas. It is interesting to note that freedom of expression in the Netherlands was strongly favored by the House of Orange of which William was its leading member. The reasons were somewhat self-serving since the press had been partially curtailed during the "Stadholderless" period when the Oranges were banned from holding office.

Émigrés, 1689-1699

The speed and competence with which Hans adapted to the new cultural and political environment was stunning. Granted, his friend placed him in a position of power. But it was his to lose should he not use it effectively. The King and his subjects sat in judgment of Hans's actions and methods; whether they served them and the country. As William's favorite, his position in the palace was naturally good. During their frequent contact, the two friends exchanged information and ideas. Hans had much control over who had access to the King. Because of the multiple duties of Stadholder and King of wealthy and powerful countries, William was overwhelmed. He used Hans as a conduit for instructions in just about all parts of all governments and had no choice but to let Hans make decisions on his own. William needed to be shielded and Hans was that shield.

Imagine the complexity. William was Stadholder of Holland and several other provinces in the Dutch Republic. These were powerful military positions that carried a lot of political weight. He was King of England, King of Scotland, and King of Ireland. In all these territories he had to deal with parliaments, assemblies, and executive governments at the national, provincial, and, in the case of large cities, municipal levels. His countrymen in the Netherlands sometimes felt slighted because William resided in England. To his subjects in Britain, he was a foreigner who favored his fellow immigrants. It could have spelled disaster.

There is little indication that Hans mastered the English language before planning the invasion. He must have learned a good deal from his correspondence with his spy network. He much preferred French as the traditional language of diplomacy. But he was not a diplomat now. He was at the center of the English political establishment. He had to be English and in order to do that he had to act, think, and speak like an Englishman. By early 1689, his written English was near perfect. But, speaking a language does not mean that you understand all its nuances and subtleties. Hans probably understood this as he continued to conduct most of his correspondence in French.

William did not allow himself to be isolated and kept channels open to political allies and advisers. The Dutch diplomat and scientist, Constantijn Huygens, confirmed that the two friends were closely working together on the administration of their vast enterprise "[The King] was having a serious conversation with Solms and [Hans], talking solemnly and silently, sometimes staring at each other long without speaking[403]." Hans frequently sat in on the Privy Council and Cabinet Council sessions and was put in charge when William could not attend. Disagreements between Hans and the ministers were rare. It appears that William and Hans were quite prepared to leave most English affairs to the English as long as England kept financing the war effort against France. Of course there was criticism from some circles that William favored his Dutch confidants. Being Dutch made them more identifiable, but criticism was nothing new. Favoritism, jockeying for position, and jealousies were all traditional ingredients of palace politics.

In dealing with the affairs of the United Provinces[404], Hans was uniquely positioned. He was not only closest to the Stadholder; he resided with him. The aforementioned Huygens took care of the routine matters while the Grand Pensionary, Heinsius, was William's most powerful confidant in the Republic. But much of the correspondence went through Hans and he was able to discuss matters with William daily. In addition, Hans's secretary was well connected and Hans maintained a network of informers. By these means he stayed involved from across the Narrow Sea.

Almost immediately after William took the reins, he delegated Scottish affairs entirely to Hans. One pamphleteer wrote:

> … Benting, who is the minion and darling of our Monarch.   Has granted unto him as well as assumed the whole Superintendency of the Kingdom of Scotland and governs it intirely by his creatures, who are the only persons there trurted with the Administration, and to whom he gives such measures, in reference both to the Legislative and to the Executive part of the Government …"[405]

But overall, Scottish contemporaries and historians agree that Hans managed the Kingdom competently. Considering all the other tasks Hans was burdened with, it follows that the Scots were pretty much left to run their own affairs. However, Hans did have his confidants positioned to keep things under control. Prominent among them were former exiles who had resided in Holland and former, pre-invasion, intelligence operatives. On balance, the Scots were pleased with their new King and his proxy, who allowed them much greater freedom than any Stuart had. It appears from surviving correspondence and reports that the Scottish politicians displayed much respect for the immigrant power broker.

Hans Bentick when Earl of Portland

Hans's influence in Ireland is sketchy. William appointed a troika of lord justices who did consult Hans in the appointments of government positions. Hans discussed such matters with William and a decision would come down. During the Jacobite uprising in 1692, Hans was intricately involved in military planning and was the conduit for communication between military and King.

William had put control of all his militaries in the hands of long-trusted confidants, many of whom had worked with Hans in the continental campaigns as well as in the invasion and in the Irish campaign. Hans was by now an experienced soldier. After his German missions, the creation of his English network, and the successful negotiation of William's ascent to the throne, he was astute in the art of politics and diplomacy. His proximity to his friend the King logically made him the, "pivotal military secretary to the King." He continuously received information of the overall strength of troops in Ireland, England, Scotland, and on the continent, intelligence that he passed on to his friend. He gave William diagrams and tables on the number of battalions and their disposition, and he made proposals for reforms when necessary. Hans's writings contained lists of available regiments, and suggestions on where to move them.[406]

As he had done on the British Isles and in the Dutch Republic, Hans established a wide network of informants throughout the parts of Europe that were important to the Protestant cause. These provided him with political and military intelligence such as troop strengths and movements. Hans was involved in all British and Dutch military decisions and was the liaison between William and allied armies on the continent. He saw all and he knew all. But he did it all for his friend and the cause. William was in charge and responsible and no one doubted it.

Because Hans was so well informed about the goings-on on the continent, he was supervising and instructing the British and Dutch diplomats and insisted on receiving frequent reports from them. Foreign requests for particular envoys went through Hans. He was involved in all appointments. He kept close tabs on special missions. Secretaries of State reported to him.

A lesser man would have buckled under the weight of his office. If it had gone to his head, he would have made many enemies. Instead he made many friends. Had he abused his position, he would have lost the lifetime friendship with William.

Until Death Do Us Part, 1700-1709

Certainly that friendship was tested when the two men lived and worked together in such close proximity. In 1695, both entered trying times. When Queen Mary died in January, William was distraught. Having his mistress, Elisabeth Villiers, still with him was likely viewed with disapproval. Whatever the reason, he married her off to the Earl of Orkney, islands so far away he might as well have sent her to the Moon. Initially, the loss of the two women in his life made William lean on Hans more. In the meantime, a younger man had slowly but surely worked himself into the graces of the King. Twenty years junior to Hans, Arnold Joost van Keppel was friendly, easy-going, and charming. William may have seen in van Keppel the son he never had. The younger man's outgoing demeanor contrasted with that of Hans, who was more reserved. Not being able to compete in the art of charms, Hans hated his rival. Another issue may have played on William's mind. As early as 1689, he had expressed to a confidant that, *"hee would discourage the falling too much upon particular men."*[407] With the wars and the affairs of state going well, this was as good a time as any to curtail the powers of the one man who fit that description, his friend Hans. The next four years van Keppel's star rose as Hans's declined. After the peace with France in 1697, Hans accepted that his favor had waned and he extricated himself more and more from the affairs of state. But he would be frequently called upon for advice. Two years later, he made his final exit from active duty to devote himself to his extensive possessions in England and the Republic.

In 1700, Hans remarried and embarked on another family. His removal from responsibility also removed any fear that William might have been too dependent on his old friend. The two spent important time together, during which William confided that his health was declining rapidly and that he expected to die soon.

It took until 1701 before the succession to the throne was settled. Queen Mary had died childless in 1695. The Act of Settlement decided that Mary's sister, Anne, would inherit the throne from William. However, possible default heirs of Anne's would be passed over for the granddaughter of King James I. She was the Electress of Hanover, Princess Sophia.

The final separation of the friends came upon William's death in 1702. Mary's sister, Anne, was crowned and Hans's involvement in government came to a complete end. But a man with such experience and knowledge would continue to attract statesmen and diplomats who valued his advice. Hans kept open his channels with correspondence. And, as the Earl of Portland, he still held a seat in the English House of Lords. He also still had a seat on the Council of Holland. The affairs of Europe kept him busy until he fell ill in late November, 1709, and died in the early morning of December 4. His body was brought to London where his funeral procession included some fifty carriages, many riders, and a large number of nobles. They carried him from his house in St. James's Square to Westminster

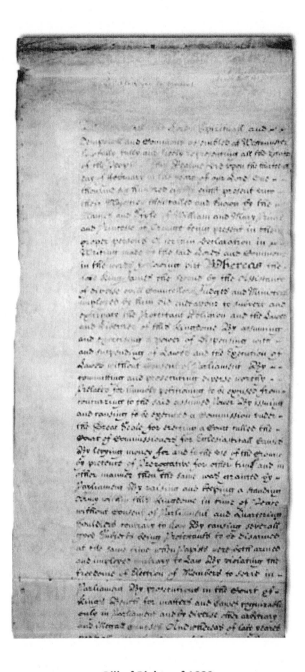

Bill of Rights of 1689

Abbey, where he was put to rest in the vault under the east window of the chapel of Henry VII.

Thus ended a most remarkable and influential alliance, the consequences of whose deeds went beyond their contemporary concerns and that helped shape the western world of today. Absolute monarchies would have lasted longer, democracy would have been delayed, and the repressive Church of Rome might have ruled with impunity had it not been for the enlightened policies of William of Orange and his trusted advisor, Hans Bentinck.

Knowledge will forever govern ignorance: and a people who mean to be their own Governors must arm themselves with the power which Knowledge gives.
James Madison to William T. Barry, 4 August, 1822.

Chapter 10: The Framework

Timeline

Year	Event
1770	Boston Massacre
1773	Boston Tea Party
1775-1783	American Revolutionary War
1777	Articles of Confederation
1781	Confederation ratified
1786	Annapolis Convention
1787	Shays' Rebellion
1787	Constitutional Convention
1788	U.S. Constitution Ratified

In April of 1787 James Madison was in New York City for another seemingly useless session of the Confederate Congress. His low opinion of the institution was surpassed only by his even lower opinion of many of its members. Back in 1780 and only one week after taking his seat in Congress, he had written to then Governor Jefferson that it suffered from inadequate statesmen[408] who were more interested in petty issues than the greater ones that plagued the nation.

The Articles of Confederation had been approved by the Continental Congress in 1777 (although it wouldn't be until 1781 that all states had ratified it). It provided for a confederation of states with a common trade and foreign policy. There was neither a federal executive nor a judiciary. There was a federal legislature, but it did not have any powers of enforcement. This model was very similar to that of the Dutch Republic, which consisted of seven states (or provinces).

In previous chapters we saw the problems that arose from that construct. Yet, jealous of their newfound independence, this is as far as the colonies were willing to go in the early days of the Revolution. The result was a system in which Congress made decisions, often with difficulty, of

James Madison, Thomas Jefferson, and Alexander Hamilton

which some had to be approved by each and every State legislature. In turn the states used the leverage they now had to extract concessions from other states with which they had an unrelated dispute. In 1786 the situation got really bad when Connecticut opened its ports to British ships to take advantage of the fact Massachusetts had closed its ports to them. The states were supposed to work in concert.

The confederation became meaningless and could well disintegrate. In addition to these interstate problems, the various states found it difficult, if not impossible, to repay their war debts to France and the Netherlands. And if that was not enough, the nation did not speak with one voice overseas and was therefore not taken seriously. The Virginia delegation in particular wanted the states to work more closely together. Of course they were advancing their own interests, among which was the free navigation of the Mississippi River. Officially, Virginia extended all the way to that river at the time. They found a fiery ally in New York by the name of Alexander Hamilton, an immigrant from the West Indies. Hamilton had been General Washington's aide-de-camp and wielded a lot of influence in New York. Already back in 1777 he had wanted a much stronger union under a federal executive and judiciary. The inability of Congress, under the current construct, to levy taxes particularly irked him.

In 1786 they had attempted to give Congress powers to regulate interstate commerce and met in Annapolis, Maryland. It came to nothing. The Virginians decided to call for a Constitutional Convention the next year to be held at Independence Hall in Philadelphia. The Annapolis Convention approved the plan unanimously. But would all States attend? Madison expected that it could make a difference if he convinced George Washington to lend his support to the Convention and raise its stature by going there in person. It took a bit of doing, but he did eventually speak with the General and received his commitment.

Now the Constitutional Convention was about to begin. Madison arrived in New York in April for a session of Congress. No doubt he met with Hamilton and discussed the upcoming debates. He had been preparing extensively by researching various confederate arrangements in history. He had read a myriad of books, many shipped to him by Jefferson from Paris. They included encyclopedias, books on human nature, studies and analyses of laws, and writings on governance. In short, he had just about everything ever written in Europe on these subjects.

His notes on the analysis of historic confederations survive. They show a thorough examination of the ancient Greek confederacies of Lycia, Amphyction, and Achaeia. Next they study the modern confederacies of the Swiss, the Germans, and the Dutch. All except the German were republics. After the Declaration of Independence, the Continental Congress had used the Dutch Republic as a prominent example for the formation of a confederation in North America[409]. It is no surprise that Madison had dedicated a lot of his attention to the Dutch. A century earlier, the Netherlands had been a world power, but its importance was now in decline. Since its independence in the 16th century, the country was a confederation of states that in the past had been nominally independent counties or duchies. Where the Dutch states were deliberating in a General Assembly (States General), the American Colonies were deliberating in a Continental Congress. There was much to learn from their experience. Fewer than ten years had passed and now the new confederation was about to become obsolete. It needed an overhaul.

Had they been wrong then? Probably not. The amount of unity that the new confederation offered was an improvement over the informal congress they had before and it was the closest form of unity they could get. With it they had been able to get help from the French and the Dutch and had achieved true independence. But now it had become inadequate, just as the Dutch Confederation had.

We saw what happened in the Netherlands in the Burgundian years and in the early years of its independence. Cities were at odds about commercial interests. So were some Dutch states. As long as there was a strong ruler – or enemy, for that matter -- to unite them, things stayed reasonably calm. The absence of a federal executive forced Barneveld to assume that role. Prince Maurice became Stadholder (military commander) and used the threat of military force to impose a measure of unity. During a period when there was no Prince of Orange, there was a somewhat stronger civil federal position (roughly coinciding with Cromwell's rule in England) that saw much turmoil and did not last very long. The Princes of Orange came back in power and created a stronger rule by nobility. The post of Stadholder was made hereditary in 1747[410]. Somewhat ironically, Madison's Montpelier was located in Orange County, Virginia, which was named after Prince William Henry Friso of Orange[411] who became the first hereditary Stadholder of all Dutch provinces. The appointment had been a serious step backward.

This was the situation Madison found and analyzed. It was the perfect example of how the confederate concept could be doomed. That is the specter he had to show to the Constitutional Convention in Philadelphia in May. Next he would present a plan for a new, federal government[412]. The legislature would be comprised of two houses. The number of members would be determined by the population of each state. The first house would be elected every three years; the second every seven years. There would be an executive in the form of a president and a judiciary that could rule on issues regarding federal law. The whole construct would be designed to provide a strong central government while preserving states' rights.

Madison's determination to save his country from a looming demise, coupled with his curiosity-driven research and great intellect, put him in the same tradition we witnessed in earlier chapters in people like Queen Balthild of the Franks, Philip van Leyden in Holland, Bradford in England, Holland and Plimoth Plantation, and countless others mentioned or not mentioned in these pages. All these received help from others. Balthild had Bishop Landri and the monk Marculf, Philip van Leyden co-opted the Count of Holland, and William Bradford learned his most important lessons regarding governance from Robertson, his minister.

Madison's foremost supporter was Thomas Jefferson. They were old friends. When the two were apart, they shortened the distance with a lively and intellectual correspondence. Jefferson, who was as curious as his friend and who had amassed an extensive library, kept feeding Madison books (Madison would eventually have over 4,000 titles[413]). During Jefferson's years in Europe, he shipped crates of books to Madison. But the small man (Madison was short) did not rely on Jefferson alone. He tested his ideas confidentially with George Washington and Edmund Randolph, the Governor of Virginia[414].

Congress's business was concluded in late April, 1787. Eager to be in Philadelphia well ahead of time, Madison departed New York on May 2nd. He hoped that others of the Virginia delegation would arrive early as well so they would have time to prepare their arguments and presentations. Also, he liked to give himself time to recuperate from the long and arduous stagecoach ride.

Madison left New York quite likely in a driving rain. According to the meteorological observations at Spring Mill near Philadelphia[415], the month of April had been dry but recorded six to eight days of precipitation (three described as tempest) followed by an extremely wet and cold month of May. Coaches were unheated, roads were unpaved, and ferries were mostly open sailboats. Madison had two alternative modes of transportation. The older of the two (opened in 1738) would take him by boat to New Brunswick, New Jersey, then by stagecoach through Princeton to Trenton[416]. From there he could travel the Old York Road to Philadelphia and cross the Delaware River at Coryell's Ferry, now Lambertville. The other route, opened in 1740, would allow him to disembark at Amboy, New Jersey, for a stage ride to Bordentown, where he had a choice of taking either a boat or another stage to Philadelphia. Neither alternative was comfortable and the bad weather would make it an ordeal. Under these conditions, he sailed from Manhattan to New Jersey. It is quite possible he spent the night since stages usually left in the very early morning hours. New Brunswick had a few taverns or guesthouses to choose from and there was at least one in Amboy.

The road was not very good in 1787. Asher Miner's newspaper, *The Correspondent* of June 4th, 1805, read,

"It is presumed a beneficial improvement might be made on the Old York Road, particularly at Sampson's Hill, Kerr's Hill, at Neshaminy, and

Watson's Hill, by reducing the ascent to the common standard of turnpike roads." Another account reads, "... a dreadful mire of blackish mud rested near the present Rising Sun Village, ... the team of Mr. Nickum, of Chestnut Hill, [was] stalled; and in endeavoring to draw out the fore horse with an iron chain to his head, it slipped and tore off the lower jaw, and the horse died on the spot."

The report goes on with other horror stories of horses, wagons, and people getting stuck on various sections of the road. Travel by coach was a challenge as it was. Another, older, anecdote[417] "laments the calling

General George Washington

of passengers from bed to get into coaches an hour or two before day. The travelers were hurried along till one, two, or three hours within the night, sitting stifled with heat in summer, and choked with dust; in the winter, starving and freezing with cold, choked with fogs, reaching inns by torchlight, too late to sit up and get supper, and the next morning into the coach too early to get breakfast. It was necessary to ride with strangers, often sick, ancient or diseased, or crying children." It goes on, "The fellow-passengers must be humored; a passenger was often poisoned with scents, and crippled with a crowd of boxes and bundles. Sometimes he was forced to wade up to the knees in mire in foul ways, and sit in cold until horses were sent to pull the coach out. The coaches were rotten, and the tackle, or perch, or axle-tree broken, causing a wait of three or four hours, sometimes half a day, and then a necessity of traveling all night to make up time lost." It is small wonder James Madison liked to give himself time to recuperate.

Madison's trip lasted three days. He must have spent two, presumably short, nights, at a guesthouse or tavern. One such was the Rising Sun Inn at the crossroads of York Road and Germantown Road. It was a stone building and a famous place where "many a cold and hungry traveler in the weary staging days left here refreshed by a hearty meal.[418]" Another was the Crooked Billet Tavern, on the York Road in Hatborough, now Hatboro, Pennsylvania. It was of some fame because of the battle of that name that took place here in 1778[419] and George Washington had his staff meetings there in 1777[420].

Weary from the trip, Madison arrived in Philadelphia on May 5th and checked in at the boardinghouse of Mrs. House on the southwest corner of Fifth and Market Streets, just a block from Independence Hall. He booked rooms for his fellow Virginia delegates and spent the next week honing his case.

The next delegate to arrive was George Washington.

Washington's Journey

Among the travelers who braved the wet, rutted, and muddy roads the second week of May was George Washington, Revolutionary War hero, Father of the Land[421], and General of the Continental Army of the United States of America. He had left Mount Vernon four days earlier, traveling huddled in his carriage. After a long first day, he arrived at Bladensburg, Maryland, with a splitting headache and feeling nauseated. At fifty-five, his mind was as strong as ever, but his body showed the effects of long rides on horseback and long days and nights in the elements, exposed to the extremes of the weather. But he had not lost his powers of recuperation yet.

Stagecoach

The next day he felt better, but delayed his departure due to rain[422]. Around eight o'clock, the rain let up and they hastily set off for Baltimore, where they entered the Fountain Inn while it was still dry outside.

The Inn, a famous landmark at the time, was a small, unassuming, three-story building on the corner of Light and Redwood Streets. Washington decided to rest a bit before visiting his old aide-de-camp, James McHenry. His friend was a skilled surgeon who had served with the Fifth Pennsylvania Battalion during the Revolutionary War before serving Washington and later Major-General Lafayette. McHenry was a fellow Federalist and convention delegate for Maryland. Washington had much to discuss with him about the upcoming convention in Philadelphia.

We can imagine the pleasant supper at McHenry's house and the retreat in the parlor with the two friends drawing smoke from cigars. Without a doubt, the discussion was dominated by proposed remedies for the ailing confederation. The country was deep in debt and the loose structure of the union made it difficult to determine shared responsibility for the repayments. That in turn had made creditors reluctant to lend more. Washington spent the night at the house and left the next morning before breakfast for the ferry at Havre de Grace to cross the Susquehanna. The weather was stormy and the winds kicked up waves too high for the ferry to safely traverse it. Washington probably lodged at the tavern of his old friend Colonel John Rogers, then 61. In his diary, Washington tells of a difficult crossing the next day. We do not know if, or how much, the General pressured the ferry operator when they made the attempt in the early morning. After the crossing, he had his breakfast at the ferry house on the east bank and then hurried onward. While he stopped for lunch at the Head of Elk, another old friend, Francis Corbin, caught up with him. Corbin was a Virginia state delegate, but not an official delegate to the

Grand Convention. But as an interested party, Corbin wanted to be there and assist his fellow Federalists as needed. It appears he was on horseback since Washington invited him to seek shelter in his carriage. Together they went on and lodged at Wilmington, Delaware.

Word of Washington's progress had traveled ahead. When he and Corbin arrived at Chester for lunch, a group of officers was waiting to greet him. Among them was the Speaker of the Pennsylvania Assembly, General Mifflin. The small group of horses and carriages went on to Gray's ferry on the Schuylkill River. On the other side, they were met by Philadelphia's Light Horse, who led them into the city. The first stretch of High Street (also called Market Street) was lined with artillery officers who saluted the General and his entourage as they rode in. It being the Sabbath, a large crowd had formed in the streets and many onlookers followed the parade to Mrs. Mary House's Boarding House on Market and Fifth Streets. They watched as Washington stepped out of his carriage and entered the brick boarding house. Loud cheers emanated from many throats. The General's chest and bags followed, but soon came back out again. Robert Morris had anticipated where his old friend would be staying and had waited inside. He insisted that Washington stay with his family in their imposing three-story house. Washington probably made a perfunctory protest, but was probably happy to exchange the cramped boarding house for the space and tranquility of the richly decorated mansion. Its beautifully landscaped grounds took up almost the whole city block between Sixth, Seventh, Chestnut, and Walnut Streets[423]. Washington would stay there all through the Convention.

The Virginia Delegation

Various notes and letters[424] show that on May 14, 1787, four members each of the Virginia and Pennsylvania delegations met at the Pennsylvania State House at the appointed time for the opening of the Constitutional Convention. Those present were disappointed in varying degrees. After having met with the same small group the next day, Washington wrote, it "is highly vexatious to those who are idly and expensively spending their time here.[425]" The general expected his troops to be on time. Madison was more forgiving, although he must have felt anxiety about the prospect of another failed convention. "... *the late bad weather has been the principal cause*[426]," he wrote to Jefferson in Paris. Since indeed the weather was bad there was no other option than to wait.

The Virginia delegation—Washington, Madison, John Blair, and George Wythe—decided to make use of the wait for a quorum. At Morris's invitation, they would get together at the mansion and work on a plan. They would first meet at the State House at 11 in the morning. If there was no quorum, they would meet at 1 in the afternoon at Morris's.

By May 17, Edmund Randolph, George Mason, and James McClurg had arrived in Philadelphia and the Virginia delegation was complete. All felt the weight on their shoulders. They had to come up with a plan that would create a strong federation and still be acceptable to the states. The future of the nation depended on it. It was a tall order considering what had gone before. The Federalists[427] had been unhappy with the Articles of Confederation soon after they had been approved by the Continental Congress. And even the Articles had been a hard sell and hadn't been ratified by all the colonies until 1781, six years after the beginning of the Revolution. Some colonies had hoped an accommodation with England could be made and postponed their vote. It wasn't until a large French army had landed in Massachusetts that they felt secure enough to put the Articles to a vote. And then there had been plenty of objections still.

As the federalist Virginians had feared, the weak union that the confederate system provided had been cause for much acrimony. Foreign policy, including engaging in treaties, was supposed to be the purview of the central government. But states were making their own arrangements, often against the interests of other states. In 1786, New Hampshire complained that Massachusetts charged duties on goods that came in through Boston[428]. In turn Massachusetts complained that Connecticut welcomed British ships it had banned from its ports. In early 1787, New Jersey accused New York of charging harbor fees on its ships and all that Congress could do was to advise that New Jersey retaliate.

James Madison saw a benefit in the delay in the start of the Convention. As we saw in the prologue, he had spent a lot of time studying various forms of government the year before. He had also read a great deal on the subject of human nature which was an awakening science in his day. As a result, he had put together a format for governance of the United States that reconciled human nature with governance. But it needed to be critiqued and honed. So he gratefully accepted Washington's suggestion to the Virginia delegation that they remove to Morris's mansion after each adjournment and work on the proposal together.

The challenge was to create a central government that was strong enough to keep the States together, but not so strong that the States had no power whatsoever and would reject it. There were voices that called for the creation of a monarchy with the House of Washington on the throne.

Fortunately the group had more imagination and looked for a new architecture of government.

The group made good progress and even George Washington was in a better mood now that the delays had actually proved useful. The meetings in the ornately decorated room at Morris Mansion allowed them to iron out any disagreements among themselves. Large glass double doors overlooking a lush spring garden let in the gray light of an unusually wet spring. Bookcases lined the walls from floor to ceiling. Richly bound books filled the shelves. The men huddled around a heavy oak table in the gloomy library of the mansion of Robert Morris. It was appropriate that they should meet in a library. These were men of books – well raised, well educated, well read, and well positioned in society. The discussion was lively. In spite of that, they were unhappy. It hadn't been that many years since they had worked so hard to wrest a nation out of thirteen English colonies and unite them into a confederation of equal States. And now that nation was in serious danger of disintegration.

The Clerk

Jacob Shallus was assistant clerk to the Pennsylvania legislature[429]. When in session, he worked at the State House where the Convention was about to open. He was born in 1750, one year after his parents arrived in America as part of a wave of German immigrants. The newcomers were probably a close knit group and, in 1771, Shallus married the daughter of a well to do German merchant named Melchior. According to publications and documents, the young couple moved to a house on Second Street near Vine where Shallus registered a business next to the Red Lion Inn. In 1774, the city tax rolls mention him as, "Jacob Shallus, gentleman," and that he owed £45. That same year his wife, Elizabeth, gave birth to their first child, a boy whom they named Francis. The outlook was good for the little family but, as we know, clouds had been gathering over the North American colonies for some time.

To counter British oppression, the First Continental Congress assembled in Philadelphia on September 5, 1774, where the delegates drew up a declaration of colonial rights. It may be that Shallus's business faced challenges of its own. That same month he put two properties up for sale, including his shop on Second Street. There are no records of a sale until a year later when the shop sold to two merchants in rum, wine, and sugar. If indeed it took that long to sell, and, if armed conflict was in the air, then the price Shallus would have received might well have been low. He may not have been cut out for a businessman. However, he must have received a good education since he could write well. He may already have worked for the Pennsylvania Land Office, as he did later.

1776

At this time the Second Continental Congress had created an American Continental Army under the command of General George Washington. The First Pennsylvania Battalion was formed in October, 1775, under the command of Colonel John Phillip de Haas. We do not know exactly when Shallus mustered as a volunteer with the Pennsylvania Brigade, but, on January 19, 1776, he had already passed the ranks of Barrack Master and Commissary and was promoted to be its Quartermaster. It was a task that required clerical and organizational skills and a great sense of responsibility.

Canada, 1776

The first American fighting force was a group of well-intentioned, but wholly unprepared men. Under the leadership of Benedict Arnold, a collection of New England and Pennsylvania militias had invaded Canada with the purpose of taking Québec and thus preventing the British from using it as a staging area for an invasion of northern New York. At last armed resistance had become the answer to British repression. Excessive taxation, trade restrictions, the quartering of military personnel in citizens' houses, and the absence of American political influence in London had raised resentment while apparent American wealth and entrepreneurial spirit had raised British resentment. Events in Massachusetts eventually sparked the powder keg and North America was at war.

On May 6 three heavily armed British vessels moored at Québec to relieve the city from the American siege. The army received orders to make an orderly retreat[430] that evening under cover of darkness. Orderly was the operative word for Jacob Shallus. As Quartermaster of the Pennsylvania brigade he was responsible for its supplies. But, as Shallus relates in his diary, the soldiers panicked, "*as soon as the Yankees saw the Enemy, and heard their Field Pieces, they flew off the ground, forgot they had the Small Pox, threw away their muskets and bayonets, but took special care of their provisions."* Shallus managed to save some of the supplies while the British were in pursuit. The Americans were no match for the superior British firepower and experience and their only option was to retreat from Canada altogether. Some days they marched as much as thirty miles. He wrote, "I was so much fatigued, hardly able to stand, and nothing to eat since the first of our retreat." They crossed many rivers in boats of various sizes. Some they commandeered as they went along, others were provided by sympathetic Québécois who had no great love for their British occupiers.

On June 2 General Arnold ordered Shallus's commanding officer, Colonel de Haas, *"to cross over with as many of the best men in his detachment, as the bateaux could carry, which would be about 300 to Connisidago, an Indian Town, surround it, and kill, burn, and destroy the whole and spare none, nor leave one stone unturned; then return to St. Anns, burn and destroy that; and then return to La Chine and wait for the General Orders."* The order to kill innocent women and children was not unusual, not then and, alas, not everywhere today. Shallus described the reaction of de Haas and the other officers. Everyone, without exception, thought the first part of the order horrific. To their credit they chose to dismiss it as too dangerous in their present condition. Shallus expended a fair amount of ink and paper on the issue. He wrote, "as the Indians were invited to a Treaty to be held in a few days at Caughnewago, humanity here I think cried aloud against an attempt to kill and destroy Women and Infants perhaps at the breast of their Mother." Next he related the Indian custom of adopting the children of the vanquished and raising them as their own. That he would write so much about the affair shows his concern for fairness and justice. His conscience was challenged by cold-blooded murder. It was not his way and it was not the way of the Pennsylvania Brigade. They did however burn St. Ann's to the ground and appeared to get great enjoyment out of the "bonfire". Eventually the troops were ordered to retreat to Montreal and join with Arnold's main force for the general retreat back to New York.

Shallus's last entry in his diary of the Québec campaign was on July 1, 1776. In it he mentioned that they had left Canada. There is no bitterness in his words. On the contrary, he relates how well he and Colonel de Haas had been treated by the *"Clergy and Noblesse"* at their *"Houses."* *"We lived like princes,"* he wrote. However, if they had expected to go home they would have been disappointed. De Haas reported in October on the conditions his soldiers endured. *"The men almost naked, as in two-thirds of the campaign."* There was a shortage of tents and, *"The Quartermaster has never been enabled by the public to supply the regiment in a proper manner.*

After the hardships of a winter campaign in Canada, with those they have since experienced, there is not the least reason to think that the men will reenlist at this place." It was a situation that would plague the war effort throughout which is very well described in Paul Lockhart's book, The Drillmaster of Valley Forge[431].

Shallus resigned his commission on January 1, 1777. He had enough. But Philadelphia was not as he had left it. The barracks, meeting houses, churches, even private dwellings were filled with soldiers on their way to the front. Hospitals overflowed with sick and wounded coming back from the battles. Washington Square had become a burial ground for hundreds in shallow graves. Shallus's wife, Elizabeth, along with so many other women, had her hands full caring for the wretched men. Half the city had fled, including Congress, in fear of a British assault. The black market thrived on the scarcity of goods. But Shallus was not easily discouraged. Possibly on the strength of his war record he secured the position of Deputy Commissary General for Pennsylvania.

The mood in the city improved when Washington defeated the British in New Jersey and marched four hundred prisoners through the streets. Congress returned in March along with thousands of refugees. But the respite was brief. A renewed British move on Philadelphia prompted the Pennsylvania Assembly and Executive Council to relocate to Lancaster. Shallus and family packed up and joined. Congress moved to York. In his new position he was responsible for purchases, a task that was in line with his experience. It appears that he may have suffered similar shortages of funds and used some of his own to fulfill his duties. In a letter to Congress he complained about not being reimbursed by the proper authorities for "Money advanced of my private property." Around the same time a bundle of cash Shallus was to forward appears to have been lost. His position was not an easy one but by all accounts he discharged his duties well.

In June, 1778, American forces entered the city, which had been abandoned by the British. Fearing retribution, some 3,000 civilians had followed the retreat. The new French-American alliance was having an impact. Congress, the Executive Council, and, presumably, Jacob Shallus, returned to Philadelphia at the end of June. The city was in a shambles. Properties had been sacked and vandalized and the British had left owing thousands of pounds in debts. British sympathizers were hunted down. Shallus participated actively in the persecution as witnessed by a statement in the *Pennsylvania Packet* of July 25, 1778, calling for testimony against collaborators. It was signed by Shallus, Thomas Paine, and 184 others. Whether he supported the execution of two Quakers (and thus pacifists) is not known but all available evidence shows he was a staunch patriot.[432]

Pennsylvania State House, now Independence Hall

Shallus was again mentioned in a notice in the *Pennsylvania Gazette* of February, 1779, which announced the sale of nail-rod irons and indigo on Second Street. The tax rolls of 1779 show that he was taxed on a holding in the Mulberry ward and on 50 acres, a horse, and two cattle in Bedford County (where his relatives Boston and Conrad Shallus lived). In September of that year he signed on to a risky venture. Together with a military officer, William Will, he formed a company to sponsor a privateer. The sloop, *Retrieve,* was to prey on enemy ships. The proceeds could be lucrative but the bond they had to post with the Secretary of Congress was substantial: $5,000. There are no records of *Retrieve's* success but Shallus's land holdings were considerable by 1782.[433]

The *Pennsylvania Gazette* of March 24, 1779, carried a statement that pointed out what was wrong with the Pennsylvania Constitution. The grievance had mainly to do with taxation and was signed by such luminaries as Thomas Mifflin and Robert Morris. The names of Jacob Shallus and that of his brother in law, Isaac Melchior, were included. Being mostly merchants, the signers were conservatives who wanted government to aid business and protect private property. They also wanted self-government for Philadelphia, presumably with a similar pro commerce slant. All this implies that Shallus had joined the ranks of well-to-do Republicans. In 1780 he owned 147 acres in Bucks County and in 1782 owned 140 acres in Falls Township and another 1,880 acres in Northumberland County.

By 1783 his fortunes seemed to have waned. He owed back taxes on one property and scrambled to hold on to another. He got the job of assistant clerk of the Pennsylvania Assembly in October. Interesting to note is that the appointment was recorded in the Minutes Book in his hand. Also in his hand is a transcription of George Washington's address of gratitude to the Assembly of December 9. The calligraphy is of high quality and especially the pseudo signature of George Washington has a beautiful flourish. These skills, as we shall see, would cause him to be given a unique honor. The Assembly reelected Shallus to his position all through the 1780s.[434]

The job did not pay enough to maintain his growing family (there were eight children by 1788). We do not know how he supplemented his income during the time the Assembly was not in session. But his post was respectable, and so were his family relations and his military record. He was a member of the historic Masonic Lodge 2 and pledged money toward the construction of a new lodge building[435].

Philadelphia, Friday, May 25, 1787

It is easy to imagine Jacob Shallus walking briskly from his home[436] in the Northern Liberties Township[437] to his office in the stately building on Chestnut Street in the brotherly city of Philadelphia. The middle-aged veteran of the Revolutionary War was almost certainly among the throng that surrounded Washington as he alighted from his carriage. Jacob Shallus was not there in an official capacity and there is no record of his attendance. However, from his diary[438] and his position of assistant clerk of the general assembly we may assume he had an above-average interest in public affairs. Quite possibly he may have felt a responsibility for the administrative aspects of the prospective proceedings. We shall develop a scenario of how the events could have taken place based on the few facts concerning George Washington that we are certain of.

Φ In spite of the dreary morning, there was expectation in Jacob's step. The Grand Convention was likely to open today. Among the delegates from the thirteen states was General George Washington, as were the delegates from Pennsylvania; men he worked with and knew so well. The rain was coming down harder but his umbrella was large. Anticipating the rain, he was wearing his gaiters, but they had not prevented muddy specks from sullying his pants. Fortunately he kept his shoes well oiled and his route could have been a lot worse had he not been familiar with the streets. He crossed Market Street, which was already busy with horse-drawn streetcars, cargo laden wagons going to and from the port; vendors' push carts – some with a draft dog underneath—a few horses with riders, and many men and women on foot. Some wore heavy capes with hoods and others carried umbrellas. But the mud was everywhere. The frequent rains of the past week[439] had taken their toll on the street surface.

As Shallus turned the corner of Fifth and Chestnut Streets, a small group of men got out of a carriage and passed through a gathering of onlookers that had braved the weather on the sidewalk on front of the State House[440]. He could hear their voices as the small group walked up the few steps and entered the doorway. After so many years, Shallus still loved the sight of the stepped tower, whose base stood on the other side of the two-story building. The building and the lower sections of the tower were made of fired red brick while the upper part of the tower was whitewashed. All four sides had a clock face. Shallus hurried on. He wanted to see who had just arrived.

Inside, he stopped at the double doors of the assembly room, where he removed his overcoat. The leather souls of his shoes knocking on the pine floor sent echoes through the dark, empty room. The six tall windows allowed little of the gray outdoor light to reach inside. He swung right to the familiar, tall narrow desk where he took his notes when the Assembly was in session. Shallus stood behind his desk and surveyed the room. A long walnut railing ran from the window near his desk across the room to the far wall. In the center it was interrupted by two swing gates. Beyond the railing were a number of large tables at which the delegates would sit. One table was placed on a low podium in the center of the opposite wall; from it the chairman directed the proceedings. The podium was flanked by two fireplaces. The smell of smoke hung in the air and the cracks and pops of burning wood softly reverberated. Weak shadows played on the walls. An attendant walked in and exchanged greetings with Shallus. The man walked through the swing gates and started to light oil lamps on the tables closest to the podium and those on the podium itself. The sparse yellow glows mixed with the fires' flames to bring a hint of cheer to the dusk. Voices started to fill the room when the visitors crossed the threshold from the central hall. They walked to the lamp lit tables, where some put down their document folders and a few pulled chairs and sat down. In the next hour more arrived. Just before eleven o'clock, George Washington entered. A loud murmur interrupted the conversations and everyone present stood. Shallus took in the scene for a moment and left the hall. ⊖

CONVENTION AT PHILADELPHIA, 1787.

The seven activists from Virginia were content with the result of their efforts. Their plan would address all the shortcomings of the Articles of Confederation. And it wasn't any too soon. As they had every morning since arriving, they met in the assembly room of the State House and this time a quorum had at last been met.

Thomas Morris, delegate of Pennsylvania, proposed that a president of the Convention be elected by ballot. Upon approval he nominated George Washington[441]. Not surprisingly the general was elected by unanimous vote. Morris and Rutledge directed Washington to the chair, where he expressed his gratitude to the delegates for the honor they had given him. Then he proceeded to remind the delegates of the unusual nature of the business he was to preside over and apologized for his lack of qualifications to do so. The humble indulgence was intended to be disarming and it set the tone for the housekeeping that followed. The meeting appointed a secretary and a committee tasked with the preparation of standing rules and orders that would govern the Convention. Then the meeting adjourned to Monday, which gave the newly appointed officers time to prepare for and work on their tasks.

According to his diary entry for the day, Washington went to the house of Thomas Willing, who lived at 100 South Third Street[442]. They could have been twins so much did they resemble each other. Willing was often mistaken for his good friend the General[443]. Washington dined there and spent the evening at his lodgings. His Saturday appears to have passed very socially. He wrote, "Returned all my visits this afternoon." He dined at the City Tavern with some club members and retreated to his quarters for an evening of letter writing. His Sunday appears much quieter. He reports going to the "Romish Church to high mass. – Dined, drank Tea, and spent the evening at my lodgings." Washington's diary contains no references to the deliberations at the Convention. It is as if the secrecy of the assembly extended to his diary. Perhaps the general was relaxed about the outcome of the Convention or, perhaps, he was determined to play the role of the confident field commander whose calm radiated into the soldiers' hearts.

We may assume that the other delegates spent their weekend much in the same fashion, although most stayed in much less comfortable quarters such as boarding houses. Many had to share their rooms and most did not have as many devoted friends as did General Washington. The members of the Rules Committee surely met to hammer out proper rules under which the deliberations were to be conducted. They may have worked in the discomfort of their boarding house.

And James Madison? We can be sure he spent his time rehearsing the arguments. He knew his fellow man. He knew the nature of the resistance some had to a closer union. He later wrote, "*It is a matter of both wonder and regret, that those who raise so many objections against the new Constitution should never call to mind the defects of that which is to be exchanged for it. It is not necessary that the former should be perfect; it is sufficient that the latter is more imperfect*[444]." But he also understood the danger, "*that in every political institution, a power to advance the public happiness, involves a discretion which may be misapplied and abused*[445]." And Madison saw the limitations of a new Constitution in that, "*time only … can mature and perfect so compound a system, can liquidate the meaning of all the parts, and adjust them to each other in a harmonious and consistent Whole*." He expected subsequent generations to make changes according to their needs. And making changes as the need arose, that is what they were embarking on now.

So, what was in the Virginia Plan?

The original handwritten document fills the two sides of one sheet. In broad lines, it proposed there be three branches of government, an executive, a legislature, and a judiciary. The legislature was to consist of two branches. The members of the first were to be elected by the people of each state while the members of the second were to be elected by members of the first, out of candidates nominated by each state's legislature. It proposed that the executive and the judiciary each be elected by the national legislature.

As the Convention wore on, there were competing plans such as the New Jersey Plan that called for a single chamber of the national legislature to be elected by the states' legislatures. Charles Pinckney of South Carolina proposed another plan and Alexander Hamilton of New York presented one of his own.

On Monday morning the 28th of May, the members again gathered at the State House, now under the presiding authority of George Washington. At 10 O'clock he stood behind the chairman's desk, lifted the gavel, and let it land on the oak surface.

Preamble of the United States Constitution

It is evident, if we do not radically depart from a [con]federal plan, we shall share the fate of ancient and modern confederacies. The amphyctionic council, like the American congress, had the power of judging in the last resort in war and peace—call out forces—send ambassadors. What was its fate or continuance? Philip of Macedon, with little difficulty, destroyed every appearance of it. The Athenian had nearly the same fate—The Helvetic confederacy is rather a league—In the German confederacy the parts are too strong for the whole—The Dutch are in a most wretched situation—weak in all its parts, and only supported by surrounding contending powers.
James Madison in his reply to the New Jersey Plan, 19 June, 1787
(according to Yates).

Epilogue

Washington's gavel fell many more times in the Convention that had started in the cold wet spring, struggled through the long hot summer, and ended just before the onset of fall on September 17, 1787. For James Madison and his supporters, it had been a long hard struggle. Several delegates had left -- some angrily and others for personal reasons. There were barely enough delegates or delegations left for the final vote.

But, the new Constitution passed. We know the opening words on the parchment so well[446]. "*We the People*" and all of the text that followed were put there in the exquisite calligraphic handwriting of Jacob Shallus, assistant clerk of the Pennsylvania Assembly (for which he received $30). It was his document that was signed by those who approved of the "more perfect Union" it described. It was a remarkable accomplishment of a group of people who had been tenacious in their convictions and who, instead of standing idly, had taken the bull by the horns and ridden the beast until it had turned in their direction. But they were not done yet. It took two years for eleven states to ratify the Constitution and another two before the Constitution, including the Bill of Rights, was adopted by all thirteen. The U.S. Bill of Rights was influenced by George Mason's 1776 Virginia Declaration of Rights, the 1689 English Bill of Rights, and other works[447].

Everyone understood that the document was a compromise. The expectation that the Convention would provide "a more perfect Union" than under the current Articles of Confederation proved a powerful argument during the Convention. Madison repeated the argument in *Federalist 38*, writing, "It is not necessary that the former should be perfect, it is sufficient that the latter is more imperfect." They understood that the perfect often was the enemy of the good. Many also understood that the document was of a temporary nature; that future generations would mold it to their needs.

Some understood that, whatever its provisions, there would be groups and individuals who would find ways to recruit the Constitution's provisions to advance narrow interests and eventually corrupt the system and gain power for themselves. Jefferson suggested that there ought to be a revolution at least every twenty years.[448]

Our Founding Fathers and Framers followed in the footsteps of activists throughout human history. There have always been people who wanted to improve the plight of their communities or societies. These good folks, and the ones that followed, all were actively pursuing their cause.

In that light we have to see our founders. We can admire them for their courage, wisdom, and stick-to-it-ism. But, as many of them would have said, they were human with human failings who did not think they deserved the pedestal on which some would place them. Certainly they would have rejected reverence, as if they were deities. They did not want their words be used as Scripture. Isn't it ironic that their words can be used by parties in support of both sides of opposing views? Does it not prove that the Framers had disagreements, too? Fortunately a large amount of writing from the years surrounding the Convention survives. That material, in turn, inspired subsequent scholars, historians, and others. Without fail, all these works show the nature of the disagreements (and disagreements on disagreements, etc.) and the arguments used. If at all, what then makes these people, whom we now address collectively in words[449] that start with the capital letters "F", special or deserving of idolatry? Or makes the United States "exceptional" to the point that the condition has become a supreme virtue, regardless of ideas or examples from elsewhere that might in fact represent improvements?

Our Founding Fathers certainly did not subscribe to such a smug, and ultimately self-defeating, attitude.

By and large the people we examined in these pages had a broad view. They addressed the big picture and attempted to improve it. Young people naturally rebel against their parents and that which their parents created. The push-back from the older generation forces the younger one to become more creative. It is a skill that requires a broad view. As the youngsters age, they develop more knowledge and wisdom and, if circumstances allow, get to implement some of their ideals. To the next generation, then, these are no longer ideals. They are now facts, and those facts in turn will be tested by time and new generations.

Society needs activists in order to advance. It also needs the participation of ordinary people. University of Denver professors Erica Chenoweth and Maria Stephan conducted a study[450] of violent and non-violent revolutions from 1900 to 2006. For non-violent revolutions, they found that participation by just 3.5 percent of the population was sufficient for success, if they were sustained and "inclusive and representative in terms of gender, race, political party, class, and the urban-rural distinction."

One should note that the Framers did not want, nor did they anticipate, the formation of political parties. They saw that in England the party system stifled innovation and activism. Ever since the formation of parties, activism has had to come from outside government. Think of the Abolitionists, the Prohibitionists, and the Tea Party of today. In the case of the latter, the strategy has been different, aiming (not yet successfully, it seems) at a partial take-over of an existing political party, the Republicans. The Tea Partiers can probably rightfully claim to be working in accordance with the Framers' intent. However, it is in method only. Although they claim to hark back to the Framers, their message of States' rights and a limited role for the federal government has a confederative ring.

The conversion of the English monarchy from Catholic to Protestant saved Protestant Europe, twice. Since at the national level limited forms of participatory government during the Reformation existed primarily in Protestant Europe, it is no stretch to conclude that the cause of democracy was preserved and strengthened by that conversion. After the defeat of the elected Saxon King Harold by the feudal Count William of Normandy in 1066, it took the English six hundred years to regain a say in matters of governance. There had been progress along the way but, as far as governance, even the much-heralded Magna Carta of 1215 addressed the rights of nobility only and, in any case, was signed by King John under duress. He almost immediately repudiated it. But it did establish Common Law, which the English built upon. Eventually the intervention from across the Narrow Sea helped restore some of the Saxon social customs and customs of governance. William of Orange was their leader and Hans Bentinck their bold executor.

As these things go, the two friends could not foresee that the modernization brought by the Glorious Revolution would strengthen English commerce to the point where it would outpace that of the Dutch Republic. Over the following century, institutional change continued and brought increased benefits to England. The system of governance in the Netherlands, first formulated in 1477, was showing its age. Unable to adapt to the changing world around them, the old institutions and confederate form of national government caused the Republic to lag behind. Their answer to the weakness of the central government was not to innovate and move forward. In the middle of the 18th century, the Dutch Republic took a step back and increased the power of the old aristocracy. The States' positions of Stadholder were unified in one hereditary post that nearly rose to the level of King. Stale institutions and the loss of commerce to an innovative England led to a weaker country. The Republic eventually fell to the French while England became the hub of international commerce. As Britain ruled the waves, most Dutch colonies were lost to them.

Eventually most North American colonies would become British Royal Colonies. Each continued its inevitable path toward independence. Individually, they were too weak to shake colonial rule. They could have waited it out and gained their freedom as all large British dominions eventually did. But they could not wait. Their citizens had become Americans, just like Adriaen van der Donck, and, when they were all aggrieved in the same way, they rose together and mustered the strength to found their own nation. They believed that the self-determination of the individual, with rights and duties, was paramount and could be attained only in a true democracy, where justice ruled and opportunities were equal for all (admittedly, their definition of "all" was at first very limited.). Where the Dutch had ultimately failed to progress, the Americans succeeded.

Logically there is no healthy way back. The Dutch tried it and failed. Humanity moves onward driven by new ideas, new technology, new ways of doing things. It demands new ways in which to be governed. Therefore the story did not end in 1787 or in 1791. It does not end here and now. The U.S. form of government is now more than 220 years old — just about as old as the Dutch Republic was. But that republic eventually failed and fell because it could not adapt to changing circumstances. Will America find a similar fate? If history is a guide, the answer is, inevitably, yes. We can ask ourselves; how far are we from that point? However, a better question is; what can we do to postpone or, better yet, prevent it?

The stories in this book should provide hope. Again we have to be reminded of Queen Balthild who rose from slavery and, together with powerful allies, introduced changes that improved the plight of her subjects. Philips van Leyden borrowed the concept of the Public Good from the Romans and sold the notion to Count William, who improved the plight of the Hollanders. William of Orange started a revolution and freed a country. The commoner John of Barneveld led the Republic to great prominence in an otherwise monarchical Europe. Edwin Sandys used his position to become the father of American republicanism. Adriaen van der Donck created the idea of Americans as a separate community with rights. And there were countless others these pages have not mentioned.

Luckily for us, these people had the right skills at the right time in the right circumstances. They participated in one form or other in the political discourse of their times. By doing so, they were responsible for our better lives today. This author would propose that we owe it to them, and not least ourselves, to participate in the processes of democracy. We have it a lot easier than they did. Our lives are not on the line – only a bit of our time. So, no matter what your cause or conviction, stand up, voice your thoughts, and be counted.

Some day our heirs will write about us; what we did with our republic, with our democracy; how we changed, added to, or subtracted from our freedoms; what wisdoms we came up with or what follies we gave into. Most of all, they will analyze, and inevitably judge, how we reacted to the change of time and the cultures or technologies it brought. I hope they will praise us. But I also hope that we and they realize that our journey will never reach an end. And that in that journey only one thing is certain: with human nature what it is: for democracy to be a constant, the interests of the many will continuously have to trump the interests of the few.

All Europe must by degrees be aroused to the recollection and assertion of the rights of human nature. Your good will to Mankind will be gratified with the prospect, and your pleasure as an American be enhanced by the reflection that the light which is chasing darkness and despotism from the old world, is but an emanation from that which has produced and succeeded the establishment of liberty in the New.
James Madison to Edmund Pendleton, 4 March, 1790.

THE END

With us [in the United States] there are more books than buyers of Books. In England there are more buyers than Readers. Hence those Gorgeous Editions, which are destined to sleep in the private libraries of the Rich, whose vanity aspires to that species of furniture; or who give that turn to their public spirit and patronage of letters.
James Madison to Edward Everett, 19 March, 1823.

Bibliography

A General Index to the Publications of the Parker Society, Cambridge University Press, Cambridge, 1855.

Ainsworth, Henry, *The Book of Psalmes*, 1612.

Ames, Azel, *The May-Flower and her Log*, Houghton Mifflin and Company, Boston, 1901.

Amesbury Archer, http://www.wessexarch.co.uk/projects/amesbury/archer.html.

Anonymous *transcript of Shallus's diary* archived at the Harvard University Library.

Anonymous, *Mourt's Relation*, Applewood Books, Bedford, 1963.

Bangs, Jeremy, *Strangers and Pilgrims, Travelers and Sojourners: Leiden and the*

Foundations of Plymouth Plantation, General Society of Mayflower Descendants, 2009.

Barton, Dennis, *James II and the Glorious Revolution*, http://www.churchhistory.org.

Baylies, Francis, *An Historical Memoir of the Colony of New Plymouth*, Vol.2, Wiggin & Lunt, Boston, 1866

Baylin, Bernard, *Atlantic History*, Concept and Contours, Harvard University Press, 2005.

Baylin, Bernard, *Soundings in Atlantic History,* Latent Structures and Intellectual Currents, 1500-1830, Harvard University Press, 2009.

Baylin, Bernard, *The Ideological Origins of the American Revolution*, Harvard University Press, 1982.

Bax, Ernest Belfort, *Rise and Fall of the Anabaptists*, Swan Sonnenschein & Co., London, 1903.

Baxter, Stephen B., *William III*, Harcourt Brace & World Inc., New York, 1966.

Bitterman, H.R., *The Council of Chalcedon and Episcopal Jurisdiction*, article in Speculum, 1938.

Blok, J.P., *Geschiedenis Eener Hollandsche Stad*, Martinus Nijhoff, 'sGravenhage, 1910.

Blok, J.P., *Geschiedenis van het Nederlandsche Volk*, J.B. Wolters, Groningen, 1902.

Bookhiser, Richard, *James Madison*, Basic Books, 2011.

Bosch, Cornelis, *Historie van het leven en sterven van Heer Johan van Oldenbarneveld*, Loevenstein, 1658

Bowen, Marjorie, *William Prince of Orange*, John Lane, The Bodley Head Ltd., London, 1928.

Bradford, William, *History of Plymouth Plantation 1620-1647, Volume I*, Massachusetts Historical Society, Houghton Mifflin Company, Boston, 1912.

Bradford, William, *Of Plymouth Plantation*, Alfred A. Knopf, 2004.

Brodhead, John R., *Documents relative to the Colonial History of the State of New York: Remonstrance and Petition of the Colonies and Villages in this New Netherland Province*, Weed Parsons and Company, Albany, 1856.

Brouwer, Maria, *Governance and Innovation,* Routledge, Abbingdon & New York, 2008.

Brown, Alexander, *The First Republic in America*, Houghton Mifflin and Company, Boston, 1898.

Brown, Nigel, *Vousden One-Name Study*, http://www.vousden.name/origins.htm, 2010.

Bunker, Nick, *Making Haste From Babylon: The Mayflower Pilgrims and Their World*, Random House, 2010.

Burt, Nathaniel, *Perennial Philadelphians*, University of Pennsylvania Press, 1999.

Caenegem, R.C. van, *An Historical Introduction to Private Law*, Cambridge University Press, Cambridge, 1992.

Campi, Emidio, *Scholarly Knowledge*, Libraire Droz S.A., Geneva, 2008.

Cannon, E. and Tonks, I., *Annuity Markets*, Oxford University Press, Oxford, 2009.

le Carré, John, *Smiley's People*, Alfred Knopf, New York, 1979.

Chandler, J.A.C. & James, T.B., *Colonial Virginia*, Times-Dispatch Company, Richmond, 1907.

Collinson, Patrick, *The Elizabethan Puritan Movement*, 1967.

Collinson, Patrick, *The Religion of Protestants: The Church in English Society 1559-1625*, 1984.

Conforti, Joseph, *Imagining New England*, University of North Carolina Press, Chapel Hill, 2001.

Congressional Serial Set, United States Printing Office, Washington DC, 1910.

Cunninghame Graham, R.B., *The life of Bernal Diaz del Castillo*, Eveleigh Nash, London, 1915.

Dam, W. Van, *Geschiedenis Ooltgensplaat*, http://www.wvandam.nl/index2.htm.

Davis, A., *History of New Amsterdam*, R.T. Young, New York, 1854.

Dean, John W., *A Memoir of the Rev. Nathaniel Ward A.M.*, J. Munsell, Albany, 1868.

Deventer, M.L. van, *Gedenkstukken van Johan van Oldenbarnevelt en zijn tijd: 1577 - 1589*, Martinus Nijhoff, 'sGravenhage, 1860.

Dotty Doughty DNA, http://www.dottydoughtydna.org.

Doyle, J.A.Y., *English Colonies in America*, Henry Holt and Company, New York, 1882.

Dreiskämper, P., *Aan de Vooravond van de Overtocht naar Engeland*, Verloren, Hilversum, 1996.

Duruy, Victor, *A History of France*; translated by M. Carey; Thomas Y. Crowell Company; New York, 1889

Edmundson, George, *History of Holland*, Cambridge University Press, Cambridge, 1922.

Farrand, Max, *The Records of the Constitutional Convention of 1787*, New Haven: Yale University Press, 1911.

Ferguson, Sandra, *Biography of the Rev. Francis Doughty*, http://wc.rootsweb.ancestry.com, undated.

Fiske, John, *The Dutch and Quaker Colonies in America*, Houghton Mifflin and Company, Boston, 1902.

Fordham, M., *A Short History of English Rural Life*, George Allen & Unwin Ltd., London, 1916.

Formulae of Marculfus in Groot Charterboek der Graaven van Holland en Zeeland, Vol.1, F. van Mieris, Leyden, 1753-1758.

Fouracre, Paul and Gerberding, Richard A., *Late Merovingian France*, Manchester University Press, Manchester, 1996.

Fraser, Antonia, *Royal Charles: Charles II and the Restoration*, Alfred A. Knopf, New York, 1979.

Frazier, A., *Cromwell*, Grove Press Books, New York, 1972.

Garrett, J.K. and Underwood, L., *Our American Constitution*, Steck-Vaughn, 1977.

George, Timothy, *John Robinson and the English Separatist Tradition*, 1982.

Gerbier, Mlle A., *Marie de Bourgogne*, Alfred Mame et Fils, Paris, 1859.

Goodrich, Charles A., *A History of the United States*, Brewer and Tileston, Boston, 1857.

Goudhurst, http://www.goudhurst.co.uk

Greene, Lorenzo Johnston, *The Negro in Colonial New England, 1620-1776*, Columbia University Press, New York, 1942.

Griffis, William Elliot, *The Pilgrims in Their Three Homes*, Houghton, Boston and New York, Mifflin and Company, The Riverside Press, Cambridge, 1898.

Hoop Scheffer, J. G. de and Griffis, W. E., *History of the Free Churchmen called the Brownists, Pilgrim Fathers and Baptists in the Dutch republic, 1581-1701*, Andrus & Church, Ithaca, 1922.

Hossell, Karen P., *The United States Constitution*, Heinemann Library, Chicago, 2003.

Hotchkin, S.F., *The York Road, Old and New*, Binder & Kelly, 1892.

http://eclipse.gsfc.nasa.gov/phase/phases1601.html.

http://www.goudhurst.co.uk.

http://www.hatboro-pa.com/hathist.htm.

http://www.pitrone.com/dawson.html.

Illustris Academia Lugd-Batava, Leiden University, Leiden, 1613.

Inns and Hotels of the Early Years of the Republic, David McKay Company, Philadelphia, 1927.

Inside the Body of Henry VIII, History Channel, 2009.

Isaack de Rasieres' *1628 letter to Blommaert* in Three Visitors to Early Plymouth, Plimoth Plantation, 1963.

Izaak Walton's Lives, *Life of Mr. Richard Hooker*, George Routledge and Sons, London, 1888.

Jacob Shallus diary, Papers in the American Philosophical Society, Philadelphia, 1831. With thanks to Harvard University Library.

James, Sydney, ed., *Three Visitors to Early Plymouth*, 1963.

Jameson, Franklin, *Narratives of the Witchcraft Cases*, American Historical Association, Charles Scribner's Sons, New York, 1914.

Janssen, G.H., *Het stokje van Oldenbarnevelt*, Verloren, Hilversum, 2001.

Jardine, Lisa, *Going Dutch*, HarperCollins, New York, 2008.

Jennings, William Henry, *A Genealogical History of the Jennings Families in England and America Volume II*, Columbus, 1899.

Johnson, Caleb, *MayflowerHistory.com*.

Johnson. Caleb, *The Mayflower and Her Passengers*, 2006.

Jonge, J.C., *De Geschiedenis van het Nederlandsche Zeewezen*, Van Cleef, 'sGravenhage & Amsterdam, 1837.

Journalen van Constantijn Huygensz Part III, By Historisch Genootschap, Kemink & Zoon, Utrecht, 1888.

Kaplan, Benjamin J., *Divided by Faith*, Harvard University Press, Boston, 2007.

Keane, John, *The Life and Death of Democracy*, W.W. Norton & Company Ltd., New York, 2009.

Kemp, John, Introduction, *Governor William Bradford's Letter Book*, Applewood Books, 2001.

Knellwof, C. & McCalman, I., *The Enlightenment World*, The Cromwell Press, London, 2004.

Kumdu, Kunal, *Article*, Asian Times, 8/21/04.

Lansdale, M.H., *Paris, its Sites, Monuments and History*, Henry T. Coates, Philadelphia, 1899.

Lawler Jr., Edward, *The President's House in Philadelphia*, www. ushistory.org, 2010.

Leading Businessmen of Back Bay, South End, Boston Highlands, Jamaica Plain and Dorchester; Mercantile Publishing Company, Boston, 1888.

Lee, Francis Bazley, *Genealogical and Memorial History of the State of New Jersey, Volume III*, Lewis Historical Publishing Company, New York, 1910.

Lindo, M.P. and others, *De Nederlandsche Spectator*, D.A. Thieme, 'sGravenhage, 1880.

Lindo, M.P. and others, *De Nederlandsche Spectator*, M. Nijhoff, Amsterdam, 1902.

Lloyd, Gordon, *Constitutional Convention, Teaching American History website*, http://teachingamericanhistory.org.

Lockhart, Paul, *The Drillmaster of Valley Forge*, HarperCollins, 2008.

Ludwig, Arnold M., *King of the Mountain*, University Press of Kentucky, Lexington, 2002.

Madison, James, *The Papers of James Madison, Vol. 9*, University of Chicago Press, Chicago 1975.

Maitland, A., H. and A. Poole Family History, http://www. antonymaitland.com, 1998.

Maitland/Poole from W.J. Hoffman, New York Genealogical Record.

Marquis de Vieileville, 1551.

Marsilje, J.W., *Het Financiele Beleid van Leiden in de Laat-Beierse en Bourgondische Periode ~1390-1477*, Verloren, Hilversum, 1985.

Mattern, David, Editor, *James Madison's "Advice to My Country"*, Rector and Visitors of the University of Virginia, 1997.

Mattern, David, *James Madison: Patriot, Politician, and President*, The Rosen Publishing Group, 2005.

May, Thomas Erskine, *Democracy in Europe*, W.J. Widdleton, New York, 1878.

Miroff, Bruce & Seidelman, Raymond & Swanstrom, Todd & Luca, Tome de, *The Democratic Debate: American Politics in an Age of Change*, Cengage Learning, 2009.

Moon Phases, http://eclipse.gsfc.nasa.gov/phase/phases1601.html.

Motley, John Lothrop, *The Life and Death of John Barneveld Vol. II*, Harper & Brothers, New York, 1874.

Motley, John Lothrop, *The Life of John of Barneveld, 1614-23, Volume II*, Harper & Brothers, New York, 1874.

Motley, John Lothrop, *The Rise of the Dutch Republic Volume I*, Harper & Brothers, New York, 1855.

Mourt's Relation, (Anon., 1622) Paper edition by Dwight Heath, Applewood, 1963.

Nationmaster, http://www.nationmaster.com.

Neill, E.D., *Virginia Carolorum*, Joel Munsell's Sons, Albany, 1886.

New England's First Fruits, London, England, 1643.

Schechter, Stephen I and Bernstein, Richard B., *New York and the Union: Contributions to the American Constitutional Experience*, Albany, NY: New York State Commission on the Bicentennial of the U.S. Constitution, 1990.

Nicolle, David and Turner, Graham, *Orléans 1429: France turns the tide*, Osprey Publishing Ltd., Oxford, 2001.

Nijs, Thimo de en Beukers, Eelco, *Geschiedenis van Holland tot 1572*, Verloren, Hilversum, 2002.

Noordam, D.J., *Riskante Relaties*, Verloren, Hilversum, 1995.

Onnekink, David M. L., *The Anglo-Dutch Favourite* (thesis), 2004.

Osgood, Herbert Levi, *The American Colonies in the Seventeenth Century, Volume I*, The Macmillan Company, 1904.

Parker, G., *The Military Revolution*, Cambridge University Press, Cambridge, 1996.

Parker, Rev. H.A., *Transactions, Volume 10*, Colonial Society of Massachusetts, Boston, 1907.

Payne, Ernest Alexander, *The Anabaptists of the 16th Century, and their influence in the modern world*. The Dr. Williams's Trust lecture at the Presbyterian College, Carmarthen, on October 5th, 1948, Presbyterian College of Carmarthen, Carmathen, 1948.

Payne, G.H., *The Child in Human Progress*, Putnam, New York, 1916.

Pedigree of Robert Bradford c1487-1552, http://www.ancestry.com.

Pennsylvania German Almanac, Francis Bailey, 1778.

Perry, James R., *The Formation of a Society on Virginia's Eastern Shore, 1615-1655*, Institute of Early American History and Culture, 1990.

Plain Dealing, Thomas Letchford, London, 1641.

Plotnik, Arthur, *The Man Behind the Quill*, National Archives Trust Fund Board, 1987.

Princeton University, http://etcweb.princeton.edu.

Putnam, Robert, *Making Democracy Work: Civic Traditions in Modern Italy*, Harvard University Press, Boston, 1993.

Putnam, Ruth, *William the Silent, Prince of Orange*, G.P. Putnam's Sons, New York, 1911.

Rabb, Theodore K., *Jacobean Gentleman: Sir Edwin Sandys*, Princeton University Press, 1998.

Quarter Millenial Celebration of the City of Taunton, City Government, 1889.

Rakove, Jack, *Revolutionaries*, Houghton Mifflin Harcourt, 2010.

Reverend Nathaniel Ward, *Massachusetts Colony*, 1647.

Ridley, Matt, *The Rational Optimist*, HarperCollins, New York, 2010.

Riemsdijk, Th. van & Muller, Johannes, *De Nederlandsche Spectator - Verslagen en Mededeelingen der Koninklijke Akademie van Wetenschappen*, Afdeeling Letterkunde, , Johannes Müller, Amsterdam, 1890.

Ritchie, Robert C., *Duke's Province: A Study of New York Politics and Society, 1664-1691*; University of North Carolina Press Books, 1977.

Ritsema, Alex, *Discover the Dutch Wadden Islands*, Lulu.com, 2008.

Belval, Brian, *A Primary Source History of the Lost Colony of Roanoke*, The Rosen Publishing Group, Inc., 2006.

Robinson, James H., *The Encyclopedea Britannica, Columbia University*, New York, 1915.

Robinson, John, *Works, 3 volumes*, edited by Robert, 1841.

Sampson, *The Life of John Bradford*, Seeley Jackson and Halliday, London, 1855.

Sandys, Edwin, *Europae Speculum*, 1629.

Saunders Smith, Sarah, *The Founders of the Massachusetts Bay Colony*, Sun Printing Company, Pittsfield, 1897.

Schechter, Frank I. & Smith, Munroe, *The historical foundations of the law relating to trade-marks*, Columbia University Press, New York, 1925.

Seabright, P., *In the Company of Strangers*, Princeton University Press, Princeton, 2004

Seelye, John, *Memory's Nation: the Place of Plymouth Rock*, 1998.

Sherman, C.P., *Roman Law in the Modern World*, The Boston Book Company, Boston, 1917.

Shorto, Russell, *The Island at the Center of the World*, Thorndike Press, Waterville, 2004.

Smiles, Samuel, *The Huguenots*, John Murray, London, 1881.

Smith & Deane, *The Journals of the Rev. Thomas Smith and the Rev. Samuel Dean*, Joseph S. Bailey, Portland, 1849.

Smith, Loren E., *The Library List of 1783*, Lisa Crane, 1969. CGU These and Dissertations. Paper 87. With special thanks to Allegra Swift, Head of Scholarly Communications and Publishing, Claremont Colleges Library, Claremont University Consortium.

Smith, William & Wace, Henry, *article in A Dictionary of Christian Biography, Literature, Sects and Doctrines*, John Murray, London, 1882.

Smolenaar, M. & Veenhoff, A., *Hugh Goodyear and his Books*, Leiden University, Leiden, 1993

Sparks, Jared, *The Life of George Washington*, Ferdinand Andrews, Boston, 1839.

St. Nicolas Center: http://www.stnicolascenter.org.

Steward, David O., *The Summer of 1787*, Simon & Schuster, New York, 2007.

Stratton, Eugene A., *Plymouth Colony: Its History and People 1620-1691*, Ancestry Press, 1986.

Tacitus, C., *Dialogus, Agricola, Germania*, translated by W. Peterson, W. Heinemann, London, 1914.

Tex, Jan Den, *Oldenbarnevelt*, Cambridge University Press, Cambridge, 1973.

The Christian Reformer, New Series, Vol.XIII, January to December, 1857.

The Complete Anti-Federalist.

The Diaries of George Washington, 1748-1799, Volume 4, Houghton Mifflin, 1925.

The Doughty Family of Long Island by P.G. Burton in Genealogies of Long Island Families, Charles J.B. Werner & Benjamin F. Thompson Editors, Werner, New York, 1887.

The Federalist Papers, facsimile of 1788 edition, American Bar Association, Chicago, 2009.

The Memoirs of Philip de Commines, translated by Andrew R. Scoble, Henry G. Bohn, London, 1855.

The Register of Pennsylvania, Volume II, Samual Hazard Editor and Publisher, 1828.

Thirsk, Joan, *Industries in the Countryside*, published in Essays in the Economic and Social History of Tudor and Stuart England, compiled by F.J. Fisher, Cambridge University Press, Cambridge, 1961.

Thomas, E.M., *The Old Way*, Farrar Straus and Giroux, New York, 2006.

Thomas, J.W., *Chronicles of Colonial Maryland*, The Eddy Press Corporation, Cumberland, 1913.

Thompson, B.F., *History of Long Island*, The Berkeley Press, New York, 1843.

Thompson, Edith, *History of England*, Henry Holt & Company, New York, 1887.

Thompson, J.C., *Zooarchaeological Tests for Modern Human Behavior at Blombos Cave and Pinnacle Point Cave 13B Southwestern Cape*, ProQuest, Ann Arbor, 2008.

Thorpe, Francis N., *The Constitutional History of the United States*, Callaghan & Company, 1901.

Timmer, Rijk, *Profeet in eigen land*, Verloren, Hilversum, 2008.

Tolman, William Howe, *History of Higher Education in Rhode Island, Issue 18*, Government Printing Office, Washington DC, 1894.

Troost, Wout, *William III the Stadholder King*, Ashgate Publishing Ltd., Burlington, 2005.

Tudorplace, www.tudorplace.com.

United States Census of 1790.

US Constitution, http://www.usconstitution.net.

Usher, Roland G., *The Pilgrims and their History*, Houghton Mifflin and Company, Boston, 1918.

Van der Donck, Adriaen, *Beschrijvinge Van Nieuw-Nederlant*, Evert Nieuwenhof, 1655.

Various authors, *The Preacher's Complete Homiletical Commentary on the Old Testament*, Funk & Wagnalls Company, New York, 1892.

Vaughn, Richard, *Philip the Good*, The Boydell Press, Woodbridge, 2002

Venema, Janny, *Killiaen van Rensselaar (1586-1643)*, Verloren, Hilversum, 2011.

Verey, David & Brooks, Alan, Gloucestershire 1: *The Cotswolds*, Penguin, London, 1999.

Wade, Robert, *The System of Administrative and Political Corruption in India*, Journal of Development Studies XVIII, World Bank, Washington DC, 1982.

Wessels, J.W., *History of Roman-Dutch Law*, African Book Company, Cape of Good Hope, 1908.

Williams Bicknell, Thomas, *History of the State of Rhode Island and Providence Plantations, Volume 3*, American Historical Society, New York, 1920.

Williams, David C., *The Mythic Meanings of the Second Amendment*, Yale University, 2003

Willison, George, *Saints and Strangers*, 1946.

Winkler Prins Geillustreerde Encyclopaedie, Winkler Prins, Elsevier, Amsterdam, 1906.

Winslow, Edward, *Good Newes From New England*, 1624.

Winslow, Edward, *Hypocrisie Unmasked*, 1646.

Young, Alexander, ed., *Chronicles of the Pilgrim Fathers*, 1844.

Gratitude is the only fund I can pay you out of which I am sensible your generosity accepts as sufficient: but at the same time Friendship likes it not to be behind hand in favours.
James Madison to William Bradford, Dec. 1, 1773.

Acknowledgements

It is amazing how life changing one human relationship and an insatiable curiosity for the human condition can be. The curiosity was always there but for that relationship I had to travel from Europe to Botswana to have an once-in-a-lifetime chance and meet the right Peace-Corps volunteer. She helped open windows to vistas of the world I couldn't have found on my own. She stimulated my feeding on them, and enjoyed the insights that we gained together. Jackie is the love of my life, my wife and, above all, my best friend. I am hugely grateful for the value she has added, and continues to add to our world.

Several years ago we visited my English cousin, Ann Lovering, at her home outside Paris and talked about the possibility of writing a book on Democracy and America. She raised the subject of the Pilgrim Fathers and the research she had done for a thesis on their pastor in Leyden[451], the Netherlands. The copy she gave me contained valuable information, myriad references to source materials, and personal perspectives. It was the perfect basis from which to start.

The people of Google Books have helped create an enormous research library of out of print books and documents. With the tools to open it, a computer and internet access, the benefits of instant gratification cannot be overstated. It allows the thought process to develop as fast as information can be gathered and vice versa. The time lost in taking wrong turns, following false leads, sorting fact and fiction, losing one's train of thought, etc. are reduced to minutes rather than the days or weeks it would have taken to visit libraries, slog through books, and travel between sources. My small budget would have put the purchase of gas and tickets out of range and made the project impossible. Thank you, people of Google Books.

And then there are the authors of all those books who so generously shared the findings of their own research, their interpretations and thoughts, and who found unmistakable joy in their own journeys of discovery. Many of the books were written a century or more ago in the beautifully constructed prose of their day; the authors long departed. Others honored those works by building on them or by expanding their underexplored avenues. I am indebted to our contemporary scholars who must have spent inordinate amounts of time digging through old manuscripts and documents, and identified their importance, and who translated and paraphrased archaic texts into modern languages while applying historic context to keep the original meanings intact.

A writer should not work in a vacuum. Having people read your prose and critique it is essential. In addition to Jackie's tireless encouragements to explain subject matter better, there were the wonderful, multidisciplinary critiques from my dear, nonagenarian friend, Helen Colgan. As a former English teacher in the days when grammar had to follow certain formats for the purpose of clarity, she scoured the text and edited every error, shortcoming, or idiosyncrasy. As a competent student of history, Helen identified the places where events, relationships, or successions were too complex or too fuzzy and advised on where to eliminate some or expand on others.

My friend and neighbor, Joe Oppenheimer, Professor Emeritus of Government and Politics at the University of Maryland, paid particular attention to the factual history and the arguments I made based on them. His comments and suggestions were invaluable to the academic quality of the narratives.

Dr. John Kemp of Plimoth Plantation, Dr. Lynn Uzzell and Sterling Howell both of Montpelier, and David Mattern of The Papers of James Madison at the University of Virginia have all been very supportive and helpful with critiques, corrections and crucial information.

The librarians at several colleges and universities have been so kind as to provide copies of documents that existed in their libraries only.

My editor, Todd McClimans, skillfully balanced critique with encouragement. With few exceptions I followed his excellent advice on punctuation, grammar, clarity, story development, and facts. As an experienced history writer his inputs were invaluable.

I am grateful to my publisher, David Poyer of Northampton House Press, who had the courage and confidence to support this project, and to my friends who patiently put up with my frequent need of a sounding board. I am certain they are as happy as I am with the completion of this project.

Lastly, I thank all those whose curiosity has encouraged me to keep delving and share the findings. The insights I have gained from this project have enriched my life enormously. It is my hope that sharing them through this book may have enriched yours.

It was at length agreed that the reference should be made without an instruction to report.
James Madison in Notes on Debates, Friday 30 March, 1787.

End Notes

1 Princeton University Website: http://etcweb.princeton.edu

2 Known here as Peter John Van Berkel

3 A "kil" is a long, narrow stretch of water and is derived from the word "kille" which means creek.

4 St. Nicholas Center: http://wwwstnicholascenter.org

5 Ritchie, Robert, *Duke's Province: A Study of New York Politics and Society, 1664-1691*, UNC Press Books, 1977

6 National Public Radio

7 Now known as the PBS Newshour.

8 Public Broadcasting System

9 John F. Kennedy

10 Robert Kennedy

11 Martin Luther King

12 Kent State

13 Levy, Leonard W., *Original Intent and the Framers' Constitution*, Ivan R. Dee, 2000.

14 The Federalist Papers, number 10.

15 Robert Yates reporting Hamilton's words at the Constitutional Convention of 1787 in Philadelphia. The Records of the Constitutional Convention of 1787, Max Farrand, New Haven: Yale University Press, 1911.

16 The Complete Anti-Federalist, 5-1.52.

17 Miroff, Bruce; Seidelman, Raymond; Swanstrom, Todd; de Luca, Tom, *The Democratic Debate: American Politics in an Age of Change,* Cengage Learning, 2009.

18 Smith, Loren Eugene, *The Library List of 1783*, Lisa Crane, 1969 "The Library List of 1783" (1969). CGU Theses & Dissertations. Paper 87. With special thanks to Allegra Swift, Head of Scholarly Communications & Publishing, Claremont Colleges Library, Claremont University Consortium.

19 Montpellier

20   *The Papers of James Madison, Vol. 9*, University of Chicago Press, 1975 and The Federalist 18 through 20.

21   Montpelier Foundation, Orange, VA.

22   Zooarcheological Tests for Modern Human Behavior at Blombos Cave and Pinnacle Point Cave 13B, Southwestern Cape, South Africa; J.C. Thompson; ProQuest; 2008.

23   Thomas, E.M., *The Old Way*, Farrar, Straus and Giroux; 2006.

24   Tacitus, C., *Dialogus, Agricola, Germania*, translated by W. Peterson; W. Heinemann; 1914.

25   Putnam, Robert, *Making Democracy Work: Civic Traditions in Modern Italy*, Harvard University Press, 1993.

26   Seabright, Paul, Prologue to Part II, *In the Company of Strangers*, Princeton University Press, 2004.

27   Ludwig, Arnold, *King of the Mountain*, University Press of Kentucky, 2002.

28   Ridley, Matt, *The Rational Optimist*, HarperCollins, 2010.

29   Loren, L.E., *The Library List of 1783*, Clairmont College, 1969.

30   Wessels, J.W., *History of Roman-Dutch Law*, African Book Company, 1908.

31   Tacitus.

32   Leaders for one hundred armed men.

33   Fordham, Montague, *A Short History of English Rural Life*, George Allen & Unwin Ltd, 1916.

34   Village.

35   In Old Saxon a churl (ceorl) was a man. Later its meaning changed to that of "lowest freeman."

36   Old Saxon word for a noble servant.

37   Fordham.

38   Children were nursed for up to four years. This is still the case in some societies with the added benefit of reduced fertility and a low birth rate.

39   Payne, G.H., *The Child in Human Progress*, G.P. Putnam's Sons, 1916.

40   Lansdale, M.H., *Paris, its sites, monuments and history*, Henry T. Coates & Co, 1899.

41   Orléans.

42   Small bridge.

43   Large bridge.

44   St. Stephen.

45 Neustria was the most powerful Frankisch kingdom.

46 Fouracre & Gerberding, *Late Merovingian France*, Manchester University Press, 1996.

47 The Nautae Parisii as it was known in Roman times was the guild of watermen who controlled the trade in the river and who formed an influential force in the city government. The Quai de la Grève was where now the Place de Hôtel de Ville meets the river. Presumably their headquarters, the Marchandise, together with two other structures evolved into the Hôtel de Ville (city hall). The guild of watermen was as powerful as it was old. They almost certainly preceded the Roman conquest and were very influential in the city's affairs under the Romans. By some accounts they had emperor Julian's house built for him and, at the site of the basilica of St. Etienne, they had devoted an altar to Jupiter. Just before the Frankish conquest they had helped bring provisions from Troyes down the Seine to the starving, beleaguered city.

48 This is the Place de la Grève of the Nautae and where later Les Halles would stand.

49 This is speculation. See *Late Merovingian France*, pp 104.

50 Fouracre & Gerberding.

51 Arminius, 1861.

52 The Franks constituted a small minority. It is therefore fair to assume that many recruits were Gauls.

53 Lansdale.

54 She exaggerates the numbers but the ratio is about right. The invaders constituted a small minority.

55 Present day Melsbroek near Brussels.

56 Noble families strove to have relatives work at the palace. Landri's uncle had a ranking household position.

57 There is something odd about this affair that needs contemplating. According to recorded history it was Clovis II who took valuable relics from the Abbey of St. Denis to buy provisions for Paris' citizens, particularly the poor. Supposedly he did this at the direction of Queen Balthild. Under that scenario you would think that it made little sense to wrest control of the monastery away from the Bishop with the excuse of protecting it from him. We may never be able to assess these events since the records are so unreliable. In addition to the few official documents of the period there are reports that were written well after the deaths of all the players. Undoubtedly these writings were heavily influenced by the biases of the authors and their desire to be noted.

This author took the liberty of making Landri the responsible person and that the liberation of the monasteries was the result of a conspiracy between Balthild and Landri.

58   The fourth canon of Chalcedon in 451 specified that "monks of the country and of the town are under the jurisdiction of the bishop." It did not specify whether this was spiritual jurisdiction only or whether the bishop had the right to interfere in the administration of monastic properties and their economy. Bitterman, H. R. (1938), *The Council of Chalcedon and Episcopal Jurisdiction*, Speculum 103: 198–203.

59   It was later named Hôtel Dieu. Today it is named Hôpital Hôtel Dieu and occupies nearly the whole width of the island.

60   The exact year of the recruitment is unknown. Other events suggest that 654 is very close.

61   The printing press had to wait another 800 years.

62   Sometimes Latinized as Marculfus and sometimes referred to as Marculph or Marcoul.

63   His ethnicity is based on speculation. Some historians identify him as a Frank as did William Smith in his entry in A Dictionary of Christian Biography, Literature, Sects and Doctrines, 1882. However, as Smith admits, traditionally monks came from the lower classes which were primarily the original Gallic people. The ruling Franks were more interested in high office.

64   Wessels.

65   The Sea Franks.

66   *Vita Domnae Balthildis*, 7th century hagiography, author unknown. For more on this see *Late Merovingian France*, Paul Fouracre, Richard A. Gerberding, Manchester University Press, 1996.

67   Translation by Fouracre & Gerberding.

68   Genesius probably stayed at Balthild's side until her retirement and his elevation to bishop of Lyons. Interesting to note is that he was buried at Kala.

69   In his letter of dedication to Landri he writes: "To Landerich, the Holy Lord, and most venerable Father, Marculfus, the lowest and humblest of monks. Would, Holy Father, that I could have fulfilled your commands as efficiently as willingly. But I have now reached my seventieth year ; my hand trembles with age ; my eyes are become dim ; and all the faculties of my mind are enfeebled ; even as the wise man."

70   She imposed her son Childeric as Prince on Austrasia, and absorbed Burgundy.

71   He was then only 15 years old!

72 Frisian name for a manmade hill that elevated farmsteads and villages above high water.

73 ***Geschiedenis van Holland***, T. de Nijs & E. Beukers, 2002.

74 at Leiden-Roomburg.

75 The term Frisian may be flexible in this period. Because of the large movement of peoples they may have been a mixture of original Frisians, Saxons, and Franks. The current Frisian language may be an indicator. It includes a very large amount of Old Saxon.

76 J.W. Wessels: The institutions of the Franks may be briefly summarised as follows:
The King, or Emperor, as he was called after the coronation of Charlemagne by the Pope. He was the executive head of the nation, but his laws were made with the consent of the Assembly of the Freemen.
The Court of the King. This consisted of the principal officers attached to his household. The Court was composed of the chancellor, the grand justicier, usually an ecclesiastic, the chamberlain, the seneschal, the constable and others.
Royal Commissioners. Each Commission consisted as a rule of two members, one a high dignitary of State, the other a bishop or abbot. They acted both as high administrative and judicial functionaries.
The National Assembly, composed of bishops, abbots, counts, dukes, and other magnates as well as of freemen.
Counts, hundredmen and vicars.
General Assemblies of Freemen for transacting legal and other business.
Special Assemblies of Freemen for judicial and other purposes.
Members of Local Courts.
The country was divided into Great Pagi, and these into pagi medii and pagi minores. The pagi were ruled over by dukes and counts, and the subdivisions of the pagi by the hundredmen and vicars.

The tenure of land was either privately owned or feudal property. These again were parceled out into plots held under servile tenure.
The various divisions of land were known as manses or small farms, casae or dwelling plots, hospitia or small rural holdings, and viluw or villages.
The people were divided into clerics and laymen. The latter were either freemen, landowners, or half- free (lites), or, lastly, serfs (Poullet, Originea, vol. 1, pp. 66-110).

77 ***Groot Charter Boek***, Mieris: formulae of Marculfus, aforementioned 7th century jurist.

78 Seabright.

79 All three were Germanic peoples. The distinction here is mostly a geographic indication of where their power centers were at the time.

80   https://www.kiesraad.nl/artikel/waterschappen. Next election is in March, 2015.

81   This heritable administrative position gave its lower noble occupant duties to represent the count or bishop, administer justice and collect taxes, and the right to sell rights to the city. Because of their relative power and isolation, the counts of Holland enjoyed a substantial independence from their monarchs.

82   About the names Holland, Netherlands, and Dutch. In the 16th century the Netherlands was the name for all 17 provinces of which Holland was one that spanned present day Belgium and the Netherlands. Holland was one of the provinces. Now the name refers to all of the modern day nation state. In the 17th century the province of Holland became by far the richest and best known of the remaining seven provinces of the Dutch Republic. The word Dutch comes from Deutsch which is the German word for German. The Dutch were known as the Nieder-Deutsch or Lower Germans since they lived in the Low Lands by the sea. The names Nederland (in Dutch) and Netherlands mean Low Lands. The Pennsylvania Dutch in the U.S. are of German origin although their religion originates in Friesland, the Netherlands.

83   Different size fish require differently gauged nets.

84   The people living inside the gates of the city, the citizens or burghers.

85   Blok, J.P., *Geschiedenis Eener Hollandsche Stad*, Martinus Nijhoff, 1910.

86   Council of wise men almost all of whom were former office holders.

87   "Finally, the allegations of enhanced propensity for corruption and unproductive activities when PSUs (public sector units) exist cannot be easily brushed aside. Pilferage of electricity, kickbacks for jobs and appointments, sharing profits with suppliers, rent seeking, and graft and grab in general, are experienced by the common man." Kunal Kumdu, Asian Times, 8/21/04.
      "...some irrigation engineers raise vast amounts of illicit revenue from the distribution of water and contracts, and redistribute part to superior officers and politicians." Robert Wade in The System of Administrative and Political Corruption" in India, 2002.

88   Sometimes annuities that the Count sold were coerced from wealthy individuals. The city's annuities were sold to willing investors that included Italian financiers and citizens of Flanders and England. It is obvious that an elaborate and reliable legal system was required to support the necessary trust.

89   Cannon, E. and Tonks, I., *Annuity Markets*, Oxford University Press, 2009.

90   This is not so different from our modern day social security where individuals buy (through installments) the right to a regular payout, starting at a certain age and for the duration of their lives.

91   Blok.

92   Blok.

      Het Financiele Beleid van Leiden in de Laat-Beierse en Bourgondische Periode ~1390-1477, J.W. Marsilje, Verloren Hilversum, 1985.

      Geschiedenis van Holland to 1572, Thimo de Nijs en Eelco Beukers, Verloren Hilversum, 2002.

93   Smaller outbreaks of plague.

94   This was quite exceptional but the city of Leyden at some point had its very own trade agreement with England.

95   ***Orléans 1429: France turns the tide,*** David Nicolle and Graham Turner, Osprey Publishing Ltd., 2001.

96   The difference between respublica and reipublica is one of case.

97   Van Riemsdijk, ***Verslagen en Mededeelingen der Koninklijke Akademie van Wetenschappen, Afdeeling Letterkunde,*** Johannes Muller, 1890.

98   Various authors, ***The Preacher's Complete Homiletical Commentary on the Old Testament,*** Funk & Wagnalls Company, 1892.

99   Philips explicitly states that the ruler has to be powerful and rich. (Rich so that he doesn't have to rely on others who could demand rights in return.

100   Medieval merchant ship with Latin or bucket rigging.

101   Pronounced Clahs.

102   A somewhat rectangular sail that is attached to the mast on one long side, has a long stake from the bottom of the mast to the free upper corner, and a line attached to the lower free corner.

103   Pronounced Yahn.

104   The rope that is attached to the sail.

105   ***Geschiedenis Ooltgensplaat,*** Willem van Dam, 2009.

106   Pronounced Mahtye.

107   Pronounced Dahngker.

108   Timmer, Rijk, ***Profeet in eigen land,*** 2008, Verloren.

109   Timmer.

110   Later to become Philips's employer.

111   This was not always true. The city of Leyden already controlled industrial and trade activities in a wide area of country around it and outlawed competition there.

112   Timmer.

113   Italic added for emphasis.

114   He means the 18th century.

115   Actually, the power of the church was somewhat in decline then
       but clergy enjoyed a worldly power through the sale of favors and
       indulgences (a kind of pay-off for sins so they would be of no
       consequence on judgment day).

116   Timmer.

117   In many developing countries it is an accepted and expected custom
       that offices are bought from the powerful for rent-seeking (corruption)
       potential. Even in the U.S. the appointment to offices can occasionally
       be smoothened through money or favors (2008 Illinois' U.S. senate seat
       vacated by Obama peddled by governor Blagojevich).

118   French for the people of Ghent.

119   Vaughn, Richard, *Philip the Good*, Boydell Press, 2002.

120   Elected or appointed representatives.

121   This resembles the long-time arrangement in Hong-Kong where elected
       officials are representing various sectors of the economy.

122   Louis' claims were based on Salic law. As king he was the guardian. See
       Chapter 2.

123   Leeuwenhof, at that time a 200 year old zoo.

124   Gerbier, Mlle A., *Marie de Bourgogne*, Alfred Mame et Fils, 1859.

125   De Commines, diplomat, historian, and writer, born in Flanders he
       served in high positions at the Burgundian court but in 1464 suddenly
       left for service with King Louis XI.

126   *The memoirs of Philip de Commines*, translated by Andrew R. Scoble,
       Henry G. Bohn, 1855.

127   At this time Germany claimed to be the heir to, or continuation of, the
       empire. Some jokingly called it neither holy, nor Roman, nor an empire.

128   The name reflects the tradition of where it originated but the
       Burgundian version of this High Court was seated at Mechlin.

129   De Commines.

130   Gerbier.

131   Knowledge of the law was a prerequisite.

132   This is perhaps a reflection of the more feudal culture of the Walloon
       lands.

133   Fiske, John, *The Dutch and Quaker Colonies in America*, Houghton
       Mifflin and Company, 1902; and Keane, John, *The Life and Death of
       Democracy*, W.W. Norton & Company Ltd., 2009.

134   May, Thomas Erskine, **Democracy in Europe**, W.J. Widdleton, 1878.

135   Gerbier.

136   Duruy, Victor, **A History of France**, translated by M. Cary; Thomas Y. Crowell Company; 1889.

137   Edmundson, George, **History of Holland**, Cambridge University Press, 1922.

138   Note that Louis had sought an alliance between his son and Margaret's mother, Mary, only five years earlier.

139   **Encyclopedia Britannica** online, www.britannica.com, 2014.

140   Amid all these events little Margaret was transferred to the French court while the sister of the dauphin took on the regency. Once of age the dauphin, now King Charles VIII, repudiated the marriage and forced one with Anne of Brittany (who originally had been betrothed to Maximilian). Margaret eventually returned to her father in 1493.

141   The Dutch still have a saying, "op zijn elfst en dertigst", literally meaning "on his 11th and 30th", and referring to the number of provinces and the number of days it took for the delegates to travel home, consult with their State's Councils, and return to the General Assembly.

142   The necessity of a strong central leadership. See Chapter 4.

143   Putnam, Ruth, **William the Silent, Prince of Orange**, G.P. Putnam's Sons, 1911.

144   Kaplan, Benjamin J., **Divided by Faith**, Harvard University Press, 2007.

145   Desiderius Erasmus Roterodamus was a Dutch Catholic priest, humanist, social critic and teacher.

146   Motley, John Lothrop, **The Life of John of Barneveld, 1614-23, Volume II**, Harper and Brothers, 1874.

147   Marquis de Vieileville, 1551.

148   The Electors of the H.R.E., composed of the rulers of the various German states, determined who their emperor would be. It was a relatively weak position anyway. The Empire was really no more than a loose confederation of states.

149   Motley, John Lothrop, **The Rise of the Dutch Republic Volume I,** David McKay, 1855.

150   Cunnighame Graham, **The life of Bernal Diaz del Castillo**, R.B. Eveleigh Nash, 1915.

151   Known as the Beeldenstorm.

152   Sherman, C.P., **Roman Law in the Modern World**, The Boston Book Company, 1917.

153   French Style of Roman Law (civil law).

154 Van Caenegem, *An Historical Introduction to Private Law*, Cambridge University Press, 1992.

155 Knellwof, C. & McCalman, I., *The Enlightenment World*, The Cromwell Press, 2004.

156 Located in France-Comté it was then ruled by Protestant Württemberg and known by its German name of Mömpelgard.

157 Both Louis's allies, Egmont and Hoorn, were beheaded.

158 Pinker, Steven, *The Better Angels of Our Nature*, Viking Books, 2011.

159 Historisch Genootschap, *Journalen van Constantijn Huygensz Part III*, Kemink & Zoon, 1888.

160 Janssen, G.H., *Het stokje van Oldenbarnevelt*, Verloren, 2001.

161 Den Tex, Jan, *Oldenbarnevelt*, Cambridge University Press, 1973.

162 Not to be confused with Erasmus.

163 Janssen.

164 Den Tex.

165 Campi, Emidio, *Scholarly Knowledge*, Libraire Droz S.A., 2008.

166 August 24 was the start of a wave of extreme violence against the Huguenots.

167 Attributed to Philip Marnix, it is the national anthem of the Netherlands.

168 Then open water but now diked in and partially dried. The remaining water is known as the IJsselmeer.

169 Major public official receiving an annual fee for his legal and administrative services.

170 Bosch, Cornelis, *Historie van het leven en sterven van Heer Johan van Oldenbarneveld*, Loevenstein, 1658. Motley, John Lothrop, *The Life and Death of John Barneveld Vol.II*, Harper & Brothers, 1874. Quotes and sources in this chapter are from these works, unless stated otherwise.

171 The Dutch use the word "inspraak" to express it.

172 The Dutch do easily criticize others and will then say, "But that doesn't concern me."

173 See Chapter Five.

174 Janssen.

175 www.kasteleninutrecht.neu/Gunterstein.htm.

176 Act of Abjuration.

177 Motley, John Lothrop, *The Rise of the Dutch Republic Volume I*, 1855.

178 Van Deventer, M.L., *Gedenkstukken van Johan van Oldenbarnevelt en zijn tijd: 1577 - 1589*, Nijhoff, 1860.

179   Van Deventer.

180   Parker, G., *The Military Revolution*, Cambridge University Press, 1996.

181   Article I of the Union of Utrecht states that a national of a province cannot be prosecuted by a jurisdiction other than its own.

182   The castle and square in The Hague that were the ancient seat of the counts and are part of the buildings that house the government of the Netherlands today.

183   Motley, John Lothrop, *The Life of John of Barneveld, 1614-23, Volume II*, Harper and Brothers, 1874.

184   James I translated, and interpreted, the bible into English. We know it today as the King James Version.

185   In this book we will not examine the theology that proved so damaging. Already too much has been written and said about it and it would distract from the impact it had on the lives of ordinary people, their leaders, and their country.

186   Van Deventer.

187   Motley, John Lothrop, *The Life of John of Barneveld, 1614-23, Volume II*, Harper and Brothers, 1874.

188   The Dutch name, *Verenigde Provincien*, translates as United Provinces. However, the provinces referred to themselves as *Staten* or states. Therefore the names "United Provinces" and United States are interchangeable.

189   Actually, over time, the freedoms of Catholics had been curtailed and they were not allowed to express their religion in public. Even Barneveld had supported constraints that were put upon Catholics by banning the Jesuits who were regarded as agents of Spain and its allies.

190   See chapter 7.

191   Member of the English government.

192   The satirical pamphlets that ridiculed the Advocate.

193   Hugo de Groot or Grotius.

194   As was customary, all of Barneveld's possessions had been confiscated.

195   Legally there was still a separation between church and state and freedom of religion was the official credo. However, from the strife that developed during the Truce we can conclude that religious tolerance had suffered a setback.

196   The church maintained that you could buy off your sins and qualify for a place in heaven.

197   The members form the church and elect officers who appoint the preacher. The church is entirely independent.

198 Thirsk, Joan, *Industries in the Countryside*, published in Essays in the Economic and Social History of Tudor and Stuart England, compiled by F.J. Fisher, Cambridge University Press, 1961.

199 Bax, Ernest Belfort, *Rise and Fall of the Anabaptists*, Swan Sonnenschein & Co., Lim, 1903.

200 Recent research (Inside the Body of Henry VIII, History Channel, 2009) suggests that a trauma in 1536 caused him to become paranoid and ill-tempered.

201 Milder central control than Catholic.

202 Schechter, Frank I. and Smith, Munroe, *The historical foundations of the law relating to trade-marks*, Columbia University Press, 1925.

203 Payne, Ernest A., *The Anabaptists of the 16th Century*, a lecture at the Presbyterian College of Carmarthen, 1948.

204 De Hoop Scheffer, J.G. and Griffis, W.E., *History of the Free Churchmen called the Brownists, Pilgrim Fathers and Baptists in the Dutch republic, 1581-1701*, Andrus & Church; 1922.

205 He traveled to the continent in the 1530s and made contact with Martin Luther and the Frisian former monk Menno Simons, the founder of the Mennonites.

206 *A General Index to the Publications of the Parker Society*, Cambridge University Press, 1855.

207 Sufficiently related to the Tudors to be a contender and beheaded at the Tower of London in 1554 at age sixteen.

208 Known in the Netherlands as the "Beeldenstorm" or Iconoclasm.

209 Belval, Brian, *A Primary Source History of the Lost Colony of Roanoke*, The Rosen Publishing Group, Inc, 2006.

210 *Congressional Serial Set*, United States Printing Office, 1910.

211 Usher, Roland, *The Pilgrims and their History*, Houghton Mifflin and Company, 1918.

212 Tudorplace (www.tudorplace.com).

213 The company grew out of the old tailor guild and founded several schools for boys and, later, for girls.

214 Walton, Izaak, *Izaak Walton's Lives, Life of Mr. Richard Hooker*, George Routledge and Sons, 1888.

215 *The Christian Reformer, New Series, Vol.XIII, January to December*, 1857.

216 A freethinking group of nobles and churchmen.

217 Kaplan, Benjamin J., *Divided by Faith*, Harvard University Press, 2007.

218 *Europae Speculum*, 1629.

219 The Christian Reformer.

220 Sampson, Seeley Jackson and Halliday, *The Life of John Bradford*, 1855. Pedigree of Robert Bradford c1487-1552, Ancestry.com.

221 Usher.

222 Brown, Alexander, *The First Republic in America*, Houghton Mifflin and Company, 1898.

223 The name Pilgrims refers to the Separatists who left England, settled in the Netherlands, and subsequently emigrated to found Plymouth Plantation in Massachusetts. They used the term in a spiritual sense (Pilgrims and Strangers). At a later date historians coined the term to identify the actual group. From Imagining New England, Joseph Conforti, University of North Carolina Press, 2001.

224 Smolenaar, M. and Veenhoff, A., *Hugh Goodyear and his Books*, Leiden University, 1993.

225 Passage from the Second Charter of Virginia, 1609.

226 Also called the Independents.

227 *Illustris Academia Lugd-Batava*, Leiden University, 1613.

228 Half Moon. They mapped the Hudson River and coastal areas from New York to Maine.

229 The Spanish murdered a group that settled there for their heresy.

230 Bradford, William, *History of Plymouth Plantation 1620-1647, Volume I*, Massachusetts Historical Society, Houghton Mifflin Company, 1912.

231 The basic summary of belief of the Church of England and drawn up in 1563.

232 Rights of settlement.

233 The Founders of the Massachusetts Bay Colony, Sun Printing Company, Sarah Saunders Smith, 1897.

234 This was the formal term used for investors.

235 In the old manorial system in England serfs had no property and no time to work for themselves. The Pilgrims had been tenants and freemen.

236 Indentured servants committed themselves to service for a specific duration in return for the paid voyage.

237 Ames, Azel, *The May-Flower and her Log*, Houghton Mifflin and Company, 1901.

238 Doyle, J.A., *English Colonies in America*, Henry Holt and Company, 1882.

239 Bradford.

240   He was a controversial military adventurer who was imprisoned for misbehavior and then took on the leadership of the precarious settlement. He befriended Pocahontas, the daughter of the local Indian chief.

241   Scholars disagree about his identity. Tradition has him as Thomas Jones who was a notoriously bad character. Later analyses presume he was a Christopher Jones.

242   *Mourt's Relation*, Applewood Books, 1963.

243   Bangs, Jeremy, *Strangers and Pilgrims, Travelers and Sojourners: Leiden and the Foundations of Plymouth Plantation*, General Society of Mayflower Descendants, 2009.

244   An open boat with oars and sails.

245   http://eclipse.gsfc.nasa.gov/phase/phases1601.html.

246   Flint lock hand gun.

247   Measuring depth with a knotted rope and lead weight.

248   Bangs.

249   Osgood, Herbert, *The American Colonies in the Seventeenth Century, Volume I*, The Macmillan Company, 1904. The book served as a guide for this chapter, Other sources will be referenced.

250   Literally a company of men, a partnership.

251   Brouwer, Maria, *Governance and Innovation*, Routledge, 2008.

252   Description of his journey on the bark Nassau from New Amsterdam via the trading post at Aptucxet. Letter to Blommaert, Isaack de Rasieres, ca. 1628.

253   Blackstone River and Sakonnet River.

254   Patuxet is the Indian name of a village on whose location Plymouth was built. It was also the name that Europeans used for the entire district.

255   Beads made of shells by Algonquian Indians. The Massasoit word for them was "wampum(peag)." It was deemed so valuable that it served as money.

256   Narragansett Bay.

257   Monomoy Point on Cape Cod.

258   De Rasiere, Isaack, *Letter to Blommaert in Of Plymouth Plantation*, William Bradford, Alfred A. Knopf, 2004, ca. 1628.

259   We think of permanent representations as an embassy, the building where an Ambassador works. In those days Ambassadors were often of the roving variety and the visit itself was referred to as an embassy.

260 Who exactly owned the trading post at Aptucxet is uncertain. Conventional theory allocates it to the Pilgrims. The only evidence available is from the writings of Bradford. What tilts it toward the Dutch is Bradford's phrase, "They came up with their bark to Manomet, to their house there." My suggested compromise of Aptucxet being Dutch owned but eventually Pilgrim staffed may well be the truthful explanation of an intentional ambiguity.

261 From the French for boss (patron).

262 See chapter 7.

263 Bradford, William, *The Letter Book*, Applewood, 2001.

264 All quotes by de Rasiere are from his letter of 1628 to his friend and protégé, Samuel Blommaert. He provides detailed descriptions of various territories with regard to flora and fauna, people, and suitability for settlement, trade opportunities, and growing crops. This information must have been the deciding factor for Killiaen van Rensselaer and Samuel Blommaert to found the colony Rensselaerwijck near the present Albany, NY, in 1629. As we shall see, van Rensselaer's colony would play an important role in further developments at New Amsterdam.

265 Going all the way around Cape Cod peninsula.

266 Sewan was the Mohawk name for wampunpeag.

267 Fort Oranje (Orange) near present day Albany, NY.

268 Letter to Blommaert.

269 Griffis, William Elliot, *The Pilgrims in Their Three Homes*, Houghton, Boston and New York, Mifflin and Company, The Riverside Press, Cambridge, 1898.

270 Bradford, *The Letter Book.*

271 Bradford, *The Letter Book.*

272 Bangs.

273 Received a Royal charter in 1629.

274 *Leading Businessmen of Back Bay, South End, Boston Highlands, Jamaica Plain and Dorchester*, Mercantile Publishing Company, 1888.

275 Verey, David and Brooks, Ian, *Gloucestershire 1: The Cotswolds*, Penguin, 1999.

276 Jennings, William Henry, *A Genealogical History of the Jennings Families in England and America Volume II*, 1899.

277 Doughty, Sandra, *Biography of the Rev. Francis Doughty*, undated.

278 Lee, Francis Bazley, *Genealogical and Memorial History of the State of New Jersey, Volume III*, Lewis Historical Publishing Company, 1910.

279   Ferguson.

280   *Transactions, Volume 10*, Colonial Society of Massachusetts, 1907.

281   Jennings. Present day Taunton.

282   Baylies, Francis, *An Historical Memoir of the Colony of New Plymouth, Vol.2*, Wiggin & Lunt, 1866 and Quarter Millenial Celebration of the City of Taunton, City Government, 1889.

283   Thompson, B.F., *History of Long Island*, 1843.

284   *New England's First Fruits*. Published at London, Eng., 1643.

285   Ibid.

286   Letchford, Thomas, *Plain Dealing*, 1641.

287   Ward, Rev. Nathaniel, *Massachusetts Colony*, 1647.

288   Jameson, Franklin, *Narratives of the Witchcraft Cases*, American Historical Association, Charles Scribner's Sons, 1914.

289   *Lee, Francis Bazley, Genealogical and Memorial History of the State of New Jersey, Volume III*, Lewis Historical Publishing Company, 1910.

290   Goodrich, Charles A., *A History of the United States*, 1857.

291   Tolman, William Howe, *History of Higher Education in Rhode Island, Issue 18*, Government Printing Office, 1894.

292   Bicknell, Thomas, *History of the State of Rhode Island and Providence Plantations, Volume 3*, American Historical Society, 1920.

293   Green, Lorenzo Johnston, *The Negro in Colonial New England, 1620-1776. N.Y.,* Columbia University Press, 1942.

294   See Chapter 7.

295   Nationmaster.com.

296   Illustrious Schools.

297   Shorton, Russell, *The Island at the Center of the World*, Thorndike Press, 2004.

298   Hugo de Groot, Dutch lawyer and philosopher.

299   Wessels.

300   After running afoul of Dutch politics and subsequent imprisonment he escaped first to settle in Paris and later in Pomerania.

301   The same who received the letter from de Rassiere in 1627 mentioned in Chapter One.

302   Later New York.

303   Traditionally the chief law enforcement officer of a city.

304   Dutch West-India Company ship The Oak Tree.

305   Shorto.

306 The Bay.

307 Davis and Young, R.T., *History of New Amsterdam*, Davis, R.T. Young, New York, 1854.

308 Lee.

309 Dutch for boss.

310 Also called Mespath, present day Newton.

311 Local tribe.

312 Lee.

313 dottydoughtydna.org.

314 Shorto.

315 Venema, Janny, *Killiaen van Rensselaar (1586-1643)*, Verloren, 2011.

316 Lindo, M.P. and others, *De Nederlandse Spectator*, M. Nijhoff, 1902.

317 Shorto.

318 Remember the case brought against John of Barneveld, his illegal trial and execution. See Chapter 7.

319 Shorto.

320 Shorto.

321 Ferguson.

322 Shorto.

323 Shorto.

324   Van der Donck, Adriaen, *Beschrijvinge Van Nieuw-Nederlant*, vert Nieuwenhof, 1655.

325 See Chapter 9

326 Parker, Rev. H.A., *Transactions, Volume 10*, Colonial Society of Massachusetts, 1907.

327 The Dutch had long established trading posts on the Connecticut coast.

328 Antonia Fraser, Cromwell, Grove Great Lives, 1972.

329 Shorto.

330 Nationmaster.

331 Shorto.

332 Eastern Long Island.

333 Remonstrance and Petition of the Colonies and Villages in this New Netherland Province.

334 Shorto.

335 Nationmaster.

336 Dutch for farm and the origin of the word bowery.

337   Shorto.

338   Burton, P.G. to E.A. Doty, *The Dogty Family of Long Island*, Washington, DC.

339   See Chapter 8.

340   J.A.C. Chandler, J.A.C. & James, T.B., *Colonial Virginia*, Times-Dispatch Company, 1907.

341   Chandler & James.

342   Chandler & James.

343   A. Maitland from H. and A. Poole Family History, 1998.

344   Maitland/Poole from W.J. Hoffman, New York Genealogical Record.

345   Maitland/Poole.

346   Parker.

347   Maitland/Poole

348   Later split up into Richmond and Essex Counties and unrelated to the current Rappahannock County which territory was then not yet settled by colonists.

349   Chandler & James.

350   The Formation of a Society on Virginia's Eastern Shore, 1615-1655, James R. Perry, Institute of Early American History and Culture, 1990.

351   Maitland.

352   Neill, E.D., *Virginia Carolorum*, Joel Munsell's Sons, 1886.

353   Thomas, J.W., *Chronicles of Colonial Maryland*, The Eddy Press Corporation, 1913.

354   Passed by a Catholic majority in 1649 and confirmed by a Protestant majority in 1650. Thomas.

355   Lee.

356   http://dotydoughtydna.org.

357   Amesbury Archer, http://www.wessexarch.co.uk/projects/amesbury/archer.html.

358   Brown, Nigel, *Vousden One-Name Study*, http://www.vousden.name/origins .htm, 2010.

359   http://www.goudhurst.co.uk.

360   See Chapter 7.

361   Smiles, Samuel, *The Huguenots*, John Murray, 1881.

362   Jardine, Lisa, *Going Dutch*, HarperCollins, 2008. English historian Lisa Jardine does an in-depth study of the Dutch influence in England.

She makes the case that England, over time, stole the Dutch wealth and culture and was largely responsible for the decline of the country to which it owed its greatness. This author highly recommends her thorough and groundbreaking work.

363 The Encyclopedea Britannica called it one of the most remarkable chapters in the industrial history of England.

364 Frazier.

365 His full name was Hans Willem Bentinck.

366 His Dutch first name was Willem.

367 Onnekink, D.M.L., *The Anglo-Dutch Favourite*, (thesis) 2004. Unless noted otherwise facts regarding Bentinck come from this source.

368 Bowen, Marjorie, *William Prince of Orange*, John Lane the Bodley Head Ltd., 1928.

369 The top military officer.

370 King Charles II of England spent the Cromwell years in the hospitality of the Orange family in the Netherlands and was restored to the English throne in 1660. England and the Republic were once again at war.

371 Junior officer.

372 Bowen.

373 Also called the Secret Treaty of Dover.

374 Passage in the Treaty of Dover.

375 Fraser, Antonia, *Royal Charles: Charles II and the Restoration*, Alfred A. Knopf, 1979.

376 For all practical purposes he was the prime-minister of the Republic.

377 Baxter, Stephen B., *William III*, Harcourt Brace & World Inc., 1966.

378 Onnekink.

379 Winkler Prins Geillustreerde Encyclopaedie, Winkler Prins, Elsevier, 1906.

380 Noordam, D.J., *Riskante relaties*, Verloren, 1995.

381 Reeve or Steward in some localities on the British Isles.

382 Bentinck.

383 Anonymous English agent through Onnekink.

384 De B.

385 Designed to exclude all except Protestants from public service, including the monarch.

386 They did not want any role for nobility such as the Oranges.

387   Holland being the largest and most powerful state or province of the Dutch Republic which was also called the United States of the Netherlands. The name The Netherlands referred to the area now covered by Belgium and the current Netherlands.

388   Troost, Wout, *William III the Stadholder King*, Ashgate Publishing Ltd., 2005.

389   A reference to author le Carré's book of that name whose protagonist George Smiley runs a spy network.

390   Onnekink.

391   The descendents of Huguenots who had fled the Spanish Netherlands a few generations earlier to settle in England.

392   Barton, Dennis, *James II and the Glorious Revolution*, ChurchHistory. org.

393   Dreiskämper, P., *Aan de Vooravond van de Overtocht naar Engeland*, Verloren, 1996.

394   For religion and freedom.

395   Onnekink.

396   Blok, P.J., *Geschiedenis van het Nederlandsche Volk*, J.B. Wolters, 1902.

397   Seven Provinces.

398   De Jonge, J.C., *Geschiedenis van het Nederlandsche Zeewezen*, Van Cleef, 1837.

399   Meant to be set alight and sent into the enemy fleet.

400   Lindo, M.P. and others, *De Nederlandsche Spectator*, D.A. Thieme, 1880.

401   Edith Thompson, *History of England*, Henry Holt & Company, 1887.

402   Onnekink.

403   Onnekink.

404   Also known as the Dutch Republic or the Northern Netherlands.

405   Onnekink from R. Ferguson, *A brief account of some of the late encroachments and depredations of the Dutch upon the English etc.* (London, 1695).

406   Onnekink.

407   Onnekink from Halifax's Spencer House Journals.

408   Hunt, Gaillard Editor, *The writings of James Madison, Volume 1*, G.P. Putnam's Sons, 1900.

409 Schechter, Stephen I. and Bernstein, Richard B., *New York and the Union: Contributions to the American Constitutional Experience*, Albany, NY: New York State Commission on the Bicentennial of the U.S. Constitution, 1990.

410 Nederlands Archief, http://www.archieven.nl/nl/.

411 Orange County Historical Society, Orange, Virginia.

412 http://avalon.law.yale.edu/18th_century/vatexta.asp

413 Sterling Howell, Interpretive Team Coordinator, Montpelier.

414 Two excellent books on the subject are: *Revolutionaries*, Jack Rakove, Houghton Mifflin Harcourt, 2010 and *James Madison*, Richard Brookhiser, Basic Books, 2011.

415 Hazard, Samuel Editor and Publisher, *The Register of Pennsylvania Volume II*, 1828.

416 Hotchkin, S.F., *The York Road*, Binder & Kelly, 1892.

417 A Lover of his Country, *The Grand Concern of England*, 1673.

418 Hotchkin.

419 http://www.hatboro-pa.com/hathist.htm.

420 http://www.pitrone.com/dawson.html.

421 First used as "Landes Vater" on the cover of the 1778 Pennsylvania German Almanac, printed by Francis Bailey.

422 Sparks, Jared, *Excerpts from G. W.'s diary published in The Life of George Washington*, Ferdinand Andrews, 1839.

423 Garrett, J.K. and Underwood, L., *Our American Constitution*, Steck-Vaughn, 1977.

424 Lloyd, Gordon, *Teaching American History website*, Constitutional Convention.

425 Ibid.

426 Ibid.

427 The movement that advocated a strong union with a central federal government.

428 Linklater, Andro, *The Fabric of America*, Bloomsbury Publishing USA, 2009.

429 Plotnik, Arthur, *The Man Behind the Quill*, National Archives Trust Fund Board, 1987.

430 *Jacob Shallus diary*, Papers in the American Philosophical Society, Philadelphia, 1831.

431 Lockhart, Paul, *The Drillmaster of Valley Forge*, HarperCollins, 2008

432 Plotnik.

436   Census of 1790.

437   This was an area north of Vine Street and separate from Philadelphia.

438   Diary of the campaign to Quebec, July 1776.

439   Smith and Deane, *The Journals of the Rev. Thomas Smith and the Rev. Samuel Dean*, Joseph S. Bailey, 1849.

440   Since renamed Independence Hall.

441   Gilpin, Henry D., *The Papers of James Madison, Volume II*, Langtree & Sullivan, 1840.

442   *The Diaries of George Washington, 1748-1799, Volume 4*, Houghton Mifflin, 1925.

443   Burt, Nathaniel, *The Perennial Philadelphians*, University of Pennsylvania Press, 1999.

444   Federalist 38.

445   Ibid.

446   Plotnik

447   http://www.constitutionfacts.com/us-constitution-amendments/bill-of-rights/.

448   Letter to William S. Smith, Nov. 13, 1787.

449   Founding Fathers and Framers.

450   Chenoweth, Erica and Stephan, Maria J., *Why Civil Resistance Works*, Columbia University Press, 2011.

451   Leyden is the spelling found in old English texts and will be used here for historic accounts. The Dutch spelling is Leiden.

Index

57, 58, 70, 71, 78, 79, 80, 81, 83, 84, 85, 87,
90, 92, 97, 99, 101, 105, 107, 109, 112, 113,
114, 116, 118, 124, 127, 129, 131, 132, 133,
156, 162, 187, 234, 239, 240, 242, 245, 246,
247, 248, 249, 251, 257, 258, 261, 264, 268,
293, 294, 297, 307, 308, 311, 313, 314
Francia 20
Frankfurt 91
Franks 5, 10, 20, 21, 30, 32, 36, 37, 40, 41,
46, 48, 50, 73, 270, 307, 308, 309
Frederick of Brandenburg 252
Freedom of Religion 4
freemen 21, 22, 210, 231, 309, 317
free speech 7
free trade 71, 99, 137, 205, 214, 229, 236
French and Indian War 12
French revolution 72, 73
Friesland 86, 94, 154, 242, 249, 310
Frisia 50, 75
Frisians 20, 46, 47, 50, 309
Fruin 72
Gainsborough 160
Gantois 88, 92
Gaul 20, 21, 32, 37, 46, 48
Gelderland 94, 99, 119, 120, 237, 241
Georgia 12, 186
Gerard Alewijnsz 59
German 4, 9, 15, 40, 58, 78, 90, 91, 95, 105,
108, 110, 114, 116, 117, 156, 195, 244, 245,
246, 252, 253, 263, 269, 276, 286, 298, 310,
313, 314, 325
Germanic 15, 16, 17, 20, 21, 32, 36, 41, 46,
48, 57, 76, 309
Germantown 272
Germany viii, 1, 4, 9, 16, 47, 49, 70, 77, 90,
101, 104, 110, 111, 114, 116, 117, 125, 127,
128, 158, 162, 165, 227, 242, 247, 252, 253,
254, 255, 257, 312
Ghent vii, 79, 80, 81, 82, 83, 84, 86, 87, 88,
91, 92, 93, 97, 99, 101, 108, 120, 121, 312
Glorious Revolution 1, 233, 288, 291, 324
Goethe 73
Golden Age 236
Golden Fleece 99, 101, 104
Gomarus 169
Goudhurst 234
governance 2, 5, 7, 8, 9, 15, 36, 48, 53, 55,
56, 59, 71, 78, 81, 82, 97, 102, 103, 104, 121,
125, 156, 163, 169, 170, 178, 187, 201, 205,

210, 250, 269, 270, 275, 288
Governor 94, 109, 120, 126, 168, 176, 200,
201, 204, 210, 214, 215, 216, 217, 218, 219,
220, 221, 222, 224, 225, 226, 229, 231, 267,
270, 295
Granvelle 109, 111, 112, 113, 114
Gray's ferry 274
Great Council 95, 96, 97, 98, 102
Great Hall 151
Great Level of the Fens 236
Great Privilege 3, 11, 92, 93, 97, 102, 103,
110, 120, 122, 155, 260
Greek 5, 40, 41, 269
Grève 34, 35, 307
Groot Privilege 94
Gruthuse 91
Guiana 171
Guildhall 257
Guilds 53, 76, 169
Guinegate 97
gun rights 7
Gunthersteyn 125
Haarlem 118, 126, 144
Hainault 37, 59, 71, 75, 86, 93, 94, 95, 98
Hamburg 125
Ham House 257
Hamilton, Alexander 8, 268, 269, 284, 305
Hampton Court 259
Hannover 252
Hans 237, 238, 239, 240, 242, 243, 244,
245, 246, 247, 248, 249, 250, 251, 252, 253,
254, 255, 256, 257, 258, 259, 260, 261, 262,
263, 264, 266, 288, 323
Hartaing 133
Hartford 225
Hatborough 272
Havre de Grace 273
Heidelberg viii, 114, 117, 126
Heinsius 169, 261
Hellevoetsluis 253, 254, 255
Hempstead 3
Hendrik Casimir II 249
Henry II 109
Henry III 46, 234
Henry VII 122, 155, 234, 264
Henry VIII 103, 156, 157, 236, 295, 316
High Council of Holland 134
Hobbes 5
Holcroft 158
Holland vii, ix, 5, 10, 11, 46, 49, 50, 51, 52,

301, 315, 316, 320, 324
Utrecht viii, 4, 8, 46, 71, 72, 77, 99, 101,
106, 109, 118, 119, 120, 125, 126, 141, 143,
147, 205, 237, 260, 295, 315
van Bergen 212
van der Donck 11, 185, 212, 215, 216, 217,
218, 222, 224, 230, 232, 289
van der Meulen 150
van Leeuwen 138
van Rensselaer 195, 214, 216, 319
van Weede van Dijkveld 244
Vatican 117
Vermigli 158
Vermuyden 236
Vienna 246
Vietnam 6
Virginia ix, x, 11, 12, 13, 159, 165, 168,
169, 171, 172, 173, 175, 176, 179, 180, 181,
185, 186, 196, 204, 206, 228, 229, 230, 232,
236, 268, 270, 272, 273, 274, 275, 282, 284,
286, 293, 296, 297, 298, 304, 317, 322, 325
Virginia Articles of Government 11, 185
Virginia Company 165, 168, 171, 172, 173,
175, 180, 206, 236
Virginia Plan 284
Vita Domnae Balthildis 308
Vlissingen 219
Volckerack 64, 66
Voorhout 147
Vorstius 136, 169
Walcheren 240
Waldeck 244
Wallaeus 142, 143, 147, 151
Wallonia 95, 195, 227
Walloon 94, 95, 312
Walton 161, 295, 316
wampunpeag 197, 198, 199, 319
Ward, Nathaniel 209
Washington, George x, 6, 12, 268, 269, 270,
271, 272, 273, 274, 275, 276, 279, 280, 281,
282, 283, 284, 285, 286, 293, 299, 300, 301,
322, 325, 326
water boards 10, 50
Watergeuzen 114
Watertown 3
Watson's Hill 271
Wessex 234
Westerburg 105
West-India Company 137, 193, 195, 196,

201, 213, 214, 320
West Munster Cathedral 61
Weston 173, 174, 176, 180
Weymouth colony 180
Whitehall 240, 259
Wijnendaal 98
Wilford 158
Wilhelmus 118
William 1, 4, 11, 46, 58, 59, 60, 63, 65, 66,
68, 69, 70, 71, 75, 76, 103, 104, 105, 106,
107, 108, 109, 110, 111, 112, 113, 114, 115,
116, 117, 118, 119, 120, 121, 122, 126, 127,
134, 140, 149, 153, 155, 157, 159, 160, 163,
164, 168, 192, 194, 221, 223, 232, 233, 234,
237, 238, 239, 240, 241, 242, 243, 244, 245,
246, 247, 248, 249, 250, 251, 252, 253, 254,
255, 256, 257, 258, 259, 260, 261, 262, 263,
264, 266, 267, 270, 280, 288, 289, 292, 294,
295, 298, 299, 301, 303, 308, 313, 317, 318,
319, 320, 323, 324, 326
William and Mary 1, 233, 259
Williamites 258
William of Nassau 11, 103, 104, 105, 110
William of Normandy 233, 234, 288
William of Orange-Nassau 11, 103, 115,
120, 121
Williamson, Hugh 8
William V 58, 59, 70, 76
Willing, Thomas 283
Wilmington 274
Wincob 173
Winslow 178, 184, 206, 302
Winthrop 206, 208, 209, 210, 219
Worcester 158
Worcestershire 161
Wythe, George 274
Yeardley 176
Yonkers 218
Zeeland 10, 48, 58, 59, 60, 61, 74, 80, 86,
94, 95, 99, 109, 118, 119, 120, 127, 195, 239,
242, 294
Zurich 158
Zutphen 94, 120

About the Author

Born in the Netherlands, Mau grew up in a family of doctors, accountants, artists and musicians; pillars of society and freebooters. During many years in international consulting as an information specialist he endeavored to serve the human element in projects as diverse as technical education, institution building, and land reform. Back in the U.S. he engaged in community service, was president of the board of a non-profit theater, and still participates in a number of local, state and national political campaigns. Mau and his wife Jackie found a haven in Accomack, Virginia.

Northampton House Press

Established in 2011, Northampton House Press publishes carefully selected fiction – historical, romance, thrillers, fantasy – and lifestyle nonfiction, memoir, and poetry. Our logo represents the Greek muse Polyhymnia. See our list at www.northampton-house.com, or Like us on Facebook – "Northampton House Press" to discover more innovative works from brilliant new writers.

CPSIA information can be obtained at www.ICGtesting.com
Printed in the USA
BVOW08*1244131215

429458BV00003B/4/P